Visual QuickStart Guide

Illustrator CS3

for Windows and Macintosh

Elaine Weinmann
Peter Lourekas

Peachpit Press

For Simona

Visual QuickStart Guide
Illustrator CS3 for Windows and Macintosh
Elaine Weinmann and Peter Lourekas

Peachpit Press
1249 Eighth Street
Berkeley, CA 94710

510/524-2178
510/524-2221 (fax)

Find us on the Web at: www.peachpit.com

Visual QuickStart Guide is a trademark of Peachpit Press, a division of Pearson Education

Cover design: Peachpit Press
Interior design: Elaine Weinmann
Production: Elaine Weinmann and Peter Lourekas
Illustrations: Elaine Weinmann and Peter Lourekas, except as noted

Colophon

This book was created with Adobe InDesign CS2 on two Power Macintosh G5s. The primary fonts used were ITC Stone Serif, Gill Sans, Myriad, and ITC New Baskerville from Adobe Systems Inc.

Notice of Rights

Notice of Liability

ISBN-13: 978-0-321-51045-7
ISBN-10: 0-321-51045-3
9 8 7 6 5 4 3

Printed and bound in the United States of America

Our heartfelt thanks to

Nancy Aldrich-Ruenzel, Publisher, Peachpit Press; **Nancy Davis**, Editor-in-Chief; **Lisa Brazieal**, Production Editor; **Gary-Paul Prince**, PTG Tradeshow and Conventions Manager; **Keasley Jones**, Business Manager; and the rest of the terrific, hardworking staff at Peachpit Press.

Victor Gavenda, sharp, funny, and indispensable technical editor at Peachpit Press, for painstakingly testing the book in Windows, and also for his work as our editor.

J.D. King, Chris Lyons, John Mattos, Daniel Pelavin, John Pirman, and **Nancy Stahl**, the artists whose work we're honored to feature in this book (see the color insert). Their contact information appears on the following page.

Diane Margolin, for her fine illustration work.

Rebecca Pepper, copy editor, for her intelligent corrections and meticulous attention to detail.

Leona Benten, proofreader, for all the last-minute "catches."

Steve Rath, for generating a great index.

Adobe Systems, Inc. and the Adobe Illustrator CS3 team, for designing software that's fun to use and to write about, and in particular **Silas Lepcha**, the Adobe Prerelease Program Coordinator.

Mies Hora, of Ultimate Symbol, for the Design Elements CD (www.ultimatesymbol.com), a valuable resource for vector graphics.

Edwards Brothers, for a fine print job.

Our friends and family, for being understanding when we're in deadline mode and for being there when we reemerge.

©DANIEL PELAVIN

Thanks!

Directory of artists

J.D. King
Rep: Gerald & Cullen Rapp 212-889-3337
www.jdkingillustration.com
Page 339, color section

Chris Lyons
14 East Park Road
Pittsford, NY 14534
Studio 585-385-5739
Cell 585-615-2781
www.chrislyonsillustration.com
Pages v, xiii, 437, color section

Diane Margolin
41 Perry Street
New York, NY 10014
Studio 212-691-9537
dimargolin@nyc.rr.com
Pages 131, 142, 162, 163, 296, 297, 300, 307, 324

John Mattos
109 Waverly Place
San Francisco, CA 94108
Studio 415-397-2138
www.johnmattos.com
john@johnmattos.com
color section

The illustrations in this book are protected by copyright, and may not be used without permission. Please respect the artists' rights.

Daniel Pelavin
80 Varick Street, #3B
New York, NY 10013
Studio 212-941-7418
www.pelavin.com
Pages ii, iii, vii, xi, xv, xvii, 69, 70, 71, 72, 104, 185, 188, 189, 309, 310, 317, 325, 332, 333, 419, 423, 425, 431, color section

John Pirman
15 West 12th Street, Apt. 11A
New York, NY 10011
www.rappart.com/john_pirman
johnpirman@aol.com
color section

Nancy Stahl
www.nancystahl.com
Page 377, color section

Photo credits

Pages 153, 159, 160, 293 © PhotoDisc (gettyimages.com)

Pages 100, 334 © photospin.com

Page 150, 294 © shutterstock.com

Page 154 © 2007 jupiterimages.com

All other photos © Peter Lourekas and Elaine Weinmann

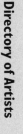

Directory of Artists

©CHRIS LYONS

CONTENTS

AT A GLANCE

1 Illustrator Interface...... 1

2 Create & Save Files..... 27

3 Bridge.................. 37

4 Manage Color 51

5 Workspace 59

6 Geometric Objects 69

7 Select.................. 79

8 Move, Copy & Align 89

9 Fill & Stroke 101

10 Transform............. 123

11 Reshape 133

12 Tracing............... 153

13 Live Paint............. 161

14 Live Color 175

15 Pen 185

16 Layers 193

17 Create Type 211

18 Style & Edit Type 225

19 Acquire............... 255

20 Appearances & Styles.. 265

21 Effects & Filters....... 279

22 Brushes............... 295

23 Blends 309

24 Gradients............. 317

25 Combine Paths 325

26 Clipping Masks........ 333

27 Transparency......... 339

28 Symbols 345

29 Preferences........... 365

30 Print................. 377

31 Export............... 399

Index 417

Contents

TOPICS IN DETAIL

New or changed features are identified by this symbol: ★

1 Illustrator Interface

The Tools panel

Using the Tools panel 1

The Tools panel ★ 2

The tearoff toolbars 3

The Illustrator menus 4

Using the panels ★ 6

The Control panel ★ 8

The other panels ★ 10

Mini-Glossary ★ 22

Measuring up 25

Undos and context menus

Multiple undos. 26

Context menus. 26

2 Create & Save Files

Launching Illustrator

Launch Illustrator in Macintosh 27

Launch Illustrator in Windows 28

Creating new documents ★ 29

Using templates

Preview the Illustrator templates 30

Open a template or nontemplate file as
   an untitled document 30

Create a template. 31

Changing the document setup

Change the artboard dimensions or
   orientation ★ 32

The artboard and printing 33

Saving files

Save a file in the Illustrator format 34

Resave a file 36

Save a copy of a file 36

Revert to the last saved version 36

Ending a work session

Close a file 36

Quit/exit Illustrator 36

3 Bridge

Opening files from Illustrator

Open a file from Illustrator. 37

Open a file from the Macintosh Desktop
   or Windows Explorer 37

Using Bridge

Launch Bridge 38

Panels and panes in Bridge ★ 39

Opening files from Bridge 40

Choosing a workspace for Bridge ★ 41

Customizing the Bridge window

Choose Appearance preferences for the
   Bridge workspace ★ 42

Customize the Bridge workspace 43

Save a Bridge workspace ★ 44

Access saved workspaces ★ 44

Moving and copying files ★ 44

Filtering the display of thumbnails

Label and rate thumbnails 45

Choose a sorting method ★ 45

Display thumbnails based on category ★ 46

Arrange thumbnails

Rearrange thumbnails manually 46

Group thumbnails into a stack ★ 46

Expand or collapse a stack ★ 47

Move a whole stack ★ 47

Add a thumbnail to a stack ★ 47

Remove a thumbnail from a stack ★ 47

Ungroup a whole stack ★ 47

Managing files

Create a new folder 47

Delete files 47

Rename a file. 47

Searching for files ★ 48

Exporting the Bridge cache

Export the cache to the current folder ★ 49

Rebuild the cache files ★ 49

Assigning keywords to files ★ 50

4 Manage Color

Choosing color settings 51

Monitor basics. 52

Calibrating your display. 52

Choose color settings 53

Synchronizing the color settings 56

Changing document profiles 57

Proofing a document onscreen 58

5 Workspace

Changing zoom levels

Change zoom levels via the Navigator panel . . 59

Choose a preset zoom level 60

Change the zoom level with the Zoom tool . . . 61

Change the zoom level with any
tool selected 61

Changing views 62

Creating custom views

Define a custom view 63

Rename or delete a custom view 63

Creating new document windows 64

Changing screen display modes ★ 65

Moving the illustration

Move the illustration with the Hand tool 65

Move the illustration via the
Navigator panel 66

Using workspaces

Choose a preset workspace ★ 66

Save a workspace 67

Rename, delete, or duplicate a workspace . . . 68

6 Geometric Objects

Deleting objects. 69

Creating rectangles and ellipses

Create a rectangle or an ellipse by dragging . . 70

Create a rectangle or an ellipse by
specifying dimensions. 70

Create a rounded rectangle 71

Round the corners of an existing object 72

Creating polygons

Create a polygon by clicking. 72

Create a polygon by dragging 73

Creating stars

Create a star by clicking 73

Create a star by dragging. 74

Creating line segments

Draw a line segment by dragging 75

Draw a line segment by entering values 75

Creating arcs

Draw arcs by dragging. 76

Draw arcs by entering values 76

Creating spirals

Create a spiral by entering values 77

Create a spiral by dragging. 78

7 Select

The five selection tools 79

Using the Selection tool

Select an object or objects. 81

Add or subtract objects from a selection. 81

Using the Direct Selection tool ★ 82

Selecting via a command ★ 82

Selecting via the Layers panel 83

Working with groups

Create a group. 84

Edit grouped objects in isolation mode ★ . . . 84

Add a new object to a group. 85

Ungroup a group 85

Using the Lasso tool 86

Saving selections 86

Contents

Using the Magic Wand tool

Choose options for the Magic Wand tool. 87

Use the Magic Wand tool 88

Selecting/deselecting all objects

Select all the objects in a document 88

Deselect all objects on all layers 88

Invert a selection. 88

8 Move, Copy & Align

Moving objects. 89

Using smart guides

Use smart guides to align objects 90

Hide or show an object's center point 91

Duplicating objects

Duplicate an object in the same document . . . 92

Drag and drop an object between files 92

Duplicate or move objects between
    documents via the Clipboard 93

Offset a duplicate of a path ★ 94

Aligning and distributing objects ★ 95

Creating ruler guides 97

Creating guide objects

Turn an object into a guide 98

Turn an guide object back into an
    ordinary object 98

Locking/unlocking guides

Lock or unlock all guides 99

Lock or unlock one guide. 99

Removing guides

Remove one guide 99

Remove all guides 99

Using the Grid

Show/hide the grid. 100

Snap objects to the grid 100

9 Fill & Stroke

Introduction to Illustrator color. 101

Colors for your output medium 102

Change the document color mode 103

Using the basic color controls

Apply a fill or stroke of black or white 104

Apply a fill or stroke of None 104

Apply a fill or stroke color 105

Saving colors as swatches ★ 106

Applying colors from a library ★ 107

Changing the tint percentage. 108

Mixing colors numerically 109

Changing stroke attributes

Change the width of a stroke 110

Change the alignment of a stroke on
    a path 110

Create a dashed stroke 111

Change the stroke caps or joins 112

Using the Eyedropper tool. 113

Using the Swatches panel

Choose display options for the Swatches
    panel ★. 114

Create a color group ★ 115

Copy swatches between Illustrator files ★ . . 116

Save a library of swatches ★ 117

Duplicate a swatch ★. 117

Delete swatches. 117

Replacing colors in your artwork

Replace the color or stroke attributes on
    multiple objects. 118

Change a color from nonglobal to global,
    or vice versa 118

Edit the values in a global process color. . . . 118

Replace a global process or spot
    color swatch 118

Inverting colors ★. 119

Colorizing images. 119

Blending fill colors ★. 120

Creating patterns

Create a pattern. 121

Use a rectangle to define a pattern 121

Edit a pattern 122

Contents

10 Transform

Transform via the bounding box. 123

Using the Free Transform tool

Use the Free Transform tool 124

Use smart guides as you transform
an object 125

**Using the Rotate, Reflect, Scale, or
Shear tool**. 126

Using the Transform panel

Move, scale, rotate, or shear objects via
the Transform panel 128

Move an object or group via the
Control panel. 129

Using the Transform Each command

Perform multiple transformations via the
Transform Each command. 130

Use the Transform effect 131

Repeating a transformation. 132

11 Reshape

The building blocks of a path. 133

Moving points and segments ★ 134

Reshaping curves 134

Converting points

Convert a corner anchor point into a
smooth anchor point ★ 135

Convert a smooth anchor point into a
corner anchor point ★ 136

Rotate direction handles independently. . . . 136

Adding points

Add anchor points to a path manually 137

Add anchor points to a path via
a command 138

Add to a path with the Pencil or
Paintbrush tool 139

Add to an open path with the Pen tool. 139

Deleting points ★ 140

Quick reshaping

Erase part of a path with the Path
Eraser tool. 141

Reshape a path with the Pencil or
Paintbrush tool 141

Use the Reshape tool 142

Exercise: Draw a brush with the
Reshape tool 143

Aligning points ★ 144

Joining endpoints

Connect two endpoints ★ 145

Join two endpoints into one point ★ 145

Reshaping objects via commands

Apply the Zig Zag effect. 146

Combine objects using a command 147

Slicing and dicing

Split a path with the Scissors tool. 148

Split a path via the Control panel ★ 148

Cut objects via the Divide Objects Below
command 149

Erasing parts of objects ★ 150

Exercises

Change a square into a star 151

Draw a light bulb 152

12 Tracing

Using the tracing features 153

Tracing a raster image 154

Applying tracing options 155

Managing tracing presets 158

Releasing a tracing. 158

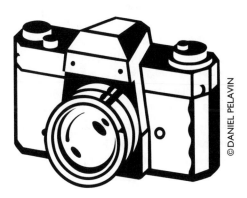

©DANIEL PELAVIN

Contents

Converting tracings to paths

Expand a live trace object 159

Convert a live trace object to a Live
Paint group 159

Exercise: Trace an object 160

13 Live Paint

What is a Live Paint group? 161

Using the Pencil tool

Draw with the Pencil tool 162

Choose preferences for the Pencil tool 163

Creating Live Paint groups. 164

Using the Live Paint Bucket tool

Choose options for the Live Paint
Bucket tool ★ 165

Recolor faces with the Live Paint
Bucket tool ★ 166

Modify edges with the Live Paint
Bucket tool 167

Using the Live Paint Selection tool

Choose options for the Live Paint
Selection tool 168

Use the Live Paint Selection tool 168

Reshaping Live Paint groups ★ 169

Adding paths to a Live Paint group ★ 170

Choosing gap options 171

Expanding and releasing Live Paint groups . . 172

Exercise: Sketch a scarf 173

14 Live Color

Using the Color Guide panel

Choose variation options for the Color
Guide panel ★. 175

Apply color variations via the Color
Guide panel ★. 176

Create a color group and variations based
on a harmony rule ★ 177

Save the active color group ★ 177

Editing colors via Live Color

Create color groups via the Live Color
command ★ 178

Use the color wheel in the Live Color
dialog box ★ 179

Assigning colors via Live Color ★ 181

Reducing colors via Live Color

Reduce colors in artwork via the Live
Color command ★ 183

Reduce selected artwork to just one spot
or process color ★ 184

15 Pen

Drawing with the Pen tool. 185

Draw a polygon with the Pen tool 186

Draw curves with the Pen tool 187

Converting points

Convert smooth points into corner points
as you draw them 189

Convert points on an existing path ★ 190

Exercise: Convert a rectangle into a
costume mask 191

16 Layers

The Layers panel

What the panel is used for 193

Object names on the Layers panel 194

Choose Layers panel options 194

Creating layers

Create a new top-level layer 195

Create a sublayer 196

Deleting layers and objects 197

Selecting Layers panel listings

Select a layer, sublayer, group, or object
listing 198

Select multiple layer listings 199

Selecting objects via the Layers panel

Select all the objects in a layer 200

Deselect all the objects in a layer 200

Select an object via the Layers panel 201

Select multiple objects on different layers . . 201

**Selecting a whole group via the
Layers panel** 202

Contents

Selecting multiple objects in a group 202

Restacking objects and layers

Restack a layer, group, or object
by dragging 203

Move an object to a layer via a command . . . 204

Duplicating layers and objects 204

Locking layers and objects 205

Hiding layers and objects 206

Collecting objects in a new layer 207

Releasing objects to layers 208

Merging layers and groups 209

Flattening artwork 210

17 Create Type

The type tools 211

Creating point type 212

Creating type in a rectangle 213

Creating area type 214

Creating path type

Place type along an object's path 215

Reposition type on a path 215

Apply options to path type 216

Rotating type

Rotate type characters on a custom angle . . . 217

Make a whole horizontal type block
vertical, or vice versa 217

Importing text 218

Threading type

Thread overflow type to another object 219

Display text threads 220

Unthread two type objects 220

Release an object from a thread and
preserve the remaining threads 220

Copying and moving type

Copy type and its object between files 221

Move type from one object to another 221

Creating type outlines 222

Exercise: Type on an ellipse 223

18 Style & Edit Type

Selecting type 225

Select type and its object 226

Select a type object but not the type 227

Select type but not its object 227

**The Character, Paragraph, and Control
panels** 228

Changing fonts

Change fonts 229

Apply underline or strikethrough styling . . . 229

Changing the point size 230

Changing leading

Change leading via the Character panel 231

Change leading via the keyboard 231

Applying kerning and tracking

Apply manual kerning or tracking 232

Fit type to its container 233

© CHRIS LYONS

Horizontal scaling

Scale type horizontally and/or vertically . . . 234

Restore normal scaling 234

Using smart punctuation

Create smart punctuation 235

Specify a quotation marks style for
future type 235

Inserting alternate glyphs

Replace or insert a glyph using the
Glyphs panel 236

Specify or insert alternate glyphs via the
OpenType panel 237

Produce fractions 238

Change case 238

Applying hyphenation 239

Changing paragraph alignment 240

Changing paragraph indentation 241

Inter-paragraph spacing 242

Character and paragraph styles

Create or edit a character or
paragraph style 243

Apply a type style 245

Remove overrides from styled text 245

Redefine a type style 245

Delete a character or paragraph style 246

Load type styles from another Illustrator
document 246

Choosing area type options 247

Baseline-shifting type 248

Hanging punctuation 249

Setting tabs

Insert tabs into text 249

Set or modify custom tab stops 250

Creating special effects with type

Wrap type around an object 251

Release a text wrap 251

Exercises

Create a shadow for point type 252

Add multiple strokes to a character 253

Create type with a rough fill area 253

Create an embossed letter 254

19 Acquire

Acquiring images 255

Using the Open command 256

Using the Place command 257

Choosing Photoshop import options 258

Managing linked images

Edit a linked image in its original
application 260

Replace a linked or embedded image ★ 261

Go to a linked or embedded image ★ 261

Update a modified linked image 262

View information about a file 262

Locate or replace images upon opening
a file 262

Choose placement options for a
linked image 263

Change a file's status from linked
to embedded ★ 263

Using drag-and-drop

Drag and drop an image from Photoshop
to Illustrator 264

Drag and drop an image into Illustrator
from Bridge 264

20 Appearances & Graphic Styles

Applying appearance attributes 265

Apply appearance attributes 266

Deciphering the Appearance panel 267

Apply multiple stroke or fill attributes 268

Choose appearance options for
future objects 268

Editing appearance attributes 269

Removing appearance attributes

Remove an appearance attribute 270

Remove a brush stroke from a stroke
attribute 270

Remove all appearance attributes from
an item 270

Contents

Applying graphic styles. 271
Apply a graphic style. 272
Copying appearance attributes. 273
Creating graphic styles
Create a graphic style from an object. 274
Duplicate a graphic style 274
Editing graphic styles 275
Merging graphic styles 276
Deleting graphic styles 276
Using graphic style libraries
Use graphic styles from other libraries ★ . . . 277
Save a graphic styles library ★ 277
Breaking the link to a graphic style 278
Expanding attributes 278

21 Effects & Filters

Effects and filters: An overview
Using effects. 279
. . .versus using filters 280
Applying filters and effects ★ 281
Applying Illustrator effects
Apply an effect 282
Edit an applied effect 282
Using effects in graphic styles
Add an effect to or edit an effect in a
graphic style 283
Remove an effect from a layer, object, or
graphic style 283
A few Illustrator effects up close
Apply Pathfinder effects 284
Apply a Convert to Shape effect 285
Apply the Inner Glow or Outer Glow effect . . 286
Apply the Scribble effect 287
Three Illustrator filters and effects up close
Apply the Drop Shadow effect or filter 288
Apply the Roughen effect or filter 289
Apply the Twist effect or filter 289
Rasterizing objects ★ 290
An Illustrator filter up close 291
Using the Filter or Effect Gallery 292

22 Brushes

Using brushes 295
Using the Paintbrush tool
Draw with the Paintbrush tool 296
Choose preferences for the Paintbrush tool. . 296
Applying brushes ★ 297
Using the Brushes panel
Add brushes from other libraries ★ 298
Choose display options for the
Brushes panel 299
Removing brush strokes 299
Expanding brush strokes 299
Creating and editing Scatter brushes 300
Creating and editing Calligraphic brushes. . . 302
Creating and editing Art brushes 304
Duplicating brushes 305
Editing brushes manually 306
Editing brush strokes on objects 307
Creating brush libraries ★ 308
Deleting brushes 308

23 Blends

Blends are live! 309
Blending objects via a command 310
Releasing a blend. 310
Choosing blend options. 311
Editing blend objects 312

©DANIEL PELAVIN

Reversing blend components

Reverse the stacking position of objects
in a blend 313

Reverse the location of objects in a blend . . 313

Using the Blend tool 314

Replacing the blend spine 315

Exercise: Use a blend to apply shading 316

24 Gradients

Applying gradients 317

Fill an object with a gradient 318

Access other gradient libraries ★ 318

Creating gradients ★ 319

Editing gradients 320

Using the Gradient tool

Use the Gradient tool 322

Spread a gradient across multiple objects . . . 323

Expanding a gradient into objects 324

25 Combine Paths

Applying Shape Mode commands 325

Apply a Shape Mode command 326

Expand a compound shape 326

Release a compound shape 327

Applying the Pathfinder commands

Apply a Pathfinder command 327

Convert a stroke or an open path into a
filled object 329

Creating compound paths

Create a compound path 329

Add an object to a compound path 331

Reverse an object's fill in a compound path . . 331

Release a compound path 332

26 Clipping Masks

Using clipping sets

Create a clipping set 334

Select a whole clipping set 335

Select an individual clipping path or
masked object ★ 335

Add an object to a clipping set 335

Restack a masked object within its
clipping set 336

Copy an object in a clipping set 336

Take an object out of a clipping set 337

Recolor a clipping path 337

Release a clipping set 338

27 Transparency

Changing the opacity and blending mode . . . 339

Change the opacity or blending mode of
an object, group, or layer 340

Change the opacity or blending mode of
an object's fill or stroke 341

Change the opacity or blending mode of
the fill and stroke on type individually . . . 341

**Controlling which objects the transparency
settings affect**

Restrict a blending mode to
specific objects 342

Knock out objects 343

Using the transparency grid

Show/hide the transparency grid 344

Choose preferences for the
transparency grid 344

28 Symbols

Using the Symbols panel 345

Create individual symbol instances 346

Accessing the symbol libraries ★ 347

Replacing symbols 348

Creating symbols ★ 348

Saving symbol libraries ★ 349

Deleting symbols 349

Using the Symbol Sprayer tool

Create instances with the Symbol
Sprayer tool 350

Delete instances from a symbol set 350

Add instances to a symbol set 350

Choosing global properties

Choose global properties for the
symbolism tools 351

Choose options for the Symbol
Sprayer tool 352

Modifying symbol instances 353

Duplicating symbols ★ 354

Editing symbols

Edit a symbol ★ 354

Create a variation of an existing symbol. . . . 355

Break the link between an instance and
the symbol ★ 355

Using the Symbol Shifter tool 356

Using the Symbol Scruncher tool 357

Using the Symbol Sizer tool 358

Using the Symbol Spinner tool 359

Using the Symbol Stainer tool 360

Using the Symbol Screener tool 361

Using the Symbol Styler tool 362

Expanding symbol instances 364

29 Preferences

General Preferences ★ 365

Selection & Anchor Display Preferences ★ . . 367

Type Preferences ★ 368

Units & Display Performance Preferences . . . 369

Guides & Grid Preferences 370

Smart Guides & Slices Preferences 371

Hyphenation Preferences 372

Plug-ins & Scratch Disks Preferences 373

User Interface Preferences ★ 374

File Handling & Clipboard Preferences 374

Appearance of Black Preferences 376

30 Print

Print dialog box: General and Setup options

Print to a black-and-white or color printer . . 378

Print (tile) a document that's larger than
the paper size 380

Marks and Bleed options

Include printer's marks in your printout 382

Choose bleed values 382

Output options

Output a composite print or
color separations 384

Change the print setting for, or convert,
individual colors. 385

Graphics options

Change the flatness setting for a file to
facilitate printing. 386

Download fonts 386

Color Management options 388

Advanced options 389

Summary options 389

Printing and exporting transparency 390

Control how transparency is flattened for
exported files. 390

Choose custom transparency
flattener options 391

Creating and editing presets

Create or edit a transparency flattener,
tracing, print, or PDF preset 393

Create a multipage PDF from page tiles 394

Creating custom crop marks

Use the Crop Area tool ★ 395

Remove a crop area created with the
Crop Area tool ★ 396

Create crop marks for an object. 396

Choosing a resolution for effects 397

Using the Document Info panel 398

Contents

©DANIEL PELAVIN

31 Export

Saving as EPS 399

Saving as Adobe PDF 402

Using the Export command

Export a file. 406

A few file formats in brief 407

Exporting as Flash (swf) ★ 408

Optimizing files for the Web 410

Image size 410

File format 410

Use the Save for Web & Devices previews . . . 411

Optimize a file in the GIF format 412

Optimize a file in the JPEG format. 413

Exporting files to Photoshop 415

Index 417

Contents

ILLUSTRATOR INTERFACE

This chapter introduces Illustrator's tools, menus, panels, and measurement systems.

Note: If you'd like to glance onscreen at the features discussed in this chapter as you read, launch Illustrator and create a new document (see pages 27–29).

Hide/show

Tab	Hide/show all currently open panels and tearoff toolbars, including the Tools panel.
Shift-Tab	Hide/show all currently open panels and tearoff toolbars, but not the Tools panel.

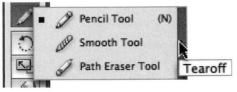

1 *Open a tearoff toolbar by choosing a **tearoff** bar.*

2 *A tearoff toolbar is created.*

The Tools panel
Using the Tools panel

The **Tools** panel contains 76 tools that are used for object creation and editing, as well as color controls and a screen mode menu. If the Tools panel is hidden, choose Window > Tools to show it. To move the Tools panel, drag the top (light gray) bar. Click once on a visible tool to select it, or click and hold on a tool that has a tiny arrowhead to choose a related tool from a pop-out menu. Some tools have a related options dialog box, which you can open by double-clicking the tool.

To create a standalone **tearoff toolbar** **1**–**2**, release the mouse when it's over the vertical tearoff bar on the far right side of a tool pop-out menu. Move a tearoff toolbar by dragging its top bar. To restore a tearoff toolbar to the Tools panel, click its close box.

To access a tool quickly, use the assigned **letter shortcut** (see the letters in parentheses on the next two pages). Some tools can be accessed temporarily via a toggle key. For example, if the Pen tool is selected, pressing Cmd/Ctrl accesses a temporary Selection tool. You'll learn more toggles as you proceed through this book.

To turn tool pointers into a **crosshair** for precise positioning, go to Illustrator (Edit, in Windows) > Preferences > General and check Use Precise Cursors. Or press Caps Lock to turn the pointer into a crosshair temporarily.

The Tools panel

Click to make the panel single column (or double column)

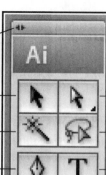

(V) Selection
Selects entire objects

(Y) Magic Wand
Selects objects by color

(P) Pen
Draws paths with curved and/or straight segments

(\) Line Segment
Draws straight lines at any angle

(B) Paintbrush
Creates Calligraphic, Scatter, Art, and Pattern brush strokes

(R) Rotate
Rotates objects

(Shift-R) Warp
Applies distortion

(Shift-S) Symbol Sprayer
Sprays symbol instances

(U) Mesh
Creates and edits multicolored mesh objects

(I) Eyedropper
Samples paint or type attributes

(K) Live Paint Bucket
Recolors faces and edges in a live paint group

(Shift-O) Crop Area NEW!
Defines a crop area for printing

(H) Hand
Moves the artboard in the document window

(X) Fill
The color, gradient, or pattern that fills the inside of a path

(D) Default Fill and Stroke
(white fill, 1 pt. black stroke)

(>) Gradient
Reapplies the last gradient fill

(<) Color
Reapplies the last solid-color stroke or fill

Direct Selection (A)
Selects parts of objects

Lasso (Q)
Selects individual points and segments by marqueeing

Type (T)
Creates and edits horizontal type

Rectangle (M)
Draws rectangles and squares

Pencil (N)
Draws paths in a freehand style

Scale (S)
Enlarges and shrinks objects

Free Transform (E)
Rotates, scales, reflects, shears, distorts, or applies perspective

Column Graph (J)
Creates column graphs

Gradient (G)
Changes the direction of existing gradients

Blend (W)
Creates shape and color blends between objects

Live Paint Selection (Shift-L)
Selects sections of a live paint group

Eraser (Shift-E) NEW!
Erases sections of objects by dragging

Zoom (Z)
Changes the zoom level of the document

Swap Fill and Stroke (Shift-X)

Stroke (X)
The color or pattern that's applied to the edge of a path (click to activate)

None (/)
Removes a stroke or a fill

Screen Mode menu (F)
Lets you change the size of the document window and the onscreen environment for Illustrator

Tools Panel Illustrated

The tearoff toolbars

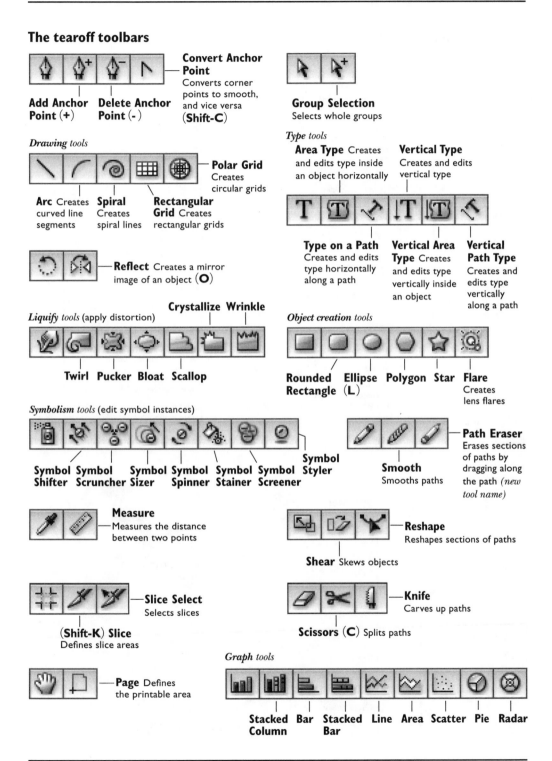

Convert Anchor Point
Converts corner points to smooth, and vice versa
(**Shift-C**)

Add Anchor Point (**+**)   **Delete Anchor Point** (**-**)

Drawing tools

Arc Creates curved line segments   **Spiral** Creates spiral lines   **Rectangular Grid** Creates rectangular grids   **Polar Grid** Creates circular grids

Reflect Creates a mirror image of an object (**O**)

Liquify tools (apply distortion)

Crystallize **Wrinkle**

Twirl **Pucker** **Bloat** **Scallop**

Symbolism tools (edit symbol instances)

Symbol Shifter **Symbol Scruncher** **Symbol Sizer** **Symbol Spinner** **Symbol Stainer** **Symbol Screener** **Symbol Styler**

Measure
Measures the distance between two points

Slice Select
Selects slices

(**Shift-K**) **Slice**
Defines slice areas

Page Defines the printable area

Group Selection
Selects whole groups

Type tools

Area Type Creates and edits type inside an object horizontally   **Vertical Type** Creates and edits vertical type

Type on a Path Creates and edits type horizontally along a path   **Vertical Area Type** Creates and edits type vertically inside an object   **Vertical Path Type** Creates and edits type vertically along a path

Object creation tools

Rounded Rectangle (**L**)   **Ellipse**   **Polygon**   **Star**   **Flare** Creates lens flares

Smooth
Smooths paths

Path Eraser
Erases sections of paths by dragging along the path *(new tool name)*

Reshape
Reshapes sections of paths

Shear Skews objects

Knife
Carves up paths

Scissors (**C**) Splits paths

Graph tools

Stacked Column **Bar** **Stacked Bar** **Line** **Area** **Scatter** **Pie** **Radar**

Tools Panel Illustrated

3

The Illustrator menus

Press any menu bar heading to access dialog boxes and commands. Many of the same commands can be chosen quickly from a context menu (see page 26) or a panel menu, or via a panel button.

Illustrator Menus *(sidebar)*

Illustrator menu

Illustrator

About Illustrator...	
Preferences	▶
Services	▶
Hide Illustrator	
Hide Others	⌥⌘H
Show All	
Quit Illustrator	⌘Q

*In Windows, there is no Illustrator menu, the **Preferences** command is on the **Edit** menu, and the **Exit** command is on the **File** menu.*

Object menu

Object

Transform	▶
Arrange	▶
Group	⌘G
Ungroup	⇧⌘G
Lock	▶
Unlock All	⌥⌘2
Hide	▶
Show All	⌥⌘3
Expand...	
Expand Appearance	
Flatten Transparency...	
Rasterize...	
Create Gradient Mesh...	
Slice	▶
Path	▶
Blend	▶
Envelope Distort	▶
Live Paint	▶
Live Trace	▶
Text Wrap	▶
Clipping Mask	▶
Compound Path	▶
Crop Area	▶
Graph	▶

File menu

File

New...	⌘N
New from Template...	⇧⌘N
Open...	⌘O
Open Recent Files	▶
Browse...	⌥⌘O
Device Central...	
Close	⌘W
Save	⌘S
Save As...	⇧⌘S
Save a Copy...	⌥⌘S
Save as Template...	
Check In...	
Save for Web & Devices...	⌥⇧⌘S
Revert	F12
Place...	
Save for Microsoft Office...	
Export...	
Scripts	▶
Document Setup...	⌥⌘P
Document Color Mode	▶
File Info...	⌥⇧⌘I
Print...	⌘P

Type menu

Type

Font	▶
Recent Fonts	▶
Size	▶
Glyphs	
Area Type Options...	
Type on a Path	▶
Threaded Text	▶
Fit Headline	
Create Outlines	⇧⌘O
Find Font...	
Change Case	▶
Smart Punctuation...	
Optical Margin Alignment	
Show Hidden Characters	⌥⌘I
Type Orientation	▶
Legacy Text	▶

Edit menu

Edit

Undo Move	⌘Z
Redo	⇧⌘Z
Cut	⌘X
Copy	⌘C
Paste	⌘V
Paste in Front	⌘F
Paste in Back	⌘B
Clear	
Find and Replace...	
Find Next	
Check Spelling...	⌘I
Edit Custom Dictionary...	
Define Pattern...	
Edit Colors	▶
Edit Original	
Transparency Flattener Presets...	
Tracing Presets...	
Print Presets...	
SWF Presets...	
Adobe PDF Presets...	
Color Settings...	⇧⌘K
Assign Profile...	
Keyboard Shortcuts...	⌥⇧⌘K

Select menu

Select

All	⌘A
Deselect	⇧⌘A
Reselect	⌘6
Inverse	
Next Object Above	⌥⌘]
Next Object Below	⌥⌘[
Same	▶
Object	▶
Save Selection...	
Edit Selection...	
Selection 1	

Filter menu

Filter

Apply Last Filter	⌘E
Last Filter	⌥⌘E

Illustrator Filters
Create	▶
Distort	▶
Stylize	▶

Photoshop Filters
Filter Gallery...
Artistic	▶
Blur	▶
Brush Strokes	▶
Distort	▶
Pixelate	▶
Sharpen	▶
Sketch	▶
Stylize	▶
Texture	▶
Video	▶

Window menu

Window

New Window	
Workspace	▶
Minimize Window	⌘M
Bring All To Front	
Adobe Labs	▶
Actions	
Align	⇧F7
Appearance	⇧F6
Attributes	⌘F11
Brushes	F5
✓ Color	F6
Color Guide	⇧F3
✓ Control	
Document Info	
Flattener Preview	
Gradient	⌘F9
✓ Graphic Styles	⇧F5
Info	⌘F8
✓ Layers	F7
Links	
Magic Wand	
Navigator	
Pathfinder	⇧⌘F9
Stroke	⌘F10
SVG Interactivity	
✓ Swatches	
Symbols	⇧⌘F11
✓ Tools	
Transform	⇧F8
✓ Transparency	⇧⌘F10
Type	▶
Variables	
Brush Libraries	▶
Graphic Style Libraries	▶
Swatch Libraries	▶
Symbol Libraries	▶
✓ AI TEST FILE.ai @ 150% (CMYK/Preview)	

Effect menu

Effect

Apply Last Effect	⇧⌘E
Last Effect	⌥⇧⌘E

Document Raster Effects Settings...

Illustrator Effects
3D	▶
Convert to Shape	▶
Distort & Transform	▶
Path	▶
Pathfinder	▶
Rasterize...	
Stylize	▶
SVG Filters	▶
Warp	▶

Photoshop Effects
Effect Gallery...
Artistic	▶
Blur	▶
Brush Strokes	▶
Distort	▶
Pixelate	▶
Sharpen	▶
Sketch	▶
Stylize	▶
Texture	▶
Video	▶

Help menu

Help

System Info...
Welcome Screen...
Illustrator Help...   F1
Registration...
Activate...
Deactivate...
Updates...

*In Windows, the **About Illustrator** and **About Plug-ins** commands are available on the Help menu.*

*In Windows, this menu contains **Cascade, Tile,** and **Arrange Icons** commands, but not the Minimize Window and Bring All to Front commands.*

View menu

View

Outline	⌘Y
Overprint Preview	⌥⇧⌘Y
Pixel Preview	⌥⌘Y
Proof Setup	▶
Proof Colors	
Zoom In	⌘+
Zoom Out	⌘-
Fit in Window	⌘0
Actual Size	⌘1
Hide Edges	⌘H
Hide Artboard	
Show Page Tiling	
Show Slices	
Lock Slices	
Hide Template	⇧⌘W
Show Rulers	⌘R
Hide Bounding Box	⇧⌘B
Show Transparency Grid	⇧⌘D
Hide Text Threads	⇧⌘Y
Show Live Paint Gaps	
Guides	▶
Smart Guides	⌘U
Show Grid	⌘"
Snap to Grid	⇧⌘"
✓ Snap to Point	⌥⌘"
New View...	
Edit Views...	

Menu shortcuts in Windows

In Windows, to activate a menu, press **Alt** + the underlined **letter** in the menu name.

Using the panels NEW!

Most of the edits you'll make in Adobe Illustrator will require the use of one or more of the 34 panels. Version CS3 introduces a clever new system for storing and accessing panels so they're easily expandable and collapsible and don't intrude on the document window when you're not using them. As expected, with enhanced flexibility, you also get greater complexity.

By default, some of the most commonly used panels are grouped into vertical docks (dark gray areas) on the right side of your screen **1**. Each dock can hold as many or as few panels or panel groups as you like. We'll show you how to reconfigure the docks to suit your working style. (The Tools panel sits in its own dock on the left side.)

Show/hide a panel: To show a panel, choose the panel name from the Window menu. The panel will display either in its default group and dock or in its last location. To bring a panel to the front of its group, click the tab (panel name). Some panels can also be shown/hidden via keyboard shortcuts, which are listed on the Window menu, and you can also open temporary versions of some panels via the Control panel (see pages 8–9).

Show/hide a panel (icon): Click the icon or panel name. If Auto-Collapse Icon Panels is checked in Preferences > User Interface and you open a panel from an icon, it collapses back to the icon when you click away from it. With this preference unchecked, the panel stays expanded. To collapse it, click the collapse/expand button on the panel bar or click the panel tab or icon.

Expand/collapse a panel (non-icon) or group vertically: Double-click the panel tab; or click the light gray bar (above the panel tabs); or click the panel or group minimize/maximize button.

Use a panel menu: Click the icon to open a menu for whichever panel is in front in a particular group.

Close a panel or group: To close (but not collapse) a panel, click the close button ✖ on its tab, as in Layers ✖. To close a panel group, click the ✖ on the gray bar. To close a group that's an icon, expand the dock first by clicking the

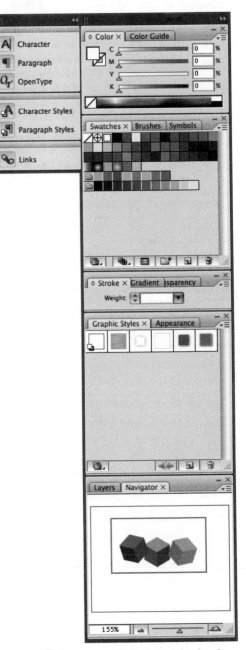

1 *There are two **docks** at the right edge of our screen: panels in the left dock are **collapsed** to icons with names; panels in the right dock are **expanded** and are organized into 4 groups.*

collapse/expand button. (To reopen a panel, use the Window menu.)

Collapse/expand a whole dock into icons with names: Click the collapse/expand button or the dark gray bar at the top of the dock. To further collapse the dock to just icons (no names), drag the vertical edge of the dock inward horizontally; to expand it, do the reverse.

Widen/narrow a dock and panels: Drag the gripper bar sideways (cursor) **1**.

Lengthen or shorten a panel, group, or dock: Position the mouse over the dark gray line at the bottom of the panel or dock (cursor), then drag upward or downward. Other panels/groups in the same group or dock will scale accordingly.

Move a panel to a different slot, same group: Drag the panel tab (name) horizontally.

Move a panel to a different group: Drag the panel tab over the bar at the top of the desired group, and release when the blue drop zone border appears **2**.

Move a panel group upward/downward in a dock: Drag the gray bar, and release when the blue drop zone line appears in the desired location.

Create a new dock: Drag a panel tab or gray bar sideways over the vertical edge of the dock, and release when the blue vertical drop zone bar appears **3**. *Note:* Depending on the current workspace settings, when you open a hidden panel from the Window menu, it may appear in a new dock.

Make a panel or group freestanding: Drag the panel tab, icon, or group bar out of the dock. To move a freestanding group, drag the group bar.

Reconfigure a dock (icon): Use similar methods as for an expanded group. Drag the group bar over the edge of a dock to create a new dock; drag it upward or downward between groups; or drag it over another gray bar to combine it with that group. The blue drop zone shows the new location for the panel or group.

To reset the panels to their default locations and show/hide state, choose Window > Workspace > Basic or Panel. To create custom workspaces that remember panel locations and which panels are showing or hidden, see pages 67–68.

To learn more about showing/hiding panels, see page 65.

➤ To change the shade of gray behind the panels, go to Preferences > User Interface.

Gripper bar

1 *The right dock was collapsed to icons, then the **gripper** bar for that dock was dragged to the left to reveal the **panel names**.*

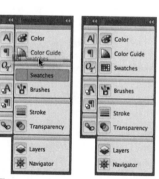

2 *You can drag a panel icon or tab from one **group** into another. Here, the Swatches panel is being moved into the Color/Color Guide panel group.*

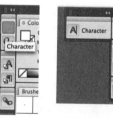

3 *To create a **new dock**, drag a panel icon or tab to the left, and release the mouse when the vertical blue drop zone bar appears.*

The Control panel

The Control panel houses many frequently used controls conveniently under one roof, and, as you can see from the screen captures on this page and the next, changes contextually depending on what type of object is selected. For example, you can use this panel to choose fill and stroke colors, change object opacity, change basic type attributes (font and point size) and paragraph alignment, align and distribute multiple objects, reposition an object, change document units, edit symbols, or embed or edit a linked image. The panel also has controls for the Live Trace and Live Paint features.

You can move the Control panel anywhere on your screen by dragging the gripper bar on the

far left side of the panel. Or choose Dock to Top or Dock to Bottom from the panel menu on the right side of the panel to move it to the top or bottom, respectively, of your screen.

Uncheck or check any of the items listed on the lower part of the panel menu to control which options display on the panel.

And finally, to go to the Bridge application, a separate application that you'll use to open and manage your Illustrator files, click the Go to Bridge button at the far right side of the panel (see Chapter 3).

Opening a temporary panel

You can click a blue **underlined** word or letter on the Control panel to open a related panel. For example, you can click Stroke to open a temporary Stroke panel, or Opacity to open a temporary Transparency panel.

You can open other temporary panels by clicking a **thumbnail** or **arrowhead.** For example, click the Brush thumbnail or arrowhead to open the Brushes panel or the Style thumbnail or arrowhead to open the Graphic Styles panel.

Click the up or down arrow to change the value one increment at a time...   *...or enter a value in the field...*   *...or choose a preset value from the menu.*

Click the Stroke or Fill color to open a temporary Swatches panel, or Shift-click it to open a temporary Color panel.

NEW! Align to Artboard/ **NEW!** Align to Crop Area button and menu

Click to open a temporary **Stroke** panel.

Stroke color   **Fill** color

Stroke weight   Click to open the **Brushes** panel.

NEW! **Recolor Artwork**

Horizontal location of the selected object, relative to the reference point

Width of the selected object

Maintain aspect ratio

Click to open the **Graphic Styles** panel.   Object **opacity**   **Select Similar Objects** menu   **Reference point** for a transformation   **Vertical location** of the selected object, relative to the reference point   **Height** of the selected object

*The Control panel when a **path, group, clipping mask, compound path, symbol,** or **symbol set** is selected*

NEW!

Click the X, Y, W, or H to open a temporary Transform panel.

Click to open a temporary **Character** panel.   **Font**   **Font style**   **Point size**

Click to open a temporary **Paragraph** panel.

Paragraph alignment

Make Envelope button and options menu

Click to open a temporary **Flash Text** panel

Type **Opacity**

*The left side of the Control panel when a **type object** is selected*

NEW!

Click to open a temporary
Transparency *panel.*

Recolor
Artwork

Align *objects*

Distribute *objects*

The left side of the Control panel when objects of **more than one kind** *are selected*

Click **Linked**
File *to open*
a temporary
Links panel.

Click to access a menu
for choosing **Relink, Go**
to Link, Update Link,
and other commands.

Embed *a*
linked image
into the file.

Edit *a linked*
image in its
original
application.

Convert an
image to a **live**
trace *object.*

Tracing
preset
menu

Mask
NEW!

The left side of the Control panel when a **linked, placed image** *is selected*

Preset *(settings) to*
be used for tracing

Open **Tracing**
Options *dialog box*

Max *(maxi-*
mum) **Colors**
for the tracing

Min Area
(size of trace-
able area)

Raster
view *for*
image
display

Vector
view *for*
tracing
display

Expand *live*
trace object
into stan-
dard paths

Convert
live trace
object to **Live**
Paint group

The left side of the Control panel when a **live trace** *object is selected*

Movie Clip

Assign an **Instance Name**

Edit Symbol
(original symbol)

Break Link
between symbol
and instance

Duplicate
instance

Replace
instance with
different symbol

The left side of the Control panel when a **symbol instance** *is selected*

NEW!
Merge Live Paint group
or **add selected paths**

Expand *Live*
Paint group into
standard paths

Open **Gap**
Options
dialog box

The left side of the Control panel when a **Live Paint group** *is selected*

Isolate Selected Group
(and Exit Isolated Group)

The left side of the Control panel when a **blend** *is selected*

Control Panel

9

The other panels

Align panel ▬ Shift-F7

Buttons on the top two rows of the Align panel let you align and/or distribute two or more objects along their centers or along their top, left, right, or bottom edges. Buttons at the bottom of the panel let you equalize (redistribute) the spacing between three or more objects.

What's illustrated, what's not

The full panels are illustrated in this section—all options visible. Double-click a panel tab to show/hide options. (To learn about the Actions, Flash Text, and SVG Interactivity panels, which aren't illustrated here, see Illustrator Help.)

Align buttons also appear on the Control panel when multiple objects are selected.

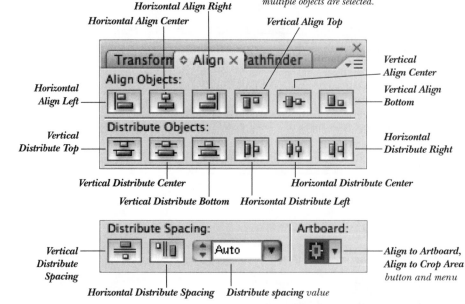

Appearance panel ⬤ Shift-F6

The Appearance panel lists in minute detail the individual appearance attributes that are applied to the currently targeted layer(s), group(s), or object(s). You can use the panel to edit, add, or remove attributes, and to edit the attributes of a graphic style in conjunction with the Graphic Styles panel. You can also use this panel to apply and edit multiple fills and/or strokes for a layer, group, or object.

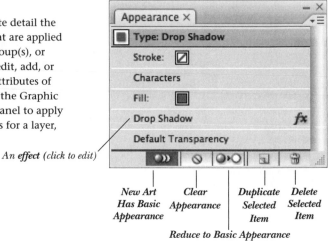

An effect (click to edit)

New Art Has Basic Appearance · Clear Appearance · Duplicate Selected Item · Delete Selected Item

Reduce to Basic Appearance

Align, Appearance Panels

Attributes panel 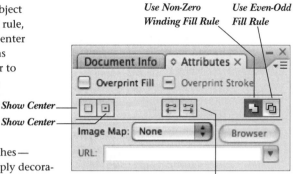 Cmd-F11/Ctrl-F11

The "catchall" Attributes panel lets you choose overprint options for an object, show/hide an object's center point, reverse the fill of an object in a compound path, change an object's fill rule, choose a shape for an image map area, and enter a Web address for an object to designate it as a hot point on an image map. Click Browser to launch the currently installed Web browser.

Use Non-Zero Winding Fill Rule *Use Even-Odd Fill Rule*

Don't Show Center
Show Center

Brushes panel 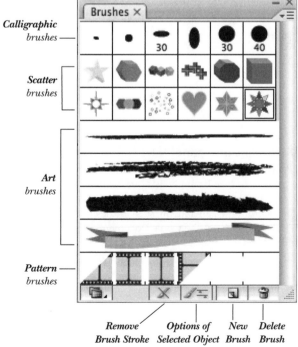 F5

You can use any of the four varieties of brushes—Calligraphic, Scatter, Art, or Pattern—to apply decorative brush strokes to paths. You can do this either by choosing the Paintbrush tool and a brush and then drawing a shape or by applying a brush stroke to an existing path. To personalize your brush strokes, you can create and edit your own brushes. If you modify a brush that's being used in a document, you'll be given the option via an alert dialog box to update the paths with the revised brush. Brushes on the Brushes panel save with the current document. To open a temporary Brushes panel, click the Brush thumbnail or arrowhead on the Control panel.

Reverse Path Direction Off and Reverse Path Direction On buttons (switch the fill between color and transparency in a compound path)

Calligraphic brushes

Scatter brushes

Art brushes

Pattern brushes

Remove Brush Stroke *Options of Selected Object* *New Brush* *Delete Brush*

Attributes, Brushes Panels

Color, Color Guide, Document Info Panels

Color panel 🎨 F6

Use the Color panel to choose Web-safe colors, remix global process or spot color tints, or switch between the fill and stroke colors. Choose a color model for the panel from the panel menu. Quick-select a color, black, white, or None from the spectrum bar at the bottom of the panel. To open a temporary Color panel, Shift-click the Fill or Stroke thumbnail or arrowhead on the Control panel.

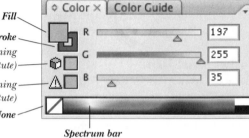

Fill

Stroke

Out of Web Color *warning*
(click box for Web-safe substitute)

Out of Gamut *warning*
(click box for printable substitute)

None

Spectrum bar

Color Guide panel 🎨 Shift-F3 NEW!

Use the Color Guide panel to generate variations (harmonies) for the current color. As is the case with the Swatches panel, you can click a variation to apply it to selected objects. You can also save variations on the Color Guide panel as a group to the Swatches panel.

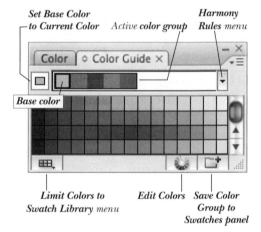

*Set Base Color
to Current Color*   *Active color group*

*Harmony
Rules menu*

Base color

*Limit Colors to
Swatch Library menu*

Edit Colors   *Save Color
Group to
Swatches panel*

Document Info panel ℹ️

Like the Info panel, the Document Info panel is noninteractive. It simply lists information about the document, based on the category you choose from the panel menu, such as the current Selection Only, the whole Document, or individual Objects, Brushes, or Fonts.

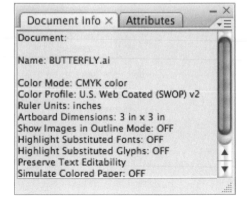

Flattener Preview panel ☑

Using the preview options in the Flattener Preview panel, you can see which objects in your document will be affected by flattening, then use the panel to adjust the flattening settings before printing. Click Refresh to preview changes to the settings in your artwork.

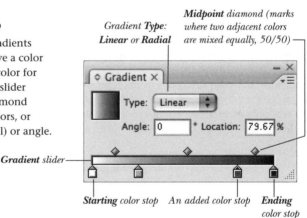

Gradient panel ▦ Cmd-F9/Ctrl-F9

Use the Gradient panel to create new gradients and edit existing gradients. You can move a color by dragging its stop, choose a different color for a selected stop, click below the gradient slider to add new colors, move a midpoint diamond to adjust the distribution of adjacent colors, or change the gradient type (linear or radial) or angle.

Gradient slider

Gradient **Type:**
Linear or *Radial*

Midpoint diamond (marks where two adjacent colors are mixed equally, 50/50)

Starting color stop   An added color stop   *Ending* color stop

Graphic Styles panel ▦ Shift-F5

The Graphic Styles panel lets you store and apply collections of appearance attributes, such as multiple solid-color and pattern fills, multiple strokes, transparency and overprint settings, blending modes, brush strokes, and effects. Like paragraph styles for type, graphic styles let you apply attributes quickly and consistently. To open a temporary Graphic Styles panel, click the Style thumbnail or arrowhead on the Control panel.

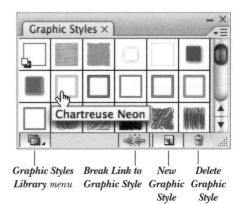

Graphic Styles Library menu   *Break Link to Graphic Style*   *New Graphic Style*   *Delete Graphic Style*

Flattener Preview, Gradient, Graphic Styles Panels

Info panel ⓘ Cmd-F8/Ctrl-F8

If no objects are selected in the current document, the Info panel lists the horizontal and vertical location of the pointer in the document window (for most tools). When an object is selected, the panel lists the location of the object on the page, its width and height, and color data about its fill and stroke. When a type tool and type object are selected, the panel displays type specifications. The Info panel opens automatically when the Measure tool is used, and lists the distance and angle the tool has calculated.

Horizontal (X) and Vertical (Y) location of the currently selected object

Object Width (W) and Height (H)

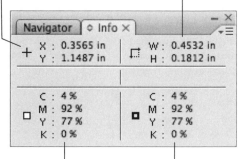

Fill info (color breakdown, or the pattern or gradient name)

Stroke info (color breakdown, or the pattern name)

Layers panel ◆ F7

The indispensable Layers panel lets you add and delete layers and sublayers from a document. You can also use this panel to select, restack, duplicate, delete, hide or show, lock or unlock, merge, change the view for, create a clipping set for, target, or dim a layer, sublayer, group, or individual object. When your artwork is finished, it can be flattened into one layer, or objects can be released to separate layers for export as a Flash animation.

*Click this icon to **target** an object or group to edit its appearances; drag the icon to **move** the object's appearance.*

Current Layer indicator

Selection square

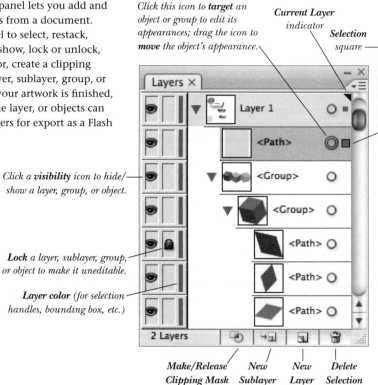

*Click a **visibility** icon to hide/ show a layer, group, or object.*

Lock a layer, sublayer, group, or object to make it uneditable.

Layer color (for selection handles, bounding box, etc.)

Make/Release Clipping Mask

New Sublayer

New Layer

Delete Selection

Links panel

When you place an image into an Illustrator document, you can either embed the image into the file (and thereby increase the file size) or merely link the image to the file. The Links panel lets you keep track of and update linked images, modify a linked image in its original application, and convert linked images to embedded images. You can also embed a linked image by clicking the Embed button on the Control panel, or edit it in its original application by clicking the Edit Original button.

Modified Linked Image indicator *Missing Image* indicator

Relink *Go to Link* *Update Link* *Edit Original*

Magic Wand panel

The Magic Wand tool selects objects that have the same or similar fill color, stroke color, stroke weight, opacity, or blending mode as the currently selected object. Using the Magic Wand panel, you can choose parameters for the tool. The Tolerance is the range within which the tool selects objects with that attribute. For example, if you check Opacity, choose an opacity Tolerance of 10%, and then select an object that has an opacity of 50%, the tool will find and select all the objects in the document that have an opacity of between 40% and 60%.

Navigator panel

The Navigator panel lets you move an illustration in the document window and change the document zoom level. Drag or click in the proxy preview area to move the illustration in the document window, or Cmd-drag/Ctrl-drag in the proxy preview area to zoom that area into view.

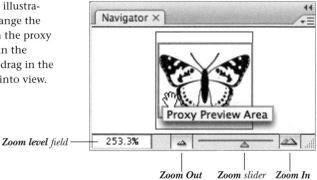

Zoom level field

Zoom Out *Zoom slider* *Zoom In*

Links, Magic Wand, Navigator Panels

Pathfinder panel

Cmd-Shift-F9/Ctrl-Shift-F9

The shape mode buttons on the top row of the Pathfinder panel create new, editable, flexible compound shapes from multiple selected objects. The Expand button converts a compound shape into either a path or a compound path, depending on the way in which the original objects overlapped. The pathfinder buttons on the bottom row of the Pathfinder panel produce flattened, cut-up shapes from multiple selected objects.

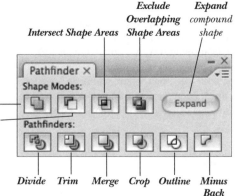

Intersect Shape Areas
Exclude Overlapping Shape Areas
Expand compound shape
Add to Shape Area
Subtract from Shape Area
Divide   Trim   Merge   Crop   Outline   Minus Back

Stroke panel Cmd-F10/Ctrl-F10

Use the Stroke panel to edit the stroke weight, style, and alignment on selected objects, and to create dashed lines or frames. To open a temporary Stroke panel, click Stroke on the Control panel.

*Stroke **Weight** (thickness)*
***Join** (bend) styles*
***Cap** (end) styles*

Align Stroke to Center,
Align Stroke to Inside, or
Align Stroke to Outside

Dashed Line segment (dash) and gap lengths (spacing between dashes)

Swatches panel

Use the Swatches panel to choose and store default and user-defined colors, patterns, gradients, and color groups. If you click a swatch, it becomes the current fill or stroke color, depending on whether the Fill or Stroke box is currently active on the Tools panel and Color panel.

Drag from the Fill or Stroke color box on the Tools or Color panel to the Swatches panel to save that color as a swatch. Double-click a swatch to open the Swatch Options dialog box, where you can change the swatch name, type (global process, nonglobal process, or spot), or mode. Via the panel menu, you can merge swatches and perform other tasks.

To open a temporary Swatches panel, click the Fill or Stroke thumbnail or arrowhead on the Control panel.

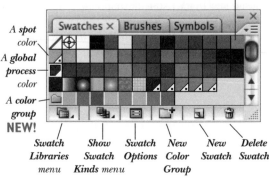

A nonglobal process color
A spot color
A global process color
A color group
NEW!

Swatch Libraries menu
Show Swatch Kinds menu
Swatch Options
New Color Group
New Swatch
Delete Swatch

Symbols panel ♣

Cmd-Shift-F11/Ctrl-Shift-F11

Using Illustrator objects that you store on the Symbols panel, you can quickly and easily create complex art, such as a bank of trees or a group of clouds. To create one instance of a symbol, you simply drag from the Symbols panel onto the artboard; to create multiple instances quickly, use the Symbol Sprayer tool. The other symbolism tools let you change the proximity (density), position, stacking order, size, rotation, transparency, color tint, or graphic style of multiple symbol instances in a symbol set, while still maintaining the link to the original symbol. If you edit the original symbol, all instances of that symbol in the document update automatically. Symbols on the panel are available for use in any document.

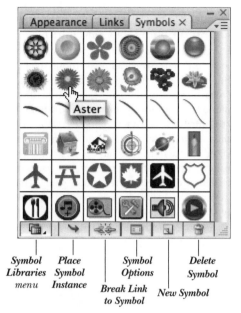

Symbol Libraries menu   *Place Symbol Instance*   *Symbol Options*   *Break Link to Symbol*   *New Symbol*   *Delete Symbol*

Transform panel ⊞ Shift-F8

The Transform panel displays location, width, and height information for the currently selected object. You can also use the panel to move, scale, rotate, or shear a selected object or objects from a reference point of your choosing. The reference point icon and X, Y, W, and H fields also appear on the Control panel when a path or paths are selected. To open a temporary Transform panel, click the X, Y, W, or H on the Control panel.

Reference point *(the part of the object the panel values are calculated from)*   *The location of the currently selected object on the* **x** *and* **y** *axes. Change either or both of these values to reposition an object.*

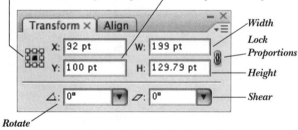

Width — *Lock Proportions* — *Height* — *Shear*

Rotate

Transparency panel ◐

Cmd-Shift-F10/Ctrl-Shift-F10

You can use the Transparency panel to change the blending mode or opacity of any layer, group, or individual object. Via a Transparency panel menu command, you can generate an editable opacity mask from two or more selected objects. You can also change the opacity of an object via the Control panel. To open a temporary Transparency panel, click Opacity on the Control panel.

Opacity mask thumbnail (click to edit)   *Object* **Opacity**

Blending mode —

Object thumbnail —

Isolate Blending *limits the blending mode to a group.*

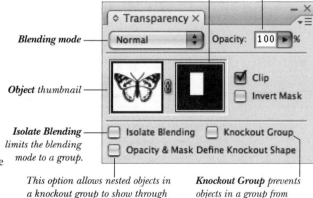

This option allows nested objects in a knockout group to show through transparent areas of an opacity mask.

Knockout Group *prevents objects in a group from showing through one another.*

The type panels

Character panel 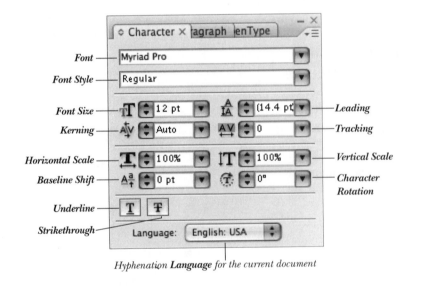 Cmd-T/Ctrl-T

Use the Character panel to apply type attributes: font, font style, size, leading, kerning, tracking, horizontal scale, vertical scale, baseline shift, character rotation, underline, and strikethrough, plus a language for hyphenation. To edit an attribute for selected text, choose a value from the menu; or click the up or down arrow; or enter a value in the field and press Return/Enter. You can open a temporary Character panel by clicking Character on the Control panel. The Control panel also provides access to some basic type controls (see below).

Shortcuts to show the type panels

Except for the Control panel, the panels that you'll use to format type open from the Window > **Type** submenu: Character, Character Styles, Glyphs, OpenType, Paragraph, Paragraph Styles, and Tabs. Four of these panels have their own shortcuts:

Character Cmd-T/Ctrl-T

OpenType Cmd-Option-Shift-T/ Ctrl-Alt-Shift-T

Paragraph Cmd-Option-T/Ctrl-Alt-T

Tabs Cmd-Shift-T/Ctrl-Shift-T

Character Panel

Font
Font Style
Font Size — — Leading
Kerning — — Tracking
Horizontal Scale — — Vertical Scale
Baseline Shift — — Character Rotation
Underline
Strikethrough

Hyphenation **Language** *for the current document*

Click to open a temporary **Character** *panel* **Font** **Font style** **Point size** **Paragraph alignment**

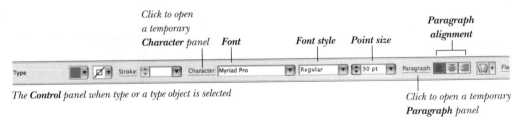

The **Control** *panel when type or a type object is selected*

Click to open a temporary **Paragraph** *panel*

Character Styles panel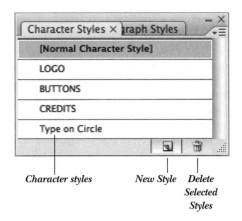

A character style is a collection of character attributes, including the font and font style and point size, leading, tracking, and kerning values. Unlike paragraph styles, which affect whole paragraphs, character styles are applied to small bits of type to make them stand out from the main text, such as bullets, boldfaced words, italicized words, or large initial caps. When you edit a character style, the text that it's associated with updates accordingly. The Character Styles panel lets you create, apply, edit, store, duplicate, and delete styles.

Character styles   *New Style*   *Delete Selected Styles*

Glyphs panel

Using the Glyphs panel, you can find out which character variations (alternate glyphs) are available for any given character in a specific OpenType font, and insert glyphs from any font into your text (including those that can't be inserted via the keyboard).

*Via the **Show** menu, you can control whether the panel displays glyphs in a specific category or for the entire font.*

__Unicode__ for the currently selected character

Font menu   *Pop-up showing **alternate glyphs** for a specific character*   *Font Style*   *Zoom Out*   *Zoom In*

OpenType panel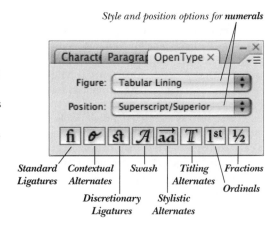

Cmd-Option-Shift-T/Ctrl-Alt-Shift-T

Amongst the Roman OpenType font families that ship with Illustrator, the fonts that contain a large assortment of alternate glyphs are labeled "Pro." By clicking a button on the OpenType panel, you can specify which alternate characters (glyphs) will appear in your text when you type the appropriate key(s), such as ligatures, swashes, titling characters, stylistic alternates, ordinals, and fractions. You can also use the panel to specify options for numerals, such as a style (e.g., tabular lining or oldstyle) and a position (e.g., numerator, denominator, superscript, or subscript).

*Style and position options for **numerals***

Standard Ligatures *Contextual Alternates* *Swash* *Titling Alternates* *Fractions*

Discretionary Ligatures *Stylistic Alternates* *Ordinals*

Paragraph panel ¶

Cmd-Option-T/Ctrl-Alt-T

Use the Paragraph panel to apply specifications that affect entire paragraphs, including horizontal alignment, indentation, space before/after paragraph, and automatic hyphenation. Via the panel menu, you can also choose hanging punctuation, justification, hyphenation, and composer options. (The Left, Center, and Right alignment buttons are also available on the Control panel when a type object is selected.) To open a temporary Paragraph panel, click Paragraph on the Control panel.

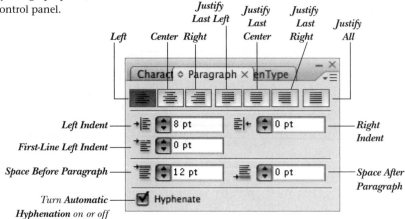

Horizontal alignment

Left *Center* *Right* *Justify Last Left* *Justify Last Center* *Justify Last Right* *Justify All*

Left Indent *First-Line Left Indent* *Space Before Paragraph* *Turn **Automatic** Hyphenation on or off*

Right Indent *Space After Paragraph*

Paragraph Styles panel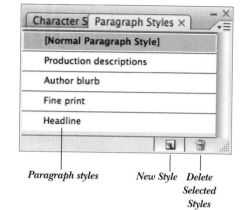

A paragraph style is a collection of paragraph specifications (including horizontal alignment, indentation, space before paragraph, word spacing, letter spacing, hyphenation, and hanging punctuation), plus character attributes, such as font and point size. When you apply a paragraph style to selected paragraphs, the type is reformatted according to the specifications in that style. When you edit a paragraph style, the type it's assigned to updates accordingly. Using styles makes typesetting easier and faster, and also helps to ensure consistent formatting throughout your document. Via the Paragraph Styles panel, you can create, apply, edit, store, duplicate, and delete paragraph styles.

Paragraph styles　　*New Style*　*Delete Selected Styles*

Tabs panel Cmd-Shift-T/Ctrl-Shift-T

If you want to create columns of text that align perfectly, regardless of the current font or point size, you need to use tabs. Using the Tabs panel, you can insert, move, and change the alignment for custom tab markers (tab stops), as well as specify optional leader and align-on characters.

*Left-, Center-, Right-, and Decimal-Justified **alignment** buttons for horizontal type (or Top-, Center-, and Bottom-Justified buttons for vertical type)*

*Numeric **Location** of the currently selected tab marker*

*Optional **Leader** character*

*Optional character to **Align On***

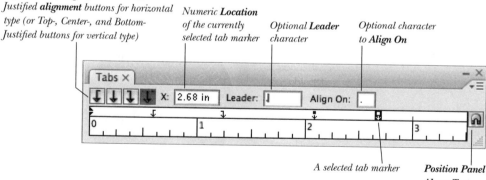

A selected tab marker　　*Position Panel Above Text*

Paragraph Styles, Tabs Panels

Mini-Glossary A brief introduction to some terms you'll encounter while reading this book.

Building blocks

Objects

Closed path   *Open path*

Straight segment   *Corner anchor point*

Direction handle

Smooth anchor point   *Curve segment*

Fill   ——*Stroke*

Selected object

Selected anchor point

Object undergoing a scale transformation

PATH (Or "object") Any individual shape you can create in Illustrator. A path can be open (a line of any shape or length with two endpoints) or closed (no endpoints).

ANCHOR POINTS Path segments are connected by smooth and/or corner anchor points. Smooth anchor points have a pair of direction handles that move in tandem and form a straight line; corner points can have no direction handles, one direction handle, or a pair of direction handles that can be moved independently to reshape adjacent segments. A curve segment can join two smooth points or a corner point and a smooth point, whereas a straight segment always joins two corner points. You can reshape any path by modifying its anchor points and/or segments.

FILL, STROKE A fill is the color, pattern, or gradient (transition between two or more colors) that you apply to the inside of an object. The stroke delineates the edge of an object; it can contain a solid color or pattern, can be of any width, and can be solid or dashed. The current fill and stroke colors display in color boxes on the Tools panel and on the Color panel. When you mix a color using the Color panel, or choose a color by using the Eyedropper tool, Swatches panel, or Color Guide panel, the new color appears in the currently active box.

LAYER A tier of a document that holds one or more objects. A document can contain multiple top-level layers, sublayers, and groups. The "actual" objects in a document (paths, type, placed images, etc.) are nested within those top-level layers, sublayers, or groups.

Basic operations

SELECT To activate an object in the document window for editing. Only selected objects can be modified. When a whole path is selected, its anchor points are solid (not hollow). You can select objects by using the Layers panel; by using the Selection, Direct Selection, Group Selection, Lasso, or Magic Wand tool; or via a menu command.

ISOLATE To isolate a group (of objects) in the document window by double-clicking or via the Isolate Selected Group button or command. Nonisolated objects are dimmed.

TRANSFORM To move, rotate, scale, reflect, or shear (slant) an object, apply distortion or perspective, or create a blend between two objects.

***Blend** created from a circle and a star*

Art **brush stroke**

Original objects   ***Compound path** made from a circle and a star*

Original objects   ***Compound shape** made from a circle, star, and triangle*

*Drop shadow **effect***

*Radial **gradient***

Other features

APPEARANCES Editable and removable attributes, such as multiple fills, strokes, effects, blending modes, opacity settings, patterns, and brush strokes.

BLEND A multistep color and shape progression between two or more objects. If you reshape, recolor, or move the original objects in a blend or reshape, move, or transform the blend path (spine), the transitional objects update automatically.

BRUSH A decorative Calligraphic, Art, Scatter, or Pattern stroke that's created when you use the Paintbrush tool or that you apply to an existing path.

CLIPPING SET The reversible clipping of parts of overlapping objects that extend beyond an object's border to prevent them from displaying and printing.

COMPOUND PATH Two or more objects that are combined into one object via a reversible command. Where the original objects overlap, a transparent hole is created, through which shapes or patterns behind the compound object are revealed.

COMPOUND SHAPE An editable (and reversible) union of overlapping objects, produced via one of the shape mode buttons on the Pathfinder panel. If you move, restack, or reshape individual objects within a compound shape, the overall compound shape readjusts accordingly.

EFFECTS Commands on the Effect menu that change the appearance of an object without changing its actual path. Unlike filters, effects can be edited or removed via the Appearance panel.

GRADIENT A gradual blending of two or more colors within an object. A gradient fill can be linear (side to side) or radial (radiate outward from a central point).

(Continued on the following page)

What is Bridge?

Bridge is a separate application that lets you locate, preview, open, read info about, sort, rename, move, rotate, assign keywords to, and delete files, edit metadata in a selected file, as well as choose global color settings for all the applications in the Adobe Creative Suite.

Mini-Glossary

*An area being filled in
a **Live Paint** group*

*A **set** of symbol instances*

Typography lingo

Font: Type characters of a particular design. In Illustrator, you'll choose a font (or font family), such as Futura, and a font style, such as Futura Light, Futura Italic, or Futura Bold.

Leading: The vertical spacing between lines of horizontal type.

Kerning: The adjustment of spacing between a pair of characters.

Tracking: The adjustment of spacing between three or more characters.

Horizontal scaling: The widening or narrowing of characters.

Baseline shift: The shifting of one or more characters upward or downward from the baseline of the type.

Glyph: A character variation.

NEW! LIVE COLOR Via the Live Color dialog box, you can edit colors and color groups or reassign or reduce the number of colors in your artwork. Via the Color Guide panel, you can generate variations on a color, and save those variations as swatches to the Swatches panel.

LIVE PAINT GROUP A group of intersecting lines (called "edges") and areas (called "faces"). Colors in the faces reflow readily when edges are added or removed, and edges can also be recolored individually.

LIVE TRACE The first step in the conversion of a raster image into editable vector artwork. Tracing options can be applied and adjusted before expanding the live trace object into editable paths or before converting it into a Live Paint group.

PREFERENCES Default settings that you choose for the current or future documents in any of the 11 option sets of the Preferences dialog box (Cmd-K/Ctrl-K), or settings that you choose for a tool via the preferences dialog box for the tool.

STYLES A collection of graphic appearance attributes, saved and applied via the Graphic Styles panel; a collection of type character attributes, applied via the Character Styles panel; or a collection of paragraph and character attributes, applied via the Paragraph Styles panel.

SYMBOLS Reusable objects that are stored on the Symbols panel and can be placed into any document. A single placed symbol is called an instance; multiple instances can also be applied in sets by using the Symbol Sprayer tool. Other symbolism tools let you modify symbol instances and sets in various ways.

WORKSPACE A saved collection of settings for the onscreen environment, such as which panels and tearoff toolbars are open, where they're located, and whether visible panels are fully expanded or collapsed to icons.

OPTIMIZE To choose a file format (such as JPEG or GIF), storage size (compression level), and color parameters for a graphic for efficient downloading on the Web.

Division the easy way

If you enter the symbol for subtraction (-), addition (+), multiplication (*), division (/), or percent (%) after the current value in any field, Illustrator will do the math for you.

Let's say you want to reduce an object's width by 25%. Select the object, highlight the entire W field on the Transform panel, type "75%", then press Return/Enter. The width will be reduced to three-quarters of its current value (e.g., 4p will become 3p). Another option is to click to the right of the current entry, type an asterisk (*), type a percentage value, then press Return/Enter.

Symbols you can use

UNIT	SYMBOL
Picas	**p**
Points	**pt**
Inches	**"** or **in**
Millimeters	**mm**
Centimeters	**cm**
Q (a type unit)	**q**
Pixels	**px**

Points vs. picas

12 pt = 1 pica
6 picas = 1 inch

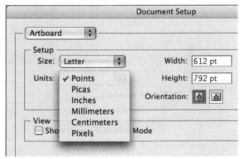

1 *You can choose **units** via a **context** menu in the document window...*

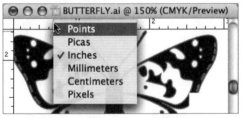

2 *...or from the **Units** menu in the **Document Setup** dialog box.*

Measuring up

The **measurement unit** that you choose for a document (see the instructions below) overrides the unit that's currently specified for the application in Preferences (Cmd-K/Ctrl-K) > **Units & Display Performance.** The current unit is used in entry fields in most panels and dialog boxes, and on the rulers in the document window.

When you enter values in dialog boxes and panels, you can use any of the units that are listed in the sidebar at left, regardless of the current default units. If you enter a value in a non-default unit, it will be translated into the default unit when you press Tab or Return/Enter.

➤ To enter a combination of picas and points, separate the two numbers with a "p". For example, 4p2 equals 4 picas plus 2 points, or 50 pt. (Be sure to highlight the entire contents of the field first.)

Follow the instructions below to change the **measurement units** for just the current **document.** Or go to Preferences (Cmd-K/Ctrl-K) > Units & Display Performance to choose a measurement unit for the whole application (current and future documents).

To change the units for the current document:

If the rulers aren't showing, choose View > **Show Rulers** (Cmd-R/Ctrl-R), then Control-click/right-click either **ruler** and choose a unit from the context menu **1**.
or
Choose File > **Document Setup** (Cmd-Option-P/ Ctrl-Alt-P); choose Artboard from the menu; choose Units: **Points, Picas, Inches, Millimeters, Centimeters,** or **Pixels 2**; then click OK.

➤ The current location of the pointer is indicated by a dotted line on both rulers. The higher the zoom level, the finer the ruler increments.

Undos and context menus

Multiple undos

To undo the last operation, choose Edit > **Undo** (Cmd-Z/Ctrl-Z). To undo the second-to-last operation, choose Edit > Undo again. Repeat, if necessary, to undo multiple editing steps. To reverse an undo, choose Edit > **Redo** (Cmd-Shift-Z/Ctrl-Shift-Z). You can also Control-click/right-click the artboard and choose either command from the context menu. You can undo or redo after saving your document, but not after you close and reopen it.

Context menus

A context menu (short for "contextual menu") lets you choose a command from an onscreen menu without having to mouse to the menu bar or even to a panel. We use them whenever we can, and list them in our instructions. To open a context menu, **Control-click/right-click** the artboard.

Context menu offerings change depending on which tool is selected and whether any objects are selected in your document **1**–**3**. If a command is dimmed on the context menu, it's not available for the type of object that's currently selected.

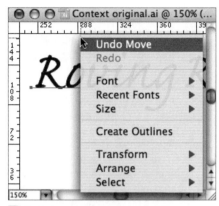

1 *Context menu when **type** is selected*

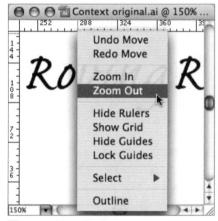

2 *Context menu when **nothing** is selected*

Hidden helpers

You can use **tool tips** to identify panel buttons, swatch names, tool names, tool shortcuts, and other application features. Simply rest the pointer (without clicking) on a button, swatch, tool, or icon, and a tip will pop up onscreen **4**. (If the tool tips don't appear, go to Preferences [Cmd-K/Ctrl-K] > General, and check Show Tool Tips.)

4 *A tool tip*

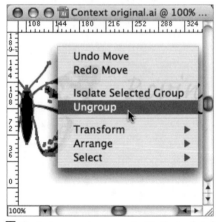

3 *Context menu when a group of **paths** is selected*

Undos, Context Menus

CREATE & SAVE FILES 2

In this chapter you'll learn how to launch Illustrator; create a new document; preview, open, and create templates; define the working and printable areas of a document; save a document in the Adobe Illustrator file format; save a copy of a document; close a document; and quit/exit Illustrator.

1 *Click the **Adobe Illustrator CS3** application icon in the **Dock** (in the Mac OS).*

2 *Double-click an Illustrator file to open it (and launch Illustrator).*

Launching Illustrator

A new document window doesn't appear automatically when you **launch Illustrator**. To create a new document after launching the application, see page 29.

To launch Illustrator in Macintosh:

On the startup drive, open the Applications > Adobe Illustrator **CS3** folder, then double-click the **Adobe Illustrator CS3** application icon.
or
Click the Illustrator application icon in the **Dock** **1**. (To create an icon, drag the application icon from the application folder to the Dock.)
or
Double-click any Illustrator **file icon 2**, or drag any Illustrator file icon over the application icon in the **Dock** to launch Illustrator and open that file.

➤ By default, a welcome screen opens when Illustrator launches **3**. If Don't Show Again was checked on the welcome screen to prevent it from appearing, you can make it reappear by choosing Help > **Welcome Screen**.

3 *The **welcome screen** for Illustrator CS3*

A new document window doesn't appear automatically when you **launch Illustrator.** To create a new document after launching the application, follow the instructions on the next page.

To launch Illustrator in Windows:

Open **My Computer**, double-click the hard drive icon where you installed Illustrator; the default is Local Disk (C:). Follow the path Program Files\Adobe\Adobe Illustrator CS3, then double-click the **Adobe Illustrator CS3** icon.
or
Double-click an Illustrator **file icon** 1 to both launch Illustrator and open that file.
or
Click the **Start** button on the taskbar, choose **All Programs**, then click **Adobe Illustrator CS3** 2.

By default, a welcome screen opens when Illustrator launches 3. If you unchecked Don't Show Again on the welcome screen to prevent it from appearing upon launch, you can make it reappear at any time by choosing Help > **Welcome Screen.**

1 *Double-click an Illustrator file icon.*

2 *Click the **Start** button, then locate and click the* **Adobe Illustrator CS3** *application.*

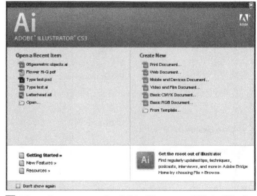

3 *The **welcome screen** for Adobe Illustrator CS3 in Windows*

Creating new documents

To create a new document: NEW!

1. Choose File > New (Cmd-N/Ctrl-N).
   or
   If the Adobe Illustrator CS3 welcome screen is displaying, under Create New, click **Print Document** or **Web Document** **1**.

2. The New Document dialog box opens **2**. Type a **Name** for the new document.

3. From the **New Document Profile** menu, choose a preset for the medium in which you plan to output your file.

4. From the **Size** menu, choose a preset size. For print output, choose Letter, Legal, Tabloid, A4, A3, B5, or B4; for Web output, choose 640 x 480, 800 x 600, or 1024 x 768.
   or
   Choose a measurement unit from the **Units** menu (use Pixels for Web output), then enter custom **Width** and **Height** values.

5. Click an **Orientation** button: Portrait (vertical) or Landscape (horizontal).

6. Click **Advanced** to expand the dialog box, if necessary, then do the following:
   Click a **Color Mode** for the document: CMYK for print output, or RGB for video or Web output.

Choose a resolution for **Raster Effects** (effects in the bottom section of the Effect menu, some Effect > Stylize commands, etc.): High (300 ppi), Medium (150 ppi), or Screen (72 ppi).

Leave the **Preview Mode** as Default.

7. Click OK. A new document window will open at the maximum window size for your display, with the full artboard displaying at the maximum zoom level for that window size. You can resize the window by dragging the lower right corner.

1 *Under **Create New**, click **Print Document** on the Adobe Illustrator CS3 welcome screen.*

2 *In the **New Document** dialog box, type a name, then choose preset or custom settings.*

Using templates

Illustrator ships with industry-standard **templates** that can be used as a starting point for creating your own projects. The templates include layouts, crop marks, objects, styles, symbols, custom swatches, and more. To get an inkling of what the templates look like via **PDF** previews, follow these instructions. If you're new to Illustrator, this is a good way to see what the program can do. (To open an actual template file, follow the next set of instructions.)

To preview the Illustrator templates:

1. Launch Bridge by clicking the **Go to Bridge** button 🎬 at the far right end of the Control panel.

2. Click the Folders tab in the left panel, navigate to the Adobe Illustrator CS3/Cool Extras/Templates folder, double-click **Basic** or **Inspiration,** then browse through the images in any of the folders **1**.

The **New from Template** command opens a template file as a new, untitled document—content, specifications, and all—which can be edited like any other document; the original file is left intact.

You're not limited to using the templates that ship with Illustrator. You can open any existing Illustrator file as an untitled document via the New from Template command, as per the instructions below. On the following page, we show you how to save a file as a template.

To open a template or nontemplate file as an untitled document:

1. Choose File > **New from Template** (Cmd-Shift-N/Ctrl-Shift-N) or under Create New on the Adobe Illustrator CS3 welcome screen, click **From Template.** The New from Template dialog box opens.

2. To open an Illustrator template in the Mac OS, navigate to Applications/Adobe Illustrator CS3/Cool Extras/Templates. In Windows, navigate to Program Files\Adobe\Adobe Illustrator CS3\Cool Extras\Templates.

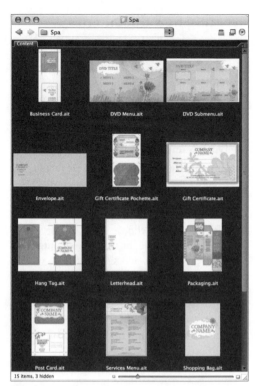

1 *You can preview the Adobe Illustrator CS3* **templates** *in Bridge.*

1 *A CD template in the Band folder*

2 *A packaging template in the Spa folder*

Click a folder in the Basic or Inspiration folder inside the **Templates** folder, click a template name, then click New. The template will open in a new, untitled document window **1**–**3**.

or

Locate and select an existing Illustrator file, then click New to open the file as an untitled document.

3. If a Missing Profile alert prompt appears, see page 54. Save the file.

You can go the extra mile and **save** any of **your own files** as a **template.** Regardless of what kind of project you're working on—CD label, business card, book cover, Web graphics—using a template can save you time and labor. When creating a template, you can choose settings and layout aids such as guides, zoom level, and artboard dimensions; and you can create brushes, swatches, symbols, graphic styles, crop marks, and, of course, path objects.

To create a template:

1. Create a new file, then create any path objects, swatches, graphic styles, symbols, etc. that you want to save in a template.

You can also choose specifications for the artboard; set a zoom level or custom views; create layers and guides; and define transparency flattener, PDF, and print presets.

You can even create text boxes containing instructions for the lucky user of your template.

2. Save the file via File > **Save as Template** (leave the format as Illustrator Template (ait). That's all there is to it.

3 *A business card template in the Club folder*

Create Template

Changing the document setup

In the center of every Illustrator document is a nonmovable artboard work area **1**. You chose the dimensions for your artboard in the New Document dialog box, but you can **change** those **dimensions** at any time via the Document Setup dialog box. In other words, the artboard size doesn't have to match the size (e.g., paper size) or orientation of the output medium.

To change the artboard dimensions or orientation:

1. Choose File > **Document Setup** (Cmd-Option-P/Ctrl-Alt-P). The Document Setup dialog box opens.

2. Choose **Artboard** from the topmost menu.

3. From the **Setup: Size** menu, choose a preset size **2**. The options listed will depend on which profile (e.g., Print, Web) you chose in the New Document dialog box.**NEW!**
   or
   To enter custom dimensions, choose a mesurement unit from the **Units** menu (for Web output, use Pixels), then enter **Width** and **Height** values. Custom will become the selection on the Size menu. *Note:* For the current document, the Units chosen here override the Units chosen in Preferences > Units & Display Performance.

4. Click a different **Orientation** icon, if desired.

5. *Optional:* Check Show Images in Outline Mode to display a low-resolution version of

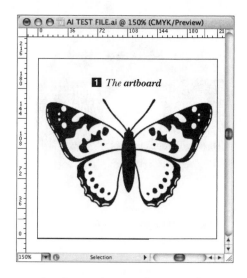

1 *The artboard*

any placed, raster images when your document is in Outline view.

6. Click OK.

7. *Optional:* If you changed the artboard orientation, you can double-click the upper left corner of the document window to reset the ruler origin (the actual ruler origin is located in the lower left corner); to show or hide the rulers, press Cmd-R/Ctrl-R.

➤ Objects (or parts of objects) that you stash outside the artboard will save with your file.

➤ Double-click the Hand tool in the Tools panel to display the entire artboard in the document window.

2 *In the **Document Setup** dialog box, you can choose a preset **Size** or enter custom **Width** and **Height** values.*

The artboard and printing

In the default setup for printing, only objects (or parts of objects) that are within the artboard area will print.

You can use the **Setup** panel in File > Print to reposition the printable page relative to the artboard. If the illustration is oversized, for example, in the Setup panel you can specify that it be tiled (subdivided) into a grid so it will print in sections on the paper size of your chosen printer (see pages 380–381).

To view the relationship between the current artboard and the paper size for the currently chosen printer, choose View > **Fit in Window**

and View > **Show Page Tiling.** The outermost dotted rectangle that you see onscreen represents the paper size; the inner, dotted rectangle represents the actual printable area, which accounts for the printer's nonprintable margins at the edge of the paper **1**.

➤ Although you could use the Page tool to reposition the printable page relative to the artboard, we recommend doing this via the Setup options in the Print dialog box.

To learn more about printing files from Illustrator, see Chapter 30.

1 *View > **Show Page Tiling** is on for this document. Here, the size and orientation of the printable page don't match the size and orientation of the artboard.*

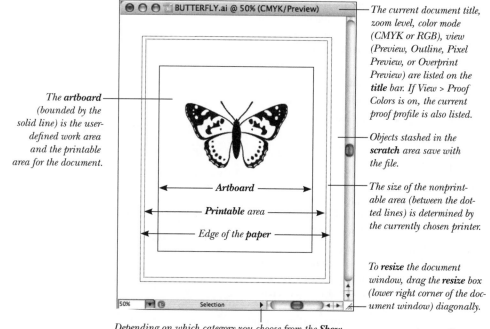

*The current document title, zoom level, color mode (CMYK or RGB), view (Preview, Outline, Pixel Preview, or Overprint Preview) are listed on the **title** bar. If View > Proof Colors is on, the current proof profile is also listed.*

*The **artboard** (bounded by the solid line) is the user-defined work area and the printable area for the document.*

*Objects stashed in the **scratch** area save with the file.*

Artboard

Printable *area*

Edge of the **paper**

The size of the nonprintable area (between the dotted lines) is determined by the currently chosen printer.

*To **resize** the document window, drag the **resize** box (lower right corner of the document window) diagonally.*

*Depending on which category you choose from the **Show** submenu on the **status** bar menu, the status bar displays the current tool name, date and time from the computer's internal clock, number of available undos, or document color profile (RGB or CMYK). A Version Cue Status option will also be available if Enable Version Cue is checked in Preferences (Cmd-K/Ctrl-K) > File Handling & Clipboard. Option-click/Alt-click the status bar menu to access the moon phase, shopping days 'til Christmas, and other vital statistics.*

Artboard and Printing

Saving files

There are 6 formats to choose from when saving an Illustrator file: Adobe Illustrator (ai), Illustrator EPS (eps), Illustrator Template (ait), Adobe PDF (pdf), SVG Compressed (svgz), and SVG (svg). Files in all 6 formats can be reopened and edited in Illustrator.

If you're going to print your file directly from Illustrator, you can stick with the **Adobe Illustrator Document** format (ai), or "Illustrator format," for short (see below). If you're going to display your file online or export it to an application that doesn't read native Illustrator files (such as a layout application, for print output), you'll need to save a copy of it in a nonnative format; see Chapter 31.

To save a file in the Illustrator format:

1. If the file has never been saved, choose File > **Save** (Cmd-S/Ctrl-S). If the file has already been saved in a different format, choose File > **Save As.** In either case, the Save As dialog box opens.

2. Enter a name in the Save As/File Name field.

3. Navigate to the desired folder or disk.

4. In the Mac OS, choose **Format: Adobe Illustrator Document.**

   In Windows, choose **Save as Type: Adobe Illustrator (*.AI).**

5. Click **Save.** The Illustrator Options dialog box opens **1**. Leave Illustrator CS3 as the choice on the **Version** menu. (For the legacy formats, see the sidebar at right.)

6. Under **Fonts,** enter a percentage in the **Subset Fonts When Percent of Characters Used Is Less Than** field to save fonts used in the illustration as part of the document. If not all the characters in a particular font are being used in your artwork, this option allows you to embed just a subset of characters, as opposed to the whole font, to help reduce the file size. For example, at a setting of 50%, the entire font will be embedded only if you use more than 50% of its characters in the file, and the Subset

Saving in other CS versions

To save a CS3 file in an earlier Illustrator CS format, in the Illustrator Options dialog box (step 5 on this page), choose the desired format under **Version: CS Formats.** Hopefully, you won't find a need to save a file in a pre-CS version of Illustrator, as those versions can't save such elements as effects, Live Paint groups, and transparency. Saving to an earlier CS version can also cause unexpected text reflows.

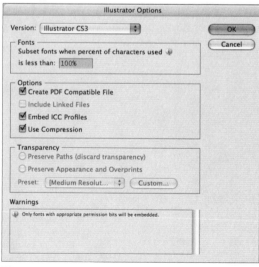

1 *The **Illustrator Options** dialog box, with options shown for the Illustrator CS3 format*

Shortcuts for saving files

Save edits in already saved file (no dialog box opens), or open Save As dialog box if file hasn't been saved	Cmd-S/Ctrl-S
Open **Save As** dialog box	Cmd-Shift-S/Ctrl-Shift-S
Open **Save a Copy** dialog box	Cmd-Option-S/Ctrl-Alt-S

option will be used if you use fewer than 50% of its characters in the file.

Characters in embedded fonts will display and print on any system, even where they aren't installed, but keep in mind that the higher the Subset Fonts... percentage, the more characters will be embedded, and the larger the file size. At 100%, all font characters will be embedded.

7. Under **Options,** you can check:

Create PDF Compatible File to save a PDF-compatible version of the file for use in other applications that support PDF. Check this option if you're planning to export your Illustrator file to Photoshop. This option increases the file size of your Illustrator file.

Include Linked Files to save a copy of any linked files with the illustration. Read about linking in Chapter 19.

If a profile was chosen in Edit > Assign Profile, check **Embed ICC Profiles** to embed those profiles in the file to properly color-manage the file.

Use Compression to compress vector data (and PDF data, if included) to help reduce the file storage size.

8. Click OK.

➤ If Enable Version Cue is checked in Preferences > File Handling & Clipboard, you can click Use Adobe Dialog in the Save dialog box to utilize the Version Cue file management features in the Adobe Creative Suite applications. Read about Adobe Version Cue in Illustrator Help.

The prior version of a file is overwritten each time you execute the **Save** command. Do yourself a favor and save often—don't be shy about it! And be sure to create backups of your work frequently, too.

To resave a file:

Choose File > **Save** (Cmd-S/Ctrl-S).

When you use the **Save a Copy** command, the original version of the file stays open onscreen, and a copy of it is saved to disk.

To save a copy of a file:

1. Choose File > **Save a Copy** (Cmd-Option-S/ Ctrl-Alt-S). The Save a Copy dialog box opens.

2. To save the file in the Illustrator (ai) format, see the previous two pages; for other formats, see Chapter 31.

To revert to the last saved version:

1. Choose File > **Revert** (F12).

2. Click **Revert**.

Ending a work session

To close a file:

In the Mac OS, click the **close** (red) button in the upper left corner of the document window (Cmd-W). In Windows, click the **close** box in the upper right corner of the document window (Ctrl-W).

If the file was modified since it was last saved, an alert dialog box will appear ▇. Click Don't Save to close the file without saving your changes; or click Save to resave the file before closing it; or click Cancel to back out of the deal.

To quit/exit Illustrator:

In the Mac OS, choose Illustrator > **Quit** Illustrator (Cmd-Q). In Windows, choose File > **Exit** (Ctrl-Q) or click the close box for the application window.

All open Illustrator files will close. If you edited any open files since they were last saved, an alert dialog box will appear. To resave the file(s), click Save, or to quit/exit Illustrator without saving your changes, click Don't Save.

Save As or Save a Copy?

You can use the Save As or Save a Copy command to save an existing file in a different format, such as Illustrator AI, Adobe PDF, or Illustrator EPS. When you use **Save As** (discussed on the previous two pages), the file with the new name stays open onscreen, while the file with the original name closes but is preserved on disk. With **Save a Copy,** discussed at left, the original file stays open onscreen, while the copy with the new name is saved to disk.

Fast close

To close **all** open Illustrator files quickly, Option-click/Alt-click the close button/box on one of the document windows, and respond to any warning prompts that appear.

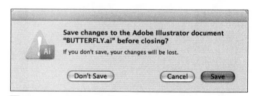

1 *If you try to close a file that you modified since it was last saved, this prompt will appear.*

BRIDGE 3

In this chapter you'll learn how to open files via the Open command and via Bridge, a separate program that serves as a conduit for all the programs in the Adobe Creative Suite. You'll also learn how to reconfigure the Bridge window and use Bridge to move, copy, rate, sort, group, find, rename, delete, and assign keywords to files.

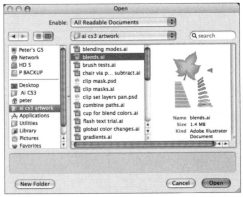

1 *The **Open** dialog box in **Mac OS X***

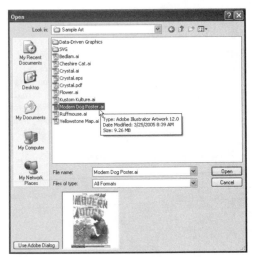

2 *The **Open** dialog box in **Windows***

Opening files from Illustrator

You can follow the instructions on this page to open Illustrator files using the **Open** command in Illustrator. Or if you'd prefer to use the Bridge application to open files—as we do—turn the page. (To learn how to import files from other programs into Illustrator, see Chapter 19.)

To open a file from Illustrator:

1. Choose File > **Open** (Cmd-O/Ctrl-O).
   or
   If the Adobe Illustrator CS3 welcome screen is onscreen, click the **Open** icon.

2. The Open dialog box appears **1**–**2**. In the Mac OS, to list files only in the formats that Illustrator can read, choose **Enable: All Readable Documents**; in Windows, to list all files, readable and not, choose **Files of Type: All Formats** or choose a format.

3. Locate and click a file name, then click **Open.** If an alert dialog box about a color profile appears, see the sidebar on page 54; for the Font Problems dialog box, see the sidebar on page 41; and for an alert dialog box about a linked image file, see page 262.

➤ To reopen a recently opened file, choose it from the File > Open Recent Files submenu.

To open a file from the Macintosh Desktop or Windows Explorer:

Double-click an Illustrator file icon. In the Mac OS, you can also open a file by dragging its icon over the Adobe Illustrator CS3 application icon on the Dock. Illustrator will launch if it isn't already running.

Using Bridge

The **Bridge** application serves as a conduit among all the programs in the Adobe Creative Suite. With its large thumbnail previews of files from Adobe Creative Suite applications, Bridge is also the best vehicle for opening files—plus it offers many other useful features. In Bridge you can display, arrange, rate, and sort thumbnails; organize thumbnails into collapsible stacks; assign keywords to files; and view data (metadata) about any file. You don't need to learn everything in this chapter at once. Master the basics in the first half of the chapter, then explore the other features at your leisure.

To launch Bridge:

In Illustrator, at the far right side of the Control panel, click the **Go to Bridge** button ![Br] (Cmd-Option-O/Ctrl-Alt-O).
or
In the Mac OS, double-click the **Adobe Bridge** application icon ![Br] in /Applications/Adobe Bridge CS3, or click the Bridge icon ![Br] on the Dock (if someone created one). In Windows, double-click the **Adobe Bridge** application icon ![Br] in C:\Program Files\Adobe\Adobe Bridge CS3.

The Bridge window opens **1**.

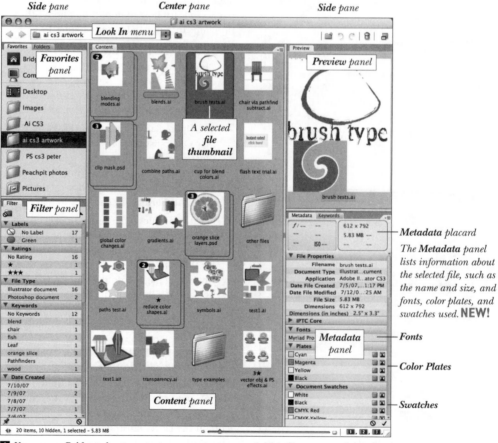

1 *You can use* **Bridge** *to locate, sort, open, move, rename, and delete files, among other tasks.*

Panels and panes in Bridge

By default, the Bridge window contains three panes: a large pane in the center and a vertical pane on either side. Each pane contains one or more panels, which are accessed via tabs: Favorites, Folders, Filter, Content, Preview, Metadata, and Keywords. Panels in the side panes let you manage files, filter the display of thumbnails, and display file data; the large central panel displays file thumbnails. You can hide/show or resize any of the panels or move any panel into a different pane.

We'll explore some of the panels in depth later in this chapter, but for now, here's a brief summary:

The **Favorites** panel displays a list of folders that you've designated as favorites, for quick access. Via check boxes in the Favorite Items area of Bridge Preferences > General, you can control which folders appear in the top part of the panel. To add a folder to the user-created list of folders in the lower part of the panel, drag the folder from the Content panel (the center pane) or from the Finder into the Favorites panel, and release the mouse when the + (plus sign) pointer displays; or click the folder and choose File > Add to Favorites. To remove a Favorites folder from the list, click it, then choose File > Remove from Favorites.

The **Folders** panel contains a scroll window with a hierarchical listing of all the top-level and nested folders on your hard drive.

NEW! The **Filter** panel is dynamic, meaning the categories listed (such as File Type, Keywords, Date Created, and Date Modified) change depending on what data is available for files in the current folder. For example, if you haven't applied ratings to any thumbnails in the current folder, you won't see a Ratings category. Should you apply a rating to a thumbnail, the Ratings category will magically appear. Click an arrowhead to expand or collapse a category.

Click a listing within a category, and only thumbnails that match the listing will display in the Content panel; click again to uncheck the listing and display the files that were filtered out. This is a new, fast way to sort and display files.

In the center pane of the Bridge window, the **Content** panel displays file and nested folder thumbnails. The file name and other file data are listed below each thumbnail.

➤ To toggle the display of metadata on or off in the Content panel, press Cmd-T/Ctrl-T.

The **Preview** panel displays a larger preview of the currently selected file (or folder) thumbnail. If you select a video file, the Preview panel will display a controller for playing the video.**NEW!** If you select a multipage PDF file, you can click the Next Page ➡ or Previous Page ⬅ button to view pages in the file.**NEW!** You can also preview two or more selected thumbnails in this panel for quick comparison.**NEW!**

The **Metadata** panel lists information about the currently selected thumbnail: a quick summary in the "placard" **NEW!** at the top, and detailed listings in categories below. The File Properties category, for example, lists the file name, format, date created, date modified, etc. To expand or collapse a category, click the arrowhead.

You can use the IPTC Core category in the Metadata panel to attach creator, description, copyright, and other information to the currently selected file. Click the field next to a listing, enter or modify the file description information, press Tab to cycle through and edit other data, then click the green Apply button ✓ in the lower right corner. To learn more about the Metadata panel, see Bridge Help.

Use the **Keywords** panel to assign descriptive keywords to files, such as an event, name, location, or other criteria. You can find file thumbnails via a keyword search, or display files based on keywords using the Filter panel.

Opening files from Bridge

You can open as many files in Illustrator as currently available RAM and scratch disk space allow. (To learn how to import files from other programs into Illustrator, see Chapter 19.)

To open files from Bridge:

1. In the **Folders** panel, navigate to the file you want to open. Scroll upward or downward, expand/collapse any folder by clicking the arrowhead, or open and display the contents of a folder by clicking its thumbnail. You can also choose from a list of Favorites or Recent Folders on the **Look In** menu at the top of the Bridge window, or click a folder that you've placed in the **Favorites** panel.

   ➤ To display the contents of a folder, double-click the folder thumbnail in the Content panel.

   ➤ To move up a level in the current folder hierarchy, click the Go Up button 🔼 at the top of the Bridge window.

2. In the Content panel, click a **thumbnail** (for a file whose format Illustrator can open). The thumbnail will now have a colored border, a preview of the file will appear in the Preview panel, and data about the file

will be listed in the Metadata panel. (To select multiple files, Cmd-click/Ctrl-click nonconsecutive thumbnails **1**; or click the first thumbnail in a series of consecutive thumbnails, then Shift-click the last.)

If a thumbnail has a number in the upper left corner, it's part of a stack (thumbnail group). To learn about stacks, see pages 46–47.

3. Double-click a thumbnail or one of the thumbnails you selected, or press Cmd-O/Ctrl-O. Illustrator will launch, if it isn't already running, and the file(s) will appear onscreen. If the Font Problems dialog box appears, see the sidebar on the next page. If an alert about a color profile appears, see the sidebar on page 54; and for an alert about a linked image file, see page 262.

What lies ahead in this chapter

There's more to Bridge than simply clicking a thumbnail or two and opening a file. Starting on the next page, you can learn how to customize your Bridge window. Or to help you manage your Illustrator files as they inevitably start to accumulate, learn how to label, sort, and filter out file thumbnails on pages 45–46.

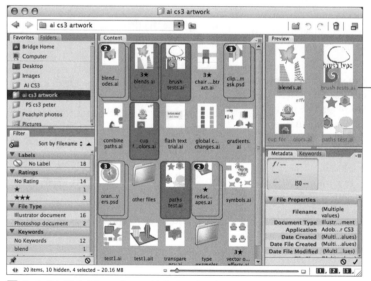

NEW! *The **Preview** panel shows enlargements of all the currently selected thumbnails. You can use this feature to compare files.*

1 *Cmd-click/Ctrl-click to select multiple thumbnails in the **Content** panel.*

Missing fonts?

If you open a file that uses a font that's unavailable to your system, the **Font Problems** dialog box will appear. Click Open to open the document as is, or click Cancel. If a missing font subsequently becomes available to the system, it will also become available on the font lists in Illustrator, and the type will redisplay correctly without any action required on your part.

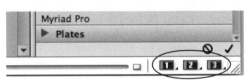

1 *Choose a predefined workspace from one of the workspace menus.*

Choosing a workspace for Bridge

To reconfigure the Bridge window automatically, you can choose from 6 **predefined workspaces**.

To choose a predefined workspace for Bridge: NEW!

From any one of the 3 workspace menus in the lower right corner of the Bridge window **1**, choose **Default, Light Table 2, File Navigator, Metadata Focus, Horizontal Filmstrip,** or **Vertical Filmstrip 3**; or use one of the shortcuts listed in the Window > Workspace submenu.

➤ If you click the preview, a loupe (magnifying lens) appears. You can move the loupe to examine different parts of the graphic. Press + to magnify further, or – to reduce the magnification. (The loupe is useful for examining raster images.)

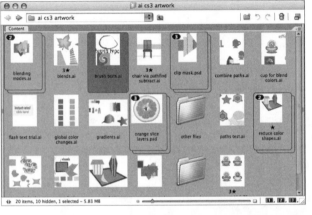

2 *In the **Light Table** workspace, the Content panel occupies the entire Bridge window, allowing you to see a large number of graphics in a folder at once.*

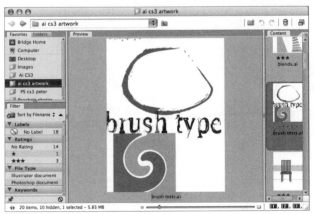

3 *To cycle through thumbnails in the current folder in the **Horizontal** or **Vertical** (shown) **Filmstrip** workspace, press the arrow keys on the keyboard. Shift-click or Cmd-click/Ctrl-click any two thumbnails to compare them in the large Preview panel.**NEW!***

Choose Predefined Workspaces

Customizing the Bridge window

To choose Appearance preferences for the Bridge workspace: NEW!

1. Choose Bridge CS3 (Edit, in Windows) > **Preferences** (Cmd-K/Ctrl-K). The Preferences dialog box opens.

2. On the left side, click General, and in the Appearance area **1**, do any of the following:

   Move the **User Interface Brightness** slider to set the gray value for the side panes.

   Move the **Image Backdrop** slider to set a separate value for the backdrop of the center pane and the Preview panel **2**. *Note:* When we work in Bridge, we use black for our Preview and Content panels (Image Backdrop) and dark gray for everything else (User Interface), but for printing reasons,

lighter colors were used for the figures in this book.

Choose an **Accent Color** for the border around the currently selected folder, thumbnail, or stack, and for selected folders in the Favorites panel.

3. Click **Thumbnails** to switch to that option set. From the **Details: Show** menus, choose to display up to four additional lines of metadata (file info) below the thumbnails. Use this option to list information that's important to you. Also check **Show Tooltips** if you want to use tool tips in Bridge.

4. Click OK.

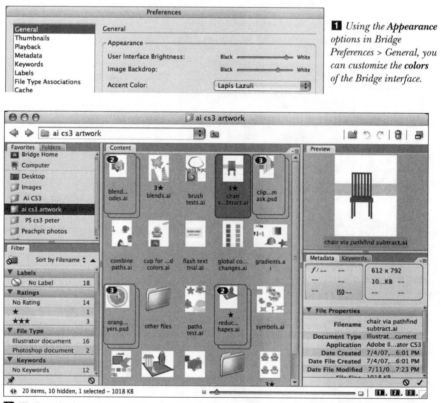

1 *Using the Appearance options in Bridge Preferences > General, you can customize the colors of the Bridge interface.*

2 *We chose the Appearance settings shown in the previous figure to make the center pane dark gray and the side panes medium gray. (This is the Default workspace.)*

To further customize the Bridge workspace, you can resize, move, or hide any of the **panels.** If you save your layout as a user-created workspace, as per the instructions on the next page, you'll be able to access it again quickly at any time.

To customize the Bridge workspace:

To make a panel **taller** or **shorter,** drag the horizontal bar upward or downward; other panels in that group will scale accordingly **1**.

To make a whole pane **wider** or **narrower,** drag the vertical bar sideways **2**; the center pane will resize accordingly.

To display only the Content panel in a compact window, click the **Compact Mode** button in the upper right corner of the Bridge window; click it again to restore the full window. To toggle the entire Bridge window between a bar and Compact mode, click the **Ultra Compact Mode** button.

To **minimize** or **collapse** any panel (except Content) to just a tab, double-click its tab.

Drag any panel tab (name) into another panel **group** (release the mouse when the blue drop zone frame appears around the desired group).

Drag a panel tab **above** or **below** another panel (release the mouse when a horizontal blue drop zone line appears in the desired location).

To change the size of the **thumbnails,** move the thumbnail slider (it's below the Content panel) **3**; or click the Smaller Thumbnail Size button or Larger Thumbnail Size button.

To display thumbnails and folders in the Content panel, check **Show Folders** on the View menu. To hide the folders, choose the command again (remove the check mark).

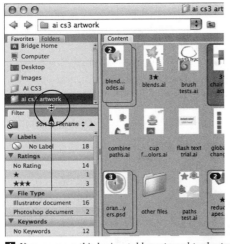

1 *You can move this horizontal bar upward to shorten the Favorites/Folder panels and lengthen the Filter panel.*

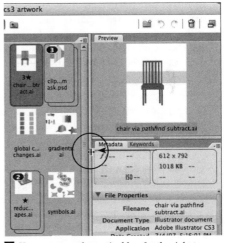

2 *You can move the vertical bar for the right pane to the left to widen the Preview and Metadata panels.*

3 *And you can move the thumbnail slider to resize the thumbnails in the center pane.*

Customize Bridge Workspace

If you **save** your customized **workspace(s)** in Bridge, you won't have to spend time reconfiguring the workspace each time you relaunch the application.

To save a Bridge workspace: NEW!

1. Choose a size and location for the overall Bridge window, a size (and groupings) for the panels, and a thumbnail size for the Content panel.

2. From any of the 3 workspace menus in the lower right corner of the Bridge window, choose **Save Workspace** 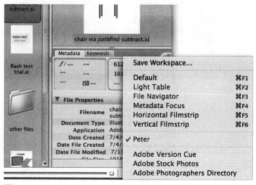. The Save Workspace dialog box opens.

3. Enter a Name for the workspace, choose a Keyboard Shortcut (or choose None), check Save Window Location as Part of Workspace and/or check Save Sort Order as Part of Workspace (both are optional), then click Save. (To learn about sorting thumbnails, see the next page.)

To access saved workspaces: NEW!

To choose any predefined or saved workspace, choose the workspace name from one of the **workspace** menus. The workspace you choose will become the default for that button. Click the button to redisplay that particular workspace.

Any changes you make to the current workspace, such as resizing a panel, will be saved to the button you assigned that workspace to. (Click a different workspace button, then click the button for the modified workspace, and you'll see what we mean.) To redisplay a saved workspace without your changes, choose it from the workspace menu instead of just clicking the button.

Moving and copying files

You can move files to a different folder by dragging them or by using a command.

To move or copy files to other folders:

Method 1 (by dragging)

1. Click the **Folders** panel tab. Display the desired subfolder (expand any folders, if necessary).

2. Select one or more thumbnails in the **Content** panel, then drag them over a folder name in the **Folders** panel to move them, or hold down Option/Ctrl and drag them over a folder name to copy them.

Method 2 (context menu) NEW!

1. Select one or more thumbnails in the **Content** panel.

2. Control-click/right-click in the Bridge window, then from the **Move To** or **Copy To** submenu on the context menu, do either of the following: select a folder name under Recent Folders; or select Choose Folder to open the Choose a Folder/Browse for Folder dialog box, locate a folder, then click Choose/OK.

➤ To locate a file in the Finder/Explorer, click a thumbnail in Bridge, then choose File > Reveal in Finder/Reveal in Explorer. The folder that the file resides in will open in a window in the Finder/Explorer and the file icon will be selected.

1 *Choose Save Workspace from any of the workspace menus.*

Rating		
✓	No Rating	⌘0
	Reject	⌥⌦
	★	⌘1
	★★	⌘2
	★★★	⌘3
	★★★★	⌘4
	★★★★★	⌘5
	Decrease Rating	⌘,
	Increase Rating	⌘.
Label		
	No Label	
	red	⌘6
	Yellow	⌘7
✓	Green	⌘8
	Blue	⌘9
	Purple	

1 *From the Label menu, choose a star Rating or Label color. (Note: In pre-2.1 versions of Bridge, you'll see Label names: Select, Second, Approved, Review, and To Do, instead of color names.)*

2 *This thumbnail has a green label (trust us).*

3 *On this thumbnail, we clicked the third dot to assign a 3-star rating.*

4 *Then we clicked to the left of the stars to remove all the stars.*

Filtering the display of thumbnails

If you assign thumbnails a **star rating** and/or **color label**, you'll be able to display them based on the presence or absence of that rating or label and find them easily via the Filter panel and Find command.

To label and rate thumbnails:

1. Select one or more thumbnails in the Content panel (Cmd-click/Ctrl-click nonconsecutive thumbnails, or Shift-click consecutive thumbnails).

2. Do any of the following:

Control–click/right-click one of the thumbnails and from the **Label** submenu on the context menu, choose a category. A colored bar will appear below the thumbnail.

From the Label menu, choose a star **Rating** and/or **Label** **1**–**2**.

Click a thumbnail, then click any one of the 5 **dots** below the thumbnail (not available if the thumbnails are small). Stars will appear **3**.

➤ To remove a star, click the star to its left. To remove all the stars from a thumbnail, click to the left of the first star **4**.

The **sorting order** you choose from the new Filter panel affects the order in which thumbnails display in the Content panel. Criteria you check in the main part of the Filter panel, which lists data specific to files in the current folder, control which thumbnails display. By filtering thumbnails, you'll be able to locate the ones you need more quickly and efficiently. The current sorting order applies to all folders and thumbnails that are displayed in Bridge, not just to one specific folder.

To choose a sorting method: NEW!

From the **Sort by Filename** menu ⬍ at the top of the **Filter** panel, choose a sorting order. Thumbnails will rearrange themselves in the Content panel.

➤ The sorting order commands won't rearrange the actual files on your hard drive.

By checking specific criteria in the **Filter** panel, such as label, rating, file type, date modified, etc., you can control which thumbnails display in a given folder.

To display thumbnails based on category: NEW!

1. Open a folder of files in Bridge.

2. If the Filter panel isn't showing, choose the **Default** workspace from a workspace menu.

3. Check (click) a listing within a category to display thumbnails that match that criterion ▮. To display thumbnails that match additional criteria, check other listings in the **same** category. To further narrow the selection of thumbnails that displays, check a listing in a **different** category.

4. To remove a check mark from the Filter panel, click the listing again. Hidden thumbnails will redisplay. (To remove all check marks from the Filter panel, click the Clear Filter ⊘ button at the bottom of the panel.)

➤ To preserve the current check marks as you display other folders, click the Keep Filter When Browsing 📌 button at the bottom of the Filter panel (the button turns greenish); to cancel this function, click the button again.

Arranging thumbnails

To rearrange thumbnails manually:

Drag a thumbnail (or multiple thumbnails) to a new location. The Sort order on the Sort By menu (Filter panel) switches to Manually.

You can group thumbnails into **stacks,** which is like sorting papers into manila folders on a desk. The center pane will look more tidy, and your thumbnails will be easier to locate.

To group thumbnails into a stack: NEW!

1. Select multiple thumbnails ▮.

2. Choose Stacks > **Group as Stack** (Cmd-G/ Ctrl-G). The stack will look like two playing cards in a pile, with the stack thumbnail on top ▮. The number in the upper left corner indicates the current number of thumbnails in the stack.

▮ *Because we've checked the 3-star option under **Ratings** in the Filter panel, only thumbnails matching that criterion (that have three stars) display in the Content panel.*

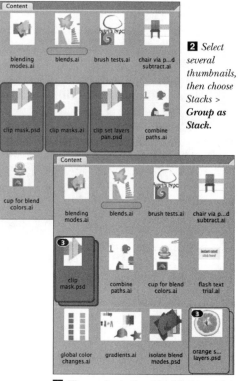

▮ *Select several thumbnails, then choose Stacks > **Group as Stack**.*

▮ *The number in the upper left corner of a stack indicates how many thumbnails it contains.*

To expand or collapse a stack: NEW!

To select and display all the thumbnails in a stack, click the stack **number.** Click the number again to collapse the stack. To select one thumbnail in an expanded stack, click that thumbnail.

To move a whole stack: NEW!

1. Option-click/Alt-click a stack that's in its collapsed state, to select the whole stack.

2. Drag the file thumbnail (not the border).

To add a thumbnail to a stack: NEW!

Click a thumbnail, then drag it onto a stack.

To remove a thumbnail from a stack: NEW!

1. Click the stack number to expand the stack.

2. Click a thumbnail, then drag it out of the stack.

To ungroup a whole stack: NEW!

Click a stack, then choose Stacks > **Ungroup from Stack** (Cmd-Shift-G/Ctrl-Shift-G). The stack number and border will disappear.

Managing files

To create a new folder:

Click the **New Folder** button at the top of the window, type a name in the highlighted field below the new folder, then press Return/Enter.

To delete files:

1. Click a thumbnail (or Cmd-click/Ctrl-click multiple thumbnails or Shift-click a series of thumbnails), then press Cmd-Delete/ Ctrl-Backspace.

2. Click OK. To retrieve a deleted file or folder, double-click the Trash icon/Recycle Bin for the operating system, then drag the item into the Content panel in Bridge.

To rename a file:

1. Click a thumbnail, then click the file name. Text to the left of the period will become selected.

2. Type a new name (don't try to delete the extension) ◆, then press Return/Enter.

◆ *Click a file name to select it, then type a new name.*

Stack Thumbnails; Manage Files

Searching for files

To find files via Bridge:

1. In Bridge, choose Edit > **Find** (Cmd-F/Ctrl-F). The Find dialog box opens **1**.

2. From the **Look In** menu, choose a folder to search through. To select a folder that's not on the list, choose Look In > Browse, locate the desired folder, then click Choose/OK.

3. From the menus in the **Criteria** area, choose search criteria (e.g., Filename, Date Created, Rating, etc.), choose a parameter from the adjoining menu, and enter data in the field. To include additional criteria in the search, click the ⊕, then choose or enter more search criteria.

4. From the **Match** menu, choose "If any criteria are met" to find files based on one or more criteria, or choose "If all criteria are met" to narrow the selection to files that meet all the chosen criteria.

5. Check **Include All Subfolders** to search all subfolders inside the folder you chose in step 2.

6. *Optional:* Check Include Non-Indexed Files to search through files that Bridge hasn't yet indexed (any folder Bridge has yet to display). This will make the search run more slowly.

7. Do either of the following:

To copy the search results and send them to a temporary folder called Search Results, click **Find.** The files will display in the Content panel and the Search Results folder will appear on the Recent Folders list on the Look In menu at the top of the Bridge window. Each time you perform a search and click Find, another generic Search Results listing appears on the menu, with no hint as to its content. This quickly becomes confusing.

To save a copy of the search results to a permanent file group, click **Save as Collection.NEW!** In the Save Collection dialog box, enter a name in the Save As field, choose a location for the found files to be copied to (the current folder is acceptable), then click Save; the files will display in the Content panel. Navigate to the folder you chose for the collection; a Collect thumbnail bearing the name you entered will display in the Content panel. Double-click the thumbnail to rerun the search and view the search results.

1 *Use the **Find** dialog box to search for and locate files according to various criteria.*

Find Files

Exporting the Bridge cache

Each time you display a folder in the Content panel in Bridge, the program automatically creates a cache file containing information about the files in that folder, such as the data for displaying ratings, labels, and high-quality thumbnails. Having the cache helps speed up the display of thumbnails when you choose that folder again. If you want to include this display information with files you copy to a removable disk or to a shared folder on a network, you'll need to copy the cache files—but before you can do so, you have to **build** the **cache files** and export them to the current folder.

To export the cache to the current folder: NEW!

1. Choose Bridge CS3 (Edit, in Windows) > Preferences, then click **Cache.** Check Automatically Export Caches to Folders When Possible, then click OK.

2. Choose Tools > Cache > **Build and Export Cache,** then click OK when the alert dialog box appears.

3. Two hidden cache files—named .BridgeCache (metadata cache) and .BridgeCacheT (thumbnail cache)—will be placed into the currently displayed folder.

   If you use the File > **Move To** (or Copy To) command in Bridge to move (or copy) selected thumbnails, the folder cache you just created will also move or copy, thanks to the export option that you turned on in Preferences > Cache.

➤ To display the cache files in the Content panel, choose View > Show Hidden Files.

If you suspect a folder cache may be causing a display problem, **purging** it may resolve the issue. Doing so will also cause Bridge to regenerate the high-quality thumbnails, so be patient while this occurs.

To rebuild the cache files: NEW!

To rebuild the cache files in the current folder, choose Tools > Cache > **Purge Cache for Folder** "[current folder name]." Two new (hidden) cache files will be generated.

Assigning keywords to files

Keywords (identifying text) are used by search utilities to locate files and by file management programs to organize them. In Bridge, you can create keywords and assign them to your files. You can also locate files in Bridge via the Find command with Keywords as a search criterion, or by checking the desired keywords under the Keywords category in the Filter panel.

Note: These instructions pertain to, and were tested in, Bridge 2.1.

To create and assign keywords to files: NEW!

I. In the **Keywords** panel, do either of the following:

Click an **existing** keyword category to select it.

Create a new category by clicking the **New Keyword** button at the bottom of the panel, ✛ type a name, then press Return/ Enter. Leave the new category selected.

2. To create a nested keyword, click the **New Sub Keyword** button. 🔖 Enter a keyword, then press Return/Enter **1**.

3. To assign a keyword to a file, click a file thumbnail (or select multiple thumbnails), then check the box to the left of a sub-keyword **2**.

➤ To rename a keyword or category, click the word or category, choose Rename from the Keywords panel menu, type a name, then press Return/Enter.

➤ To remove a keyword or category, click the word or category, click the Delete Keyword button, 🗑 then click Yes in the alert dialog.

➤ You can drag a keyword into a different category.

Note: If you import a file that has keywords assigned to it already, those keywords will be listed separately (with check boxes) in the Other Keywords category in the Keywords panel and will also be listed under Keywords in the Filter panel.

1 *We created a new* **Keyword** *category called Objects, kept the category selected, then via the* **New Sub Keyword** *button, added 6 nested keywords to that category.*

2 *After clicking a file thumbnail, check the* **keywords** *that you want to assign to that file.*

MANAGE COLOR | 4

In this chapter you'll learn how to use color settings to manage and maintain color consistency between documents and output devices; synchronize the color settings of all the programs in the Adobe Creative Suite; change document color profiles; and finally, soft-proof your artwork onscreen.

Choosing color settings

Problems with color can creep up on you when various hardware devices and software packages you use treat color differently. If you open a file in several different imaging programs or Web browsers, the colors in the image might look completely different in each case, and thus may not match the color of the picture you originally scanned in. Print the image, and you'll probably find that your results are different yet again. In some cases, you might find these differences to be slight and unobjectionable, but in other cases, such color changes can wreak havoc with your design and turn your project into a disaster.

A **color management system** can solve most of these problems by acting as a color interpreter. Such a system knows how each device and program understands color, and by using color profiles (mathematical descriptions of the color space of each device), makes the proper adjustments so the colors in your files look the same as you move them from one program or device to another. Illustrator, Photoshop, and other programs in the Adobe Creative Suite use the standardized ICC (International Color Consortium) profiles to tell your color management system how specific devices use color. Whether you're planning a traditional print run or will be using the same graphic for multiple purposes (such as for Web and print), you'll benefit from using color management.

In Illustrator, you'll find most of the color management controls in Edit > **Color Settings.** This dialog box gives you access to preset management settings for various publishing situations, including press and Web output, and also lets you choose custom settings. There are three main areas in the dialog box:

➤ The **Working Spaces** govern how RGB and CMYK colors are displayed in your document and serve as the default color profile for new Illustrator documents.

➤ The **Color Management Policies** for RGB and CMYK color files govern how the program deals with color when opening files that don't have an attached color profile, or when a file's profile doesn't match the current color settings of your working space.

➤ The **Conversion Options** (available when Advanced Mode is checked) control which color management engine is used for converting colors between color spaces.

Choosing the correct color settings will help keep your colors consistent from the first document version to the final output. The abundance of options may appear complex at first, but you and your documents will benefit if you take the time to learn about them.

➤ For high-end print output, ask your print shop to recommend specific color management settings to ensure that your color management workflow runs smoothly.

(Continued on the following page)

Color Management

Monitor basics

There are two basic types of computer displays: CRT (cathode ray tube, as in a traditional TV set) and LCD (liquid crystal display, or flat panel). The display performance of a **CRT** fluctuates due to its analog technology and the fact that its display phosphors (which produce the glowing dots onscreen) fade over time. Also, it must be calibrated at least once a month using its built-in brightness and contrast controls. A CRT display can be calibrated reliably for only about 3 years.

An **LCD** display uses a grid of fixed-sized liquid crystals that filter color coming from a back-light source. Although you can adjust only the brightness on an LCD (not the contrast), the LCD digital technology offers more reliable color conisistency than a CRT without the character-istic flickering of a CRT. The newest LCD models provide good viewing angles, display accurate color, and use a daylight temperature of 6500K for the white point. They're produced under tighter manufacturing standards than CRTs. Plus, in most cases the color profile that's provided with an LCD display (and that is installed in your system automatically) describes the display characteristics accurately.

Calibrating your display

The first step toward achieving color consistency is to calibrate your display by adjusting the con-trast and brightness, gamma, color balance, and white point.

In the Mac OS, Illustrator relies on the Calibrate utility, which is found in the Displays panel (Color tab) in System Preferences. The utility generates an ICC profile that the operating system refers to in order to display colors accurately onscreen.

If you're using a Windows machine, or you want to generate a more complete profile in the Mac OS, you'll need to use a hardware calibrator. You have to calibrate your display and save the settings as an ICC profile just once; thereafter, the profile will be available to all your applica-tions. (For more information about calibrating a display, see Illustrator Help or our *Photoshop CS3: Visual QuickStart Guide.*)

Color spaces and profiles

Each device can capture and reproduce only a limited range (gamut) of colors. This is known as the **color space** of that device. The mathematical description of the color space of each device is called the **color profile**. The color management system uses the color profile to define the colors in your document. Illustrator uses the document profile to display and edit artwork colors; or if the document doesn't have a profile, Illustrator uses the current working space instead (the color space profile you'll choose in Color Settings).

To choose color settings:

1. Choose Edit > **Color Settings** (Cmd-Shift-K/ Ctrl-Shift-K). The Color Settings dialog box opens (**1**, page 55).

2. Choose a preset from the **Settings** menu. We'll summarize the four basic presets:

   Monitor Color sets the RGB working space to your display profile. This is a good choice for video output, but not for print output.

   North America General Purpose 2 meets the requirements for screen and print output in the United States and Canada. All profile warnings are off.

   North America Prepress 2 manages color to conform with common press conditions in the United States. The default RGB color space assigned to this setting is Adobe RGB. When CMYK documents are opened, their values are preserved.

   North America Web/Internet is designed for online output. All RGB images are con-verted to the sRGB color space.

3. At this point you can click OK to accept the predefined settings or you can proceed with the remaining steps to choose custom settings.

   The **Working Spaces** menus control how RGB and CMYK colors will be treated in a document that lacks an embedded profile. You can either leave these settings as is or choose other options. The RGB options are discussed below. For the CMYK setting, you should ask your output service provider which working space to choose.

   Choose one of these RGB color spaces:

   Monitor RGB [current monitor name] sets the RGB working space to your display pro-file, which is useful if you know that other applications you'll be using for your project don't support color management. Keep in mind, however, that if you share files that use your monitor profile (as the working space) with another user, their monitor pro-file will be substituted for the RGB working

space. This may undermine the color consistency you're aiming for.

Adobe RGB (1998) contains a wide range of colors and is useful when converting RGB images to CMYK images. This working space is recommended for output to a photo inkjet printer, but not for online output.

Apple RGB is useful if you need to work with older desktop publishing files for output to Macintosh displays, as it reflects the characteristics of older standard Apple 13-inch monitors.

ColorMatch RGB contains a smaller range of colors than Adobe RGB (1998) but, because it matches the color space of Radius Pressview displays, is useful for print work.

ProPhoto RGB contains a very wide range of colors and is useful for output to high-end dye sublimation and inkjet printers.

sRGB IEC61966-2.1 is a good choice for Web output, as it reflects the settings on the average computer display. Many hardware and software manufacturers are using this as the default space for scanners, low-end printers, and software.

ColorSync RGB–Generic RGB Profile (Mac OS only) matches the Illustrator RGB space to the space specified in the Apple ColorSync Utility. (This can be the profile you created using System Preferences > Displays when you calibrated your display.) If you share this configuration with another user, it will utilize the ColorSync space as specified in that user's system.

4. To choose a color management policy that will tell Illustrator how to deal with artwork that doesn't match your current color settings, from the **RGB** and **CMYK** menus in the **Color Management Policies** area:

   Choose **Off** to prevent files from being color-managed when imported or opened.

   Choose **Preserve Embedded Profiles** if you think you're going to be working with both

(Continued on the following page)

color-managed and non-color-managed documents. This option ties each color file's profile to the individual file. Remember, in Illustrator, each open document can have its own profile.

Choose **Convert to Working Space** if you want all your documents to reflect the same color working space. This is usually the best choice for Web work.

For **Profile Mismatches,** check **Ask When Opening** to have Illustrator display an alert if the color profile in a file you're opening doesn't match the application's working space. If you choose this option, you can override your color management policy when opening documents.

Check **Ask When Pasting** to have Illustrator display an alert when color profile mismatches occur as you paste color images into your document. If you choose this option, you can override your current color management policy when pasting.

For files with **Missing Profiles,** check **Ask When Opening** to have Illustrator display an alert offering you the opportunity to assign a profile to the file you're opening.

5. *Optional:* If you've chosen custom color settings that you want to save for later use, click Save. To have your custom file name display on the Settings menu, save it in the default location. In the Mac OS, that location is Users/[user name]/Library/ Application Support/Adobe/Color/Settings; and in Windows, it's C:\Documents and Settings\[user name]\Application Data\ Adobe\Color\Settings.

6. Click OK.

➤ To reuse your saved settings, choose the file name from the Settings menu in the Color Settings dialog box. To load a settings file that wasn't saved in the Settings folder (and thus isn't listed on the Settings menu), click Load.

Responding to a profile alert

If you open an Illustrator document, and its embedded color profile doesn't match the current RGB or CMYK working space, the **Embedded Profile Mismatch** alert dialog box opens. We suggest that you click one of the first two options in the dialog box, and click OK.

If you open an Illustrator document that doesn't contain an embedded color profile, the **Missing Profile** alert dialog box opens. Here too, we suggest that you click one of the first two options in the dialog box, and click OK.

Color Settings

Unsynchronized: Your Creative Suite applications are not synchronized for consistent color. To synchronize, select Suite Color Settings in Bridge.

OK

Cancel

Load...

Save...

Settings: North America Prepress 2

☐ Advanced Mode

Working Spaces

RGB: Adobe RGB (1998)

CMYK: U.S. Web Coated (SWOP) v2

*The **Working Spaces** options govern the display of RGB and CMYK colors and provide a default color profile for new documents.*

Color Management Policies

RGB: Preserve Embedded Profiles

🔒 CMYK: Preserve Numbers (Ignore Linked Profiles)

Profile Mismatches: ☑ Ask When Opening

☑ Ask When Pasting

Missing Profiles: ☑ Ask When Opening

*The **Color Management Policies** govern how colors are treated when you open a file that lacks a color profile or that contains a profile that conflicts with the current color settings.*

Description:

Preparation of content for common printing conditions in North America. CMYK values are preserved. Profile warnings are enabled.

*Rest the pointer over a menu or option, and read about it in the **Description** area.*

Color Settings

1 *When you choose a preset from the Settings menu in the **Color Settings** dialog box, the options below the menu are chosen for you automatically. You can choose custom settings for any preset.*

Synchronizing the color settings

If the color settings in another Adobe Creative Suite program (such as Photoshop CS3) don't match the current settings in Illustrator, an alert will display at the top of the Color Settings dialog box in Illustrator **1**. If you don't own the complete Adobe Creative Suite, you'll have to start up the errant application and fix its color settings by hand. If you are lucky enough to have the whole suite installed, you can use the **Suite Color Settings** dialog box in Bridge to **synchronize** the color settings of all the programs in the suite.

Color Settings

Unsynchronized: Your Creative Suite applications are not synchronized for consistent color. To synchronize, select Suite Color Settings in Bridge.

1 *This alert tells us that the color settings in our* **Creative Suite** *applications aren't synchronized.*

To synchronize color settings using Bridge:

I. In Bridge, choose Edit > **Creative Suite Color Settings** (Ctrl-Shift-K/Cmd-Shift-K). The Suite Color Settings dialog box opens **2**, showing the same list of settings as found in the Color Settings dialog box when Advanced Mode is unchecked.

2. Click one of the settings to select it, then click **Apply.** Bridge will change (synchronize) the color settings of the other Adobe Creative Suite applications to match.

Suite Color Settings

Not Synchronized
Your Creative Suite applications are not synchronized for consistent color. "Apply" will synchronize Creative Suite Color Settings.

Monitor Color
Preparation of content for video and on-screen presentation. Emulates color behavior of most video applications. This setting is not recommended for documents with CMYK data.

North America General Purpose 2
General-purpose color settings for screen and print in North America. Profile warnings are disabled.

North America Prepress 2
Preparation of content for common printing conditions in North America. CMYK values are preserved. Profile warnings are enabled.

North America Web/Internet
Preparation of content for non-print usage like the World Wide Web (WWW) in North America. RGB content is converted to sRGB.

VG print
Preparation of content for common press conditions in the U.S.

☐ Show Expanded List of Color Settings Files

[Show Saved Color Settings Files]   (Apply)   (Cancel)

2 *Use the* **Suite Color Settings** *dialog box to synchronize the color settings of the applications in the Adobe Creative Suite.*

Embedding profiles

When you use File > Save As to save a file in a format that supports embedded profiles, such as Adobe Illustrator Document (ai), the **Illustrator Options** dialog box opens. There, you can check **Embed ICC Profiles** to embed a profile with the document, if one has been assigned.

Changing document profiles

When a file's profile doesn't match the current working space or is missing a color profile altogether, you can use the **Assign Profile** command to assign the correct profile. You may notice visible color shifts if the color data of your file is reinterpreted to match the new profile, but rest assured, the color data in the actual document is preserved.

To change or remove a file's color profile:

1. Choose Edit > **Assign Profile.** The Assign Profile dialog box opens **1**.

2. To remove a color profile from your document, click **Don't Color Manage This Document.** The current working space will now control the appearance of colors in your artwork.
   or
   If your document doesn't have an assigned profile or if its profile is different from the current working space, click **Working** [document color mode and name of current working space] to assign that profile.
   or
   To assign a different profile to your document, click **Profile**, then choose the desired profile from the menu. This won't change or convert any color data in your artwork.

3. Click OK.

Assign Profile

Assign Profile
○ Don't Color Manage This Document
◉ Working RGB: Adobe RGB (1998)
○ Profile: [ColorMatch RGB   ▲▼]

[OK]
[Cancel]

1 *Use the **Assign Profile** dialog box to change a file's color profile. The Profile chosen here will also be listed as the Document Profile in the Color Management panel of the File > Print dialog box.*

Proofing a document onscreen

Specifying a color management setup is all well and good, but once you start creating some Illustrator files, you will need to get an idea of how they're going to look in print or online. You can do this by viewing a **soft proof** of your document onscreen. Although this method is less accurate than actually making a print or viewing your Web artwork on different displays, it can give you a general idea of how your work will look in different settings. You can choose either a preset soft-proof setup or custom settings.

To proof your document onscreen:

1. From the View > **Proof Setup** submenu, choose the output display type to be simulated:

To simulate output from your current CMYK printing device, choose the **Working CMYK** profile.

If your document is in RGB Color mode and you want colors to be simulated using the Macintosh display gamma of 1.8 or the Windows display gamma of 2.2 as the proofing space, choose **Macintosh RGB** or **Windows RGB.** Or choose **Monitor RGB** to use your display profile as the proofing space.

To create a proofing model for a specific output device, choose **Customize.** The Proof Setup dialog box opens **1**. From the **Device to Simulate** menu, choose the color profile for your target output device, then check or uncheck **Preserve CMYK** (or RGB) **Numbers.** This option is available only when the document color mode of the current file matches the mode of the output device profile currently chosen on the Device to Simulate menu (e.g., if the document color mode is CMYK and the proofing profile is a CMYK profile). With this option checked, colors will look as if they're not converted to the proofing space. With this option unchecked, Illustrator colors will appear as if converted, and you'll need to choose a **Rendering Intent** (see the sidebar). Click OK.

2. *Optional:* The Display Options (On-Screen) are available for some profiles. Simulate Paper

The Rendering Intents

Perceptual changes colors in a way that seems natural to the human eye, while attempting to preserve the appearance of the overall document. This is a good choice for continuous-tone images.

Saturation changes colors with the intent of preserving vivid colors but compromises color fidelity in order to do so. This is a good choice for charts and business graphics.

Absolute Colorimetric maintains color accuracy only for colors that fall within the destination color gamut (i.e., the color range of your printer) but sacrifices the accuracy of out-of-gamut colors.

Relative Colorimetric, the default intent for all the Adobe predefined settings in the Color Settings dialog box, compares the white, or highlight, of your document's color space to the white of the destination color space (the white of the paper, in the case of a printer), shifting colors where needed. This is the best Intent choice for documents in which most of the colors fall within the color range of your printer (the destination gamut), because it preserves most of the original colors.

1 *Use the **Proof Setup** dialog box to choose custom options for soft-proofing.*

Color simulates the soft white of actual paper, based on the current proof profile. Simulate Black Ink simulates the dark gray that many printers produce when printing black.

3. View > **Proof Colors** will be checked automatically, allowing you to see the soft proof onscreen. Uncheck this option at any time to turn off soft-proofing.

Proof Document Onscreen

In this chapter you'll learn how to change document zoom levels and document views (Preview, Outline, or Pixel Preview), save and choose custom view settings, display a document in more than one window, change screen display modes, move an illustration in its window, and save and manage custom workspace settings.

Changing zoom levels

To change zoom levels via the Navigator panel:

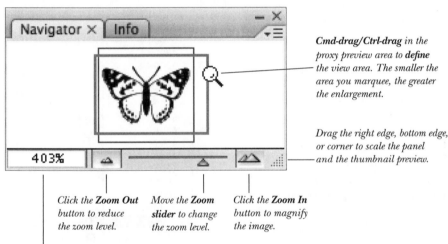

*Cmd-drag/Ctrl-drag in the proxy preview area to **define** the view area. The smaller the area you marquee, the greater the enlargement.*

Drag the right edge, bottom edge, or corner to scale the panel and the thumbnail preview.

*Click the **Zoom Out** button to reduce the zoom level.*

*Move the **Zoom slider** to change the zoom level.*

*Click the **Zoom In** button to magnify the image.*

*Enter the desired **zoom percentage** (between 3.13% and 6400%), then press Return/Enter. Or to zoom to a percentage and keep the field highlighted, press Shift-Return/Shift-Enter.*

➤ To separate the Navigator panel from its group, drag its tab (panel name).

By changing the **zoom level** for the document window, you can display the entire illustration and artboard, a magnified detail, or something in between. The current zoom level is listed as a percentage (3.13%–6400%) on the title bar and in the lower left corner of the document/ application window.

To choose a preset zoom level:

Do any of the following:

Choose View > **Zoom In** (Cmd-+/Ctrl-+). Repeat to further magnify the document.

Choose View > **Zoom Out** (Cmd--/Ctrl--). Repeat, if desired.

Make sure no objects are selected, then Control-click/right-click the document and choose **Zoom In** or **Zoom Out** 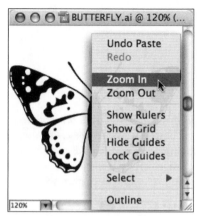.

Choose a preset percentage from the **zoom menu** in the lower left corner of the document/ application window 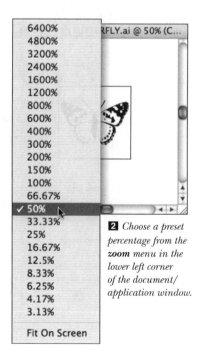. Or choose **Fit on Screen** from the menu to make the entire artboard fit within the current document window size.

Double-click the **zoom field** in the lower left corner of the document/application window, type the desired magnification, then press Return/Enter.

➤ To display the entire artboard in the document window, you can also press Cmd-0/ Ctrl-0 or double-click the Hand tool.

➤ To apply a new zoom value without exiting the zoom field, press Shift-Return/ Shift-Enter.

➤ The zoom level doesn't affect the output size.

1 *Make sure no objects are selected, then Control-click/right-click in the document window and choose* **Zoom In** *or* **Zoom Out** *from the context menu.*

2 *Choose a preset percentage from the* **zoom** *menu in the lower left corner of the document/ application window.*

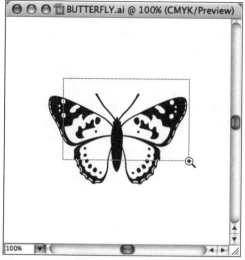

1 *Drag with the **Zoom** tool.*

2 *The illustration is **magnified** onscreen.*

To change the zoom level with the Zoom tool:

1. Choose the **Zoom** tool (Z).

2. In the document window, click in the center of, or drag a marquee across, the area you want to **magnify** **1**–**2**. The smaller the marquee you drag, the greater the degree of magnification.

or

Option-click/Alt-click in the document window to **reduce** the zoom level.

or

Drag a marquee and then, without releasing the mouse, press and hold down the Spacebar, **move** the **marquee** over the area you want to magnify, and release the mouse.

➤ To display an illustration at actual size (100%), double-click the Zoom tool or choose View > Actual Size (Cmd-1/Ctrl-1).

➤ To reposition your illustration in the window, drag in the Navigator panel or use the Hand tool (see pages 65–66).

➤ You can click to change the zoom level while the screen is redrawing.

The fastest method for changing the **zoom level** is via the **keyboard**, because you can do it with any tool selected.

To change the zoom level with any tool selected:

To **increase** the zoom level, Cmd-Spacebar-click/Ctrl-Spacebar-click or -drag in the document window.

or

To **reduce** the zoom level, Cmd-Option-Spacebar-click/Ctrl-Alt-Spacebar-click in the document window.

Zoom Tool, Shortcuts

Changing views

A document can be displayed and edited in four different views: **Preview, Outline, Pixel Preview,** and **Overprint Preview.** In all views, the other View menu commands—Hide/Show Edges, Artboard, Page Tiling, Slices, Guides, and Grid—are accessible, and you can use any selection tool. (Overprint Preview view is discussed on page 385.)

To change the view:

From the View menu, choose **Preview** to display objects with all their fill and stroke colors and all placed images, or choose **Outline** to display all objects as wireframes with no fill or stroke colors. You can press Cmd-Y/Ctrl-Y to toggle between the two views. The screen redraws more quickly in Outline view.
or
Make sure no objects are selected (click a blank area of the artboard), then Control-click/right-click in the document window and choose **Outline** or **Preview** ❶–❷.
or
To activate a 72-ppi preview for Web graphics, choose View > **Pixel Preview** (Cmd-Option-Y/ Ctrl-Alt-Y toggles it on and off) ❸, and also choose View > Actual Size. See also the sidebar at right.

➤ Let's say you're working on a large file, on a slow machine, and you start to view it in all its glory in Preview view—nah, on second thought, you decide you'll preview it later. Press Esc to cancel the preview in progress.

➤ You won't learn much about layers until you get to Chapter 16, but just to give you a glimpse of what's to come, Cmd-click/Ctrl-click the visibility (eye) icon for a layer (not an object) on the Layers panel to toggle between Preview and Outline views for just that layer.

It's a snap

When you choose **Pixel Preview** view (and also View > Actual Size), you can get a good idea of what your vector graphics will look like if you were to rasterize them for the Web, but it's more than just a preview. When you choose this view, View > **Snap to Pixel** is turned on automatically, and edges of objects will snap to the nearest pixel edge as you move or reshape them. Snap to Pixel reduces the need for anti-aliasing and helps keep edges crisp. (Anti-aliasing adds pixels along the edges of objects to make them look smoother but can also diminish their crispness.)

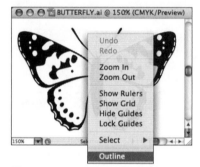

❶ *Deselect all objects, then choose* **Outline** *(or* **Preview***) from the context menu. This is* **Preview** *view.*

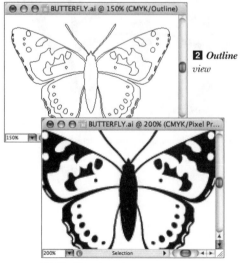

❷ *Outline view*

❸ *Pixel Preview view*

1 *Type a Name for a custom view in the **New View** dialog box.*

2 *In the **Edit Views** dialog box, highlight a view, then change the **Name** or click **Delete**.*

Creating custom views

You can save up to 25 **custom views**, and you can switch among them by using either the View menu or their assigned shortcuts. Each custom view can include a zoom level, scroll bar positions, and a choice of Preview view or Outline view.

To define a custom view:

1. Choose a zoom level for your illustration and choose scroll bar positions.

2. Put your illustration into Preview or Outline view (Cmd-Y/Ctrl-Y).

3. Choose View > **New View**. The New View dialog box opens **1**.

4. In the **Name** field, type a descriptive name for the new view for easy identification (as in "160% view, Preview").

5. Click OK. You can now choose the view name from the bottom of the **View** menu.

➤ You can switch between Outline and Preview views at any time, even for a custom view.

➤ You can assign a keyboard shortcut to any custom view via Edit > Keyboard Shortcuts. In the dialog box, choose Menu Commands from the menu, expand the listing for View, then scroll down to the Custom View listings.

To rename or delete a custom view:

1. Choose View > **Edit Views**.

2. Click the name of the view you want to rename or delete **2**.

3. Change the name in the **Name** field.
   or
   Click **Delete** to delete the view.

4. Click OK. The View menu will update to reflect the changes.

➤ If you want to rename more than one view, you have to click OK and then reopen the dialog box for each one.

Custom Views

Creating new document windows

To make it easier to edit your document, you can display it simultaneously in **two** (or more) **windows.** For one window, you could choose a high zoom level (such as 200%) to edit small details, and for another window, choose a lower zoom level to display the overall composition. Or for one of the windows you could hide individual layers and in the other window you could preview all the layers together.

To create an extra document window:

1. Open an illustration.

2. Choose Window > **New Window.** A new window of the same size will appear directly on top of the first one, bearing the same title, followed by ":2" .

3. In the Mac OS, reposition the new window by dragging its title bar, and resize either or both windows as desired.

   In Windows, you can choose one of these commands from the Window menu: **Cascade** to arrange all currently open windows in a stair-step configuration; **Tile** to arrange them side by side; or **Arrange Icons** to relocate any minimized windows to the bottom of the application window. *Note:* These commands arrange all windows, whether they're displaying a single document or multiple documents.

➤ If you choose Outline view for one window and Preview view for the same illustration in another window, objects will redraw at the same speed in both windows (that is, at the speed of the document in Preview view).

1 *One illustration is displayed in **two windows.***

New Document Windows

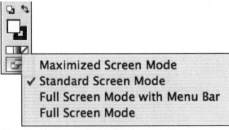

Maximized Screen Mode
✓ Standard Screen Mode
Full Screen Mode with Menu Bar
Full Screen Mode

1 *Choose a screen mode from the **Screen Mode** menu at the bottom of the Tools panel.*

2 *In **Maximized Screen mode**, the document window resizes automatically when you show or hide the panels.*

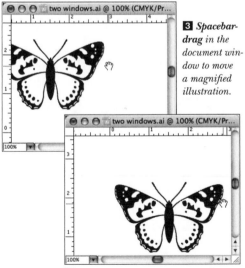

3 *Spacebar-drag in the document window to move a magnified illustration.*

4 *The illustration is **moved** to the lower right.*

Changing screen display modes
To change the screen display mode:
From the **Screen Mode** menu at the bottom of the Toolbox, choose one of the following: **1**

Maximized Screen Mode NEW! to display the illustration in a maximized window with the menu bar and scroll bars accessible, but no title bar **2**. In this mode, the document window resizes dynamically if you expand or collapse a panel dock or press Tab to hide or show the panels. If the panels are hidden and you move the pointer to the very edge of the screen/application window, they'll redisplay temporarily; move the pointer away from the panels, and they'll disappear again (the document window resizes accordingly!).

Standard Screen Mode (the default mode) to display the illusration in a manually resizable document window, with the title bar, menu bar, and scroll bars visible.

Full Screen Mode with Menu Bar to display the illustration in a maximized window with the menu bar visible, but not the title bar or scroll bars.

Full Screen Mode to display the illustration in a maximized window without the title bar, menu bar, or scroll bars (or Dock, in the Mac OS).

➤ Press F to cycle through the 4 modes.

➤ Press Tab to hide (or redisplay) all the currently open panels and docks, including the Tools; press Shift-Tab to hide (or redisplay) all the panels and docks except Tools.

Moving the illustration
To move a different part of an illustration into view, you can use either the Hand tool (see below) or the Navigator panel (next page).

To move the illustration with the Hand tool:
Choose the **Hand** tool (H) 🖐 (or hold down the Spacebar to turn any other tool into a temporary Hand tool), then drag the illustration to the desired position **3**–**4**.

➤ You can also move the illustration by clicking any of the scroll arrows at the edge of the document window.

To move the illustration via the Navigator panel:

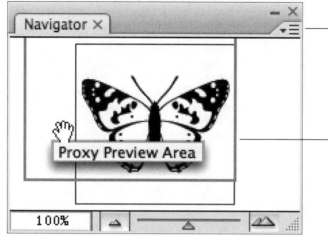

*Choose **View Artboard/Crop Area Only** from the Navigator panel menu to have the panel display only objects that are on the artboard (within the default printable area).*

*Move the illustration in the window by dragging the **proxy preview area** (red rectangle) in the panel, or click the illustration thumbnail to display that area of the illustration.*

➤ To change the color of the view box frame from its default light red, choose Panel Options from the Navigator panel menu, then choose a preset color from the Color menu, or double-click the color swatch and choose a color from the system Colors panel. Check Draw Dashed Lines as Solid Lines to have dashed lines display as solid lines on the panel.

➤ The proportions of the colored view box match the proportions of the document window. Resize the document window, and you'll see what we mean.

➤ The Navigator panel will display multiple pages, if any, and tiling of the imageable area.

Using workspaces

To change your onscreen environment quickly, you can choose one of the three **preset workspaces.**

To choose a preset workspace: NEW!

From the Window > **Workspace** menu, choose one of the following:

[**Basic**] to display icons for 11 panels on a dock on the right side of your screen.

[**Panel**] to display 9 expanded panels for color work and object creation on a dock on the right side of your screen.

[**Type**] to display 11 expanded panels for creating and editing type on a dock on the right side of your screen.

Move Illustration; Choose Preset Workspace

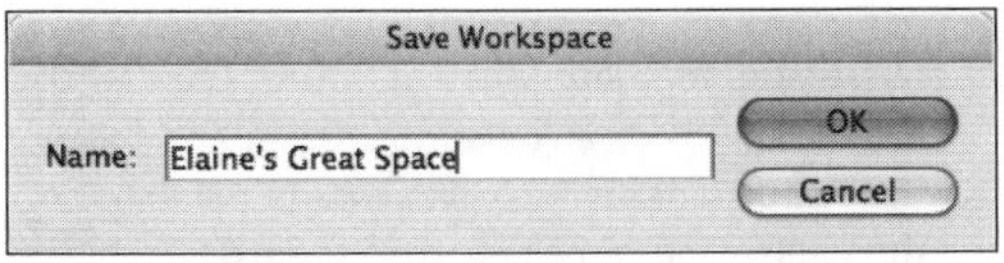

1 *Type a name for the workspace in the Save Workspace dialog box.*

Dual displays

The arrangement of panels on a computer with dual displays is saved as one workspace. You could put all the panels in one display, or put the ones you use most often in one display and the ones you use less often in the other.

If the preset workspaces don't do the trick, you can hide/show or collapse/expand any of the panels or docks and reconfigure the dock to suit your working style. Even better, instead of tediously repeating these steps each time you start a work session, save your **custom settings** as a **workspace**, then simply choose that setting name from the Window > Workspace submenu. In fact, you can save a different workspace for each type of work you do—such as type, drawing, Web work, color work, etc.

To save a workspace:

1. Configure your workspace by doing any or all of the following:

   Position all the panels where you want them, including the Tools panel and any library panels (such as a PANTONE color book), in the desired groups and in the desired location in the dock.

   Expand the panels that you use frequently in one dock and **collapse** the ones you use less frequently to icons in another dock.

   Resize any of the panels, including any panels that open from the Control panel.

   Choose a **thumbnail** or **swatch size** from any panel menu, including any that open from the Control panel. For example, you can choose a different swatch size for the Swatches panel that opens from the Control panel than for the Swatches panel that opens from the Window menu.

   Open any **tearoff toolbars** for tool groups that you use frequently (such as the toolbar for the type tools).

2. Choose Window > Workspace > **Save Workspace**.

3. Enter a **Name** for the workspace **1**. You could use your own name or, if there are multiple custom workspaces, enter a more descriptive title.

4. Click OK. Your workspace (and any other workspaces that you've saved) will be listed on, and can be chosen from, the Window > **Workspace** submenu.

Choose, Save Workspace

To rename, delete, or duplicate a workspace:

1. Choose Window > Workspace > **Manage Workspaces.**

2. Do any of the following:

   To **rename** a workspace, click the workspace name, then type the desired name in the field **2**.

   To delete a workspace, click the workspace name, then click the **Delete Workspace** button.

   To duplicate a workspace, click an existing workspace, then click the **New Workspace** button. Rename the duplicate workspace, if desired.

3. Click OK.

➤ If no workspaces are selected in the Manage Workspaces dialog box when you click the New Workspace button, the new workspace will be based on the current state of your display, panels, etc.

Editing a workspace

If you want to edit an **existing workspace,** follow the instructions on the previous page, but enter the same name in the Save Workspace dialog box. When the alert dialog box appears **1**, click Yes to overwrite the existing workspace.

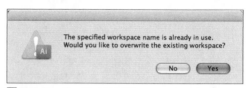

The specified workspace name is already in use. Would you like to overwrite the existing workspace?

No   Yes

1 *This prompt will appear if you try to save a new workspace under an* ***existing name.***

Manage Workspaces

Elaine's Great Space
Peter's Cool Space
Type-related space
Workspace for Color work

Workspace for Color work

OK   Cancel

2 *Use the* ***Manage Workspaces*** *dialog box to rename or delete your custom workspaces.*

GEOMETRIC OBJECTS | 6

In Illustrator, the paths you create consist of anchor points connected by straight and/or curved line segments. Paths can be closed, such as polygons and ovals, or open, such as arcs and straight lines. In this chapter, you're going to be creating a lot of objects, so we'll start off by telling you how to get rid of the ones you don't need. Then you'll learn how to create geometric objects quickly and easily with the Rectangle, Rounded Rectangle, Ellipse, Polygon, Star, Line Segment, Arc, and Spiral tools. Once you've learned the basics in this chapter, your next step is to learn how to select paths for editing (Chapter 7), copy and align them (Chapter 8), apply colors to them (Chapter 9), and change their shape (Chapters 10 and 11).

*Master illustrator **Danny Pelavin** built these crisp, effective graphics from basic **geometric** shapes.*

Deleting objects

You'll be creating lots of different shapes in this chapter, and your artboard may start to become crowded with junk. To remove an object you've just created, choose Edit > Undo (Cmd-Z/Ctrl-Z). To **remove** an **object** that's been lying around, follow these instructions.

To delete objects:

1. Choose the **Selection** tool (V), then click the object you want to delete, or drag a marquee around multiple objects. (Other methods for selecting multiple objects are described in the next chapter.)

2. Press Delete/Backspace.

➤ If you're using the Direct Selection tool and only some of the object's points are selected, you'll have to press Delete/Backspace twice to delete the whole object.

Creating rectangles and ellipses

To create a rectangle or an ellipse by dragging:

1. Choose the **Rectangle** tool (M) ▆ or the **Ellipse** tool (L).◗

2. Drag diagonally ▐1▌. As you drag, you'll see a wireframe representation of the rectangle or oval. When you release the mouse, the rectangle or oval will be selected, and it will be painted with the current fill and stroke settings (Preview view).

   You can also use these modifiers:

   To draw the object from its **center**, Option-drag/Alt-drag.

   To **move** the rectangle or ellipse as you draw it, Spacebar-drag.

   To draw a **square** with the Rectangle tool or a **circle** with the Ellipse tool, Shift-drag.

To create a rectangle or an ellipse by specifying dimensions:

1. Choose the **Rectangle** tool (M) ▆ or the **Ellipse** tool (L).◗

2. Click on the artboard where you want the object to appear. The Rectangle or Ellipse dialog box opens ▐2▌.

3. Enter **Width** and **Height** values. To create a circle or a square, enter a value in the Width field, then click the word Height (or vice versa)—the value in one field will copy to the other field.

4. Click OK.

➤ Values in dialog boxes in the current document display in the measurement units currently chosen on the Units menu in File > Document Setup > Artboard.

➤ The last-used dimensions display when the Rectangle or Ellipse dialog box is opened.

Recoloring: A sneak preview

You'll learn how to apply colors in Chapter 9, but meanwhile, here's a sneak preview. Select an object, click the **Fill** or **Stroke** thumbnail or arrowhead on the **Control** panel, then click a swatch on the **Swatches** panel. You could also Shift-click the thumbnail to bring up the **Color** panel, then click a color on the color bar.

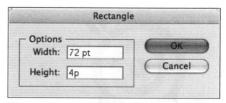

▐1▌ *With the **Rectangle** (or Ellipse) tool, drag diagonally.*

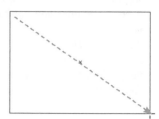

▐2▌ *Enter Width and Height values in the **Rectangle** (or **Ellipse**) dialog box.*

© DANIEL PELAVIN

This illustration contains several ellipses and rectangles.

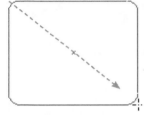

2 *Drag diagonally with the **Rounded Rectangle** tool.*

3 *The rectangle is automatically painted with the current fill and stroke colors (see Chapter 9).*

To create a rounded rectangle:

1. Choose the **Rounded Rectangle** tool **1**.

2. Drag diagonally. As you drag, you'll see a wireframe representation of the rounded rectangle **2**. When you release the mouse, the rounded rectangle will be selected and painted with the current fill and stroke settings (Preview view) **3**.

➤ As you create an object with the Rounded Rectangle tool, keep the mouse button down and keep pressing the up arrow to make the corners more round, or the down arrow to make them more square. Press (don't hold) the left or right arrow to toggle between square and round corners.

➤ To draw a rounded rectangle of a specific size, choose the Rounded Rectangle tool, click on the artboard, then enter Width, Height, and Corner Radius values. The Corner Radius value (0–8192 pt), which controls the degree of curvature in the corners of rounded rectangles, can also be specified in Preferences (Cmd-K/Ctrl-K) > General. When this value is changed in one location, it updates automatically in the other.

©DANIEL PELAVIN   *Great uses for **rounded rectangles!***

Rounded Rectangle Tool

Here's a quick introduction to one of the many Illustrator filters: **Round Corners.**

To round the corners of an existing object:

1. Select an object.

2. Choose **Filter** > Stylize > **Round Corners** (under Illustrator Filters).
or
Choose **Effect** > Stylize > **Round Corners** to create an editable appearance (not a permanent change to the object). To learn about effects and filters, see Chapter 21.

3. Enter a **Radius** value (the radius of the curve, in points). When using an effect, you can check Preview, then make adjustments before closing the dialog box.

4. Click OK ∎.

Creating polygons

There are a number of tools, such as **Polygon, Star,** and **Spiral,** that make light work of drawing geometric objects. All you have to do is draw a marquee in the artboard or enter values in a dialog box. As you can see from the wonderful graphics by Daniel Pelavin in this chapter, you can create illustrations using basic geometric objects as building blocks.

To create a polygon by clicking:

1. Choose the **Polygon** tool ∎.

2. Click where you want the center of the polygon to be located. The Polygon dialog box opens ∎.

3. Enter a **Radius** value (0–8192 pt) for the distance from the center of the object to the corner points.

4. Choose a number of **Sides** for the polygon by clicking the up or down arrow or by entering a number (3–1000). The sides will be of equal length.

5. Click OK ∎. A polygon will appear where you clicked on the artboard. The current fill and stroke settings will be applied to it automatically (see Chapter 9).

1 *Top row: the original objects; second row: after applying the* **Round Corners** *filter (30 pt)*

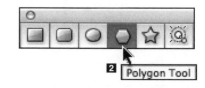

2 Polygon Tool

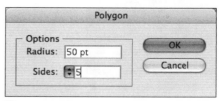

3 *In the* **Polygon** *dialog box, enter a Radius and choose the desired number of Sides.*

4 *A polygon drawn with the* **Polygon** *tool*

©DANIEL PELAVIN

Polygons, ellipses, and rectangles

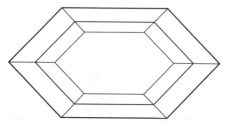

1 *To create these gemstones, we started with a* **polygon**, *created copies with the Scale tool, then added connecting lines with the Line Segment tool.*

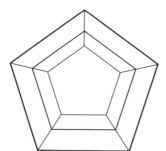

2 *Enter or choose Radius 1, Radius 2, and Points values in the* **Star** *dialog box.*

3 *We started with a classic five-pointed* **star.**

4 *We put circles on top of the points, then clicked the Add to Shape Area button on the Pathfinder panel to unite the shapes.*

To create a polygon by dragging:

1. Choose the **Polygon** tool.⬭

2. Drag on the artboard, starting from where you want the center of the polygon to be located.

   While dragging, do any of the following:

   To **scale** the polygon, drag away from or toward the center.

   To **rotate** the polygon, drag in a circular direction.

   To **constrain** the bottom side of the polygon to the horizontal axis, hold down Shift.

   To **add sides** to or **delete sides** from the polygon, press or hold down the up or down arrow key.

   To **move** the polygon without scaling it, hold down the Spacebar.

3. When you release the mouse, the polygon will be selected, and it will be painted with the current fill and stroke settings **1**.

➤ To align a new object with an existing object as you draw it, use smart guides (see pages 90–91).

Creating stars

To create a star by clicking:

1. Choose the **Star** tool. ☆

2. Click where you want the center of the star to be located. The Star dialog box opens **2**.

3. Enter **Radius 1** and **Radius 2** values (0–8192 pt). The higher value is the distance from the center of the star to its outermost points; the lower value is the distance from the center of the star to its innermost points. The greater the difference between the two values, the thinner the arms of the star.

4. Choose a number of **Points** for the star by clicking the up or down arrow or by entering a number (3–1000).

5. Click OK **3**–**4**.

➤ You can rotate the completed star via its bounding box (see page 123).

To create a star by dragging:

1. Choose the **Star** tool. ☆

2. Drag on the artboard, starting from where you want the center of the star to be located **1**.

   While dragging, do any of the following:

   To **scale** the star, drag away from or toward its center.

   To **rotate** the star, drag in a circular direction.

   To **constrain** two points to the horizontal axis, hold down Shift.

   To **add points** to or **delete points** from the star, press the up or down arrow key.

   To **move** the star, hold down the Spacebar.

   To make pairs of shoulders (opposite segments) **parallel** to each other, hold down Option/Alt **2**.

   To increase/decrease the **length** of the **arms** of the star while keeping the inner radius points constant, hold down Cmd/Ctrl and drag away from or toward the center.

3. When you release the mouse, the star will be selected and it will be painted with the current fill and stroke settings **3**–**4**.

➤ Hold down ~ (tilde) while dragging quickly with the Star or Polygon tool to create progressively larger copies of the shape **5**. You can apply stroke colors and settings to the copies afterward.

1 *Drawing a star*

2 *Parallel segments*

3 *The **Stars** were scaled and copied via the Scale tool dialog box and rotated via the Rotate tool dialog box — no drawing required!*

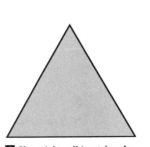

4 *You might call it a **triangle**, but actually it's a three-pointed **star**.*

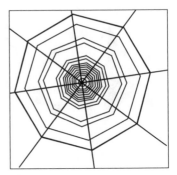

5 *To draw **multiple** polygons with the **Polygon** tool, drag with ~ held down.*

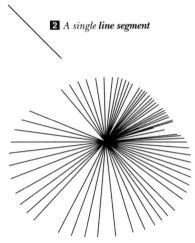

1 *The Line Segment tool and its related tools on the tearoff toolbar*

2 *A single line segment*

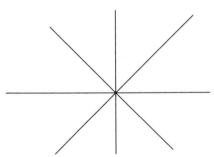

3 *Lines drawn with the Line Segment tool with ~ (tilde) held down*

4 *Lines drawn with the Line Segment tool with Shift-~ (tilde) held down*

Line Segment Tool Options

Length: 175 pt

Angle: 135°

☐ Fill Line

OK

Cancel

5 *Choose settings for the Line Segment tool in its options dialog box.*

The **Line Segment, Arc, Spiral, Rectangular Grid,** and **Polar Grid** tools **1** on the Line Segment tool pop-out menu create independent objects or groups of objects.

Creating line segments

The **Line Segment** tool (and the Arc tool, discussed on the next page), create either one line or multiple separate lines. Each time you drag with either tool, you create a new, separate path.

To draw a line segment by dragging:

1. Choose the **Line Segment** tool (\).

2. Drag to draw a line **2**. As you drag, you can do any of the following:

   To **extend** the line outward from both sides of the origin point, hold down Option/Alt.

   To **constrain** the line to the nearest 45° increment, hold down Shift.

   To **move** the line, hold down the Spacebar.

   To create **multiple** lines of **varied** lengths from the same center point at any angle, hold down ~ (tilde) **3**. Move the mouse quickly to spread the lines apart.

   To create **multiple** lines at **45°** increments, hold down Shift-~ (tilde) **4**.

To draw a line segment by entering values:

1. Choose the **Line Segment** tool (\).

2. Click where you want the segment to begin. The Line Segment Tool Options dialog box opens **5**.

3. Enter the desired line **Length**.

4. Enter an **Angle** or move the dial.

5. *Optional:* Check Fill Line to assign the current fill color to the line (see Chapter 9). If the line is later joined to another line or segment, that color will be used as the fill. With this option unchecked, the line will have a fill of None (you can apply a color later).

6. Click OK.

➤ When you open the Line Segment Tool Options dialog box, the last used values display. To restore the default values, Option-click/Alt-click Reset.

Creating arcs

The **Arc** tool creates smooth, perfect arcs.

To draw arcs by dragging:

1. Choose the Arc tool.

2. Drag to create arcs . As you drag, you can do any of the following:

   To toggle between an **open** and a **closed** arc, press C.

   To **flip** the arc while keeping the origin point constant, press F.

   To increase or decrease the **slope** of the arc, press (or press and hold) the up arrow or down arrow key.

   To **extend** the arc outward from both sides of the origin point, press Option/Alt.

   To **move** the arc, drag with the Spacebar held down.

   To create **multiple** arc segments from the same origin point, drag with ~ (tilde) down.

   To toggle between a **concave** and **convex** arc, press X.

To draw arcs by entering values:

1. Choose the Arc tool.

2. Click where you want the arc segment to begin. The Arc Segment Tool Options dialog box opens 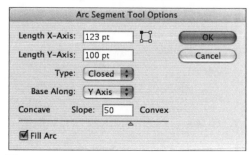.

3. Enter a **Length X-Axis** value for the width of the arc and a **Length Y-Axis** value for the height of the arc. (If desired, click a different point on the reference point locator to control the orientation of the arc.)

4. From the **Type** menu, choose whether the arc will be Open or Closed (the default).

5. From the **Base Along** menu, choose whether the arc will be measured from the X Axis or the Y Axis.

6. Move the **Slope** slider or enter a value for the steepness of the curve.

7. Leave **Fill Arc** unchecked for no fill, or check this option to have the arc fill with the current fill color.

8. Click OK.

> ## Using arc segments
>
> In Chapter 15 you'll learn how to draw curves "from scratch" with the **Pen** tool. You can use the Join command (see page 145) to combine **pen** and **arc** segments into a single object, or you can add segments to an arc by using the Pen tool.

1 *The veins on this lovely oak leaf were drawn with the Arc tool.*

2 *Choose options for the Arc tool in its options dialog box.*

Arc Tool

1 *In the **Spiral** dialog box, enter Radius and Decay values, choose the desired number of Segments, and click a Style button.*

2 *The snail shell and Ionic capital were drawn with the **Spiral** tool.*

Creating spirals

To create a spiral by entering values:

1. Choose the **Spiral** tool. @

2. Click roughly where you want the center of the spiral to be located. The Spiral dialog box opens **1**.

3. Enter a **Radius** value (1–1892 pt) for the distance from the center of the spiral to the outermost point (the overall scale).

4. Enter a **Decay** percentage (5–150) to control how tightly the spirals wind toward the center. (A Decay value greater than, say, 110% will produce overly large spirals.)

5. Choose or enter the number of **Segments** (quarter revolutions around the center point) for the spiral (2–1000). (For a Segment value greater than 50, try a Decay value of 80%.)

6. Click a **Style** button for the direction the spiral will wind from the center point.

7. Click OK **2**.

8. Apply stroke attributes to the spiral (see pages 110–112).

➤ The default Decay value is 80 and the default Segments value is 10.

Spiral Tool

To create a spiral by dragging:

1. Choose the **Spiral** tool.

2. Drag in the document window, starting from where you want the center of the spiral to be located.

3. While dragging, do any of the following:

   To **scale** the spiral, drag away from or toward the center.

   To control how **tightly** the spirals wind toward the center (the Decay value), Cmd-drag/Ctrl-drag slowly away from or toward the center.

   To **add segments** to or **delete segments** from the center of the spiral, press the up or down arrow key.

   To **rotate** the spiral, drag in a circular direction.

   To **constrain** the rotation of the entire spiral to an increment of 45°, hold down Shift.

   To **move** the spiral, drag with the Spacebar held down.

4. When you release the mouse, the spiral will be selected, and it will be painted with the current fill and stroke settings **1**–**3**.

1 *A spiral*

2 *We applied Effect > Distort & Transform > Pucker & Bloat (Bloat 15%).*

3 *And then we reversed the fill and stroke colors.*

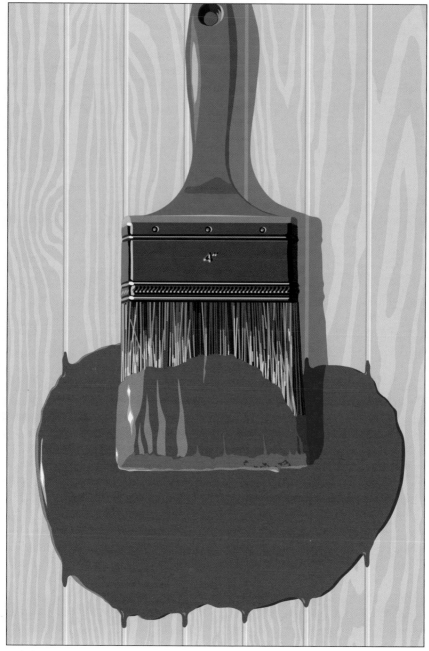

Chris Lyons

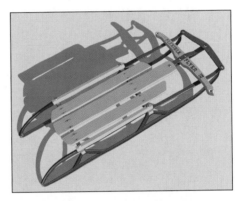

All artwork above ©Chris Lyons

Nancy Stahl

©Nancy Stahl

Nancy Stahl

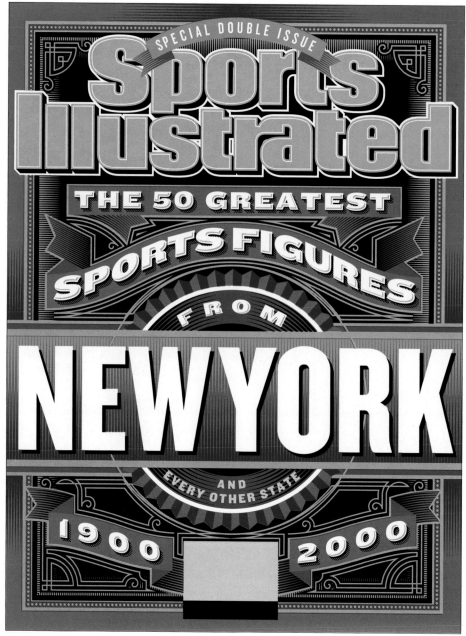

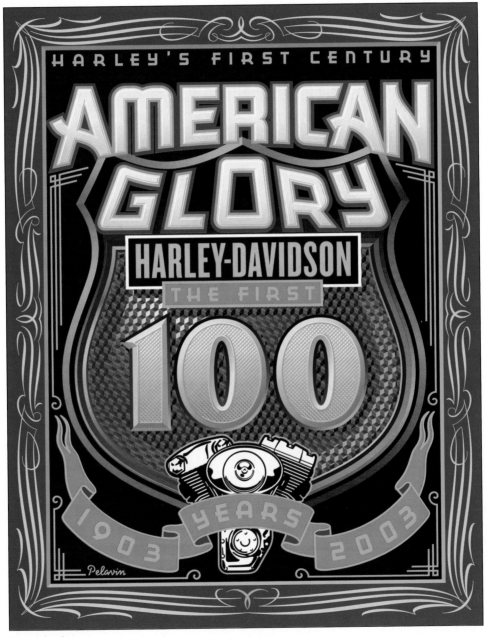

John Mattos

©John Mattos

John Mattos

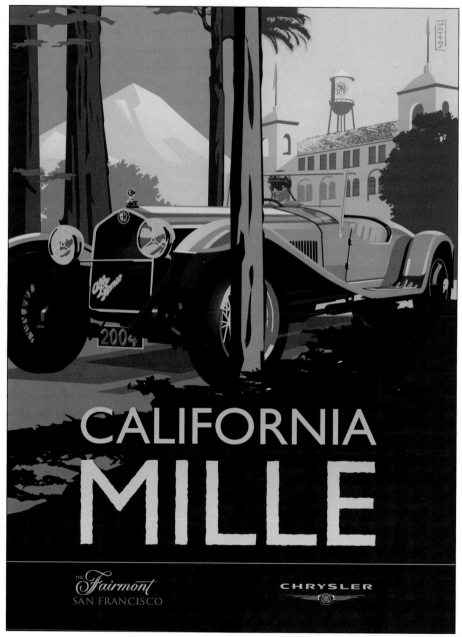

In this chapter, you'll learn many methods for selecting objects for editing, including five tools, a host of Select menu commands, and the Layers panel. You'll also learn how to group objects and isolate them for editing. Once you master these fundamental skills, you'll be ready to learn how to copy and align objects (next chapter), and from there you can plunge into all the fun stuff: recolor, transform, reshape, apply effects, etc.

A few pointers

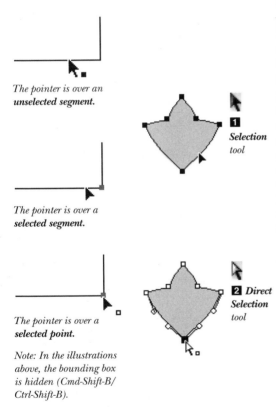

The pointer is over an **unselected segment.**

The pointer is over a **selected segment.**

The pointer is over a **selected point.**

Note: In the illustrations above, the bounding box is hidden (Cmd-Shift-B/ Ctrl-Shift-B).

1 *Selection tool*

2 *Direct Selection tool*

The five selection tools

Only selected objects can be modified, so before you learn how to modify objects, you need to know how to select and deselect them. This description of the basic functions of the selection tools will help prepare you for the step-by-step instructions that follow.

Use the **Selection** tool (V) to select or move a whole path or group (or to scale or rotate a path via its bounding box). If you click the edge of an object with the Selection tool, all the points on the object will become selected. You can also select an object with this tool by clicking the object's fill, if any, provided Object Selection by Path Only is unchecked in Preferences (Cmd-K/ Ctrl-K) > Selection & Anchor Display **NEW!** (this is the default setting) and your document is in Preview view **1**.

Use the **Direct Selection** tool (A) to select one or more individual anchor points or segments on a path. If you click a curve segment with the Direct Selection tool, the direction handles and anchor points for that segment will become visible. (Straight segments don't have direction handles—they just have anchor points.) If Object Selection by Path Only is unchecked in Preferences > Selection & Anchor Display and you click an object's fill (solid color, gradient, or pattern) in Preview view using this tool, all the points and direction handles on the object will become selected **2**.

(Continued on the following page)

Although the **Group Selection** tool can be used to select all the anchor points on a single path, its main purpose in life is for selecting groups of objects that are nested inside larger groups. Click once with this tool to select an object; click twice to select that object's group; click three times to select the next group that was added to the larger group, and so on .

➤ The easiest way to access the Group Selection tool is by holding down Option/ Alt when the Direct Selection tool is being used (note the plus sign in the pointer).

A better way to edit a group is to put it in **isolation mode.** An advantage of this method is that it prevents you from editing other objects unintentionally. To learn about this great (and improved) feature, see pages 84–85.

Use the **Lasso** tool (**Q**) to select path points and segments by dragging a freeform marquee around them .

Use the **Magic Wand** tool (**Y**) to select objects of the same or a similar fill color, stroke color, stroke weight, opacity, or blending mode as those of the object you click on (depending on which of those options are chosen for the tool on the Magic Wand panel) **3**.

➤ If Use Precise Cursors is checked in Preferences > General, you'll see a crosshair pointer -¦- onscreen instead of an icon for the current tool.

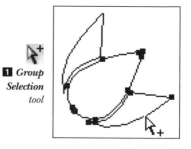

1 *Group Selection tool*

2 *Lasso tool*

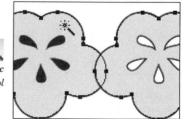

3 *Magic Wand tool*

Selection Tools

Object selection by path only

With **Object Selection by Path Only** unchecked in Preferences > Selection & Anchor Display, you can select an object in Preview view by clicking with a selection tool anywhere inside the object's bounding box. When this option is checked, to select an object with the Selection, Direct Selection, or Magic Wand tool, you must click a path segment or anchor point.

Using the Selection tool
To select an object or objects:

1. Choose the **Selection** tool (V).

2. Click the **edge** of the path **1**.
   or
   If the path has a color fill, your document is in Preview view, and the Object Selection by Path Only option is off (see the sidebar at left), click the **fill.**
   or
   Position the pointer outside the path(s) you want to select, then drag a **marquee** across all or part of it **2**. The whole path will be selected, even if you marquee just a portion of it. If the document is in Outline view, you can either use this marquee technique or click the edge of the path.

With the Selection tool, you can **add** or **subtract** whole objects from a **selection.**

To add or subtract objects from a selection:

Choose the **Selection** tool (V), then Shift-click or Shift-drag (marquee) any unselected objects to include them in the selection, or do the same for any selected objects to deselect them **3–4**.

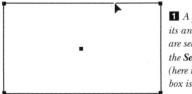

1 *A **path** and all its anchor **points** are selected with the **Selection** tool (here the bounding box is hidden).*

2 *Two paths are marqueed with the **Selection** tool.*

3 *One of two **selected** objects is marqueed with the Selection tool, in order to **deselect** it.*

4 *One path is **deselected**.*

Using the Direct Selection tool

You'll learn how to reshape objects in Chapter 11. But before you can begin reshaping, you have to know how to **select** individual **points** and **segments.** It's important to be precise about which components you select.

To select or deselect anchor points or segments with the Direct Selection tool:

1. Choose the **Direct Selection** tool (A).

2. Click the edge of the path (not the fill) to select a **segment** ▮. Click an **anchor point** on the path, if desired.
   or
   To select anchor points without having to select the path, pass the pointer over the edge of a path. When the pointer is over an **anchor point**, the point enlarges temporarily; click any point **NEW!** ▮–▮.
   or
   Position the pointer outside the object or objects whose **anchor points** you want to select, then drag a marquee across them (a dotted marquee will define the area as you drag over it). Only the points you marquee will become selected ▮–▮.

3. To select additional anchor points or segments or to deselect selected anchor points or segments individually, Shift-click or Shift-marquee those points or segments with the Direct Selection tool.

➤ To access the last-used selection tool (Selection or Direct Selection) temporarily when using a nonselection tool, hold down Cmd/Ctrl (the pointer changes).

Selecting via a command

The **Select commands** select objects whose characteristics are similar to those of the last or currently selected object. Each command is aptly named for the attributes it searches for.

To select objects via a command:

Do any of the following:

Select an object to base the search on, or deselect all objects to base the search on the last

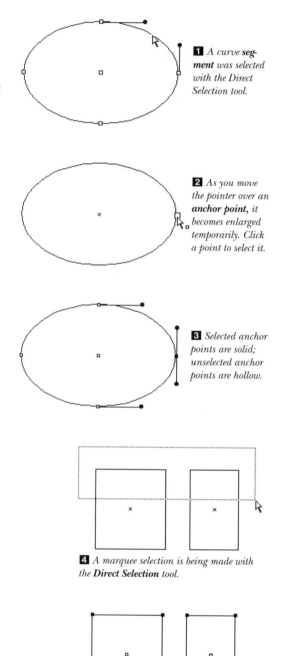

▮ *A curve **segment** was selected with the Direct Selection tool.*

▮ *As you move the pointer over an **anchor point,** it becomes enlarged temporarily. Click a point to select it.*

▮ *Selected anchor points are solid; unselected anchor points are hollow.*

▮ *A marquee selection is being made with the **Direct Selection** tool.*

▮ *Only the four points within the marquee became selected.*

1 *Choose from the Select > Same submenu.*

2 *Or choose from the Select Similar Objects menu on the Control panel.*

3 *Choose from the Select > Object submenu.*

4 *Click the selection area for an object on the Layers panel.*

object that was selected. Then from the Select > **Same** submenu **1**, choose **Blending Mode, Fill & Stroke, Fill Color, Opacity, Stroke Color, Stroke Weight, Style, Symbol Instance,** or **Link Block Series.** Some of these commands are also available on the Select Similar Objects menu on the Control panel **2** **NEW!** (the menu isn't available for all objects).

or

Select an object or objects, then from the Select > **Object** submenu **3**, choose: **All on Same Layers** to select all the objects on the layer the object resides on (or if you initially selected objects from more than one layer, to select those layers); or choose **Direction Handles** to select all the direction handles on the currently selected object or objects.

or

With or without selecting an object first, from the Select > **Object** submenu, choose one of the following: **Brush Strokes** to select all objects that have a brush stroke; **Clipping Masks** to select masking objects (this is helpful for getting the edges of a masking object to display onscreen); **Stray Points** to select lone points that aren't part of any path (so they can be deleted easily); or **Text Objects** to select all the type objects in the document.

Selecting via the Layers panel

You'll learn more about the Layers panel in Chapter 16.

To select an object via the Layers panel:

1. Display the Layers panel (F7).

2. If the name of the object that you want to select isn't visible on the Layers panel, click the expand/collapse triangle for the top-level layer, sublayer, or group.

3. At the far right side of the panel, click the **selection area** for the object you want to select (a colored square will appear) **4**. Or to select all the objects on a layer or sublayer, click the selection area for the whole layer. To learn more about selecting objects via the Layers panel, see pages 200–202.

83

Working with groups

When you collect objects into a **group**, you can easily select, isolate, cut, copy, paste, transform, recolor, or move them as a unit. When objects are grouped, they're automatically placed on the top-level layer of the frontmost object in the group, and are assigned the same selection color. You can group any types of objects together (e.g., type objects with placed images), and you can select and edit individual objects in a group without having to ungroup them first.

To create a group:

1. Choose the **Selection** tool (V). Then, in the document window, Shift-click or marquee all the objects to be grouped **1**.
   or
   Shift-click the **selection area** at the far right side of the Layers panel for each object to be put in the group. A selection square will appear for each object **2**. (You'll learn more about selection squares in Chapter 16.)

2. Control-click/right-click in the document window and choose **Group** from the context menu, or choose Object > Group (Cmd-G/Ctrl-G).

The easiest and fastest way to edit objects in a group is to put it into **isolation mode.**

To edit grouped objects in isolation mode: NEW!

1. Choose the **Selection** tool (V), then double-click a group in your artwork. *(Note:* For this method to work, Double Click to Isolate must be checked in Preferences > General.)
   or
   Choose the **Selection** tool (V), click a group, then click the **Isolate Selected Group** button on the Control panel.

2. A gray bar and the name of the group will appear at the top of the document window, and all objects outside the group will be dimmed and uneditable **3**. (Note the "Isolation Mode" listing on the Layers panel.) You can select and edit whole objects in the group with the Selection tool, or select and

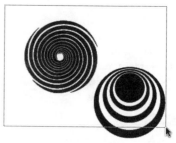

1 *To select the objects to be grouped, either draw a marquee around them...*

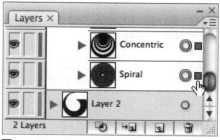

2 *...or Shift-click the selection area on the Layers panel for each object.*

3 *In isolation mode, objects in an isolated group are editable and all other objects are dimmed.*

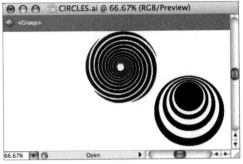

1 *A group is isolated.*

2 *Two new objects are added to the isolated group.*

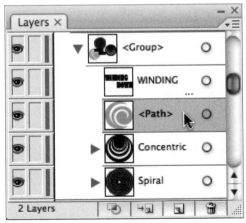

3 *The new type and path are nested within the same group on the Layers panel.*

edit individual path components with the Direct Selection tool.

3. To exit isolation mode, click the gray bar at the top of the document window.

Before creating an object or placing an image into an Illustrator document, you can **choose** the **group** you want it to belong to.

To add a new object to a group:

1. Choose the **Selection** tool (V), ⬚ then double-click a group to isolate it **1**.

2. Draw a new object or objects **2**. A listing for each new object will appear at the top of the nested group on the Layers panel **3**.

3. *Optional:* On the Layers panel, expand the group that you added an object to, then drag the new object name to any other stacking position in the group list.

4. Exit isolation mode by clicking the gray bar at the top of the document window.

➤ To add an existing object to a group, select it in the document window with the Selection tool, choose Edit > Cut (Cmd-X/Ctrl-X), double-click the group to isolate it, then choose Edit > Paste (Cmd-V/Ctrl-V).

Sometimes a group has to be disbanded — er, **ungrouped.**

To ungroup a group:

1. To select the group, choose the **Selection** tool (V), ⬚ then click the group in the document window, or click the selection area for the group on the Layers panel.

2. Control-click/right-click the artboard and choose **Ungroup** from the context menu.
or
Choose Object > **Ungroup** (Cmd-Shift-G/Ctrl-Shift-G).

The group listing will disappear from the Layers panel.

➤ Keep choosing the same command to ungroup nested groups (groups inside a larger group).

➤ To learn how to select groups and grouped objects, see page 202.

Add New Object to Group; Ungroup

Using the Lasso tool

Let's say you need to select a few points on one path and a couple of points on a nearby path. You could grab the Direct Selection tool and click the points individually (tedious) or you could marquee them (works only if the points in question fall conveniently within the rectangular marquee). With the **Lasso** tool, you can weave an irregular pathway around just the points and segments you want to select. This is especially helpful for creating selections among overlapping paths. Just don't try to use it to select whole paths.

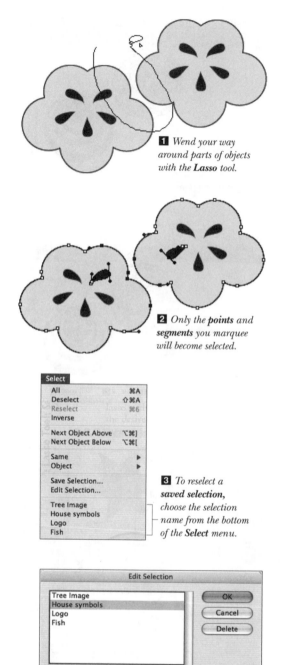

1 *Wend your way around parts of objects with the **Lasso** tool.*

To select/deselect points or segments with the Lasso tool:

1. Deselect (click a blank area of the artboard).

2. Choose the **Lasso** tool (Q), then drag to encircle the segments or points you want to select **1**–**2**. You can drag right across a path. You don't need to close the lasso selection; simply release the mouse when the desired points have been lassoed.

3. *Optional:* Shift-drag around any unselected points or segments anywhere in the document window to add them to the selection, or Option-drag/Alt-drag around any selected points or segments to deselect them.

2 *Only the **points** and segments you marquee will become selected.*

Saving selections

Via the **Save Selection** command, you can save any selection under a custom name, then reselect those objects quickly by choosing the name from the Select menu.

To save a selection:

1. Select only the objects you want to save as a selection.

2. Choose Select > **Save Selection.** The Save Selection dialog box opens.

3. Enter a descriptive name, then click OK. To reselect those objects at any time, simply choose the selection name from the bottom of the **Select** menu **3**.

➤ To rename or delete a saved selection, choose Select > Edit Selection. Click a selection, then change the name or click Delete **4**.

3 *To reselect a **saved selection,** choose the selection name from the bottom of the **Select** menu.*

4 *You can use the **Edit Selection** dialog box to rename or delete a saved selection.*

1 *The Magic Wand panel*

Using the Magic Wand tool

The Magic Wand tool selects all the objects in a document that have the same or a similar fill color, stroke color, stroke weight, opacity, or blending mode as the object you click on, depending on which options are currently checked on the **Magic Wand panel**. To use the Magic Wand tool, follow the instructions on the next page.

To choose options for the Magic Wand tool:

1. To show the **Magic Wand** panel, double-click the **Magic Wand** tool or choose Window > **Magic Wand**.

   If all three option areas aren't showing (as in **1**), click the up/down arrowhead on the panel tab until they're all visible, or choose Show Stroke Options and Show Transparency Options from the panel menu.

2. On the left side of the panel, check the attributes you want the tool to select: **Fill Color, Stroke Color, Stroke Weight, Opacity,** or **Blending Mode.**

3. For each option you checked in the previous step (except Blending Mode), choose a **Tolerance** range. Choose a low value to select only objects with colors, weights, or opacities that match or are very similar to the one you'll click; or choose a high value to allow the tool to select a broader range of those attributes. For Fill Color or Stroke Color, choose a specific color value (the range is 0–255 for RGB or 0–100 for CMYK, depending on the document color mode); for Stroke Weight, choose a width Tolerance (0–1000 pt); and for Opacity, choose a percentage (0–100).

4. To permit the Magic Wand tool to select objects on all layers, make sure **Use All Layers** has a check mark on the panel menu, or uncheck this option to permit the tool to select objects on just the current layer.

➤ The Reset command on the Magic Wand panel menu resets all fields on the panel to their default values and unchecks all the attributes except Fill Color.

Magic Wand Panel

To use the Magic Wand tool:

1. Choose the **Magic Wand** tool (Y).

2. To create a **new** selection, click an object in the document window. Depending on which options are checked on the Magic Wand panel, other objects with the same or a similar fill color, stroke color, stroke weight, opacity, or blending mode may become selected **1**–**2**.

3. To **add** to the selection, Shift-click another object.
   or
   To **subtract** from the selection, Option-click/Alt-click a selected object.

Selecting/deselecting all objects

To select all the objects in a document:

Choose Select > **All** (Cmd-A/Ctrl-A). All unlocked objects in your document will be selected, regardless of whether they're on the artboard or in the scratch area. The command won't select hidden or locked objects or objects on hidden layers (for which the visibility icon on the Layers panel is off).

➤ If the text cursor is flashing in a text block, the Select > All command selects all the text in the block instead of all the objects in the document.

To prevent objects from being modified, you must remember to **deselect** them.

To deselect all objects on all layers:

Choose Select > **Deselect** (Cmd-Shift-A/Ctrl-Shift-A).
or
Choose any **selection** tool, then click a blank area of the artboard.

➤ To deselect an individual object within a multiple-object selection, Shift-click it with the Selection tool. To deselect an object within a group, see page 202).

The **Inverse** command deselects all selected objects and selects all unselected objects.

To invert a selection:

Choose Select > **Inverse**.

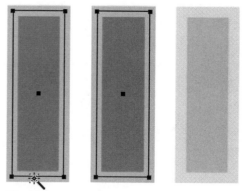

1 *All three rectangles have the same stroke color, but the one on the far right has a lower opacity (50%) than the other two. The **Opacity** option is **on** for the **Magic Wand** tool, and the stroke of the leftmost object is clicked. Only the objects that have the same stroke color and opacity became selected.*

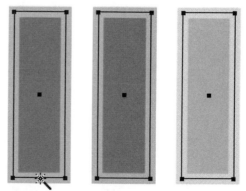

2 *This time, the **Magic Wand** tool is used with the **Opacity** option **off**. All three objects became selected, because opacity was ignored as a factor.*

MOVE, COPY & ALIGN 8

In this chapter you'll learn how to move objects; use smart guides to align objects; duplicate objects; align and distribute objects via buttons; and create and use ruler guides, guide objects, and the grid to position objects manually.

1 *To move an object, drag its **edge** with the Selection tool.*

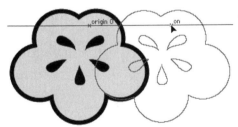

2 *If an object contains a fill, the document is in Preview view, and the Object Selection by Path Only preference is off, you can also move an object by dragging its **fill**. Here, with the aid of smart guides, an object is being moved sideways along the horizontal axis.*

More ways to move
To learn other techniques for moving objects, such as the Transform panel, Control panel, and Transform Each command, see pages 128–130.

Moving objects

Below, we discuss the simplest and most direct method for **moving objects**: by **dragging**. In conjunction with a great feature called smart guides (see the next page), dragging can easily take care of most of your moving needs.

To move an object by dragging:

1. Choose the **Selection** tool (V).

2. Drag the **edge** of the object (you can do this in Outline or Preview view) **1**.
   or
   If the document is in Preview view, the object has a fill, and Object Selection by Path Only is off in Preferences > Selection & Anchor Display, you can drag the object's **fill 2**. You can also do this with the Direct Selection tool.

➤ Hold down Shift while dragging an object to constrain the movement to a multiple of 45° (or to the current Constrain Angle in Preferences > General, if the latter is a value other than 0).

Using smart guides

Smart guides are temporary guides that appear when you draw, move, duplicate, transform, or simply move the pointer over an object. They're designed to help you align objects with one another or along a preset axis. Smart guides also have magnetic pull, which you'll discover when you start using them (they're easier done than said). To start, try using them to move an object along an axis or to align one object with points on another object.

To use smart guides to align objects:

1. Make sure View > **Smart Guides** (Cmd-U/ Ctrl-U) is on (has a check mark), and make sure View > Snap to Grid is off.

2. Go to Preferences > (Cmd-K/Ctrl-K) **Smart Guides & Slices** 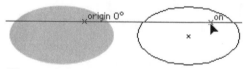. For Display Options, check **Text Label Hints** ❷, **Transform Tools**, and **Object Highlighting** ❸, then click OK. (Construction Guides, Transform Tools, and other smart guides options are also discussed on page 371.)

3. Choose the **Selection** tool (V).

4. Do any of the following:

   To use **angle guides** to position an object, start dragging the object—guides will appear as you move it (e.g., at 0°, 45°, 90°). To position the object on that angle, release the mouse any time the word "**on**" appears next to the pointer. You don't need to hold down Shift to constrain the movement—that's the whole point!

   To align **one object to another,** as you drag an object, position the pointer over the edge (path) of another object, and release the mouse when the word "**anchor**" or "**path**" appears next to the pointer (❶, next page). You can also drag an object over a point on another object to "pick up" an **angle guide**, then drag along that guide. Or to align an object's **center** point or path to the center point or path of another object, release the mouse then you see the word "center." *Note:* In order for "center" to appear as a smart guide, the object's center point must be visible (see the next set of instructions).

Smart Guides

Use smart guides to find things

Smart guides aren't used just for aligning objects. With **Text Label Hints** checked in Preferences > Smart Guides & Slices, you can also use smart guides to help you locate individual points on any object, whether the object is selected or not. And with **Object Highlighting** checked, you can use smart guides to locate the edges of objects, such as irregularly shaped objects or objects in a group. Object Highlighting works even when View > Hide Edges is enabled.

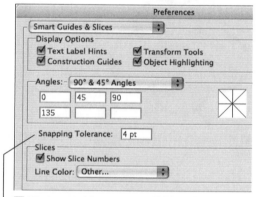

❶ The **Snapping Tolerance** *is the farthest distance the pointer can be from an object for the snap function to work.*

❷ *Text label hints and angle guides display when an object is moved along an axis.*

❸ *The edge of an object highlights when the pointer is moved over it (with the mouse button up).*

Interesting angle

In Preferences > **Smart Guides & Slices,** you can specify the angles for smart guides: Choose a pre-defined **Angles** set from the menu or enter custom angles. If you switch from Custom Angles to a pre-defined set and then switch back to Custom Angles at any time, the last custom settings you entered will be listed.

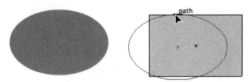

1 *As an ellipse is dragged over the edge of a rectangle, the word "**path**" appears on the unselected object.*

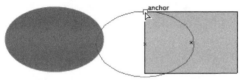

2 *An ellipse is dragged by an anchor point and is aligned with an anchor point on the rectangle (as indicated by the word "**anchor**") on the rectangle.*

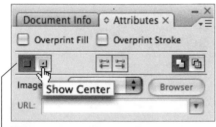

3 *Use the **Don't Show Center** and **Show Center** buttons on the Attributes panel to reveal or hide the center point on one or more selected objects.*

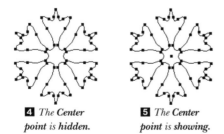

4 *The **Center** point is hidden.*

5 *The **Center** point is showing.*

To align objects by their **anchor points,** make sure the object you want to move isn't selected, then position the pointer over one of its anchor points (the word "**anchor**" will appear). Drag the object over an anchor point on another object, then release the mouse when the point becomes selected and the word "anchor" appears **2**.

You can also align a path of one object to an anchor point or the center point on another object, or align an anchor point of one object to the path of another object.

➤ You can't lock smart guides—they vanish as quickly as they appear. To create a guide that stays onscreen, drag from the horizontal or vertical ruler onto the artboard; a guide will appear (see page 97).

➤ Smart guides display in the same color as ruler guides. This color can be changed in Preferences > Guides & Grid if, say, you need the guides to contrast better with objects in your artwork.

Not only can you drag an object by its center point, you can also align objects via their center points, with the assistance of smart guides. In order to do so, however, the **center point(s)** must be **visible.**

To hide or show an object's center point:

1. Select an object (or objects). Or to show or hide the center point for all the objects in the document, choose Select > All (Cmd-A/Ctrl-A).

2. Show the **Attributes** panel (Cmd-F11/Ctrl-F11) **3**.

3. If you don't see the Show Center buttons on the panel, choose Show All from the panel menu or click the up/down arrowhead on the panel tab.

4. Click the **Don't Show Center** button **4** or the **Show Center** button **5**.

5. Deselect the object(s).

Hide or Show Center Point

Duplicating objects

To **duplicate** objects, you can use any of the following techniques:

➤ Duplicate by **dragging** (this page)

➤ **Arrow keys** (sidebar at right)

➤ The **Clipboard** (next page)

➤ The **Offset Path** command (page 94)

➤ A **transform** tool (page 126), the Transform panel (page 128), the Transform Each command (page 130), or the Transform effect (page 131)

➤ The **Layers** panel (page 204)

To duplicate an object in the same document:

1. Choose the **Selection** tool (V).

2. Option-drag/Alt-drag the fill or edge of an object (not the bounding box) **1**–**2**. The pointer will turn into a double arrowhead. Release the mouse before you release Option/Alt.

   You can use smart guides for positioning.

➤ To constrain the position of the copy to a multiple of 45°, start dragging the object, then hold down Option-Shift/Alt-Shift and continue to drag.

➤ To repeat the last transformation (such as drag-duplicate), press Cmd-D/Ctrl-D as many times as you like.

➤ If you drag-duplicate an object in a group (start dragging with the Direct Selection tool, then continue dragging with Option/Alt held down), the copy will be a member of that group. If you use the Clipboard to copy and paste an object in a group (see the following page), the object will paste outside the group.

To drag and drop an object between files:

1. Open and position two windows so you'll be able to drag from one window into the other.

Copy using the arrow keys

Choose the Selection tool, select an object, then press **Option-arrow/Alt-arrow** to copy the object and move the copy in the direction of the arrow by the current Keyboard Increment in Preferences > General. The default increment is 1 pt. To copy the object and move the copy by 10 times the current increment, press **Option-Shift-arrow/Alt-Shift-arrow.**

1 *The fastest way to copy an object is to Option-drag/Alt-drag it. Note the double-arrowhead pointer.*

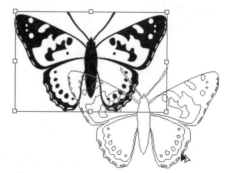

2 *A copy is made.*

Remembering layers

If you want to paste an object to the top of the same layer or sublayer rather than to a different layer, turn the **Paste Remembers Layers** option on via the Layers panel menu. If this option is on and you copy an object, delete the object's layer, then use the Paste command, the object will paste onto a brand new layer.

Hiding the box

On page 123, you'll learn how to transform an object via its bounding box 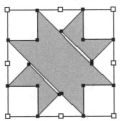–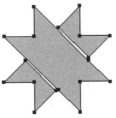. In the meantime, if you want to hide (or show) the bounding boxes, choose View > **Hide Bounding Box** (or Show Bounding Box) or press Cmd-Shift-B/Ctrl-Shift-B.

1 *The bounding box is visible.*

2 *The bounding box is hidden.*

2. With the Selection tool, drag an object or group from one document to the other. A duplicate will appear in the target document.

If you select an object or a group and then choose the **Cut** or **Copy** command, the object or group will be placed onto the **Clipboard,** a temporary storage area in memory. The previous contents of the Clipboard are replaced each time you choose Cut or Copy.

The **Paste** command places the current Clipboard contents in the center of the currently selected layer in the active document window. The **Paste in Front** and **Paste in Back** commands paste an object in its original x/y location in front of or behind the current selection, and are handy for positioning an object in a particular stacking position.

Objects are copied to the Clipboard in the PDF and/or AICB format, depending on the options currently chosen in Preferences > File Handling & Clipboard (see page 375). You can paste the current Clipboard contents an unlimited number of times.

To duplicate or move objects between documents via the Clipboard:

1. Open two documents.

2. With the Selection tool, select the object or group that you want to copy or move.

3. To place a copy of the object or group on the Clipboard, while leaving the original in the current document, choose Edit > **Copy** (Cmd-C/Ctrl-C).
   or
   To move the object or group, and delete it from the current document, choose Edit > **Cut** (Cmd-X/Ctrl-X).

4. Click in the target document.

5. Choose Edit > **Paste** (Cmd-V/Ctrl-V).
   or
   Select an object to paste the copied object in front of or behind, then choose Edit > **Paste in Front** (Cmd-F/Ctrl-F) or **Paste in Back** (Cmd-B/Ctrl-B).

Duplicate, Move Objects via Clipboard

The **Offset Path** command duplicates a path and offsets the duplicate around or inside the original path by a specified distance. The command also reshapes the duplicate automatically so it fits nicely around the original path. The fill and stroke attributes of the duplicate will match those of the original object.

To offset a duplicate of a path:

1. Select an object **1**. For your first try, we recommend using a path that has a stroke color but a fill of None.

2. Choose Object > Path > **Offset Path.** The Offset Path dialog box opens **2**. Check Preview.**NEW!**

3. In the **Offset** field, enter the distance you want to offset the duplicate path from the original. Be sure your Offset value is larger or smaller than the stroke weight of the original path so the duplicates will be visible. A positive value will create a path that's larger than the original; a negative value will create a smaller path.

4. Choose a **Joins** (bend) style: **Miter** (pointed) **3**, **Round** (semicircular) **4**, or **Bevel** (square-cornered) for the shape of the joints in the duplicate.

5. *Optional:* Change the Miter limit (1–500) value for the point at which a miter (pointed) corner becomes a beveled corner. A high Miter limit creates long, pointy corners; a low Miter limit creates beveled corners.

6. Click OK. The offset path will be a separate path from, and stacked behind or in front of, the original path **5**. And regardless of whether the original object was open or closed, the resulting offset path will be closed.

➤ You can also apply the Offset Path command as an editable effect via Effect > Path > Offset Path (to learn more about effects, see Chapter 21).

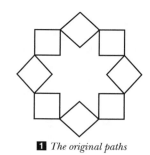

1 *The original paths*

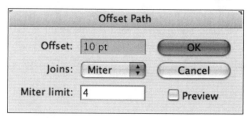

2 *In the **Offset Path** dialog box, choose options for the duplicate path.*

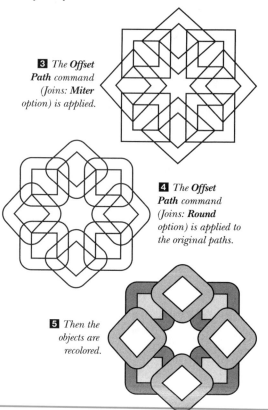

3 *The **Offset Path** command (Joins: **Miter** option) is applied.*

4 *The **Offset Path** command (Joins: **Round** option) is applied to the original paths.*

5 *Then the objects are recolored.*

Offset Path

Aligning and distributing objects

Buttons, blocks of point type—any objects that are lined up in a row or column—will require aligning and distributing in order to look neat and tidy. With commands on the **Align** 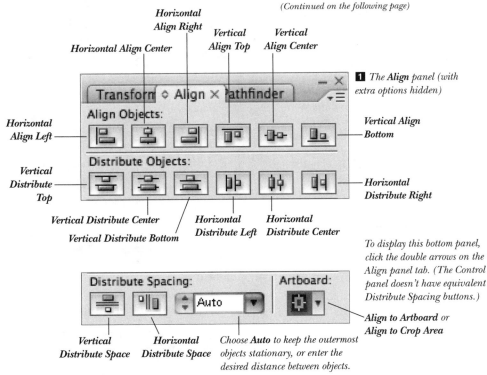 and **Control** panels, this is easy to do, and it's more precise than doing it by eye.

To align or distribute objects:

1. To align, select two or more objects or groups; to distribute, select three or more objects. Display the **Align** panel (Shift-F7) or the **Control** panel. (If the align buttons aren't visible on the Control panel, choose Align from the Control panel menu.)

2. Turn **Use Preview Bounds** on from the Align panel menu or in Preferences > General to have Illustrator factor in an object's stroke weight and any effects when calculating the alignment or distribution, or turn this option off to have Illustrator ignore the stroke weight and any effects. By

default, the stroke straddles the edge of the path, halfway inside and halfway outside.

3. *For occasional use:* Choose **Align to Artboard** from the Artboard menu on the Align or Control panel, **NEW!** then click the **Align to Artboard** button to turn the feature on. Objects will align along the top, right, bottom, or left edge of the artboard, depending on which Align Objects button you click in step 5. If Align to Artboard is on and objects are distributed vertically, the topmost object will move to the top edge of the artboard, the bottommost object will move to the bottom edge of the artboard, and the remaining objects will be distributed between them. If objects are distributed horizontally with this option on, they will be aligned between the leftmost and rightmost edges of the artboard. Or if you've set up a Crop Area, you can choose **Align to Crop Area** from the Artboard menu to align objects to the edges

(Continued on the following page)

(Continued on the following page)

Horizontal Align Right

Horizontal Align Center

Vertical Align Top

Vertical Align Center

1 *The **Align** panel (with extra options hidden)*

Horizontal Align Left

Vertical Align Bottom

Vertical Distribute Top

Horizontal Distribute Right

Vertical Distribute Center

Horizontal Distribute Left

Horizontal Distribute Center

Vertical Distribute Bottom

To display this bottom panel, click the double arrows on the Align panel tab. (The Control panel doesn't have equivalent Distribute Spacing buttons.)

Align to Artboard or Align to Crop Area

Vertical Distribute Space

Horizontal Distribute Space

*Choose **Auto** to keep the outermost objects stationary, or enter the desired distance between objects.*

Align, Distribute Objects

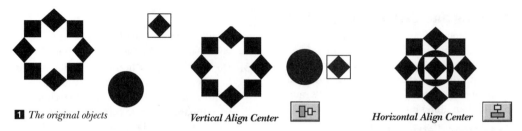

1 *The original objects* **Vertical Align Center**  **Horizontal Align Center**

of the crop area. Click the Align to Artboard button again to turn the option off.

4. *Optional:* By default (with Align to Artboard off), and depending on which Align Objects button you click, the topmost, bottommost, leftmost, or rightmost object will remain stationary. To choose another object to remain stationary (known as the "key" object), click that selected object now—that is, after all the objects are selected and before you click an Align Objects button. To go back to the default object, choose Cancel Key Object from the panel menu.

5. Click an **Align Objects** button **1** and/or a **Distribute Objects** button **2**–**4** on the Align panel or the Control panel.

   Or for **Distribute Spacing** **5**, choose Auto from the menu on the Align panel to keep the two objects that are farthest apart stationary (the topmost and bottommost or leftmost and rightmost) and redistribute the remaining objects evenly between them, or enter the exact desired distance between objects (the outermost objects will probably move); then click one of the two Distribute Spacing buttons.

➤ If you change your mind and want to apply a different Align panel option, Undo the last one first.

2 *The original objects*

3 *The **Vertical Align Bottom** button is clicked.*

4 *The **Horizontal Distribute Center** button is clicked.*

The original objects

5 *The **Horizontal Distribute Spacing** button is clicked.*

Snap for Web graphics

When View > **Pixel Preview** is on, View > Snap to Grid becomes View > **Snap to Pixel,** and Snap to Pixel is turned on automatically. With Snap to Pixel on, any new objects you create or any existing objects you drag or transform will snap to the invisible pixel grid, and anti-aliasing will be removed from any horizontal or vertical edges of those objects (they'll become more crisp).

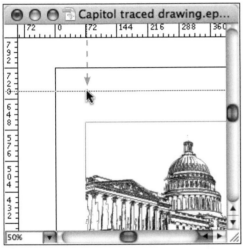

1 *A **guide** is dragged from the horizontal **ruler.***

Creating ruler guides

For most purposes, smart guides work quite well for arranging objects. But if you need guides that stay onscreen, follow these instructions to create **ruler guides.** Ruler guides don't print.

To create ruler guides:

1. Choose View > Guides > **Show Guides** (Cmd-;/Ctrl-;), or if the command is Hide Guides, leave it as is.

2. *Optional:* Create a new top-level layer expressly for the guides, label it "Guides," and keep it selected.

3. If the rulers aren't showing, choose View > **Show Rulers** (Cmd-R/Ctrl-R).

4. Drag one or more guides from the horizontal or vertical **ruler** onto your page **1**. The guide will be locked. (Guides are listed on the Layers panel as <Guide> on the currently active layer.)

5. If View > **Snap to Point** is on, as you drag an object near a guide or anchor point, the black pointer will turn white and the part of the object that's under the pointer will snap to that guide or point (see also the sidebar). You can change the Snapping Tolerance (the maximum distance between object and target) in Preferences > Smart Guides & Slices.

➤ If View > Snap to Grid is on, as you create or move a guide, it will snap to the nearest subdivision as set in Preferences > Guides & Grid. (If Pixel Preview is on, Snap to Grid won't be available.) To learn about the grid, see page 100.

➤ Option-drag/Alt-drag from the horizontal ruler to create a vertical guide, or from the vertical ruler to create a horizontal guide.

➤ After creating ruler guides, you can lock them to prevent them from being selected as you select and edit your artwork (see page 99).

Ruler Guides

Creating guide objects

So far we've shown you how to work with two kinds of guides: smart guides and ruler guides. Next, you'll learn how to convert standard Illustrator paths into guides. **Guide objects** are reversible, meaning they can be converted back to standard objects at any time.

To turn an object into a guide:

1. Select an object, a group of objects 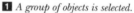, or an object within a group (but not a symbol, an object in a blend, or a Live Paint group). You can copy the object and work off the copy, if you like. *Note:* If the object you turn into a guide is part of a group, the guide will also be part of that group.

2. Choose View > Guides > **Make Guides** (Cmd-5/Ctrl-5) .
or
Control-click/right-click and choose **Make Guides** from the context menu.

➤ You can transform or reshape a guide object, provided guides aren't locked (see the following page). Guide objects can be selected using the Layers panel (look for <Guide>). Relock them when you're done.

When you **release** a **guide object**, the former fill and stroke attributes are restored to the object.

To turn a guide object back into an ordinary object:

1. If guides are locked, Control-click/right-click and choose **Lock Guides** from the context menu to uncheck that option.

2. On the Layers panel, make sure none of the guides to be released have a lock icon.

3. To release **one** guide, in the document window, Cmd-Shift-double-click/Ctrl-Shift-double-click the edge of the guide.

To release **multiple** guides, choose the Selection tool (V), Shift-click or marquee the guides you want to release, then Control-click/right-click and choose **Release Guides** from the context menu (Cmd-Option-5/Ctrl-Alt-5).

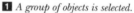

1 *A group of objects is selected.*

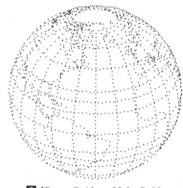

2 *View > Guides > Make Guides converted the paths to guide objects.*

Tips for working with guides

➤ If you drag all your guides into one **layer** (or sublayer), you'll be able to lock or unlock all of them at once by clicking the lock icon for that layer, and yet still be able to lock/unlock them individually.

➤ To make it easier to tell when your guides are selected, make the selection color for the layer that contains the <Guide> listings different from the **guide color**. Double-click the layer name, then in the Layer Options dialog box, choose a Color. To change the guide color, choose Preferences (Cmd-K/Ctrl-K) > Guides & Grid, and change the Guides: Color.

Locking/unlocking guides

To select or move ruler guides or guide objects, you must unlock them first. By default, the **Lock Guides** command is on.

To lock or unlock all guides:

Deselect all objects, then Control-click/right-click in the document window and choose **Lock Guides** from the context menu (Cmd-Option-;/Ctrl-Alt-;).

➤ To hide (or show) guides, choose Hide Guides (or Show Guides) from the context menu.

You can **lock** or **unlock** (or hide or show) ruler guides and guide objects **individually**, because each one has its own <Guide> listing on the Layers panel.

To lock or unlock one guide:

1. Make sure the Lock Guides command is off (see the previous set of instructions).

2. On the Layers panel, click in the **edit** (lock) column for any guide you want to lock or unlock.

Removing guides

To remove one guide:

1. Make sure either all guides are unlocked or the guide you want to remove is unlocked.

2. Choose the **Selection** tool (V), then click the ruler guide or guide object to be removed.

3. In the Mac OS, press Delete; in Windows, press Backspace or Del.

4. To relock all the remaining guides, deselect all objects, then Control-click/right-click in the document window and choose **Lock Guides.**

The **Clear Guides** command removes all ruler guides and guide objects.

To remove all guides:

Choose View > Guides > **Clear Guides.**

Lock, Remove Guides

Using the grid

The **grid** is like nonprinting graph paper. You can use it as a framework to arrange objects on, either by eye or by using the Snap to Grid feature. The first step, logically, is to display the grid.

To show/hide the grid:

Choose View > **Show Grid** (or Hide Grid) (Cmd-"/Ctrl-") 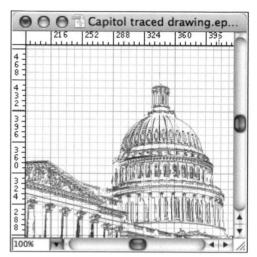.

or

Deselect, then Control-click/right-click and choose **Show Grid** (or Hide Grid) from the context menu.

➤ You can change the grid style (lines or dots), color, or spacing in Preferences > Guides & Grid. Check Grids in Back in that dialog box (the default setting) to have the grid appear in back of all objects, instead of in front.

To snap objects to the grid:

1. Choose View > **Snap to Grid** (Cmd-Shift-"/ Ctrl-Shift-") to make the check mark appear.

2. Move an object near a gridline; the edge of the object will snap to the gridline. This feature works whether the grid is displayed or not.

1 *The **Grid** is displayed.*

FILL & STROKE 9

In this chapter you'll learn the difference between process and spot colors, learn which colors to choose for your output medium, and learn how to fill the inside and/or edge of an object with a solid color or pattern by using various panels and tools. You'll also learn how to save and organize color swatches in the Swatches panel; copy swatches between files; choose stroke attributes; replace and edit colors in your artwork; invert colors; colorize images; blend fill colors between objects; and create and modify patterns.

Opening the panels

Stroke panel ≡ Click <u>Stroke</u> on the Control panel* or press Cmd-F10/ Ctrl-F10.

Swatches panel ⊞ Click the Fill or Stroke color or arrowhead on the Control panel* or choose Window > Swatches.

Color panel ✎ Shift-click the Fill or Stroke color (or arrowhead) on the Control panel* or press F6.

*When opened from the Control panel, these panels stay open only temporarily.

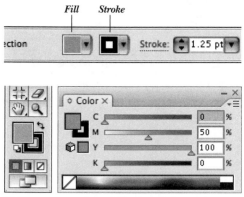

Fill   Stroke

1 The current **stroke** and **fill** colors display on the **Control**, **Tools**, and **Color** panels.

Introduction to Illustrator color

The **fill**, which you apply to the inside of a closed or open path, can be a solid color, pattern, or gradient (or None). The **stroke**, which you apply to the edge of a closed or open path, can be a solid color (or None), dashed (Stroke panel), or a scatter, calligraphic, art, or pattern brush stroke (Brushes panel), but not a gradient.

The color boxes on the **Tools, Color,** and **Control** panels display the colors of the current or most recently selected object, or new colors that you choose when no objects are selected **1**. The current fill and stroke colors are applied to new objects automatically as you create them.

In this chapter, you'll learn how to apply solid colors, patterns, and gradients via the **Color** and **Swatches** panels, the **Color Picker, library** panels, and the **Eyedropper** tool. And using the **Stroke** panel, you'll change the stroke thickness (weight), style (dashed or solid), alignment (position on the path), and endcaps.

In Chapter 13, you'll learn how to apply colors with the Live Paint Bucket tool. In Chapter 14, you'll use the Color Guide panel to apply variations on a color or color group **NEW!** and the powerful Live Color dialog box to edit and assign colors and color groups to selected artwork.**NEW!** In Chapter 20, you'll apply multiple fill and stroke attributes, and in Chapter 24, you'll create and save gradients.

Colors for your output medium

Before you choose colors, you need to know what type of colors are appropriate for your artwork and output medium.

Colors for commercial printing

Spot color inks are mixed in specific percentages for commercial printing. Each spot color is printed from a separate printing plate. To choose a spot color, you'll flip through a fan book for a matching system (such as PANTONE), pick a named, numbered spot color, then locate that color in Illustrator. You can use spot colors exclusively if your document doesn't contain any continuous-tone images, but bear in mind that each spot color incurs an added expense at the print shop.

In commercial process printing, tiny dots of four **process** colors—cyan (C), magenta (M), yellow (Y), and black (K)—are printed from four separate plates. On the printout, your eyes read the dots as solid colors. Examine a photograph in a magazine or catalog with a magnifying lens or loupe, and you'll see a mixture of those different colored dots. You can choose premixed process colors from a matching system, such as TRU-MATCH or PANTONE Process, or enter process color percentages yourself 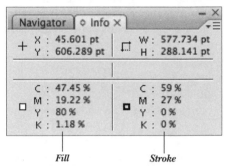–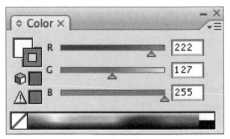. To print the graduated tones in a photographic image, you have to use four-color process printing. If your budget allows, you can have it all: process printing, plus a spot color (or two) for an important graphic, such as a logo.

Colors for the Web

For Web output, you should choose **RGB** colors (the acronym stands for red-green-blue) 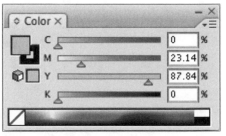. For viewers whose monitors display millions of colors (now the majority), the RGB colors you choose will look pretty much as you intend.

If you must cater to the handful of viewers still using 8-bit monitors, choose colors using the Web Safe RGB color model on the Color panel. With your artwork restricted to Web-safe colors, no color substitutions will occur in the browser. If you mix a non-Web-safe color, an Out of Web Color Warning button 🟦 appears on the Color panel; click the cube or swatch, and the color is converted to its closest Web-safe cousin.

1 *Use the CMYK color model for **print** output.*

Fill   Stroke

2 *The **Info** panel lists the color breakdowns for the currently selected object. If the currently selected objects contain different color values, these areas will be blank.*

3 *Use the **RGB** color model for **Web** output.*

Colors for Your Output Medium

Getting in the mode

➤ Any **process** colors that you create in a document will conform to the current document color mode, regardless of which mode you choose from the Color Mode menu in the Swatch Options dialog box (see page 118). In other words, you can create process CMYK or process RGB colors in a document, but not both.

➤ Colors in a **blend** or **gradient** conform to the current document color mode automatically.

➤ Embedded placed and pasted **images** are converted to the current document color mode automatically.

➤ The **Rasterize** dialog box displays options only for the current document color mode.

When you created your new document, you had the option to choose CMYK or RGB as the Color Mode. Any colors you mix or choose in your document conform to that mode automatically. When you change the **document color mode**, all the colors in the document convert to the new mode. (The current document color mode is listed in the document title bar.)

To change the document color mode:

1. Use File > **Save As** to create a copy of your file (Cmd-Shift-S/Ctrl-Shift-S).

2. Choose File > Document Color Mode > **CMYK Color** or **RGB Color.**

➤ If you need to reverse a document color mode change, don't rechoose the prior color mode. Instead, use Edit > Undo.

➤ If you need two versions of a document, say, one in RGB mode for Web output and one in CMYK mode for print output, copy the file, then change the color mode in the copy.

Document Color Mode

Using the basic color controls

Just to get the ball rolling, we'll show you how to apply **black** or **white** as a fill or stroke color.

To apply a fill or stroke of black or white:

1. Select an object or objects.

2. Do either of the following:

   Click the **Fill** or **Stroke** color (or arrowhead) on the **Control** panel to open a temporary Swatches panel, then click the White or Black swatch on the panel **1**.

   To apply a white fill and a 1-pt. black stroke, click the **Default Fill and Stroke** button on the Tools panel (or press D).

➤ You can also apply white or black by clicking the white or black selector in the bottom right corner of the Color panel **2**.

To apply a fill or stroke of None:

1. Select an object or objects by any method, and make sure your document is in Preview view.

2. Click the **Fill** or **Stroke** color (or arrowhead) on the Control panel, or the Fill or Stroke box on the Color panel.

3. Click the **None** button on the Tools, Swatches, or Color panel, or press /.

1 *Click the Fill or Stroke color or arrowhead on the* **Control** *panel to open a temporary Swatches panel, then click the* **White** *or* **Black** *swatch below.*

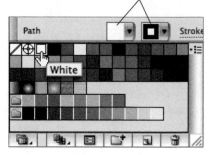

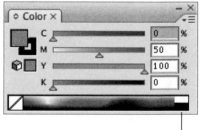

2 *White and Black selectors on the Color panel*

Recolor by dragging

When you apply a color by dragging, you don't need to choose any particular tool or select any objects. To see how this works, deselect all. Click the Fill or Stroke box on the Tools or Color panel, then drag a color from the **Swatches** or **Color Guide** panel over an object. Bing! (If an object is selected, simply clicking a color swatch or a color on the spectrum bar will change its fill or stroke automatically, depending on whether the Fill or Stroke box is active.)

©DANIEL PELAVIN

White fill, black stroke

Selecting type for recoloring

➤ To recolor all the type in a block, select it with the **Selection** tool.

➤ To recolor only a portion of a type block, select those characters or words with a **Type** tool.

➤ To recolor a path that contains path type or an object that contains area type, select it with the **Direct Selection** tool.

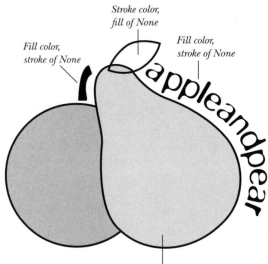

Stroke color, fill of None

Fill color, stroke of None

Fill color, stroke of None

Fill color, stroke color

1 *Fill and **stroke** combinations*

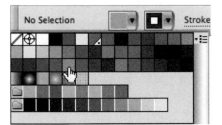

2 *Click the Fill color on the **Control** panel to open a temporary **Swatches** panel, then click a color.*

3 *A question mark signifies that the currently selected objects contain **different colors.***

You have many methods at your disposal for applying colors **1**. We'll introduce you to the **basic color controls** first.

To apply a fill or stroke color:

1. Select an object; or to choose colors for an object you're about to create, deselect all. To select type, see the sidebar at left.

2. Click the Fill color or arrowhead on the **Control** panel to open a temporary Swatches panel, then click a color, gradient, or pattern swatch **2**. If you chose a spot color ▣ or global process color ▣, you can move the **T** (Tint) slider on the Color panel 🎨 to adjust the percentage of that color.
or
Double-click the Fill box on the **Tools** or **Color** panel to open the Color Picker. Click a hue on the vertical bar in the middle of the dialog box, then click a variation of that color in the large square. If your document is going to be printed and the Out of Gamut icon ⚠ appears, click the swatch below the icon to substitute the closest printable color. Click OK.

3. To apply a stroke color, click the **Stroke** color on the Control panel to open a temporary Swatches panel, then click a color or pattern swatch. To make the stroke wider or narrower, click the up or down **Stroke Weight** arrow on the Control panel.

4. Just for the heck of it, display the **Color Guide** panel, 📊 then click a variation of the current color (see pages 175–177).**NEW!**

➤ You can't apply a gradient as a stroke color. To work around this limitation, see page 329.

➤ If the fill or stroke colors differ among currently selected objects, a question mark **3** will appear in the Fill and/or Stroke box on the Tools, Color, and Control panels, but you can go ahead and apply a new fill and/or stroke color to all the selected objects.

Saving colors as swatches

The **Swatches** panel is used for storing and applying process colors, spot colors, patterns, and gradients. Swatches that you add to the panel save just with the current file. (To learn more about this panel, see pages 114–117.)

To save the current fill or stroke color as a swatch:

1. Select an object that contains the color you want to save as a swatch; or with no objects selected, choose a color via the Color Picker (see the previous page) or specify values via the Color panel (see page 109).

2. Drag the Fill or Stroke box from the **Color** or **Tools** panel (or drag a color from the Color Guide panel) to the Swatches panel ▦ **1**.
   or
   Click the Fill or Stroke box on the Color or Tools panel, then Option-click/Alt-click the **New Swatch** button 🔲 at the bottom of the Swatches panel. **NEW!** The new swatch will appear on the palette.

➤ To choose options for a new swatch as you save it, click the New Swatch button on the Swatches panel, type a Swatch Name, keep the Color Type as Process Color, check or uncheck Global, leave the Color Mode as is, then click OK.

➤ When you apply a color from a matching system to an object directly from a library panel, that color is also added to the Swatches panel (see the next page).

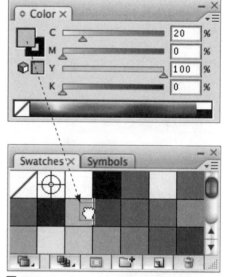

1 *To save a color as a swatch, drag it from the Color panel (or Tools panel) to the* **Swatches** *panel.*

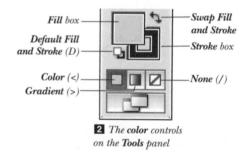

2 *The* **color** *controls on the* **Tools** *panel*

Save Color as Swatch

Shortcuts for applying colors **2**

Toggle between the Fill and Stroke boxes on the Tools or Color panel	Press X
Make the fill color the same as the stroke color, or vice versa	Drag one color box over the other on the Tools panel or Color panel
Swap the fill and stroke colors	Press Shift-X or click the Swap Fill and Stroke button 🔄 on the Tools panel
Apply a fill of None	Click the None button 🔲 (/) on the Tools panel
After applying fill or stroke of None, reapply the last solid color	Click the Last Color button ⬑■ on the Color panel or click the Color button 🔲 (<) on the Tools panel
Reapply the last gradient	Click the Gradient button 🔲 (>) on the Tools panel

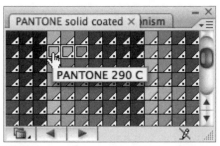

1 *Select a swatch or swatches on a library panel, then choose* **Add to Swatches** *from the library panel menu to add them to the Swatches panel.*

The color books

ANPA colors are used in the newspaper industry.

DIC Color Guide and **TOYO Color Finder** colors are used in Japan.

FOCOLTONE process colors are used in the U.K. This system was designed to reduce registration problems and the need for trapping.

HKS process colors and HKS spot colors (no "Process" in the name) are used in Europe.

PANTONE process colors and PANTONE spot colors (no "Process" in the name) are used widely in the U.S.

TRUMATCH process colors are organized differently from PANTONE colors.

Avoid nasty surprises!

As you learned in Chapter 4, the Color Settings command in Illustrator uses monitor and printer device profiles and output intents in conjunction with the system's color management utility to ensure accurate color matching between the onscreen display of your artwork and the final output. Unfortunately, even with the best color management system in place, for commercial printing, you can't proof process and spot colors onscreen — however tempted you may be to trust what you see. Instead, always pick spot colors and look up process color formulas in a printed fan book for a **color matching system**. And before you give the go-ahead for a print run, be sure to tell your print shop that you'll need to see a color proof (or two, if you need to make changes).

Applying colors from a library

In these instructions, you'll learn how to access and apply spot or processs colors from a matching system (such as PANTONE), from an Adobe library of process colors, or from the Web library of 216 Web-safe RGB colors.

To access colors from a library: NEW!

1. *Optional:* Select an object to apply a color to, and click the Fill or Stroke box on the Tools or Color panel.

2. From the **Swatch Libraries** menu ▣. at the bottom of the Swatches panel, choose a library name. To open a library from a matching system (for print output), choose that system from the **Color Books** submenu on the Swatch Libraries menu (see the sidebar at left). To reload default swatches, choose from the **Default Swatches** submenu.

   The chosen library will open in a separate panel. Scroll or enlarge the panel, if necessary, to reveal the desired color.

3. If you click a swatch in a **Color Books** library or click a **color group** icon ▣ in any library, that color or color group will appear on the Swatches panel automatically. Otherwise, do either of the following:

   On the library panel, click a swatch or Cmd-click/Ctrl-click multiple swatches **1**, then choose **Add to Swatches** from the library panel menu.

   Drag a swatch or multiple swatches from the library panel to the Swatches panel.

4. To view other, related swatch libraries, click the **Load Next Swatch Library** ▶ or **Load Previous Swatch Library** ◀ button on the library panel.

➤ To have a library panel reappear when you relaunch Illustrator, choose Persistent from the library panel menu. To close a whole library panel, click its close box; to close a single library on the panel, click the close box on its tab.

➤ You can't modify swatches on a library panel (note the non-edit icon ✗ in the lower right corner). However, you can edit any swatch once you've saved it to the Swatches panel.

Changing the tint percentage

You can achieve a pleasing range of tints (and keep a job within budget) with just a black plate and one spot color plate by applying an assortment of **tint percentages** of the spot color. You can also change the percentage of a global process color.

To change the tint percentage of a spot or global process color:

1. On the **Swatches** panel, click a spot color (dot in the lower right corner) or a global process color (white triangle in the corner).

2. On the Color panel, move the T (Tint) slider or click the Tint ramp at the bottom of the panel **1**.

➤ If Select Same Tint % is checked in Preferences > General, the Fill & Stroke, Fill Color, and Stroke Color commands on the Select Similar Options menu (Control panel) will select only objects containing the same color and tint percentage as the selected object. With this option unchecked, the commands will select the same color in any tint percentage.

Printing spots as spots

When color-separating a file from Illustrator, you can choose to either preserve spot colors as such or convert all spot colors into process colors. To ensure that the spot colors in your document color-separate properly to their own plates, choose File > Print, click Output on the left side, choose a Separations option from the Mode menu, and leave **Convert All Spot Colors to Process** *unchecked.*

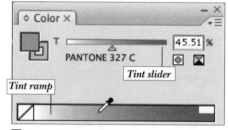

1 *On the Color panel, move the **Tint slider** or click the **Tint ramp.***

New registration color

The **[Registration]** color is used for crop marks and other marks that a commercial printer uses to align their printing plates **2**. If you need to change this color (perhaps your artwork is very dark and the marks will show up better in white), click the Registration swatch, then move the Tint slider on the Color panel.

2 *The **[Registration]** color appears on every plate when a file is color-separated.*

Staying in the gamut

An **Out of Gamut** warning ⚠ below the color boxes on the Color panel signifies that the current RGB or HSB color has no CMYK equivalent, and therefore can't be printed on a commercial press. If you click the icon or swatch, Illustrator will substitute the closest printable equivalent color.

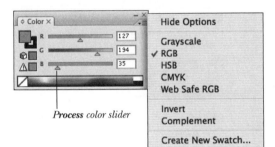

Process color slider

1 *On the Color panel, click the Fill or Stroke box, choose a color model from the panel menu, then move the sliders or enter percentages.*

Mixing colors numerically

Follow these instructions to mix an **RGB** color for Web output or a **CMYK** color for print output by specifying numeric values.

To mix a color numerically:

1. Select an object; or to choose colors for an object you're about to create, deselect all.

2. Do either of the following:

   On the **Color** panel, click the Fill or Stroke color.

   On the **Control** panel, Shift-click the Fill or Stroke color (or arrowhead) to open a temporary Color panel.

3. Choose a color **model** from the Color panel menu **1**:

   Grayscale to convert all the colors in any selected objects to grayscale, or to choose a gray shade.

   RGB to mix a color for video or Web output, or for output to a desktop color printer.

   HSB to mix a color by its hue (location on the color wheel), saturation (purity), and brightness values; this model has no practical use for print output.

   CMYK to create a process color for output on a commercial printing press.

   Web Safe RGB to mix colors for Web output using hexadecimal values (see page 102).

4. Move the available sliders (0–255 for RGB; 0–100% for CMYK) or enter values. For print output, get the percentages for the desired color from a printed fan book for a matching system, such as PANTONE process coated.

5. *Optional:* To save the new color as a swatch, click the New Swatch button 🔳 on the Swatches panel, check or uncheck Global in the Swatch Options dialog box, then click OK.

➤ Shift-click the color bar on the Color panel to cycle through the color models.

➤ To enter HSB, RGB, or Web color values or CMYK percentages by way of the Color Picker, double-click the Fill or Stroke box on the Tools or Color panel.

Changing stroke attributes

Next, you'll learn to change the weight (width) of a stroke, its position on the path, and its style (dashed or solid, rounded or sharp corners, flat or rounded ends). Remember, you can open a temporary Stroke panel by clicking Stroke on the Control panel.

First, you'll change the **stroke width**.

To change the width of a stroke:

1. Select one or more objects.

2. In the **Weight** area of the **Stroke** panel ≡ ❶ or the **Stroke** area of the **Control** panel ❷, do one of the following:

   Click the up or down arrow, or Shift-click either arrow to change the weight by a larger interval.

   Choose a preset value from the menu.

   Enter a value ❸. *Note:* A stroke that's narrower than .25 pt. may not print. A weight of 0 makes a stroke invisible.

➤ Don't apply a wide stroke to small type—it will distort the letterforms.

➤ You can enter a stroke weight in points (pt), picas (p), inches (in), millimeters (mm), centimeters (cm), or pixels (px). When you press Return/Enter or Tab, the value will be converted automatically to the Stroke unit currently chosen in Preferences > Units & Display Performance.

To change the alignment of a stroke on a path:

1. Select one or more closed objects. To see the effect of the align options, make the stroke fairly wide, or zoom in on your artwork.

2. On the **Stroke** panel, click the **Align Stroke to Center** ▣, **Align Stroke to Inside** ▣, or **Align Stroke to Outside** button ▣ ❹–❻.

   Note: If the buttons aren't showing, double-click the Stroke tab until they appear.

Stroke Width, Alignment

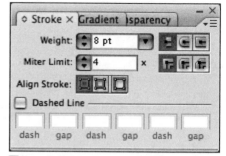

❶ On the **Stroke** panel, enter a **Weight** value, or click the up or down arrow, or choose from the menu.

❷ You can also choose a stroke weight via the **Control** panel.

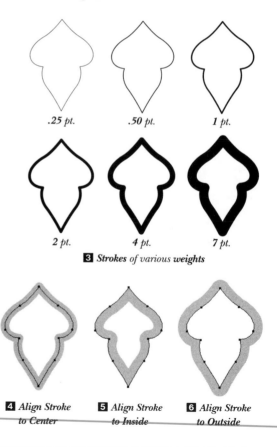

.25 pt.　　.50 pt.　　1 pt.

2 pt.　　4 pt.　　7 pt.

❸ *Strokes of various weights*

❹ *Align Stroke to Center*　　❺ *Align Stroke to Inside*　　❻ *Align Stroke to Outside*

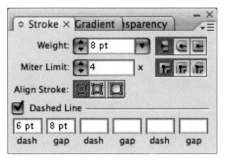

1 *The* **Dashed Line** *settings chosen here will create 6-pt.* **dashes,** *with 8-pt.* **gaps** *between them.*

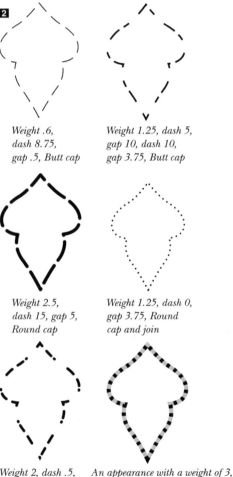

Weight .6,
dash 8.75,
gap .5, Butt cap

Weight 1.25, dash 5,
gap 10, dash 10,
gap 3.75, Butt cap

Weight 2.5,
dash 15, gap 5,
Round cap

Weight 1.25, dash 0,
gap 3.75, Round
cap and join

Weight 2, dash .5,
gap 12, dash 6,
gap 5, dash 5,
gap 3, Round cap

An appearance with a weight of 3,
dash 2.5, gap 3.75, Butt cap; and
a second stroke appearance with a
gray stroke, 3 pt. (see Chapter 20)

Using the **Dashed Line** feature, you can easily create dashed strokes.

To create a dashed stroke:

1. Select an object. Make sure it has a stroke color and a Weight greater than zero.

2. Make sure the full options are showing on the **Stroke** panel. If not, double-click the Stroke tab until they appear **1**.

3. Click a **Cap** button for the dash shape (see the following page).

4. Check **Dashed Line.**

5. Enter a value in the first **Dash** field (for the length of the first dash), then press Tab. If you don't enter values in the other dash fields, the first dash value will be used for all the dashes **2**.

> The default Stroke unit in Preferences > Units & Display Performance, Points, is used in the Dash and Gap fields, but you can enter values in another unit, such as centimeters (cm) or pixels (px).

6. *Optional:* Enter a value in the first Gap field (the length of the first gap after the first dash), then press Tab to proceed to the next field or press Return/Enter to exit the panel. If you don't enter a gap value, the dash value will also be used as the gap value.

7. *Optional:* To create dashes (or gaps) of varying lengths, enter values in the other dash (or gap) fields. The more different values you enter, the more irregular the dashes or gaps.

> To create a dotted line, click the second Cap button, enter a dash value of 0, and enter a gap value that's greater than or equal to the stroke Weight.

> To save a dashed stroke as a graphic style, drag a path to which the stroke is applied to the Graphic Styles panel (see page 274).

Dashed Stroke

111

To change the stroke caps or joins:

1. Select an object, and apply a fairly wide stroke to it.

2. Make sure the full options are showing on the **Stroke** panel. If not, double-click the Stroke tab until they appear. You can use tool tips to identify them.

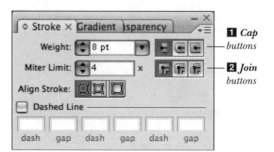

1 Cap buttons

2 Join buttons

3. Click a **Cap** button to modify the endpoints of a solid line or all the dashes in a dashed line **1**–**3**:

Butt Cap to create square-cornered ends in which the stroke stops at the endpoints, or to create thin, rectangular dashes. Use this option if you need to align your paths very precisely.

Round Cap to create semicircular ends or elliptical dashes.

Projecting Cap to create square-cornered ends in which the stroke extends beyond the endpoints, or to create rectangular dashes.

4. Click a **Join** button to modify the bends on corner points (not curve points) of the path:

Miter Join to produce pointed bends.

Round Join to produce semicircular bends.

Bevel Join to produce beveled bends. The sharper the angle of the path, the wider the bevel.

5. *Optional:* Change the Miter Limit (1–500) value to control when a mitered (pointed) corner becomes a beveled corner. Don't worry about how it works; just use a high Miter Limit value to create sharp, pointy corners or a low Miter Limit value to create beveled corners.

➤ To learn the difference between corner and curve points, see page 133.

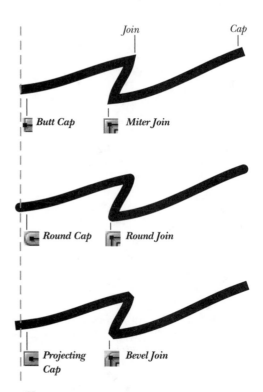

3 The **Join** buttons affect the **bends** in a stroke; the **Cap** buttons affect the **ends** of a stroke.

Stroke Caps and Joins

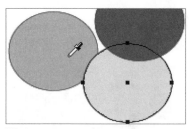

1 *Select an object or objects, then click with the **Eyedropper** tool on an object that contains the attributes you want to **sample**.*

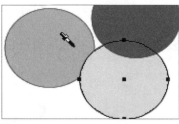

2 *The attributes you sample will be applied instantly to the **selected** object.*

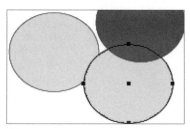

3 *Or **Option-click/Alt-click** with the Eyedropper tool to apply attributes from the currently **selected** object to the one you **click** on.*

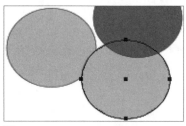

4 *These are the results after Option/Alt-clicking with the **Eyedropper** tool.*

Using the Eyedropper tool

When you click an object with the **Eyedropper** tool, it samples the object's color and stroke attributes, displays them on the Color and Stroke panels, and applies them to any currently selected objects — in one quick step.

To sample and apply colors with the Eyedropper tool:

1. *Optional:* To change which attributes the Eyedropper tool picks up, double-click the tool. The Eyedropper Options dialog box opens. Check the attributes to be picked up and applied (all are checked by default), uncheck the attributes to be ignored, then click OK.

2. *Optional:* Select an object or objects. They'll be recolored instantly with the attributes you'll sample with the Eyedropper in step 4.

3. Choose the **Eyedropper** tool (I).

4. Click an object in any Illustrator window that contains the attributes you want to sample **1**. It can be any kind of object (even a placed image), and it can contain a solid color, pattern, or gradient. The object doesn't have to be selected. Depending on the current Eyedropper options, the sampled colors will appear in the Fill and/or Stroke boxes on the Tools and Color panels, and the sampled Stroke settings will appear on the Stroke panel.

   If you selected any objects before using the Eyedropper tool, the sampled attributes will be applied to those objects **2**.

➤ Option-click/Alt-click any objects to do the opposite of the above: Apply color attributes from the currently selected object to the object you click **3**–**4**.

➤ To have the Eyedropper tool sample only the color it clicks on (no other attributes), click the Fill or Stroke box on the Tools or Color panel, then Shift-click the color to be sampled.

➤ To preserve a sampled color to use again, drag from the Fill or Stroke box on the Tools or Color panel to the Swatches panel.

Using the Swatches panel

Via the Swatches panel menu, you can control the **categories** and **size** of swatches the panel displays.

To choose display options for the Swatches panel: NEW!

1. To control which categories of swatches are displayed on the Swatches panel, ▦ from the **Show Swatch Kinds** menu ▦ at the bottom of the panel, choose **Show All Swatches** for all types (colors, gradients, patterns, and groups) **1**; **Show Color Swatches** for just solid colors and color groups; **Show Gradient Swatches** for just gradients; **Show Pattern Swatches** for just patterns; or **Show Color Groups** for just color groups.

2. From the panel menu, choose a view for the currently chosen category of swatches: **Small Thumbnail View, Medium Thumbnail View, Large Thumbnail View, Small List View,** or **List View.** The medium and large thumbnail views are useful for identifying gradients and patterns. In the two list views, the panel displays icons representing the color type and mode for each solid color **2**.

3. *Optional:* From the panel menu, choose Sort by Name to sort the swatches alphabetically by name or numerically by their color contents; or choose Sort by Kind (when all swatch categories are displayed) to sort swatches in this order: solid colors, gradients, patterns, color groups.

➤ To locate a particular swatch, choose Show Find Field from the panel menu, click in the field, then start typing the swatch name. Choose the command again to hide the field.

➤ You can drag a swatch, or multiple selected swatches, to a new location on the panel; note the location of the white vertical line before releasing the mouse.

➤ To learn the difference between global and nonglobal colors, see page 118.

see page 118.

Display Options for Swatches Panel

Global process colors have a white corner but no dot.   ***Nonglobal process*** *color are plain.*   ***Spot*** *colors have a dot.*

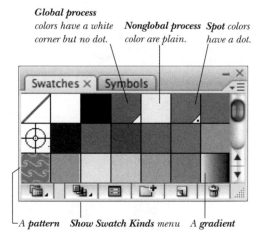

—*A* **pattern**   **Show Swatch Kinds** *menu*   *A* **gradient**

1 ***All categories*** *of swatches are currently displayed on this* **Swatches** *panel.*

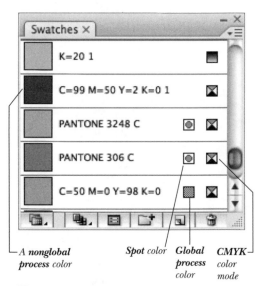

—*A* ***nonglobal*** *process color*   ***Spot*** *color*   ***Global*** *process color*   ***CMYK*** *color mode*

2 *When the Swatches panel is in a list view, on the right side, you'll see icons representing the* **color type** *and* **document color mode.**

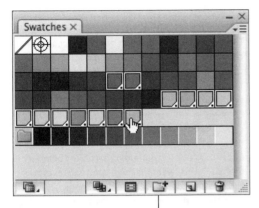

1 *Select the solid-color swatches you want to gather into a color group, then click the **New Color Group** button.*

2 *In the **New Color Group** dialog box, enter a name for the new color group.*

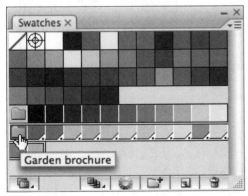

3 *The new **color group** appears on the panel.*

Color groups are a new—and very useful—organizational tool for the Swatches panel. When the panel is in a thumbnail view, the colors in each group are lined up in their own tidy little row, with a folder icon on the left side, and you can identify the groups via tool tips. When the panel is in a list view, the name of the color group is listed next to the folder icon, with the colors listed below it. If you're coordinating a group of solid colors for a client, for a specific design, or by a theme, you'll be able to locate them more easily if they're in a group.

To create a color group: NEW!

1. On the Swatches panel, ⊞ Shift-click to select contiguous swatches or Cmd-click/Ctrl-click to select multiple swatches **1**. Only solid colors can be put in a group (sorry, no gradients or patterns).

2. Click the **New Color Group** button ⊡ at the bottom of the panel. The New Color Group dialog box opens **2**.

3. Enter a Name, keep Selected Swatches as the Create From setting, then click OK. The new swatches group will appear on the panel **3**.

➤ You can also create a color group based on harmonies via the Color Guide panel or the Live Color dialog box (see Chapter 14).

➤ To rename a group, double-click the group folder icon, change the name at the top of the Live Color dialog box, click OK, then click Yes in the alert dialog box.

➤ You can restack a color group by dragging the folder icon upward or downward.

Color Groups

To copy swatches between Illustrator files: NEW!

1. Open the file that you want to load swatches into.

2. Choose **Other Library** from the Swatch Libraries menu 📖. at the bottom of the Swatches panel. The Select a Library to Open dialog box opens.

3. Locate and click the Illustrator file you want to copy swatches from, then click Open. A swatch library panel will appear onscreen, bearing the name of the source file in its tab.

4. Drag a swatch or color group icon from the library panel into the Swatches panel **1**–**2**. Or Cmd-click/Ctrl-click or Shift-click multiple swatches, then choose Add to Swatches from the swatch library menu. (If the Swatch Conflict dialog box appears, see the sidebar.)

➤ To append colors between files quickly, copy and paste or drag and drop an object from one Illustrator document window to another; the object's colors will appear on the Swatches panel of the target document.

Resolving a swatch conflict

The **Swatch Conflict** dialog box will appear as you copy swatches between files if a global process color that you're trying to copy has the same name but different color percentages as an existing swatch in your document. Click **Merge Swatches** to let the existing swatch take precedence, or click **Add Swatches** to add the new swatch and have a number be appended to its name. If you're appending colors by dragging an object between files, click Add Swatches if you want to prevent colors in the copied objects from changing. (To have the current Options setting apply to any other name conflicts that crop up and prevent the alert dialog box from opening repeatedly, check Apply to All in the Swatch Conflict dialog box.)

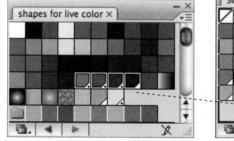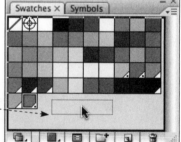

1 *Open a swatch library from another file, then **drag** a swatch or swatches from the library panel to the Swatches panel.*

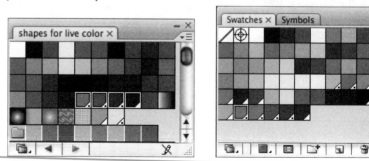

2 *The **duplicate** swatches appear on the **Swatches** panel.*

By saving your swatches and color groups to **custom libraries**, you'll be able to load them onto the Swatches panel for use in any document.

To save a library of swatches:

I. Make sure the Swatches panel contains only the swatches or color groups that you want to save in a library.

➤ To remove the swatches that aren't being used in your artwork, choose Select All Unused from the Swatches panel menu, click the Delete Swatch button 🗑 on the panel, then click Yes in the alert dialog.

2. From the **Swatches Libraries** menu 🔖, at the bottom of the Swatches panel, choose **Save Swatches.NEW!** The Save Swatches as Library dialog box opens.

3. Type a name for the library in the Save As field, keep the default location, and click Save.

4. The new library will be listed on, and can be opened from, the **User Defined** submenu on the Swatches Libraries menu, along with any other user-defined libraries.

Quick retrieval

If you unintentionally delete a solid color, gradient, or pattern that's being used in the current file, you can retrieve it by selecting an object that contains it, then dragging the Fill and/or Stroke box from the Tools or Color panel to the Swatches panel.

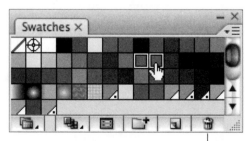

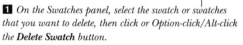

1 *On the Swatches panel, select the swatch or swatches that you want to delete, then click or Option-click/Alt-click the **Delete Swatch** button.*

To duplicate a swatch: NEW!

I. On the Swatches panel, click the swatch you want to duplicate, then click the **New Swatch** button 🔲 on the panel (or drag the swatch over the button). The New Swatch dialog box opens.

2. Change the name, if desired, check Global or not, then click OK. The duplicate swatch will appear next to the original swatch.

➤ To duplicate a swatch without opening a dialog box, click the swatch, then Option-click/Alt-click the New Swatch button.

To delete swatches:

I. Click a **swatch** or the **icon** for a color group that you want to delete, or Shift-click or Cmd-click/Ctrl-click to select multiple swatches or color groups.
or
To select only the swatches that aren't being used in your artwork, choose **Show All Swatches** from the Show Swatch Kinds menu, then choose **Select All Unused** from the Swatches panel menu.

2. Click the **Delete Swatch** button 🗑 at the bottom of the Swatches panel, then click Yes in the alert dialog box **1**.
or
To bypass the prompt, Option-click/Alt-click the **Delete Swatch** button.
or
Drag the swatch(es) you want to delete over the **Delete Swatch** button.

➤ To restore a deleted swatch or swatches, choose Undo right away.

➤ If you delete a global process color that's being used in your artwork, you won't be able to edit the object colors globally. If you delete a spot color that's currently applied to an object, a nonglobal process color equivalent of the deleted color will be applied to that object (see the following page).

➤ If you want to restore swatches from one of the default libraries, see page 107.

Replacing colors in your artwork

If you edit a **nonglobal process** color swatch (Global is unchecked for the color in the Swatch Options dialog box), the color will update where it's being used—but only on selected objects.

To replace the color or stroke attributes on multiple objects:

1. Select an object that contains the nonglobal process color(s), stroke weight, or other attributes that you want to change.

2. From the **Select Similar Options** menu [icon] on the Control panel, **NEW!** choose Same > **Fill & Stroke, Fill Color, Opacity, Stroke Color,** or **Stroke Weight.**

3. Click the Fill or Stroke box on the Tools or Color panel, then do any of the following:

   Click a different swatch on the **Swatches** or **Color Guide** panel (see page 176), or mix a new color using the **Color** panel.

   Choose a new Weight or other attributes on the **Stroke** panel.

If you edit the values in a **global process** color, the color will update automatically in all the objects where it's being used—whether those objects are selected or not.

To change a color from nonglobal to global, or vice versa:

1. Double-click a process or nonglobal process color swatch on the Swatches panel. Global process color swatches have a white corner and no dot; nonglobal process colors are plain (no corner, no dot).

2. The Swatch Options dialog box opens **1**. Check or uncheck **Global,** then click OK.

To edit the values in a global process color:

1. Double-click a global **process** color swatch on the Swatches panel.

2. In the Swatch Options dialog box, check Preview, move the sliders to modify the color, then click OK. Tint percentages are preserved.

To change a **spot** or **global process** color that's being used in multiple objects, instead of recoloring one object at a time, simply **replace** the color swatch with a new color, and it will update automatically in all the objects where it's being used (even when no objects are selected). Existing tint percentages are preserved.

To replace a global process or spot color swatch:

1. Deselect all objects.

2. From the **Swatch Libraries** menu [icon] on the Swatches panel, choose a library name (or choose from a submenu, such as Color Books). Click a color on the library panel, then Option-drag/Alt-drag it over the swatch on the **Swatches** panel that you want to replace.
   or
   Click the Fill or Stroke box on the Tools or Color panel, then mix a new color using the **Color** panel (or double-click either box, then mix a color in the Color Picker); or click a color on the **Color Guide** panel. (Be sure to create a new color, not just a tint variation of an existing color.) Option-drag/Alt-drag the Fill or Stroke box over the global process color swatch on the Swatches panel that you want to replace.
   or
   On the **Swatches** panel, Option-drag/Alt-drag one swatch over another swatch. If you Option-drag/Alt-drag a nonglobal process swatch over a global process swatch, the resulting swatch will be a global process color.

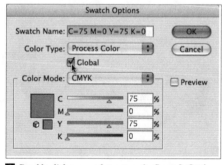

1 *Double-click a swatch to open the **Swatch Options** dialog box, then check or uncheck **Global.***

1 *The original group of objects*

2 *All the colors are **inverted**.*

Inverting colors

The **Invert Colors** command converts multiple nonglobal process colors in selected objects to their opposite values on the color scale, whereas the **Invert** command converts just the fill or stroke color (of any type) in a selected object to its opposite values on the color scale.

To invert colors:

To invert multiple nonglobal process colors, select an object or objects, then choose Edit > Edit Colors > **Invert Colors NEW! 1**–**2**. This command doesn't convert spot colors, global process colors, gradients, or patterns.
or
To invert a single solid color (spot, global process, or nonglobal process), click an object, click the Fill or Stroke box on the Color panel, then from the Color panel menu, choose **Invert.**

Colorizing images

You can colorize a **grayscale** EPS, JPEG, PCX, PDF, PSD, or TIFF image that you open or place in an Illustrator document. Select a grayscale image that you've imported into Illustrator via File > Open or Place, click the **Fill** box on the Colors or Tools panel, then apply any type of fill color via the Color, Swatches, or Color Guide panel. Gray areas will be recolored; white background areas will remain opaque white.

Another option is to convert an imported image to grayscale via Edit > Edit Colors > **Convert to Grayscale** in Illustrator, then colorize it as per the instructions in the previous paragraph. You can also do this to an image that you drag and drop into Illustrator.

Notes: To learn about the Open and Place commands, see Chapter 19. You can't colorize a linked EPS image, but you can colorize an embedded EPS file (uncheck the Link option in the Place dialog box).

Invert Colors; Colorize Images

Blending fill colors
To blend fill colors between objects:

1. Select **three or more** objects that contain fill colors (make sure none of them have a fill of None) 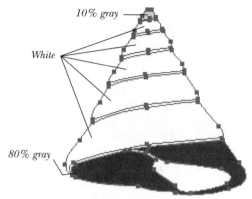. The more objects you use, the more gradual the blend. The stroke colors and widths will remain the same, and the objects will stay on their respective layers.

   The two objects that are either farthest apart or frontmost and backmost can contain only nonglobal colors or different tints of the same spot color, but no global process colors, patterns, or gradients (and they can't be type objects).

2. From the Edit > **Edit Colors** submenu, **NEW!** choose:

   Blend Front to Back to use the fill colors of the frontmost and backmost objects as the starting and ending colors in the blend (this works irrespective of the x/y location of the objects in the artwork).

   Blend Horizontally to use the fill colors of the leftmost and rightmost objects as the starting and ending colors in the blend.

   Blend Vertically to use the fill colors of the topmost and bottommost objects as the starting and ending colors in the blend .

   Selected objects that are stacked or located between the frontmost and backmost objects, the leftmost and rightmost objects, or the topmost and bottommost objects will be assigned intermediate blend colors.

➤ Compare these commands with the commands that blend object colors and shapes, which are discussed fully in Chapter 23.

10% gray

White

80% gray

1 *Seven objects are selected.*

2 *The **Blend Vertically** command is applied.*

1 *Select one or more objects. You can use anything from geometric objects to freehand lines.*

➤ *For a rough-and-tumbled look, apply Effect > Distort & Transform > Roughen (use a low setting) to the objects.*

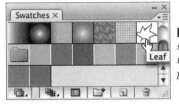

2 *Drag the selected object(s) to the* **Swatches** *panel.*

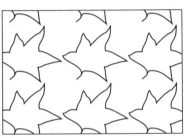

3 *An object is* **filled** *with the new pattern.*

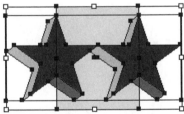

4 *We copied the star, and arranged the objects symmetrically. Then a rectangle was drawn, and stacked behind the other objects.*

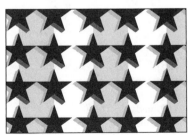

5 *The new pattern is used as a fill.*

Creating patterns

To create a pattern:

1. Draw an object or objects to be used as a pattern **1**. They can contain brush strokes or a gradient, can be part of a mask or blend, and can include a bitmap image, but simple shapes are less apt to cause a printing error.

2. Choose the Selection tool (V), then Shift-click or marquee all the objects.

3. Choose Edit > **Define Pattern.**
   or
   Drag the selection onto the **Swatches** panel, deselect the objects, then double-click the new swatch.

4. The New Swatch or Swatch Options dialog box opens. Type a Swatch Name, then click OK **2**–**3**. You can apply the new pattern as a fill or stroke to any object.

You can use a **rectangle** to control the amount of white space around a **pattern** or to crop away parts of objects that you want to exclude.

To use a rectangle to define a pattern:

1. Draw objects of any type for the pattern. To create a symmetrical pattern of geometric objects, use the Rectangle, Ellipse, Polygon, Spiral, or Star tool. To copy an object along an axis, Option-Shift-drag/Alt-Shift-drag it with the Selection tool. You can use the grid, smart guides (see pages 90–91), or the Align buttons (see pages 95–96) to position the objects.

2. Deselect all, then choose the **Rectangle** tool ▨ (M).

3. Choose a fill and stroke of None. ▧

4. Drag a rectangle (or Shift-drag to draw a square) around the objects, roughly a half-inch to an inch wide and high; use the Info panel to check the dimensions **4**. If the pattern is complex, keeping the rectangle small will help prevent a printing error. Fit the rectangle closely around the objects if you don't want any blank space to be part of the pattern (use smart guides). For a geometric pattern, draw the rectangle carefully so the

(Continued on the following page)

Create a Pattern

pattern will be symmetrical and will repeat correctly.

5. On the **Layers** panel, drag the rectangle listing below the pattern object listings.

6. Leave the fill and stroke as None ⊿ for the rectangle if you don't want it to become part of the pattern, or apply a fill color to the rectangle if you do.

7. Follow steps 2–4 in the previous set of instructions (**5**, previous page).

You can **edit** any **pattern**, including any of the patterns that are supplied with Illustrator.

To edit a pattern:

1. Drag a pattern swatch from the Swatches panel onto a blank area of the artboard **1**. The objects will consist of a group or nested groups, with a bounding rectangle (fill and stroke of None) as the bottommost layer **2**.

2. Double-click the group to isolate it, then edit the pattern objects. Use the **Direct Selection** tool (A) to select individual components **3**.

3. Double-click outside the group to exit isolation mode.

4. Choose the Selection tool (V), then Option-drag/Alt-drag the group over the original pattern swatch. The pattern will update in any objects where it's being used **4**.

➤ To add an edited pattern as a new swatch, drag the selection onto the Swatches panel without holding down Option/Alt, then double-click the new swatch to rename it.

➤ Read about transforming patterns on pages 125 and 128.

➤ To expand a pattern into individual objects, select an object that contains the pattern, then choose Object > Expand. In the Expand dialog box, check Fill and/or Stroke. The pattern will be divided into the original shapes that made up the pattern tile, nested as groups below a clipping mask (which is listed on the Layers panel as <Clipping Path>). You can release the mask (Object > Clipping Mask > Release), change the mask shape, or delete it altogether.

Read about transforming patterns on pages 125 and 128.

Edit a Pattern

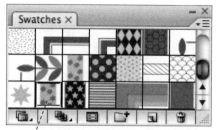

1 Drag the pattern that you want to edit from the **Swatches** panel to the artboard.

2 The pattern objects appear on the artboard.

3 Edit the pattern objects, then select and drag them back over the original swatch.

4 The edited pattern is used as a fill in these objects.

Move just the pattern

To **reposition** the **pattern** fill or stroke in an object without moving the object **5**, hold down ~ (tilde) and drag inside it with the Selection tool.

5 A pattern (applied as a stroke) is being moved, while the object remains stationary.

TRANSFORM 10

In this chapter, you'll learn several methods for transforming objects, including manipulating an object's bounding box and using the multipurpose Free Transform tool, the individual transformation tools, the Transform panel, the Control panel, the Transform Each command, and the Transform effect.

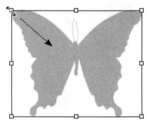

1 *Option-drag/ Alt-drag to **scale** an object from its center.*

2 *The object is scaled down.*

3 *To **reflect** an object, drag a bounding box handle all the way across it.*

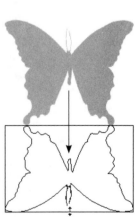

4 *The object is **reflected**.*

Transform via the bounding box

One of the fastest ways to **transform** an object is by using its **bounding box.** With this method, though, you can't copy an object or move the reference point.

To transform an object via its bounding box:

1. If bounding boxes are currently hidden, choose View > **Show Bounding Box** (Cmd-Shift-B/Ctrl-Shift-B).

2. With the Selection tool, select an object (or objects). A rectangular bounding box with eight handles will appear around the object(s).

3. To **scale** the object(s) along two axes, drag a corner handle; to scale it along one axis, drag a side handle. Or Shift-drag to scale the object proportionally; Option-drag/Alt-drag to scale it from its center **1**–**2**; or Option-Shift-drag/Alt-Shift-drag to scale it proportionally from its center.
   or
   To create a **reflection** (mirror image) of the object, drag a side handle all the way across it **3**–**4**.
   or
   To **rotate** the object, move the pointer slightly outside a corner handle (the pointer will be a curved double arrow), then drag in a circular direction.
   or
   To **rotate** the object 180°, drag a corner handle diagonally all the way across the object. Smart guides are helpful when doing this. (To square off the bounding box after rotating an object, see the tip on page 132.)

Using the Free Transform tool

The multipurpose **Free Transform** tool lets you rotate, scale, reflect, or shear an object, or apply perspective or distortion. However, unlike the other transformation tools, with this tool, you can't move the reference point or make copies.

To use the Free Transform tool:

1. Select one or more objects or a group. The Free Transform tool can't make clones, so copy the object now if you want to transform a copy of it.

2. Choose the **Free Transform** tool (E).

3. To **scale** the object(s) along two axes, drag a corner handle; to scale along one axis, drag a side handle. Shift-drag to scale the object proportionally; Option-drag/Alt-drag to scale it from its center; or Option-Shift-drag/Alt-Shift-drag to scale it proportionally from its center.

To **rotate** the object, position the pointer outside it, then drag in a circular direction. Shift-drag to rotate in 45° increments. To rotate the object 180°, drag a corner handle all the way across it; to rotate it proportionally, Shift-drag a corner handle.

To **shear** the object, start dragging a side handle then hold down Cmd/Ctrl and continue to drag **1**–**2**. To constrain the movement, drag a side handle, then Cmd-Shift-drag/Ctrl-Shift-drag. To shear the object from its center, start dragging, then hold down Cmd-Option/Ctrl-Alt and continue to drag.

To **reflect** the object, drag a side handle all the way across it; to reflect the object from its center, Option-drag/Alt-drag a side handle.

To **distort** the object, start dragging a corner handle, then hold down Cmd/Ctrl and continue to drag **3**–**4**. *Note:* You can't distort editable type.

To apply **perspective** to the object (not to editable type), start dragging a corner handle, then hold down Cmd-Option-Shift/ Ctrl-Alt-Shift and continue to drag **5**–**6**. The perspective will occur along the *x* or *y* axis, depending on the direction you drag.

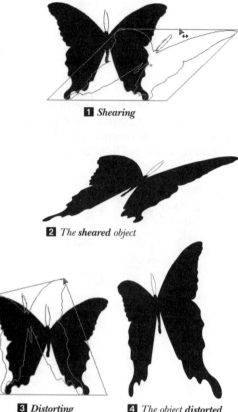

1 *Shearing*

2 *The* **sheared** *object*

3 *Distorting*   **4** *The object* **distorted**

5 *Applying* **perspective**

6 *After applying* **perspective**

Free Transform Tool

Preferences for transformations

When performing transformations, there are three options in Preferences (Cmd-K/Ctrl-K) > General that you should know about:

➤ When transforming objects, the default Horizontal angle is 0° and the default Vertical angle is 90°. The default starting point for measuring the degree of an angle is the horizontal (x) axis (the three o'clock position). You can enter a custom **Constrain Angle.**

➤ If **Transform Pattern Tiles** is checked when you transform an object that contains a pattern fill or stroke, the pattern will also transform.*

➤ For scale transformations, check **Scale Strokes & Effects** to scale an object's stroke and appearances proportionately, or uncheck this option to allow disproportionate scaling.*

This option can also be turned on or off on the Transform panel menu.

As we showed you in Chapter 8, **smart guides** can be a great help when aligning objects or points onscreen. In these instructions, you'll use smart guides as you **transform** an object. (To read more about smart guides, see pages 90–91.)

To use smart guides as you transform an object:

1. In Preferences (Cmd-K/Ctrl-K) > Smart Guides & Slices, make sure **Transform Tools** is checked. You can also choose a different Angles set for the guides or enter custom angles.

2. Make sure View > **Smart Guides** is on (Cmd-U/Ctrl-U).

3. Select the object(s) or group to be transformed.

4. Choose the **Free Transform** ▦ tool (or the Rotate (R) ⟳, Reflect (O) ◨, Scale (S) ▦, or Shear tool ▱; see the instructions on the following page).

5. As you drag the mouse to transform the object, smart guides will appear onscreen temporarily **1**–**3**. Move the pointer along a smart guide to apply the transformation on that axis. The rotate angle and other readouts will appear on the Info panel as you apply a transformation.

Transform Using Smart Guides

1 *Smart guides used with the **Reflect** tool*

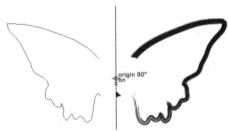

2 *Smart guides used with the **Scale** tool*

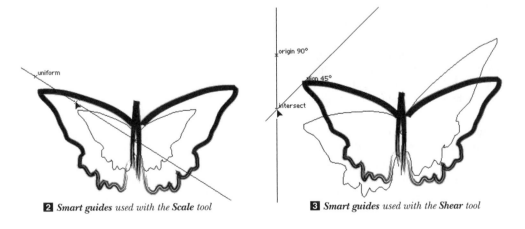

3 *Smart guides used with the **Shear** tool*

Using the Rotate, Reflect, Scale, or Shear tool

To rotate, reflect, scale, or shear an object by dragging:

1. Select an object(s) or group.

2. Choose the **Rotate** (R) , **Reflect** (O) , **Scale** (S) , or **Shear** tool.

3. Do any of the following:

To transform the object from its **center**, move the mouse (button up) far away from the center for better control, then drag. To **scale** the object, drag away from or toward it; to **rotate** the object, drag around it; or to **shear** the object **1**–**2**, drag away from it. Don't forget to use smart guides!

To transform the object from a **reference point** of your choosing, click near the object (the pointer will turn into an arrowhead), move the mouse (button up) away from the reference point for better control, then drag (**1**–**2**, next page).

To **reflect** the object, click to establish a reference point, then click again to define the axis of reflection (or Shift-click to place the second point along the nearest 45° angle) (**3**–**4**, next page).

To transform a **copy** of the object, start dragging, then hold down Option/Alt and continue to drag (release the mouse first).

To transform the object along a multiple of **45°** or to **scale** it **proportionally**, start dragging, then hold down Shift and continue to drag (release the mouse button before releasing Shift) (**5**, next page).

To transform a **copy** of the object along a multiple of **45°**, or to **copy** and **scale** it **proportionally**, start dragging, then hold down Option-Shift/Alt-Shift and continue to drag.

To **flip** and **scale** the object simultaneously, drag completely across it with the Scale tool.

➤ To transform a pattern but not the object when using the Rotate, Reflect, Scale, or Shear tool, hold down ~ (tilde) while dragging.

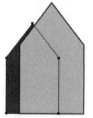

1 *The shadow object is selected.*

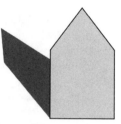

2 *The shadow object is **sheared** along the horizontal axis.*

Transforming via a dialog box

To apply a transformation via a dialog box, select one or more objects or a group, then Control-click/ right-click in the document window and choose Transform > **Rotate, Reflect, Scale,** or **Shear** from the context menu. The dialog box opens; check Preview. After choosing values, you may check Copy instead of OK to transform a copy of the selected object(s). (To transform an object from a reference point of your choosing instead of the center, choose the Rotate , Reflect , Scale , or Shear tool, then Option-click/Alt-click on or near the object.)

If an object's fill or stroke contains a pattern and you want the pattern to transform along with the object, make sure both **Patterns** and **Objects** are checked in the transform dialog box; or to scale just the pattern and not the object, uncheck Objects. These options are also available on the Transform panel menu.

Rotate, Reflect, Scale, Shear Tools

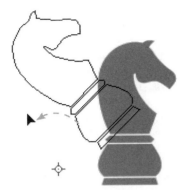

1 *After clicking a point of origin with the* **Rotate** *tool, the mouse is repositioned, then dragged in a circular direction.*

2 *After clicking a point of origin with the* **Shear** *tool, the mouse is repositioned, then dragged to the left.*

3 *A point of origin is clicked with the* **Reflect** *tool…*

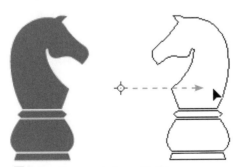

5 *After clicking a point of origin with the* **Scale** *tool, the mouse is repositioned, then dragged to the upper right with Shift down.*

4 *…then the mouse is dragged to the right with Option-Shift/Alt-Shift down.*

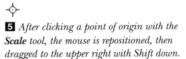

Rotate, Reflect, Scale, Shear Tools

Using the Transform panel

Use the **Transform panel** to move, scale, rotate, or shear objects based on exact values or percentages.

To move, scale, rotate, or shear objects via the Transform panel:

1. Select one or more objects or a group.

2. Show the **Transform** panel.⊟ To open a temporary Transform panel, click the blue X, Y, W, or H on the Control panel; in Windows, if your application window is too narrow to display those letters, click <u>Transform</u>.

3. Choose a reference point for the transformation by clicking a handle on the **reference point locator** on the left side of the panel ❶.

4. From the Transform panel menu, choose **Transform Object Only**, **Transform Pattern Only**, or **Transform Both** (to transform the object and pattern).

5. If you're going to scale the object, check **Scale Strokes & Effects** on the panel menu to scale the object's stroke and appearances proportionately, or uncheck this option to allow disproportionate scaling. This option can also be turned on or off in Preferences (Cmd-K/Ctrl-K) > General.

6. Enter or choose a value as per the instructions below, then apply it via one of the shortcuts listed in the sidebar on this page:

To move the object **horizontally**, enter a new X position. Enter a higher value to move the object to the right, or a lower value to move it to the left.

To move the object **vertically**, enter a new Y position. Enter a higher value to move the object upward, or a lower value to move it downward. You can also enter a plus or minus sign, then the amount you want the object to move.

To **scale** the object, enter the desired width and/or height as percentage or absolute values. To scale the object proportionally, first click the **Constrain Proportions** button ⊟ (a bracket will appear next to the button).

Applying Transform panel values

Apply the current value and **exit** the panel	Return/Enter
Apply the current value and select the **next** field	Tab
Apply the current value and reselect the **same** field	Shift-Return/ Shift-Enter
Apply the current value, **exit** the panel, and **clone** the object	Option-Return/ Alt-Enter
Highlight the **next** field and **clone** the object (Mac only)	Option-Tab
Repeat the last transformation (after exiting the panel)	Cmd-D/Ctrl-D

❶ *Reference point (the part of the object that Transform panel values are calculated from)*

Width and Height of selected object

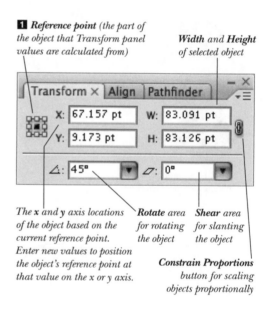

The x and y axis locations of the object based on the current reference point. Enter new values to position the object's reference point at that value on the x or y axis.

Rotate area for rotating the object

Shear area for slanting the object

Constrain Proportions button for scaling objects proportionally

Transform Panel

X: 200 pt   Y: 9.173 pt   W: 78.99

1 *On the Control panel, enter the desired X and/or Y location for an object or group.*

Let Illustrator do the math

In the W or H field on the **Transform** panel, you can perform simple math to scale an object (and you can use any of these units of measure: p, pt, in, mm, q, or cm).

➤ After the current number, type an asterisk * and then a **percentage** value or whole number. For example, to reduce an object's scale by half, click to the right of the current value, then type "*50%" (e.g., 4p would become 2p).

➤ Replace the entire field with a **percentage.** Enter "75%," for example, to reduce the W or H to three-quarters of its current value (e.g., 4p becomes 3p).

➤ Enter a **positive** or **negative** value to the right of the current number, as in "+2" or "-2," to increase or decrease the current value, respectively, by that amount.

To apply the new value, use one of the keystrokes listed in the sidebar on the previous page.

Enter a positive **Rotate** value to rotate the object counterclockwise, or a negative value to rotate it clockwise. Or choose a preset rotation angle from the menu.

To shear (slant) the object to the right, enter or choose a positive **Shear** value. To shear an object to the left, enter or choose a negative Shear value.

7. From the panel menu, you can also choose **Flip Horizontal** or **Flip Vertical**.

➤ To apply a transformation as an editable and removable effect, see page 131.

➤ If Use Preview Bounds is checked in Preferences (Cmd-K/Ctrl-K) > General, the full dimensions of an object, including the stroke and any applied effects, will be listed in the W and H fields on the Transform, Control, and Info panels.

To move an object or group via the Control panel:

1. Select an object or group.

2. In the X (horizontal) and/or Y (vertical) field on the Control panel **1**, enter the desired axis locations for the object. (In Windows, if the size of your application window doesn't allow the X and Y to appear on the Control panel, click Transform and enter values on the temporary Transform panel.)

Transform via Control Panel

Using the Transform Each command

The transformation tools transform multiple objects relative to a single, common reference point, whereas the **Transform Each** command modifies one or more selected objects relative to their individual center points **1**. To make your artwork look less regular and more hand-drawn, try applying this command to a bunch of objects with the Random option checked.

To perform multiple transformations via the Transform Each command:

I. Select one or more objects (preferably two or more). Objects in a group can't be transformed individually.

2. Control-click/right-click and choose Transform > **Transform Each** (Cmd-Option-Shift-D/Ctrl-Alt-Shift-D).

3. Check Preview, and move the dialog box out of the way, if necessary.

4. Do any of the following **2**:

Move the Horizontal or Vertical **Scale** slider (or enter a percentage then press Tab) to scale the objects horizontally and/or vertically from their reference points.

Choose a higher Horizontal **Move** value to move the objects to the right or a negative value to move them to the left; and/or choose a higher Vertical Move value to move the objects upward, or vice versa.

Enter a **Rotate: Angle** value and press Tab, or rotate the dial.

Check the **Reflect X** or **Reflect Y** box to create a mirror reflection of the objects.

Check **Random** to have Illustrator apply random transformations within the range of the values you've chosen for Scale, Move, or Rotate. For example, at a Rotate Angle of 35°, a different angle between 0° and 35° will be used for each selected object. Uncheck and recheck Preview to get different random effects.

Click a different **reference point** ▦ (the point transformations are calculated from).

5. Click **OK** or **Copy** (**1**–**2**, next page).

The original formation

The formation rotated 15° via the Rotate tool

*The formation rotated 15° via the **Transform Each** command with the **Random** option **unchecked***

1 *The results of the **Transform Each** command, compared with results from using the **Rotate** tool*

2 *The **Transform Each** dialog box*

(sidebar) **Transform Each Command**

DIANE MARGOLIN

1 *The original objects*

2 *The* ***Transform Each*** *command was applied using these values: Horizontal Scale 120, Vertical Scale 80 (nonmatching Horizontal and Vertical Scale values), Horizontal Move 13, Vertical Move –13, and Rotate 17°.*

Transform Effect

- Scale
  - Horizontal: 130 %
  - Vertical: 100 %

- Move
  - Horizontal: –24 pt
  - Vertical: 0 pt

- Rotate
  - Angle: 54 °

OK
Cancel

5 copies

☐ Reflect X
☐ Reflect Y

☐ Random
☑ Preview

3 *Use the* ***Transform Effect*** *dialog box to apply* ***editable*** *effects.*

Appearance ×

☐ **Path**
　Stroke: ■ 1 pt
　Fill: ☐
　Transform　*fx*

Double-click to edit effect

4 *To edit a transform effect, double-click the* ***Transform*** *listing on the* ***Appearance*** *panel.*

If you apply transformations via the **Transform Effect** dialog box, you will be able to edit (not just undo) those transformations long after you've closed the dialog box, and even after you close and reopen the file!

To use the Transform effect:

1. Select one or more objects.

2. Choose Effect > Distort & Transform > **Transform**.

3. The Transform Effect dialog box looks like the Transform Each dialog box, with one exception: In the Transform Effect dialog box, you can specify how many copies you want **3**. Follow the instructions for the Transform Each dialog box on the previous page.

4. To edit the transformation after you click OK, select the object, then double-click Transform on the Appearance panel ⬤ **4** to reopen the Transform Effect dialog box. This is a sneak preview of what's to come in Chapter 20, Appearances & Styles.

Transform Effect

131

Repeating a transformation

By using the **Transform Again** command, you can quickly repeat the last transformation (using the last-used values) on any selected object. If you copied an object while transforming it, Transform Again will produce another transformed copy.

To repeat a transformation:

1. Transform an object or group .

2. Keep the object selected, or select another object or group.

3. Control-click/right-click and choose Transform > **Transform Again** (Cmd-D/Ctrl-D) .

1 *An object is copy-rotated...*

2 *...and then the **Transform Again** command (Cmd-D/ Ctrl-D) is applied twice.*

Reset the bounding box

After rotating an object by using a tool or by dragging the corner of the bounding box, the bounding box will no longer align with the x/y axes of the page. If you like, you can square off the bounding box to the horizontal axis while preserving the new orientation of the object. Select the object, then Control-click/right-click and choose Transform > **Reset Bounding Box** (or choose Object > Transform > Reset Bounding Box).

RESHAPE ‖

In Chapter 6 you learned how to draw closed and open geometric paths without thinking about their individual components. In this important chapter, you'll learn how to reshape a path's contour by manipulating the nuts and bolts that all paths are composed of: direction handles, anchor points, and segments. Once you learn how to change the position, number, or type (smooth or corner) of anchor points on a path, you'll be able to create just about any shape imaginable.

In addition, you'll learn how to quickly reshape all or part of a path with the Path Eraser, Pencil, Paintbrush, and Reshape tools; align anchor points; join endpoints; reshape objects via an Effect command; combine paths; split and cut paths; and erase objects with the Eraser tool. This chapter also includes three practice exercises.

Building Blocks of a Path

The building blocks of a path

Paths can be open or closed, and consist of anchor points connected by straight and/or curved **segments** ∎. **Smooth** anchor points have a pair of direction handles that move in tandem; **corner** anchor points have no direction handles, one direction handle, or a pair of direction handles that move independently. Each direction handle has a direction point at the end, which you can drag to change the shape of the adjacent curve ❷–❸.

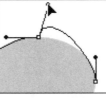

❷ *The **angle** of a direction handle affects the **slope** of the curve leading into the anchor point.*

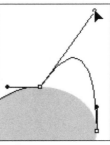

❸ *The **length** of a direction handle affects the **height** of the curve.*

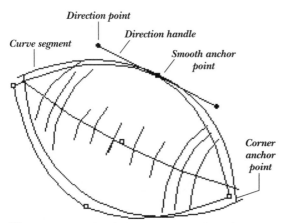

Direction point

Direction handle

Curve segment

Smooth anchor point

Corner anchor point

❶ *You can manipulate the basic components of a path manually, or with special reshaping tools and commands.*

Moving points and segments

If you **move** an **anchor point**, the segments that are connected to it reshape, lengthen, or shorten accordingly. If you move a **straight segment**, the anchor points it's connected to will move with it; if you move a **curve segment**, the curve will reshape but the connecting anchor points will remain stationary.

Note: For the instructions in this chapter, make sure **Highlight Anchors on Mouse Over** is checked in Preferences > Selection & Anchor Display.**NEW!** In the same option set, you can also choose preferences for the anchor and/or handle display.

To move an anchor point or a segment:

1. Choose the **Direct Selection** tool (A), and deselect all by clicking a blank area of the artboard. (If all the anchor points on a path are selected, you won't be able to move any individual points or segments.)

2. **Drag** an anchor **point** **1**; or **drag** the middle of a **segment** **2**; or **click** an anchor **point** or **segment**, then press an arrow key. You can use smart guides for positioning.

➤ Shift-drag a point or segment to constrain the movement to a multiple of 45°.

➤ You can move more than one point at a time, even if they're on different paths. To select them first, Shift-click them individually or drag a marquee around them.

Reshaping curves

In the instructions above, you learned that you can drag a curve segment or an anchor point to reshape a curve. A more precise way to reshape a curve is to lengthen, shorten, or change the angle of its **direction handles.**

To reshape a curve segment:

1. Choose the **Direct Selection** tool (A).

2. Click an anchor point or a curve segment **3**.

3. **Drag** a **direction point** (at the end of the direction handle) toward or away from the anchor point **4**.
   or

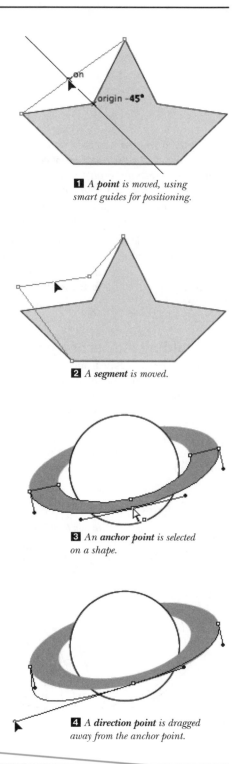

1 A **point** is moved, using smart guides for positioning.

2 A **segment** is moved.

3 An **anchor point** is selected on a shape.

4 A **direction point** is dragged away from the anchor point.

1 *To convert a corner point into a smooth point, click with the **Direct Selection** tool on the anchor point…*

2 *…then click the **Convert Selected Anchor Points to Smooth** button on the Control panel.*

3 *Direction handles appear for that anchor point.*

4 *You can drag either of the direction handles to modify the curve.*

5 *The original object has sharp corners.*

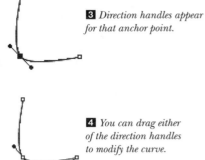

6 *Effect > Stylize > **Round Corners** rounded off the corners (and the effect is removable).*

Tearoff toolbar

To practice the techniques in this chapter, we recommend tearing off the toolbar for the **Pen** tool **7** so the Pen and its related tools are visible and easily accessible. (Once you memorize the shortcuts for accessing these tools, you won't need to use the toolbar.)

Rotate the **direction point** around the anchor point. You can use Shift to constrain the angle, or use smart guides for positioning.

➤ Direction handles on a smooth point always rotate in tandem and stay in a straight line, but can be different lengths.

Converting points

To convert a corner anchor point into a smooth anchor point: NEW!

1. In Preferences > Selection & Anchors, make sure **Highlight Anchors on Mouse Over** is checked.

2. Choose the **Direct Selection** tool (A).

3. Pass the pointer over a corner of the path; the anchor point will be highlighted (enlarged); click to select it **1**.

4. On the Control panel, click the **Convert Selected Anchor Points to Smooth** button **2**–**3**. Direction handles will appear for the selected anchor point.

5. *Optional:* To modify the curve further, with the Direct Selection tool, drag either of the direction handles that are attached to the anchor point **4**.

➤ You can also convert a corner point to a smooth point using the Convert Anchor Point tool (Shift-C). Click the corner point with the tool, then drag away from the anchor point. Direction handles will appear as you drag.

➤ To round the corners on a path via a vector filter, use Filter > Stylize > Round Corners (under Illustrator filters); or to do it via a removable effect, use Effect > Stylize > Round Corners **5**–**6** (to straighten out the rounded corners, simply remove the effect).

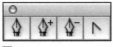

7 *Keep the tearoff toolbar for the **Pen** tool handy.*

Convert Corner Point to Smooth

To convert a smooth anchor point into a corner anchor point: NEW!

1. Choose the **Direct Selection** tool (A).

2. Deselect all, then pass the pointer over an anchor point on a path to highlight that point, or click the edge of a path to display its anchor points.

3. Click a smooth point to select it **1**.

4. On the Control panel, click the **Convert Selected Anchor Points to Corner** button **2**. Direction handles for that anchor point will disappear.

➤ You can also click a smooth point with the Convert Anchor Point tool (Shift-C) to convert it into a corner point.

In these instructions, you'll learn how to convert a point so its **direction handles**, instead of remaining in a straight line, can be **rotated independently** of each other.

To rotate direction handles independently:

1. Choose the **Direct Selection** tool (A).

2. Deselect all, click the edge of an object to display its anchor points, then click a smooth point **3**.

3. Choose the **Convert Anchor Point** tool (Shift-C).

4. Drag a direction point at the end of one of the direction handles. The curve segment will reshape as you drag **4**.

5. Choose the Direct Selection tool again (A), click the anchor point, then drag the other direction point for that anchor point **5**.

➤ To restore independently rotating direction handles back to their original straight-line alignment (and thereby produce a smooth, unpinched curve segment), click the anchor point with the Direct Selection tool, then click the Convert Selected Anchor Points to Smooth button on the Control panel. NEW!

➤ If the Pen tool (P) is selected, you can hold down Option/Alt to access a temporary Convert Anchor Point tool.

1 *With the* **Direct Selection** *tool, click a smooth anchor point...*

2 *...then click the* **Convert Selected Anchor Points to Corner** *button on the Control panel.*

3 *A point is selected on an object.*

4 *A single* **direction handle** *is moved with the* **Convert Anchor Point** *tool.*

5 *The second* **direction handle** *is moved.*

Convert Smooth to Corner; Rotate Handles

1 *Click a* ***segment*** *to add a* ***new point.***

2 ***Move*** *the new point, if desired.*

Getting nice curves

By paying attention to the placement of points, you can achieve smoother curves. When reshaping paths (and when drawing them in Chapter 15), try to remember to place points at the ends of a curve instead of at the midpoint **3**–**4**.

3 *It's hard to draw symmetrical curves if you place points at the high point of a curve.*

4 *You'll get a more symmetrical curve by placing points just at the* ***ends.***

Adding points

Another way to reshape a path is by manually **adding anchor points** to it.

To add anchor points to a path manually:

1. Choose the **Selection** tool (V), then select the object to which you want to add a point or points.

2. Do either of the following:

   Choose the **Add Anchor Point** tool (+).

   Choose the **Pen** tool (P), and make sure Disable Auto Add/Delete is unchecked in Preferences > General.

3. Click the edge of the object. A new, selected anchor point will appear **1**. Repeat, if desired, to add more points to the path.

   An anchor point that you add to a curve segment will be a smooth point with direction handles; an anchor point that you add to a straight segment will be a corner point with no direction handles.

4. *Optional:* With the Direct Selection tool (A), move the new anchor point, or lengthen or rotate its direction handles **2**.

➤ If you don't click precisely on a segment with the Add Anchor Point tool, an alert dialog box may appear. Click OK, then try again. If you want to use smart guides to help you find anchor points, check Text Label Hints in Preferences > Smart Guides & Slices.

➤ Hold down Option/Alt to use a temporary Delete Anchor Point tool when the Add Anchor Point tool is selected, and vice versa.

Add Anchor Points Manually

The **Add Anchor Points** command inserts one point midway between every pair of existing anchor points in a selected object.

To add anchor points to a path via a command:

1. Choose the **Selection** tool (V), then select the object or objects that you want to add points to.

2. Choose Object > Path > **Add Anchor Points** **1**–**3**. Repeat, if desired.

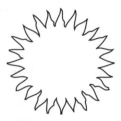

1 *The original object*

Handy shortcuts	
Pen tool	P
Add Anchor Point tool	+
Delete Anchor Point tool	-
Convert Anchor Point tool	Shift-C
Pencil tool	N
Paintbrush tool	B
Scissors tool	C
Lasso tool	Q
Disable Auto Add/Delete function of Pen tool	Shift
Pen tool to last-used selection tool	Cmd/Ctrl
Add Anchor Point tool to Delete Anchor Point tool, and vice versa	Option/Alt
Average endpoints	Cmd-Option-J/ Ctrl-Alt-J
Join endpoints	Cmd-J/Ctrl-J
Average and join endpoints	Cmd-Option-Shift-J/ Ctrl-Alt-Shift-J

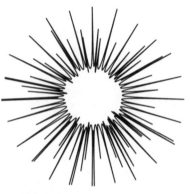

2 *After applying Filter > Distort > Pucker & Bloat (Pucker –70%)*

3 *After applying the **Add Anchor Points** command to the original object, then applying Filter > Distort > Pucker & Bloat (Pucker –70%). With more points on the original path, the filter produced more rays.*

1 *The* **Paintbrush** *pointer is positioned over an* **endpoint** *of an arc.*

2 *An* **addition** *to the path is drawn.*

3 *The pointer is positioned over an* **endpoint** *(note the slash next to the pen icon).*

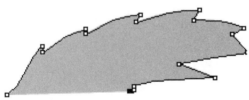

4 *After the endpoint is clicked, it becomes solid.*

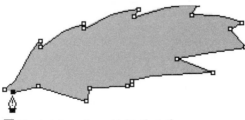

5 *New points are then added to the path.*

You can **add** a **segment** to a path with the **Pencil** tool, regardless of which tool the path was drawn with; the existing path can have an applied brush stroke. If a path has a brush stroke, another option is to add to it with the **Paintbrush** tool.

To add to a path with the Pencil or Paintbrush tool:

1. Choose the **Selection** tool (V), then select a path.

2. Double-click the **Pencil** tool (N) to open the preferences dialog box for that tool. Or if the path has a brush stroke, you can double-click the **Paintbrush** tool (B) instead.

3. In the tool preferences dialog box, make sure Edit Selected Paths is checked, then click OK.

4. Position the pointer directly over an end-point, then draw an addition to it **1**. When you release the mouse, the path will remain selected **2**. If you added to an open path, it will remain open. If you added to a closed path, it will now be an open path; you can drag either endpoint with the Direct Selection tool.

➤ If you end up with a new, separate path instead of an addition to an existing path, delete the new one and try again.

To add to an open path with the Pen tool:

1. Choose the **Pen** tool (P).

2. Position the pointer over the **endpoint** of the path that you want to add a segment to (the path doesn't have to be selected). A slash appears next to the Pen pointer when the tool is positioned correctly **3**.

3. Click the endpoint to make it a corner point, or drag from it to make it a smooth point. The point will become solid **4**.

4. Position the pointer where you want the additional anchor point to appear.

5. If desired, continue to click to create more corner points or drag to create more smooth points **5**. Choose another tool when you're done adding to the path.

Deleting points

When you **delete points** from a closed path, it stays closed.

To delete anchor points from a path:

Method 1 (Pen tools)

1. Choose the **Delete Anchor Point** tool (-).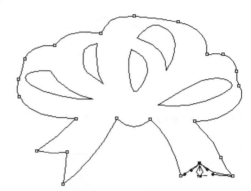
   or
   Choose the **Pen** tool (P), and make sure Disable Auto Add/Delete is unchecked in Preferences > General.

2. Cmd-click/Ctrl-click the edge of the object that you want to delete anchor points from.

3. Click an anchor point (don't press Delete!). The point will be deleted ■–■. Repeat to delete other anchor points, if desired.

➤ Hold down Shift to disable the add/delete function of the Pen tool. Release Shift before releasing the mouse button.

➤ If you don't click precisely on an anchor point with the Delete Anchor Point tool, an alert dialog box will appear. Click OK and try again.

■ *Click an anchor point with the **Delete Anchor Point** tool (or the Pen tool).*

Method 2 (Control panel) NEW!

1. Choose the **Direct Selection** tool (A).

2. Deselect all, click the edge of an object to display its anchor points, then click a point.

3. Click the Anchors: **Remove Selected Anchor Points** button on the Control panel.

■ *The point is deleted.*

1 *The original objects*

2 *The **Path Eraser** tool is being used to erase points.*

3 *A path is being reshaped with the **Pencil** tool. (To get a crosshair pointer, check Use Precise Cursors in Preferences > General, or press Caps Lock.)*

4 *The path has a new shape.*

Quick reshaping

The **Path Eraser** tool deletes points, too—but you don't have to click them individually.

To erase part of a path with the Path Eraser tool:

1. Choose the **Path Eraser** tool. It's the last tool on the Pencil tool pop-out menu.

2. Cmd-click/Ctrl-click a path (not a type object) to select it.

3. Position the eraser of the pencil pointer directly over the path, then drag along the part of the path you want to erase **1**–**2**. If you erase part of a closed path, you'll end up with an open path; if you erase part of an open path (not the endpoints), you'll end up with two separate paths.

Next, we'll show you how to use the **Pencil** and **Paintbrush** tools to quickly and easily reshape an existing path.

To reshape a path with the Pencil or Paintbrush tool:

1. To reshape a path that doesn't have a brush stroke, choose the **Pencil** tool (N).
   or
   To reshape a path that does have a brush stroke, choose the **Pencil** tool (N) or the **Paintbrush** tool (B).

2. Cmd-click/Ctrl-click a path to select it.

3. Position the pointer **directly** over the edge of the path, then start dragging **3**. The path will reshape instantly! **4** *Note:* Be sure to position the pointer precisely on the edge of the path. If you don't, you'll create a new path instead of reshaping the existing one.

➤ Press Caps Lock to turn the pointer into a Precise Cursor (crosshair). Press Caps Lock again to restore the default cursors.

➤ To add to a path using the Pencil or Paintbrush tool, see page 139.

Path Eraser; Reshape with Pencil, Paintbrush

The **Reshape** tool is the best tool for gentle reshaping because it causes the least amount of distortion, but it's hard to describe in words. Our favorite way to use this tool is to select a handful of points with it, then drag. That selected portion of the path will keep its overall contour while it elongates or contracts, and the rest of the path will stay put.

To use the Reshape tool:

1. Choose the **Direct Selection** tool (A), dese-lect all, then click the edge of a path. Only one point or segment should be selected.

2. Choose the **Reshape** tool 🐦 (it's on the Scale tool pop-out menu).

3. Drag any visible **point**. A tiny square border will display around the point when you release the mouse.
   or
   Drag any **segment** of the path. A new square border point will be created.
   or
   Try this: Shift-click or marquee **multiple points** on the path with the Reshape tool (squares will display around these points), then drag one of the square points. The unselected points on the path (the ones without a square around them) will serve as anchors for the shape **1**–**2**.

➤ To reshape multiple paths at once with the Reshape tool, select some points on each path.

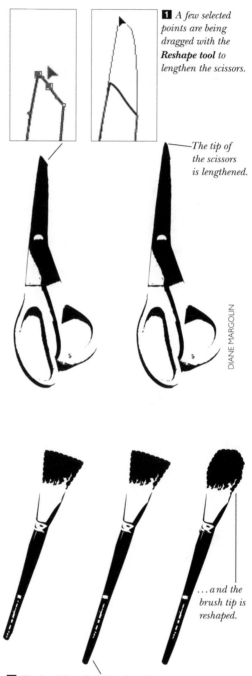

1 *A few selected points are being dragged with the* **Reshape tool** *to lengthen the scissors.*

The tip of the scissors is lengthened.

DIANE MARGOLIN

...and the brush tip is reshaped.

2 *The brush handle is lengthened...*

Reshape Tool

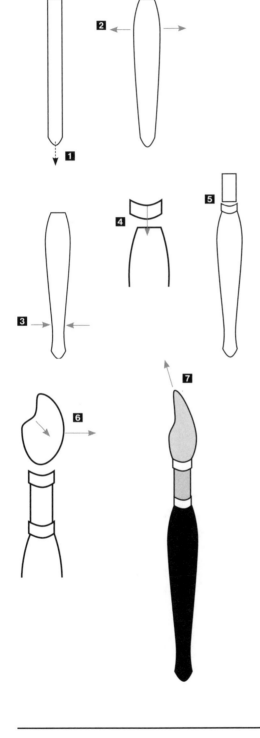

Exercise
Draw a brush with the Reshape tool

1. Using the **Rectangle** tool (M), draw a narrow vertical rectangle, and press D to apply white fill and a black stroke.

2. Choose the **Direct Selection** tool (A), deselect the path, then click on its edge.

3. With the **Reshape** tool, ☝ Shift-drag the bottom segment downward **1**.

4. Drag the upper part of the right vertical segment slightly outward, and drag the upper part of the left vertical segment outward by the same distance **2**.

5. Drag each side of the bottom vertical segments inward to pinch the stem **3**.

6. Using the **Rectangle** tool (M) again, draw a small horizontal rectangle. Choose the **Direct Selection** tool (A), deselect, then click the edge of the rectangle.

7. Choose the **Reshape** tool again, click the middle of the top segment of the new rectangle, Shift-click the middle of the bottom segment, then drag downward **4**.

8. Choose the **Selection** tool (V), ☝ move the rectangle over the top of the brush stem, and scale it to fit (use the bounding box).

9. Draw a slightly thinner vertical rectangle above the horizontal rectangle **5**. Then, on the Layers panel, drag the new path below the curved rectangular path.

10. Using the **Selection** tool, Option-Shift/ Alt-Shift drag the horizontal rectangle up to the top of the vertical rectangle.

11. Using the **Ellipse** tool (L), ⬭ draw an oval for the brush bristles. Choose the **Direct Selection** tool (A), deselect the oval, then click the edge of the oval path.

12. Choose the **Reshape** tool, drag the right middle point outward, drag the upper left segment inward **6**, and drag the top point upward to lengthen the tip **7**.

13. With the **Selection** tool (V), move the brush tip over the brush stem, then Control-click/right-click and choose Arrange > Send to Back. Apply fill colors.

Exercise: Reshape Tool

Aligning points

The **Align** buttons on the Control panel reshape one or more paths by precisely realigning selected endpoints or anchor points along the horizontal and/or vertical axis.

To align points: NEW!

1. Choose the **Lasso** tool (Q).

2. Drag to select two or more endpoints or anchor points **1** on one path or on different paths.

3. On the Control panel, do any of the following:

   Click one of the **Horizontal Align** buttons to align the points by moving them along the horizontal (*x*) axis.

   or

   Click one of the **Vertical Align** buttons to align the points by moving them along the vertical (*y*) axis.

   or

   Click a **Horizontal Align** button, then a **Vertical Align** button to overlap the points along both the horizontal and vertical axes. Choose this option if you're planning to join them into one point (instructions on the following page).

   If you click a left or right, or top **2**, or bottom **3** align button, points will align to the leftmost, rightmost, topmost, or bottommost selected point, respectively. If you click a center align button **4**, points will align to an equidistant location between the points.

➤ If you Shift-select points with the Direct Selection tool (instead of dragging a selection marquee) before clicking an align button, points will align with and move toward the last selected point, regardless of which Horizontal or Vertical Align button you click.

➤ You can also align selected points by choosing Object > Path > Average (Cmd-Option-J/ Ctrl-Alt-J), then clicking Axis: Horizontal, Vertical, or Both in the Average dialog box (this has fewer options than are offered on the Control panel).

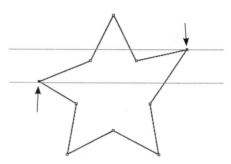

1 *Two anchor points are selected.*

2 *The **Vertical Align Top** button is clicked.*

3 *The **Vertical Align Bottom** button is clicked.*

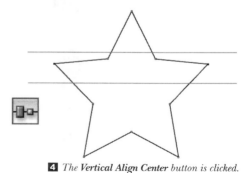

4 *The **Vertical Align Center** button is clicked.*

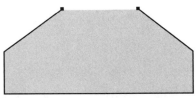

1 *Two endpoints are selected.*

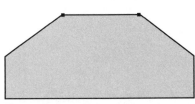

2 *The **Connect Selected End Points** button created a straight segment between them.*

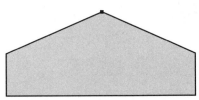

3 *If you click the **Connect Selected End Points** button when one selected endpoint is right on top of another, the Join dialog box will open.*

4 *This is the first figure on this page, after clicking the **Horizontal Align Center** and **Vertical Align Center** buttons, then clicking the **Connect Selected End Points** button.*

Average and join in one fell swoop
To average and join two selected endpoints via one keystroke, press **Cmd-Option-Shift-J/Ctrl-Alt-Shift-J.** Don't try this on a fully selected path!

Joining endpoints NEW!
The Connect Selected End Points button connects two selected endpoints via a new straight segment or joins endpoints into one point. The endpoints you connect or join can be on separate open paths or on the same open path.

To connect two endpoints:
1. With the **Direct Selection** tool (A) or **Lasso** tool (Q), select two endpoints **1**.
2. Click the **Connect Selected End Points** button on the Control panel. A straight line segment will connect the points **2**.

To join two endpoints into one point:
1. With the **Direct Selection** tool (A) or **Lasso** tool (Q), select two endpoints.
2. On the Control panel, click one of the three **Horizontal Align** buttons and one of the three **Vertical Align** buttons. To have the endpoints meet in the middle, click the Horizontal Align Center and Vertical Align Center buttons.

   The two selected endpoints should now be aligned right on top of each other.
3. Click the **Connect Selected End Points** button on the Control panel. The Join dialog box opens **3**.
4. Click **Corner** to join corner points into one corner point with no direction handles; or to connect two smooth points into one smooth point with moving direction handles that move independently.
   or
   Click **Smooth** to connect two smooth points into a smooth point with direction handles that move in tandem.
5. Click OK **4**.
➤ The Join command doesn't add direction handles to the resulting anchor point.

Join Endpoints

145

Reshaping objects via commands

Some of the Illustrator filters and effects can be used to explode simple shapes into more complex shapes, with almost no effort. Effect menu commands are reeditable; Filter menu commands are not. The **Zig Zag** filter, for example, adds anchor points to a path and then moves those points to produce waves or zigzags. The version on the Effect menu applies the Zig Zag effect without actually altering the path. Learn more about effects and filters in Chapter 21.

To apply the Zig Zag effect:

1. Select a path.

2. Choose Effect > Distort & Transform (under Illustrator Effects) > **Zig Zag**. The Zig Zag dialog box opens 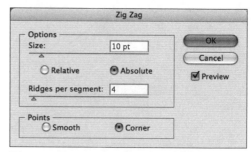. Check Preview.

3. Click Points: **Smooth** (at the bottom of the dialog box) to create curvy waves, or **Corner** to create sharp-cornered zigzags.

4. To move the added points by a percentage relative to the size of the object, click **Relative**, then move the **Size** slider (0–100).
   or
   To move the added points by a specified distance, click **Absolute**, then choose or enter that distance (0–100 pt) via the **Size** slider or field.

5. Choose a number of **Ridges** per segment (0–100) for the number of anchor points to be added between existing points. If you enter a number, press Tab to preview.

6. Click OK **2**–**7**.

1 *The* **Zig Zag** *dialog box*

2 *The original star*

3 *After applying the* **Zig Zag** *effect (Size 45, Ridges 4, Smooth)*

4 *The original circle*

5 *After applying the* **Zig Zag** *effect (Size 24, Ridges 20, Corner)*

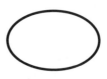

6 *The original ellipse*

7 *After applying the* **Zig Zag** *effect (Relative, Ridges 4, Smooth)*

Zig Zag Effect

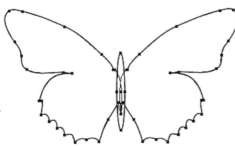

1 *Arrange two or more objects so they overlap, then select them.*

2 *Clicking the **Add to Shape Area** button on the Pathfinder panel united the separate shapes into a single compound shape.*

3 *The original objects*   **4** *After applying the **Add to Shape Area** command*

5 *The original objects*   **6** *After applying the **Add to Shape Area** command*

Using the tools that create shapes, such as the Rectangle, Ellipse, Star, or even the Pencil or Paintbrush, together with the reshaping functions covered in this chapter and occasionally some of the commands on the Pathfinder panel, you can create complex objects without having to draw with the notoriously difficult Pen tool. For example, rather than joining points pair by pair, you can use the Shape Mode buttons on the Pathfinder panel to combine whole objects. In these instructions, you'll use the **Add to Shape Area** button.

To combine objects using a command:

1. Position two or more objects so they overlap one another at least partially **1**.

2. Choose any selection tool.

3. Marquee at least some portion of all the objects.

4. Display the **Pathfinder** panel ▥ (Cmd-Shift-F9/Ctrl-Shift-F9).

5. Click the **Add to Shape Area** (first) button ▥ on the panel. The individual objects will combine into one closed compound shape, and will be painted with the attributes of the topmost object **2**–**6**. To learn more about compound shapes, see Chapter 25.

   Note: If you apply a stroke color to the new object, it will appear only on the perimeter of the overall combined shape, not on the interior segments. The interior segments are editable, but you can't apply a stroke color to them. If you want to delete those interior segments, select the object, then click Expand on the Pathfinder panel.

➤ Although you can't use multiple objects as a mask, you can use a closed object produced by the Add to Shape Area command as a masking object (see page 334).

Slicing and dicing

The **Scissors** tool can open a closed path or split an open path into two paths. You can split a path either at an anchor point or in the middle of a segment.

To split a path with the Scissors tool:

1. Choose any selection tool.

2. Click an object to display its points. *Note:* You can split a closed path that contains type (area type), but not an open path that has type along or inside it.

3. Choose the **Scissors** tool (C). ✂

4. Click the object's path 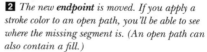 **1**: If you click once on a **closed** path, it will turn into a single, open path; if you click once on an **open** path, it will split into two paths.

   If you click a **segment**, two new endpoints will appear, one on top of the other. If you click an anchor **point**, a new anchor point will appear on top of the existing one, and it will be selected.

5. To move the two new endpoints apart, choose the **Direct Selection** tool (A), then drag the selected point away to reveal the second one below it **2**.

To split a path via the Control panel:
NEW!

1. Choose the **Direct Selection** tool (A).

2. Click a path to display the anchor points, then click an anchor point to select it.

3. Click the **Cut Path at Selected Anchor Points** button on the Control panel. A new anchor point will appear on top of the existing one, and it will be selected.

4. To move the two new endpoints apart, drag the selected point; the second point will be revealed below it.

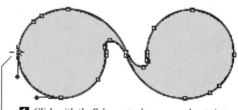

1 *Click with the* **Scissors** *tool on an anchor point or segment.*

There is no segment, and thus no stroke, between these endpoints.

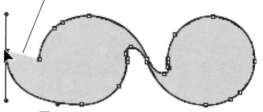

2 *The new* **endpoint** *is moved. If you apply a stroke color to an open path, you'll be able to see where the missing segment is. (An open path can also contain a fill.)*

Split Path

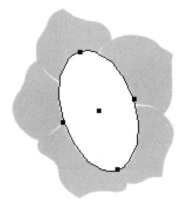

1 *The white oval (on top) will be the cutting object.*

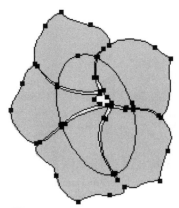

2 *The **Divide Objects Below** command caused the oval to cut through the underlying objects.*

3 *Fill colors were applied to five of the paths.*

The **Divide Objects Below** command uses an object like a cookie cutter to cut the objects below it, and deletes the cutting object.

To cut objects via the Divide Objects Below command:

1. Create or select an object that contains a solid-color fill and/or stroke (not a group or a Live Paint group) to be used as a cutting shape. The Slice command will delete this object, so make a copy of it now if you want to preserve it.

2. Place the cutting object on top of the object(s) to be cut **1**.

3. Make sure only the cutting object is selected.

4. Choose Object > Path > **Divide Objects Below.** The topmost shape (cutting object) will be deleted automatically and the underlying objects will be cut into separate paths where they met the edge of the cutting object **2**–**3**.

5. Deselect, then move any of the objects with the Selection tool. Any objects that were in a group will remain so.

➤ To prevent an object below the cutting shape from being affected by the Divide Objects Below command, lock it (see page 205) or hide it (see page 206).

Divide, or Divide Objects Below?

Compare the Divide Objects Below command, discussed above, with the Divide button on the Pathfinder panel, which is discussed on pages 327–328. **Divide Objects Below** deletes the top cutting object and leaves the resulting objects ungrouped, whereas **Divide** preserves the paint attributes of all the objects, including the topmost object, and groups the resulting paths. Divide usually produces smaller pieces than Divide Objects Below. (To apply the Divide command, you need to select two or more overlapping paths. To separate the resulting objects, ungroup them, then move them with the Selection tool.)

Divide Objects Below

Erasing parts of objects

The **Eraser** tool removes parts of objects that it passes over, and the remaining parts of the objects are reconnected to form closed paths.

To erase parts of objects: NEW!

1. *Optional:* To limit the Eraser tool to specific objects, select them first (say, if there are many objects close together in the artwork, and you want to erase only some of them).

   Note: To erase type, convert it to outlines first (choose Type > Create Outlines).

2. Choose the **Eraser** tool (Shift-E).

3. Drag across parts of objects that you want to erase  – . (Shift-drag to constrain the Eraser strokes to an increment of 45°.)
   or
   Option-drag/Alt-drag to create a marquee. Any parts of the artwork that fall within the marquee will be erased completely.

➤ Press [or] to decrease or increase the Eraser tool diameter. Double-click the tool icon to change the tool shape (see pages 302–303).

➤ Dragging the Eraser tool over the inside of a filled object is the fastest way to create a hole in an object. The result will be a compound path.

➤ When the Live Trace command is used on a photo or drawing, you invariably end up with complex artwork. The Eraser tool is handy for quick cleanup afterward  – **5**.

1 *The original mountain shape was drawn with the Pen tool.*

2 *Parts of objects were erased using the **Eraser** tool, to create details on the mountains and lake.*

3 *Additional erasures were done with a smaller **diameter** chosen for the **Eraser** tool.*

4 *This tracing of a photo of an ice cream cone is overly complex.*

5 *To simplify the drawing, we erased the entire background and some paths on the ice cream with the **Eraser** tool.*

Eraser Tool

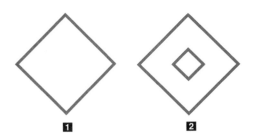

1 **2**

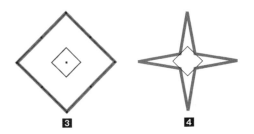

3 **4**

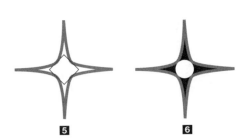

5 **6**

7

Exercise

Change a square into a star

1. Choose the **Rectangle** tool (M). Choose a fill of None and a 3-pt. stroke.

2. Click on the artboard. The Rectangle dialog box opens.

3. Enter 2" in the Width field, click the word Height, then click OK.

4. Double-click the **Rotate** tool, enter 45 in the Angle field, then click OK **1**.

5. Double-click the **Scale** tool, enter 30 in the **Uniform: Scale** field, then click Copy **2**.

6. Choose View > Guides > **Make Guides** (Cmd-5/Ctrl-5) to turn the smaller diamond into a guide.

7. Choose the **Selection** tool (V), then select the large diamond. Choose Object > Path > **Add Anchor Points 3**.

8. Choose the **Direct Selection** tool (A). Deselect, then click the edge of the diamond.

9. Drag each of the new midpoints inward to meet the guide. Use smart guides to align the points at 45° angles **4**.

10. Choose the **Convert Anchor Point** tool (Shift-C), then drag each of the inner midpoints to create a curve. Drag clockwise and along the edge of the guide shape **5**.

11. Choose the **Ellipse** tool (L), position the pointer over the center point of the star shape, then Option-Shift-drag/Alt-Shift-drag until the circle touches the inner curves of the star.

12. To the circle, apply a white fill and a stroke of None; to the star shape, apply a black or dark fill and a lighter stroke **6**.

13. *Optional:* Select the circle. Choose the Scale tool (S). Start dragging diagonally, hold down Option-Shift/Alt-Shift, and continue to drag until the copy of the circle touches the outer tips of the star. Fill the large circle with None, and apply a 2-pt. stroke **7**.

14. Group the objects.

Exercise: Square to Star

Exercise

Draw a light bulb

1. *With the **Ellipse** tool (L), click the artboard and create a circle 1 inch in diameter; and with the **Rectangle** tool (M), click the artboard and create a .5 inch square. Apply a fill of None and a 3-pt. black stroke to both objects.*

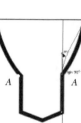

2. *Choose the **Direct Selection** tool (A), select the bottom point of the circle, then drag that point downward. Using the **Selection** tool (V), select **both** objects.*

3. *Click the **Add to Shape Area** button 🔲 on the Pathfinder panel, then click the Expand button. Use the **Add Anchor Point** tool (+) to add a point on the bottommost segment, then use the **Direct Selection** tool to drag the new point downward.*

4. *Click on each point where the curve meets the straight segment (A). Using smart guides, rotate the direction handle upward to 90° vertical.*

5. *Apply a fill of white to the bulb.*

6. *With the **Rounded Rectangle** tool, draw an oval that's wider than the base of the bulb. With the **Selection** tool, drag slightly outside a corner of the bounding box to rotate the rectangle, then Option-Shift-drag/Alt–Shift-drag a copy of the path downward. Press Cmd-D/ Ctrl-D to repeat the duplication.*

7. *Apply a dark fill color and a stroke of None to the ovals, and place them on the bottom part of the bulb.*

8. *Use the **Star** tool to create a 20-point star (click with the tool on the artboard; enter Radius 1: .4 in., Radius 2: .69 in. Apply a light fill color and a stroke of None. Scale the star, if necessary, so it's a bit larger than the bulb.*

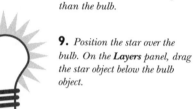

9. *Position the star over the bulb. On the **Layers** panel, drag the star object below the bulb object.*

10. *Select the star. Apply Effect > Distort & Transform > **Roughen** (Size: 2, Relative, Detail: 8, Corner). Deselect.*

11. *Choose the **Pencil** tool (N), a fill of None, a black stroke, and a stroke weight of 1–2 pt. Draw a filament line inside the bulb. It should be the topmost object on the Layers panel.*

12. *Select the bulb. On the **Transparency** panel, set the Opacity slider to 60–70% (Normal mode).*

13. *Select the bulb, star, and filament. Apply Effect > Stylize > **Drop Shadow** (Opacity 50–60%, Blur 1–3 pt).*

Exercise: Light Bulb

TRACING 12

In this chapter, you'll learn how use the tracing features in Illustrator to convert raster images into editable vector art, apply custom tracing settings before and after tracing, create custom tracing presets, release a tracing, expand a tracing into separate paths, and convert a tracing into a Live Paint group. A practice exercise is also included.

1 A **raster** image is placed into an Illustrator file.

2 The image is **traced**.

3 The tracing is **expanded** into separate objects (shown here in Outline view).

Using the tracing features

The **Live Trace** command can detect and trace the color and shade areas in any raster image that you open or place into Illustrator, such as a Photoshop EPS, TIFF, JPEG, or PSD image, or scanned artwork, such as a logo. You can choose from a wide array of custom tracing options prior to tracing—and because traced objects are "live," you can also fine-tune the tracing results via the **Tracing Options** dialog box before converting them into editable paths or a Live Paint group. You can use a built-in tracing preset (set of presaved settings) as a starting point, or create and save your own presets. Among the numerous settings that you can specify are the precision with which the image is traced, the stroke weight and length, the number of colors, and a color palette **1**–**3**.

With such a wide range of tracing controls at your fingertips, you can produce everything from a close simulation of your original artwork to a loose rendering. Regardless of the type of imagery you trace, the end result will be editable paths with a restricted number of fill and/or stroke colors. Although the Live Trace command doesn't have the natural editing power of the human eye and brain, it does a decent job, and you may find the results—albeit after some cleanup work—to be useful. For creating complex, nongeometric artwork, it's much faster to start with a tracing and make adjustments afterward than to draw a gazillion intricate shapes by hand.

153

Tracing a raster image

In these instructions, you'll **trace** a raster **image** using **preset** settings. In the instructions that begin on the next page, you'll learn how to choose custom settings for tracing or apply custom settings to an existing tracing.

After tracing the image, you can either convert the results into editable paths via the Expand command or convert the artwork to a Live Paint group (see page 159).

To trace a raster image:

1. Using File > **Open,** open a raster image, such as a TIFF, JPG, or PSD file; or with an Illustrator document open, use File > **Place** to place a raster image . *Note:* If you open or place a PSD (Photoshop) file that contains layers, the Photoshop Import Options dialog box will open. Click Convert Photoshop Layers to Objects to import the image as a series of objects on multiple layers, or Flatten Photoshop Layers to a Single Image to import the image as one flattened layer.

2. Select the image that you want to trace.

3. To trace the object using preset settings, from the **Tracing Presets and Options** menu ▼ on the Control panel **2**–**3**, choose a preset based on how detailed you want the end result to be.

   or

   To trace the object using the last-used (or default) settings, click **Live Trace** on the Control panel. If an alert dialog box appears, click OK (some presets take longer to process than others).

   A progress bar will appear onscreen as Illustrator traces the object, then new options will appear on the Control panel when the tracing is complete.

4. *Optional:* To customize the tracing, follow the instructions that begin on the next page.

1 *Place a raster **image** into an Illustrator document.*

2 *Choose one of the **tracing presets** from the **Control** panel.*

3 *The [Default] tracing preset produced this vector art.*

Trace Using Preset Settings

Applying tracing options

By choosing settings in the **Tracing Options** dialog box or from the Control panel, you can make your tracing conform closely to the original artwork or simplify it dramatically. And because tracings are live, you can choose these options before or after using the Live Trace command.

To apply tracing options:

1. *Optional:* To apply colors to the resulting vector art from a custom library, open that library via the Swatches Libraries menu. If you click the Load Previous or Load Next Swatch Library button, each library you display will be listed on the Palette menu in the Tracing Options dialog box.

2. Select a tracing object in your document.

3. Choose a different preset from the **Preset** menu on the Control panel, and ignore the remaining steps.
   or
   Click the **Tracing Options Dialog** button ▦ on the Control panel. The Tracing Options dialog box opens **1**. Check Preview (or to speed up processing, don't check it until step 5), then follow any of the remaining steps.

Choose options before tracing

To choose custom options prior to tracing, click an image in your Illustrator document. From the Tracing Presets and Options menu on the Control panel, choose **Tracing Options,** then follow steps 3–9, starting on this page.

---

4. Choose a different **Preset** (the choices are the same as on the Preset menu on the Control panel).

5. Choose options in the **Adjustments** area to control how the image is prepped for retracing:

   From the **Mode** menu, choose Color, Grayscale, or Black and White, depending on how many colors you want the final tracing to contain.

   For Black and White mode only, choose a **Threshold** value (0–255; the default is 128). All pixels darker than this value will be converted to black; all pixels lighter than this value will be converted to white. You can also change the Threshold value on the Control panel.

   (Continued on the following page)

Tracing Options

If you forget which feature is which, you can use the tool tips in the Tracing Options dialog box to remind yourself.

1 *Choose custom settings in the **Tracing Options** dialog box.*

For Grayscale or Color mode, from the **Palette** menu, choose Automatic to have Illustrator use colors from the image in the tracing, or choose the name of any swatch library you opened in step 1 (above) to have the final tracing contain only colors from that library.

For just Grayscale or Color mode and the Palette menu choice of Automatic, choose a **Max Colors** value for the maximum number of colors the final tracing may contain (2–256; the default is 6). For a hand-drawn look or a screen-printed look with fewer fill areas, keep this value low (say, 12 or less); this will also speed up the retracing. (You can also change the Max Colors value on the Control panel after exiting the dialog box.)

Optional: Click Output to Swatches to save the colors in the resulting tracing as new global color swatches on the Swatches panel.

Choose a **Blur** value (0–20 pixels; the default is 0) to reduce artifacts, noise, and extraneous marks. This simplifies the image for retracing, but also diminishes the sharpness of the image.

Click **Resample** and change the resolution for the tracing. A lower resolution will speed up the retracing but also produces fewer image details and less precise outlines. Choose Vector: Tracing Result (see the next step) to verify the result.

6. In the **View** area, make choices from the Raster and Vector menus to compare the source image and the result (make sure Preview is checked when you do this):

The **Raster** options control how the underlying raster image displays: **No Image** hides the original image; **Original Image** shows the original image unchanged; **Adjusted Image** shows how the image will be preprocessed for tracing (e.g., colors or shades reduced); and **Transparent Image** dims

the image so you can see the tracing results more clearly on top.

The **Vector** options control how the tracing results are displayed: **No Tracing Result** hides the tracing; **Tracing Result** displays the tracing; **Outlines** shows the tracing paths only, without fills or strokes; and **Outlines with Tracing** displays the resulting paths on top of a dimmed version of the resulting fills and strokes.

(These view settings can also be chosen via the **Preview Different Views of Raster Image** ▲ and **Preview Different Views of Vector Result** △ menus on the Control panel **1**.)

7. Choose the **Trace Settings** options to control the resulting paths:

➤ As you choose Adjustments and Trace Settings, monitor the number of Paths, Anchors, Colors, and Areas in the resulting artwork via the readouts on the right side of the dialog box.

For Black and White mode only, check **Fills** to create filled paths and/or **Strokes** to create stroked paths.

If Strokes is checked, specify a **Max Stroke Weight** value (0–100 px; the default is 10). Areas at this width or narrower will become strokes; wider areas will become outlined areas.

If Strokes is checked, specify a **Min Stroke Length** value (0–200 px; the default is 20). Areas this length or longer will be converted to strokes; areas shorter than this length will be ignored.

Specify a **Path Fitting** value to control how closely traced paths will follow the edges of shapes in the image (0–10 px; the default is 2). A low Path Fitting value yields a more accurate fit but also produces more anchor points.

Preset: | Custom | ▲▼ | ▦ | Threshold: ▲▼ 128 ▲▼ | Min Area: ▲▼ 10 px ▲▼ | ▲ | △ | (Expand) | (Live Paint)

1 *These options are available on the **Control** panel when a **tracing** object is selected.*

Change the **Minimum Area** setting to minimize the number of extraneous small paths. Specify the smallest area that you will permit the program to trace (0–3000 pixels square). For example, a 5 x 5-pixel object would occupy a 25-pixel area. For Grayscale or Color mode, a small Minimum Area value (10–60 px) produces a detailed, "photographic" tracing, whereas a larger area (144–300 px) produces a looser, more "hand-drawn" tracing. Adjust the Max Colors and Minimum Area settings to control the tightness or looseness of the tracing **1**–**2**. (You can also change the **Min Area** value on the Control panel after exiting the dialog box.)

Choose a **Corner Angle** for the minimum angle a path must have to be defined by a corner anchor point as opposed to a smooth point (0–180°; the default is 20°).

8. *Optional:* If you save your settings as a preset, you'll be able to apply them to any image and use them as a starting point when choosing custom settings. Click Save Preset, type a name for the preset in the Save Tracing Preset dialog box, then click

OK. (The Resample and View settings aren't saved.) Saved presets can be chosen from the Preset menu on the Control panel when a raster image or tracing object is selected, and from the Preset menu in the Tracing Options dialog box.

9. Click **Trace.** A progress bar will appear onscreen while Illustrator traces the image (be patient!), then a "Tracing" listing for the tracing object (maybe nested) will appear on the Layers panel. If you're happy with the results, you can either expand the tracing into editable paths or convert it into a Live Paint group (see page 159).

➤ To produce a simple tracing, in the Tracing Options dialog box, check Resample and enter a value of 72 px, and choose Mode: Color, Max Colors 10–16, Path Fitting 4–6, and Minimum Area 200–300. Or for a more detailed color tracing, place a 150–200 ppi color image into your document, then choose Mode: Color, Max Colors 50–64, Path Fitting 2, and Minimum Area 5–10 as tracing values.

1 *Tracing options of **Max Colors 45** and **Minimum Area 10 px** produced a detailed, "photographic" tracing.*

2 *Tracing options of **Max Colors 12** and **Minimum Area 490 px** produced a tracing with a more painted or screen-printed look.*

Managing tracing presets

You can use the **Tracing Presets** dialog box to create, edit, delete, import, or export custom tracing presets.

To create, delete, edit, import, or export a tracing preset:

1. Choose Edit > **Tracing Presets**. The Tracing Presets dialog box opens 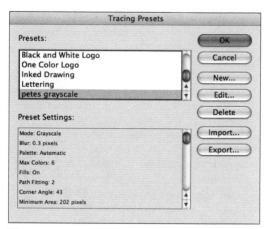.

2. To create a new preset based on an existing one, click a preset on the **Presets** scroll list, then click **New.** The Tracing Options dialog box opens. Enter a name, choose settings, then click Done. (To create a new preset based on the default settings, click [Default] on the Presets scroll list.)

To export the current settings as a preset file, click **Export.** In the Export Presets File As dialog box, keep the default location, then click Save.

To edit an existing preset, click the preset on the Presets scroll list, then click **Edit.** The Tracing Options dialog box opens. Choose settings, then click Done.

To delete a user-saved preset, click the preset name, then click **Delete.**

To import a user-saved preset, click **Import.** In the Import Presets File dialog box, locate and click the desired presets file, then click Open.

3. Click OK.

Releasing a tracing

Clicking Cancel in the Tracing Options dialog box cancels only changes made in that dialog box. To restore a tracing object to its virgin bitmap state, use the **Release** command, as per the instructions below.

To release a tracing object:

1. Select the tracing object.

2. Choose Object > Live Trace > **Release.** The listing on the Layers panel will change from Tracing to Image, or to the file name of the original image.

1 *Use the* **Tracing Presets** *dialog box to create, edit, delete, import, or export tracing presets (settings).*

Tracing the paleolithic way

If you want to trace an image manually, first place it into your Illustrator document. Double-click the new layer, and in the Layer Options dialog box, click **Template** to dim the placed image on the layer and make it uneditable. Create a new layer above the template layer, then with any drawing tool, such as the Pencil or Pen, trace the image.

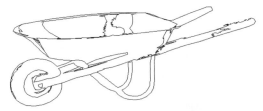

2 *The same **expanded** objects are shown in Preview view.*

3 *Some of the expanded objects are recolored.*

1 *A tracing is **expanded** (shown in Outline view).*

Converting tracings to paths

The **Expand** command converts a tracing into standard paths that can be selected via the Layers panel and then recolored, reshaped, transformed, etc. Once you expand a tracing, it's no longer "live," meaning you can't adjust the Tracing Options settings for it.

To expand a live trace object:

1. Select a live trace object.

2. To expand the tracing, on the Control panel, click **Expand 1**–**3**. On the Layers panel, you'll now see a group containing a gazillion paths (or maybe fewer, depending on the tracing settings used).

➤ You can also trace and expand an image in one step, but this has limited usefulness because you can't choose the tracing options (the default tracing settings are applied). Open or place a raster image, select it, then choose Object > Live Trace > Make and Expand. Or to trace an image and convert it to a Live Paint group instead, choose Object > Live Trace > Make and Convert to Live Paint.

Follow these instructions to convert a live trace object to a **Live Paint** group. This is a good route to take if your tracing is relatively simple and you want to utilize such Live Paint features as the ability to hide or recolor edges or quickly recolor faces (fill areas). To learn about the Live Paint features, see the next chapter.

To convert a live trace object to a Live Paint group:

1. Select a live trace object.

2. On the Control panel, click **Live Paint**. Ta-da!

Expand Tracing: Convert to Live Paint

Exercise

In this practice exercise, you'll trace a photograph of an object that's on a white background.

Trace an object

1. Place a raster image into an Illustrator document , and keep it selected. A product shot of an object on a white background would be a good choice for this exercise.

2. From the **Tracing Presets and Options** menu on the Control panel, choose **Tracing Options**, then click OK if an alert dialog opens.

3. From the **Preset** menu in the Tracing Options dialog box, choose **Photo Low Fidelity.**

4. Set the **Max Colors** value to 25–30. (The lower the Max Colors value, the simpler the tracing and the fewer the number of areas created.) Check Preview.

5. To preview the tracing lines, choose **Outlines** from the **Vector** menu, then reselect Vector: **Tracing Results.**

6. To add more tracing lines, raise the **Max Colors** value to 50. Or to remove tracing lines, lower the Max Colors value to 10–16 and raise the Minimum Area value to 100.

7. When you're satisfied with the settings, click **Trace 2**.

8. On the Control panel, click **Expand.**

9. *Optional:* To remove the fill colors and produce a line art tracing instead, keep the expanded objects selected, and via the Control panel, choose a Fill of None, a Stroke of black, and a Stroke Weight of .3 to .5 pt. **3**.

➤ To produce **4**, from the Preset menu in the Tracing Options dialog box, we chose Technical Drawing, then adjusted the Threshold value, but we think the method described in the steps above yielded better results.

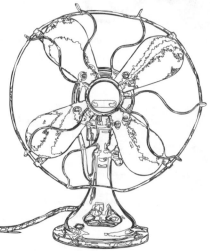

1 *The original placed image*

2 *The image was traced using the **Photo Low Fidelity** preset (Max Colors 28; Minimum Area 100).*

3 *This is the same tracing, after applying a Fill of None and a Stroke of black.*

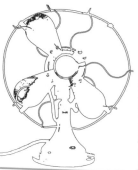

4 *This tracing was produced using the **Technical Drawing** preset at a Threshold value of 170. We think the results shown in the previous figure are superior.*

Exercise: Trace an Object

LIVE PAINT | 13

In this chapter, first you'll learn to draw in a freehand style using the Pencil tool. Then you'll learn how to convert objects to a Live Paint group, apply colors to faces and edges in the group, reshape the group, and finally, expand it into standard paths. A practice exercise is included at the end of the chapter.

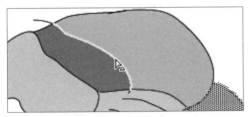

1 A pencil sketch was converted to a **Live Paint** group.

2 A **face** is selected.

3 An **edge** is selected.

What is a Live Paint group?

The Live Paint features offer a novel method for filling paths. To create the "armature" for a Live Paint group, you can either create some open or closed paths with the Pencil tool or another drawing tool, then convert the whole drawing into a **Live Paint** group **1**; or you can convert a tracing into a Live Paint group and use the Live Paint group features to apply colors to the resulting objects.

With the **Live Paint Bucket** tool, you simply click any area formed by intersecting lines (called a **face**) **2**, and the current paint attributes are applied. Add to or reshape the Live Paint objects at any time, and the fill color flows into the new shape; that's what makes the whole process "live." Another unique feature of Live Paint groups is that you can recolor (or leave unpainted) individual line segments, called **edges** **3**, instead of whole paths. This method of recoloring sketches and tracings is quick and flexible.

When you're done using the Live Paint features, you can expand the group into normal Illustrator objects. The result will be a group of paths with strokes and a group of closed, filled paths.

Before delving into the Live Paint features, we'll explore the Pencil tool, the ultimate electronic sketching tool.

Using the Pencil tool

If you enjoy sketching objects by hand, you'll gravitate to the **Pencil** tool, especially if you own a pressure-sensitive tablet. This tool has three distinct functions. If you drag in a blank area of the artboard, you'll create a new, open path. If you drag along the edge of an existing, selected path (open or closed), the tool will reshape the path (see page 141). And if you drag from an endpoint of an existing open path, you'll add new segments to the path (see page 139). Paths drawn with this tool can be reshaped like any other paths (see Chapter 11).

Note: If you want to draw straight lines or smooth curves, you'll go mad trying to do it with the Pencil tool. For that, we recommend using the Line Segment, Arc, or Pen tool instead.

To draw with the Pencil tool:

1. Choose the **Pencil** tool (N).

2. Choose stroke attributes (color and width), and a fill color of None.

3. Draw a line (a dotted line will appear while you draw). Choose Preview view to see the line with the current Stroke settings **1**, or choose Outline view to see the line as a bare-bones, wireframe representation **2**. Continue to draw additional lines, as needed.

   To choose preferences for the Pencil tool, see the next page.

➤ To create a closed path with the Pencil tool, start drawing the path, then finish drawing it with Option/Alt held down.

➤ To close an existing Pencil line with a straight segment, choose the Selection tool (V), click the line, then choose Object > Path > Join (Cmd-J/Ctrl-J).

1 *A blue-footed booby, drawn with the **Pencil** tool*

2 *The booby in **Outline** view*

Pencil Tool

DIANE MARGOLIN

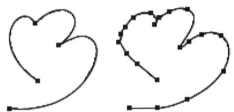

1 *The **Pencil** tool has its own **Preferences** dialog box.*

Use the **Pencil Tool Preferences** dialog box to customize the Pencil tool. If you change these settings, only subsequently drawn lines will be affected—not existing lines.

To choose preferences for the Pencil tool:

1. Double-click the **Pencil** tool 🖉 (or press N to choose the tool, then press Return/Enter). The Pencil Tool Preferences dialog box opens **1**.

2. In the **Tolerances** area:

   Choose a **Fidelity** value (.5–20) **2**–**3**. The lower the Fidelity value, the more closely the line will follow the movement of the mouse and the more anchor points the tool will produce. A high Fidelity value produces fewer anchor points and a smoother path.

   Choose a **Smoothness** value (0–100). The higher the Smoothness value, the smoother the curves; the lower the Smoothness value, the more small bends and twists in the path.

3. Check any of the following options:

   Fill new pencil strokes to fill new paths (open or closed) with the current fill color automatically.

   Keep selected to have Pencil paths stay selected after they're created. This comes in handy if you tend to add to your paths right after drawing them.

   Edit selected paths to activate the reshaping function of the Pencil tool (see page 141). The Within: [ ] pixels value (2–20) is the minimum distance the pointer must be from a path for the tool to reshape it. Uncheck this option if you want to be able to draw multiple Pencil lines near one another without reshaping any existing selected paths.

4. Click OK **4**.

➤ Click Reset in the Pencil Tool Preferences dialog box to restore the default settings for the tool.

2 *This line was drawn with the Pencil tool at a **high Fidelity** setting.*

3 *This line was drawn with the Pencil tool at a **low Fidelity** setting.*

4 *This figure was drawn with the **Pencil** tool by Diane Margolin.*

Creating Live Paint groups

To **create** a **Live Paint** group, you can either click some existing paths with the Live Paint Bucket tool or choose the Live Paint command. To draw paths for a Live Paint group, we like to use the Pencil tool, but you can use any drawing tool. The important thing is to draw lines that intersect, because the Live Paint Bucket tool, which you'll also use for coloring, detects and fills only faces, which are areas bounded by intersecting lines.

To convert a bitmap image into a Live Paint group, trace it via the Live Trace command (see Chapter 12), then click Live Paint on the Control panel. When you **convert path objects** into a **Live Paint** group (instructions below), basic fill and stroke settings are preserved, but other attributes, such as transparency settings, brush strokes, and live effects, are removed.

1 *Draw an illustration, making sure most or all of your **segments intersect**. This illustration was drawn with the Pencil tool.*

To create a Live Paint group:

1. Draw some open or closed paths using any tool, such as the Pencil, Pen, Arc, Line Segment, or Ellipse, and apply stroke colors and weights **1**. As you create your sketch, be sure to let the segments **intersect**.

2. Select all the paths.

3. Choose the **Live Paint Bucket** tool (K), then click any of the selected objects **2**.
   or
   Choose Object > Live Paint > **Make** (Cmd-Option-X/Ctrl-Alt-X).

   If a lavishly illustrated alert prompt appears, make sure your objects are still selected, then click again with the Paint Bucket tool. On the Layers panel, the paths will now be nested in a Live Paint group.

➤ To make a Live Paint group from a symbol or blend, you must apply Object > Expand first. To use a clipping set in a Live Paint group, release the set first. To create a Live Paint group from type, convert it to outlines via Type > Create Outlines first.

➤ Some Illustrator commands aren't available for Live Paint groups, such as the Clipping Mask, Pathfinder, and Select > Same commands.

Click to make a Live Paint group

2 *Click the selected paths with the **Live Paint Bucket tool** to convert them to a **Live Paint** group.*

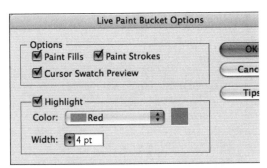

 *Use the **Live Paint Bucket Options** dialog box to specify the default behavior for the tool.*

 *If the **Cursor Swatch Preview** option is on for the **Live Paint Bucket** tool and you mix a color via the **Color** panel, the pointer displays that swatch.*

*If the **Cursor Swatch Preview** option is on for the **Live Paint Bucket** tool and you click a swatch on the **Swatches** panel, that color and two adjacent swatches preview above the pointer.*

Using the Live Paint Bucket tool

On the next page, you'll learn how to use the Paint Bucket tool to recolor a Live Paint group. But before you do that, familiarize yourself with the **Live Paint Bucket Options** dialog box so you can customize it for your working style.

To choose options for the Live Paint Bucket tool:

1. Double-click the **Live Paint Bucket** tool.
   or
   Click the **Live Paint Bucket** tool (K), then press Return/Enter.

2. The Live Paint Bucket Options dialog box opens **1**. For **Options:**

   Click **Paint Fills** and/or **Paint Strokes**, depending on the desired default behavior for the tool. (For your first use of the tool, we recommend checking both options.)

   ➤ If you click just one of these options, you can Shift-click with the tool to switch its function between painting fills (faces) and applying stroke (edge) colors and weights.

   Check **Cursor Swatch Preview** to display, in a tiny strip above the tool pointer, the current color (if you're using the Color panel), or the last chosen swatch on the Swatches panel and two adjacent swatches **2**–**3**.**NEW!** We recommend keeping this option checked; the color strip is helpful and not too obtrusive.

3. *Optional:* If the current highlight color is too similar to colors in your artwork (or colors you're going to apply), check Highlight, then, from the Color menu, choose a preset color for faces and edges the tool passes over, or click the color swatch and choose a color from the Colors dialog box. You can also change the highlight Width.

4. Click OK. Now you're ready to use the tool; see the following page.

Live Paint Bucket Options

When you apply fill or stroke attributes to a Live
Paint group, you recolor faces or edges—not the
actual paths. If you reshape a Live Paint group
in any way, such as by editing the paths, colors
will flow instantly into the new faces. In these
instructions, you'll recolor faces with the **Live
Paint Bucket** tool.

To recolor faces with the Live Paint Bucket tool:

1. Have a Live Paint group at the ready (you
don't need to select it), **1** and choose the
Live Paint Bucket tool (K).

2. Click a swatch or color group icon on the
Swatches panel, or choose a fill color via the
Control panel. If the Cursor Swatch Preview
option is checked in the tool options dialog
box, the currently selected swatch will display as the middle of the three colors above
the pointer. You can press the left or right
arrow key to select the previous or next
swatch on the Swatches panel as your fill
color; keep pressing the key to move along
the current row in the Swatches panel.**NEW!**

3. Move the pointer over any **face** (area where
two or more paths intersect; the face will
become highlighted), then click **2**.
or
Drag across **multiple faces.**

➤ To have the Live Paint Bucket tool use colors
from a color group, first create a group that
contains the colors you want to apply (see
page 115). Make sure Paint Fills is checked
in the Live Paint Bucket Options dialog
box, then with the tool selected, click the
color group on the Swatches panel. Colors
from the new color group will display in the
cursor swatch preview, and the left or right
arrow keys will select swatches only from
that color group.**NEW!**

➤ Hold down Option/Alt to turn the Live Paint
Bucket tool into a temporary Eyedropper
tool, and use it to sample a fill color from
anywhere in the document window.

➤ The Arrange commands (Bring to Front, etc.)
don't work on Live Paint groups.

1 *This **Live Paint group** was created from lines drawn with the Pencil tool.*

2 *When the **Live Paint Bucket** tool is clicked on a **face** (an area where paths intersect) in a Live Paint group, the current fill color is applied.*

Flood fill

➤ Double-click a face with the Live Paint Bucket
tool to fill adjacent faces across all unstroked
edges (this process is called "flood fill").

➤ Triple-click a face to recolor all faces that already
have the same color as the one you click,
whether adjacent or not.

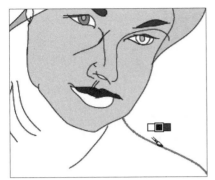

1 *Stroke attributes are being applied to an edge with the **Live Paint Bucket** tool.*

2 *Additional paths were drawn on the neck, lips, and face to create more fillable faces.*

3 *The **Live Paint Bucket** tool was used to fill the new faces and to apply a stroke of None to edges on the neck, cheeks, and forehead.*

You can also use the **Live Paint Bucket** tool to apply **stroke** colors and/or line **weights.** Each edge can have a different color, weight, and other stroke attributes, or a stroke color of None. Only the edges you click will be modified—not the whole path.

To modify edges with the Live Paint Bucket tool:

1. Double-click the **Live Paint Bucket** tool, check **Paint Strokes** in the Live Paint Bucket Options dialog box, then click OK.

2. Choose a stroke color, and choose a stroke weight and other attributes via the Stroke panel (access it via the Control panel, if desired). Or to remove colors from edges, choose a color of None.

3. Move the pointer over an **edge** in a Live Paint group (the bucket icon turns into a brush icon), then click **1**–**3**.
   or
   Drag across **multiple edges.**
   or
   Double-click an edge to **flood-stroke**— that is, apply the current stroke attributes to all contiguous edges that have the same color and weight.

➤ If the current Live Paint Bucket option setting is just Paint Fills or Paint Strokes, you can hold down Shift to toggle between the two functions.

➤ Triple-click an edge to apply the current stroke color and Stroke panel attributes to all edges—contiguous or not—that have the same attributes as the one you click.

➤ You can also recolor a Live Paint group by using the Live Color dialog box (Chapter 14).

➤ You can apply transparency settings, brush strokes, and effects to an entire Live Paint group, but not to individual faces or edges. For example, if you drag a brush from the Brushes panel over a Live Paint group, that brush will be applied to all the edges in the group.

Using the Live Paint Selection tool

The **Live Paint Selection** tool lets you select edges and/or faces in a Live Paint group. Choose options for the tool before using it.

To choose options for the Live Paint Selection tool:

1. Double-click the **Live Paint Selection** tool.
   or
   Click the **Live Paint Selection** tool (Shift-L), then press Return/Enter.

2. The Live Paint Selection Options dialog box opens 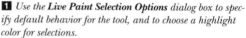. Check **Select Fills** and/or **Select Strokes** (and choose a different Highlight Color and/or Width for selections, if desired), then click OK.

   ➤ To avoid confusion, choose a different highlight color for the Live Paint Bucket tool than for the Live Paint Selection tool (in the options dialog box for each tool).

To use the Live Paint Selection tool:

1. Choose the **Live Paint Selection** tool (Shift-L), and choose options for the tool as per the instructions above.

2. Click an edge or face in a Live Paint group, then Shift-click additional edges or faces 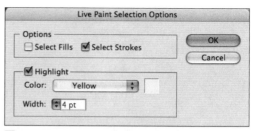. (Shift-click to deselect individual edges or faces.) The selections display as a gray pattern.

3. Do any of the following:

   For the **fill**, choose a solid color , gradient, or pattern. You can modify a gradient fill with the Gradient tool (see pages 322–323).

   Change the **stroke color, weight,** or other stroke attributes. Apply a stroke of None to any edges that you want to hide.

   Press **Delete/Backspace** to remove the currently selected edge(s) or face(s).

4. When you're done making changes, click outside the Live Paint group to deselect it.

1 Use the **Live Paint Selection Options** dialog box to specify default behavior for the tool, and to choose a highlight color for selections.

2 Three areas of the woman's hair are selected with the **Live Paint Selection** tool.

3 A new fill color is applied to the selected faces.

Live Paint Selection Tool

1 *A path is selected in a Live Paint group with the Selection tool, then lengthened until it crosses another path, thereby creating a new face.*

2 *With the **Live Paint Bucket** tool, a fill is applied to the new face (behind the neck).*

Reshaping Live Paint groups

If you **isolate** a **Live Paint** group, you can transform or move whole paths in the group, manipulate points on a path, and add new faces. Colors will reflow into the new shapes.

To reshape or move paths in a Live Paint group:

1. Choose the **Selection** tool (V), and make sure the Bounding Box feature is on (View menu).

2. To isolate a Live Paint group:

   Double-click a **path** or **face** in the group.
   or
   Click a path or area in the group, then click the **Isolate Selected Group** button on the Control panel.

   A gray bar will display at the top of the document window and all other artwork will be dimmed.**NEW!**

3. Choose the **Selection** tool, then either click a face that contains a fill color or click a path. A bounding box with star-filled selection handles will display. Drag the path to move it; drag a handle to transform it **1**–**2**. You can also delete a selected path by pressing Delete.
   or
   Choose the **Direct Selection** tool (A), click the edge of a path to make its anchor points and direction points visible, and manipulate any of those points to reshape the path (see Chapter 11). You can use the Align buttons (Control or Align panel) to align selected anchor points.**NEW!**

   Fill colors will reflow automatically into any areas you reshape or transform. You can also change the stroke color and/or weight for any selected path.

4. To exit isolation mode, click the gray bar at the top of the document window; or with a selection tool, double-click outside the Live Paint group.

Adding paths to a Live Paint group

Here are three ways to add **paths** to an existing **Live Paint** group.

To add paths to a Live Paint group:

Method 1 (Layers panel)

1. Create the path you want to add.

2. On the **Layers** panel, drag the new path into the Live Paint Group listing.

Method 2 (isolate group)

1. Choose the **Selection** tool (V), then double-click the Live Paint group to isolate it.

2. Draw the path you want to add **1**–**2**; it will be part of the Live Paint group.

3. To exit isolation mode, click the gray bar at the top of the document window.

➤ To add an existing object to a Live Paint group, select the object in the document window with the Selection tool, choose Edit > Cut (Cmd-X/Ctrl-X), double-click the group to isolate it, then choose Edit > Paste (Cmd-V/Ctrl-V). Exit isolation mode.

Method 3 (Control panel)

1. Deselect the Live Paint group, then draw a new path (or paths) on any layer.

2. Choose the **Selection** tool (V), then select both the new path(s) and the Live Paint group.

3. Click **Merge Live Paint** on the Control panel.**NEW!**

Fuzzy rules of Live Paint

➤ Faces in a Live Paint group are repainted instantly if you reshape a face or delete an edge. If you delete an edge that borders two faces, the fill color from the larger of the two faces is usually applied — but not in every case.

➤ If you move a closed path that's part of a Live Paint group over filled faces in the group, the fill from the closed path won't initially interact with colors in the faces. If you then move the closed object away from the filled faces, some of the small faces will refill with the fill color from the closed path. If you don't like the results, Undo.

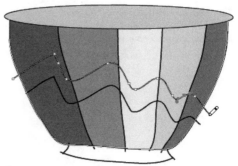

1 *With the Live Paint group in* **isolation mode,** *two new paths are drawn across existing edges to create new faces.*

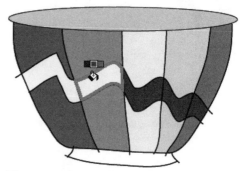

2 *With the* **Live Paint Bucket** *tool, fill colors are applied to the new faces.*

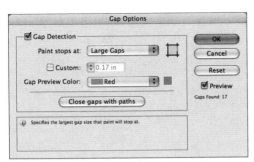

1 *Choose **Gap Options** to control color leakage in your Live Paint groups.*

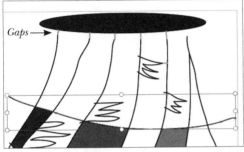

2 *The **Paint stops at: Large Gaps** option is chosen. The gaps preview in the current Gap Preview Color.*

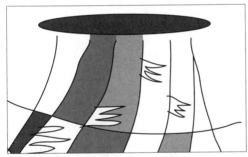

3 *With the **Large Gaps** option chosen, we were able to fill the small- to medium-sized gaps in the open areas.*

Minimize the gap

The more you allow lines to **intersect** in the original objects, the fewer the gaps in the Live Paint group. As shown in step 11 on page 174, you can delete or apply a stroke of None to any overhanging edges.

Choosing gap options

If you reshape an edge so as to create a gap in a formerly closed area (face), any fill color in that face will disappear, because in the world of Live Paint, fills can't be applied to areas that have large gaps. Via the **Gap Options** dialog box, you can specify a gap size to stop the fill colors from leaking. Different gap options can be chosen for each Live Paint group.

To choose gap options for a Live Paint group:

1. Choose the **Selection** tool (V), then click a Live Paint group.

2. Click the **Gap Options** button on the Control panel. The Gap Options dialog box opens **1**.

3. Check Preview, then do any of the following:

   Make sure **Gap Detection** is checked, then from the **Paint Stops At** menu, choose a gap size that colors can't flow through, or check **Custom** and enter a specific gap size (.01–72 pt). We like to set our menu to Large Gaps **2**, which enables us to draw lines freely but also fill faces.

   From the **Gap Preview Color** menu, choose a preview color for the invisible (nonprinting) gap "lines" that stop paint leakage. You can also click the color swatch and choose a color from the Colors dialog box. Gap lines display onscreen in a selected Live Paint group while the Gap Options dialog box is open, or when View > **Show Live Paint Gaps** is on.

   Click the **Close Gaps with Paths** button to have Illustrator close up any existing gaps with actual unpainted edge segments (click Yes in the alert dialog box). This can improve the processing time.

4. Click OK. If you increased the gap size, try using the Live Paint Bucket tool to fill areas that couldn't be filled before **3**. Colors will still leak from gaps that are larger than the gap size you specified.

Gap Options

Expanding and releasing Live Paint groups

You can't apply appearances (such as brush strokes, transparency settings, or effects) selectively to individual parts of a Live Paint group; you have to **expand** or **release** it into normal Illustrator objects first. You also may need to expand or release a Live Paint group if you're planning to export it to a non-Adobe application. Use these commands when you're done editing the group.

To expand or release a Live Paint group:

1. Using the Selection tool or the Layers panel, select a Live Paint group. *Optional:* Option-drag/Alt-drag the group to create a copy of it, for future edits.

2. On the Control panel, do either of the following:

   Click **Expand** to convert the Live Paint group into two nested groups on the same layer . The former faces will become filled paths in one group , and the former edges will become paths with strokes in the other group.
   or
   Choose Object > Live Paint > **Release** to convert the Live Paint group into separate paths, each with a .5-pt. black stroke and no fill (not in a group). Use this option if, say, you want to remove the fill colors and start your sketch over with just linework.

➤ After applying the Expand command, you can easily apply stroke or fill attributes en masse to each group (e.g., apply a brush stroke or an effect) 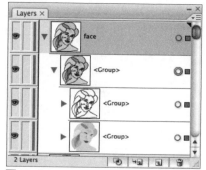. See Chapter 20.

1 *The Live Paint group is* **expanded,** *and two nested groups appear on the Layers panel.*

2 *After expanding the Live Paint group, we hid the <Group> layer that contains the stroked paths. Now only the filled paths are visible.*

3 *Finally, we applied a .5 pt. brush stroke to the group of stroked paths to make the line work look more hand drawn.*

Expand, Release Live Paint Group

1 *Draw the perimeter of the scarf with 4 pencil lines.*

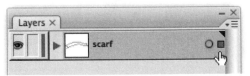

2 *Click the selection area for the scarf layer.*

3 *Click with the **Live Paint Bucket** tool to apply a fill color to the scarf face.*

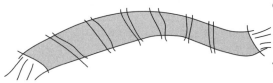

4 *Draw stripes with the **Pencil** tool.*

5 *Click with the **Live Paint Bucket** tool to fill the stripes.*

Exercise

In this exercise, you'll use the Live Paint feature to create a loosely drawn sketch of a striped scarf.

Sketch a scarf

1. Create a new layer on the Layers panel. Double-click the layer name, enter the name "scarf," then click OK.

2. Press D to choose a black stroke of 1 pt. Double-click the **Pencil** tool, uncheck Fill New Pencil Strokes, check Edit Selected Paths, then click OK.

3. Draw the top and bottom edges of a scarf, and a line at each end of the scarf shape that crisscrosses the first two **1**.

4. On the Layers panel, click the selection area for the scarf layer (far right) to select all the objects on that layer **2**, then choose Object > Live Paint > **Make** (Cmd-Option-X/ Ctrl-Alt-X).

5. Choose the **Selection** tool (V), then double-click any path in the Live Paint group to isolate the group. A gray bar will display at the top of the document window and all other artwork will be dimmed.

6. Choose a fill color for the background of the scarf. Double-click the **Live Paint Bucket** tool, check **Paint Fills** and **Paint Strokes**, then click OK. Click inside the scarf face **3**.

7. Choose a stroke color. Choose the **Pencil** tool (N). Draw lines for stripes across the scarf, making sure your new lines cross over the existing edges **4**. Cmd-click/Ctrl-click to deselect the last line.

8. Choose the **Live Paint Bucket** tool (K), choose a fill color, then click within each stripe area **5**. Zoom in, if necessary, to help you click precisely on the correct faces.

(Continued on the following page)

9. Click the gray bar at the top of the document window to exit isolation mode, then save your document 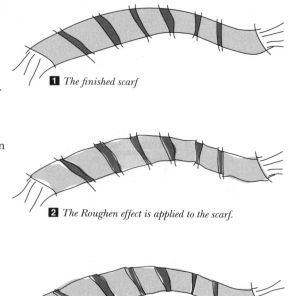.

10. *Optional:* For a more irregular, hand-drawn look, on the Layers panel, click the circle for the Live Paint group to target the group. Choose Effect > Distort & Transform > Roughen, check Preview, click Absolute, move the Size slider to around 3–4 and the Detail slider to around 4, click Smooth, then click OK **2**.

11. *Optional:* To hide the scraggly lines on the scarf, choose the Live Paint Selection tool (Shift-L) and Cmd-Spacebar-click/Ctrl-Spacebar-click to zoom in on the scarf. Click one of the edges that juts out from the long sides of the scarf, Shift-click the others, then choose a stroke of None (or press Delete/Backspace to delete them) **3**. *Note:* If you applied the Roughen effect, a gray selection pattern will appear where the original edges were, and the effect will also update automatically.

1 *The finished scarf*

2 *The Roughen effect is applied to the scarf.*

3 *A stroke of None is applied to the edges that jut out from the scarf.*

LIVE COLOR 14

In this chapter, you'll learn how to create color variations and color groups via the Color Guide panel first. Then you'll learn how to use the powerful Live Color dialog box to edit colors in, and assign new colors to, your artwork, and also how to reduce the number of colors in your artwork.

New Chapter!

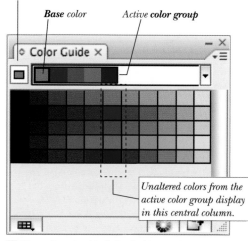

1 *Via the Variation Options dialog box, specify the number of Steps (variations to be displayed) and the degree of Variation for colors on the Color Guide panel.*

Set Base Color to Current Color

Base *color*

Active *color group*

Unaltered colors from the active color group display in this central column.

2 *The options for this Color Guide panel are set to 5 Steps (5 on either side of the central column) and the maximum amount of Variation (More).*

The new color controls

Via the **Color Guide** panel and the **Live Color** dialog box, you can generate color schemes based on harmony rules and variation types, and save the resulting colors as a group to the Swatches panel. You'll find these features to be useful if your projects require you to work with an approved group of colors, if you want to apply a set of coordinated colors quickly, or if you simply want to see how a new range of hues, tints, or saturations would look in your artwork.

First, you'll learn how to use the Color Guide panel to display and apply variations for a color. Then you'll delve into the complex (and impressive) Live Color dialog box, which lets you edit colors in an active group or in selected artwork, apply new harmony rules, save modified colors as a swatch group, and, should the need arise, reduce the number of colors in your artwork.

Using the Color Guide panel NEW!

To get acquainted with the **Color Guide** panel, start by choosing options for it.

To choose variation options for the Color Guide panel:

1. Show the **Color Guide** panel (Shift-F3), then choose **Color Guide Options** from the panel menu. The Variation Options dialog box opens **1**.

2. Click the up/down arrow to set the number of variation **Steps** (columns of colors) to be displayed on either side of the central column, and move the **Variation** slider to control the degree of variation.

3. Click OK **2**.

To apply color variations via the Color Guide panel: NEW!

1. From the **Limit Colors to Swatch Library** menu at the bottom of the **Color Guide** panel, ⊞, choose None.

2. To make a color appear on the panel: 🔲

   Select an object, click the fill or stroke color on the Color or Tools panel, then in the upper left corner of the **Color Guide** panel, click the **Set Base Color to Current Color** button. 🔲
   or
   With no objects selected, click a swatch on the **Swatches** panel or mix a color on the **Color** panel.

3. The active color group is displayed at the top of the Color Guide panel. To control what types of variations are derived from the active color group, choose a variation type from the panel menu:

   Show Tints/Shades adds black to variations on the left side of the central column and white to variations on the right.

   Show Warm/Cool adds red to variations on the left and blue to variations on the right.

   Show Vivid/Muted adds gray to variations on the left and increases the saturation for variations on the right.

4. To recolor a selected object, click the Fill or Stroke box on the Tools panel, then **click** a variation on the Color Guide panel or click a color in the active group.
   or
   Drag a variation swatch over any unselected object **1**–**2**.

➤ Clicking a variation on the Color Guide panel makes that color the current color. If you then click the Set Base Color to Current Color button, the active color group will change and new variations will be generated.

➤ To limit the variations that display on the Color Guide panel to a specific color library, see the sidebar at right. To replace a spot color in a selected object with a new spot color, click a variation that has a dot in the lower right corner.

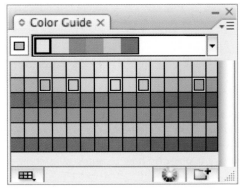

1 *We chose the **Show Warm/Cool** variation type for the **Color Guide** panel.*

2 *To use some of the new variations, we dragged five colors (shown selected in the panel above, in the order used) individually over objects in the artwork to create a progression from warm to cool.*

Limiting colors to a library

To limit the harmony and variation colors on the Color Guide panel to colors in a library, from the **Limit Colors to Swatch Library** menu, ⊞, choose a library name (e.g., Color Books > PANTONE Solid Coated). The library name will be listed at the bottom of the panel, and only colors from that library will display as variations on the Color Guide panel, on the Harmony Rules menu, and also on the color wheel in the Live Color dialog box. (To remove the current restriction, choose None from the Limit Colors to Swatch Library menu.)

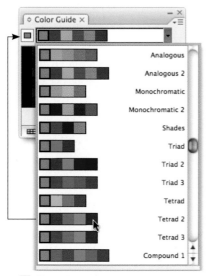

1 *Choose from the **Harmony Rules** menu on the **Color Guide** panel. (The base color will stay the same, but the color group will change to abide by the new rule.)*

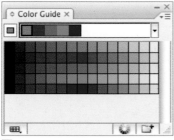

2 *A new color group and variations appear on the panel, based on the chosen **harmony rule.***

3 *Some of the new color **variations**, based on the current **harmony rule**, were dragged onto objects in this artwork.*

Another way to change the variations on the Color Guide panel is by choosing one of the preset **Harmony Rules**, such as Complementary, Analogous, or High Contrast. A new color group and variations will be generated from the same base color, in accordance with the chosen rule.

To create a color group and variations based on a harmony rule: NEW!

1. Follow step 2 on the previous page to establish the base color on the Color Guide panel.

2. On the **Color Guide** panel, ▲ click the **Harmony Rules** arrowhead next to the active color group to open the menu **1**. The base color is shown as the first color in each rule. Click a rule. The menu closes, and a new color group for that base color, in accordance with that rule, displays at the top of the panel and, below that, a new set of variations that Illustrator generated from the new color group **2**.

3. *Optional:* At any time, you can change the base color to generate a new color group and variations based on the current harmony rule, or choose a different rule.

4. To recolor an object, select it, then click a variation **3**.

The active color group changes when you change the base color, choose a new harmony rule, or click a swatch on the Swatches panel. Whenever you create an **active color group** to your liking, it's best to **preserve** it for future use.

To save the active color group: NEW!

Click the gray area below the variations on the Color Guide panel, then click the **Save Color Group to Swatches Panel** button.◻ The new group will display on the Swatches panel.

➤ To save a single variation instead of a whole color group, drag that variation from the Color Guide panel to the Swatches panel.

Editing colors via Live Color NEW!

The remaining pages of this chapter are devoted to the **Live Color** dialog box, which gives you the power to change multiple colors in your artwork simultaneously by editing and applying color groups. There are so many features in this dialog box, we've decided to break it down into 4 manageable sets of instructions.

The first step is to save the existing colors in selected artwork as a **group** for safekeeping. Then you'll be ready to apply a new **harmony rule** and perform basic **color adjustments**.

To create color groups via the Live Color command:

1. Select the objects that you want to recolor.

2. Click the **Edit or Apply Colors** button 🎨 at the bottom of the Color Guide panel.
or
Click the **Recolor Artwork** button 🎨 on the Control panel.

3. The Live Color dialog box opens **1**. Click the **Edit** tab. Check **Recolor Art** at the bottom of the dialog box to preview changes in your artwork (and to have your color edits be applied to the artwork when you exit the dialog box).

4. If the list of Color Groups isn't showing on the right side of the dialog box, click the **Show Color Group Storage** button.▐

5. Click the **Get Colors from Selected Art** button 📷 to create a color group from the selected objects, and enter a descriptive name in the adjacent field. Click the **New Color Group** button.📷 The new group will appear on the list of **Color Groups**. You can click this group to restore the original object colors at any time.

6. To try out some new colors on the selected objects, start by choosing a rule from the **Harmony Rules** menu (click the arrowhead at the top of the dialog box). You may recognize the rules from the Color Guide panel.

7. To adjust all the colors in the selected objects:

Use the tool tip to find out whether the slider below the color wheel is in **brightness** or **saturation** mode, click the button if you want to switch modes, then move the slider.
and/or
From the **Color Mode** menu,⊙ choose **Global Adjust**, then move the Saturation,

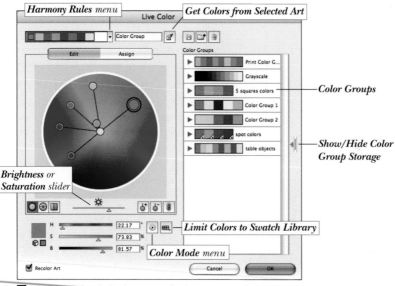

1 *The **Live Color** dialog box is complex but very powerful.*

1 *The original artwork*

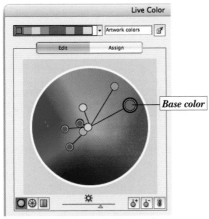

2 *These are the original **color wheel** settings in the **Live Color** dialog box.*

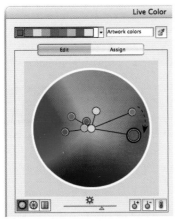

3 *Drag the **base color** marker around the wheel to change all the **hues**.*

Brightness, Temperature, and Luminosity sliders to adjust all the colors.

8. Click the **New Color Group** button to save the active color group to the list of Color Groups and to the Swatches panel.

9. Continue to create as many new groups as you like by following steps 6–8 on the previous page, and recolor your artwork at any time by clicking a different group on the Color Groups list.

10. Click OK.

➤ To delete a color group, click the group, then click the Delete Color Group button.

Next you'll learn how to use the **color wheel** in the Live Color dialog box to adjust the hue, saturation, and brightness in process colors.

To use the color wheel in the Live Color dialog box: NEW!

1. Select the objects that you want to recolor **1**.

2. Click the **Edit or Apply Colors** button on the Color Guide panel or the **Recolor Artwork** button on the Control panel. The Live Color dialog box opens.

3. Check **Recolor Art**, then click the **Edit** tab.

4. If you don't see a color wheel, click the **Display Smooth Color Wheel** button.

5. Edits to the color wheel affect the active color group. To choose the active color group, click the **Get Colors from Selected Art** button or click a group on the **Color Groups** list. You can also choose a new rule from the **Harmony Rules** menu.

6. Each round marker on the color wheel represents a color in the current group **2**; the largest marker represents the base color. The arrangement of markers reflects the current harmony rule relationships. Choose **HSB** from the Color Mode menu. To edit the current color group, do any of the following:

   Drag a color marker around the wheel to shift **hues 3** (and **1**, next page) (the H slider moves as you do this). The current harmony rule is preserved.

   (Continued on the following page)

Color Wheel

Drag a color marker inward or outward to adjust the **saturation** or **brightness** ▮, depending on the current status of the Show Saturation/Brightness and Hue button,☀ ☀ (the saturation [S] or brightness [B] slider will move, too).

➤ Move the base color marker to adjust all the colors in the group, or move a non-base marker to adjust an individual color.

To add a color to the group, click the **Add Color** tool,◑⁺ then click any color on the wheel. To remove a color from the group, click the **Remove Color** tool,◑⁻ then click the marker you want to remove ▮.

➤ Double-click an individual color marker to open the Color Picker, click a hue in the vertical bar, then click or drag in the big square to adjust the saturation and brightness.

7. To choose colors independently from the current harmony rule, click the **Unlink Harmony Colors** button ▯ (the lines leading to the markers are now dashed) ▮. When you're ready to relink the markers, click the **Link Harmonies** button.▧

8. Although you could click the Save Changes to Color Group button ▮ to save your changes to the existing group, that can't be undone, so a better way to save your edited colors is by modifying the group name, then clicking the **New Color Group** button.▭ The new group displays on the list, and your original group is preserved. Win-win.

9. To save any new color groups to the Swatches panel and **recolor** the selected objects, click OK; or to save any new color groups **without recoloring** the selected objects, uncheck Recolor Art, then click OK.

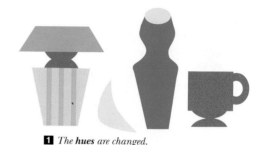

▮ *The **hues** are changed.*

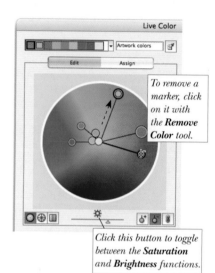

*To remove a marker, click on it with the **Remove Color** tool.*

*Click this button to toggle between the **Saturation** and **Brightness** functions.*

▮ *Drag a color marker inward or outward to adjust either the **brightness** or the **saturation**.*

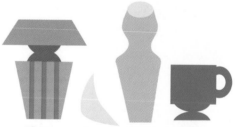

▮ *These are the results after increasing the **saturation** for the yellow marker and **removing** the red marker.*

▮ *This is the illustration after clicking the **Unlink Harmonies** button, then moving some of the markers independently.*

1 *The original artwork*

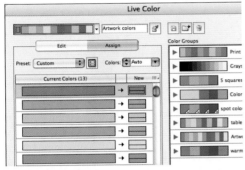

2 *In the **Assign** tab of the Live Color dialog box, colors from the selected artwork display in the **Current Colors** column; replacement colors are shown in the **New** column.*

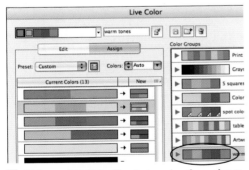

3 *Click one of the **Color Groups** to assign those colors to the active color group. The group we clicked contains just five colors; similar colors were combined automatically into three multicolor rows in the Current Colors column.*

4 *The new **color group** is assigned to the artwork.*

Assigning colors via Live Color NEW!

Using the Assign tab of the Live Color dialog box, you can control not only which colors in a group will replace existing colors in your artwork, but **how.** The features in this tab can be confusing, so don't worry if it takes a few editing sessions to get accustomed to using them. We'll cover just the main features of this tab.

To assign colors to artwork via the Live Color command:

1. Select the objects that you want to recolor **1**.

2. Click the **Edit or Apply Colors** button 🎨 on the Color Guide panel, or the Recolor Artwork button on the Control panel. The Live Color dialog box opens. Check **Recolor Art**, and note how the artwork changes as you make edits in the dialog box.

3. Click the **Assign** tab **2**. Colors from the currently selected objects display in the **Current Colors** column, and colors from the current color group display in the **New** column.

4. To change the active color group, click a group on the **Color Groups** list on the right side of the dialog box, and/or choose a new rule from the **Harmony Rules** menu at the top of the dialog box.

5. If the new active color group contains fewer colors than the current colors, the current colors that are close in hue, shade, or tint to one another will be grouped in the same row and will be assigned the same active color, thereby reducing the number of colors. The solid colors and tints to be assigned to a row will display in the New column **3**–**4**.

   Click a color in the **New** column (a white border will display around it); this selects the whole row. To edit this color, move the sliders below the columns, or double-click the color to edit it via the Color Picker.

   (Continued on the following page)

Assign Colors

6. To assign a color to a different **New** color, drag a Current Color from one row to another row **1**–**2**. You can drag a color from a multicolor row into another row, or to move a whole row, drag the selector bar (located at the left edge of the row) into another row **3**.

To assign a New color to a different **Current Colors** row, drag it upward or downward in the New column.

7. To prevent a row in the Current Colors column from being reassigned to a new color, click the **arrow** between the two columns **4**–**5**. Those current colors won't be changed in the artwork. (To permit the colors to be assigned, click between the two columns again.)

8. *Optional:* Click the New Color Group button to save the active color group to the Color Groups list and to the Swatches panel.

9. Click OK.

➤ To locate one of the Current Colors in your artwork, click the Click Colors Above to Find in Artwork button, then click a color in the Current Colors column. Just that color will display fully; other current colors will be dimmed. To locate all of the colors in a multicolor row, click the selector bar (located at the left edge of the row) first. Reclick the Click Colors Above to Find in Artwork button to turn the feature off.

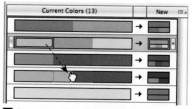

1 *Drag one of the **Current Colors** into another row to reassign it to a different **New** color.*

2 *The tabletop and window are now blue-green.*

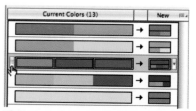

3 *You can drag the **selector bar** to move a whole row.*

4 *Click between two columns to remove the arrow, and thereby **prevent** colors in that row from being reassigned.*

5 *Because we prevented the reds and oranges from being reassigned, the original color of the cup was preserved.*

Assign Colors

1 *The original artwork*

The colors in our artwork will be reduced to the first 4 colors in this active color group.

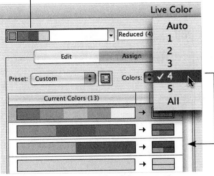

2 *When you select a value from the Colors menu, the Current Colors are reduced to that number.*

3 *The number of Current Colors in the artwork was reduced to 4.*

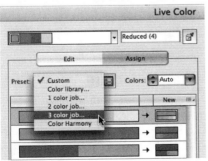

4 *You can also reduce the Current Colors by choosing a Color Job option from the Preset menu.*

Reducing colors via Live Color NEW!

Yet another use for the Live Color dialog box is to **reduce** the **number of colors** in selected artwork. This is helpful, say, if you're planning to print your artwork using one, two, or three spot colors instead of the usual four-color process.

To reduce colors in artwork via the Live Color command:

1. *Optional:* If you're going to reduce colors in your artwork to specific colors (process or spot), open the desired swatch library and copy those colors onto the Swatches panel. Keep the colors selected, then click the New Color Group button.

2. Use File > **Save As** (Cmd-Shift-S/Ctrl-Shift-S) to copy your file.

3. Select the objects for color reduction **1**.

4. Click the **Edit or Apply Colors** button on the Color Guide panel or the **Recolor Artwork** button on the Control panel. The Live Color dialog box opens.

5. Click the **Assign** tab. Check **Recolor Art** to preview changes in your artwork (this also allows your changes to apply to the artwork when you exit the dialog box).

6. From the **Colors** menu, choose the desired number of colors **2**–**3**. That number of colors from the active color group will be applied to your artwork, starting from the first color. If you created a color group (step 1, above), you can click that group now, and you can also choose a new harmony rule. Or click a different color group. (Auto, the default setting, resets the colors to those in the active group.)

   or

   From the **Preset** menu, choose **1-**, **2-**, or **3 Color Job** **4**. When the dialog box opens, from the **Limit Colors to Swatch Library** menu, choose a matching system library or choose None, then click OK. If you chose a library, the active color group will now be limited to colors in the chosen library (**1**, next page).

(Continued on the following page)

7. To control whether black is recolored or preserved, click the **Color Reduction Options**
button ▤ (next to the Preset menu). The
Recolor Options dialog opens **2**. Check or
uncheck **Preserve: Black,** then click OK.

8. Follow steps 5–7 on pages 181–182 to
reassign colors.

➤ If you need to restore the original colors
to your artwork at any time, click the Get
Colors from Selected Art button.▣

9. *Optional:* Click the New Color Group button
▣ to add the reduced color group (now the
active color group) to the Swatches panel.

10. Click OK.

➤ The Recolor Options dialog box contains
the same Colors and Preset menus as
the Live Color dialog box, plus Colorize
Method options. To learn more about these
options, see "Reducing colors in artwork" in
Illustrator Help.

You can get really minimal and reduce your
artwork to just a single **spot** or **process color.**
The color will appear in various tint percentages in your selected artwork, depending on the
brightness values of the original colors.

To reduce selected artwork to just one spot or process color:

1. Select the objects for color reduction.

2. Click the **Edit or Apply Colors** button ▣
on the Color Guide panel or the **Recolor
Artwork** button on the Control panel. The
Live Color dialog box opens.

3. Click the **Assign** tab.

4. From the Preset menu, choose **1 Color Job.**
The 1 Color Job dialog box opens. Choose a
color library, then click OK.

5. Double-click the color in the **New** column,
choose a matching system color from the
Color Picker, then click OK.

6. Click OK in the Live Color dialog box.

➤ To reduce selected artwork to just grayscale
shades, click the Grayscale color group
in the Color Groups area of the Live Color
dialog box.

1 *The same artwork is reduced to 3 colors via the 3 Color Job preset.*

2 *In the **Recolor Options** dialog box, you can specify, among other things, whether Black is recolored or preserved.*

Reduce Colors

PEN | 15

Mastering the Pen tool—Illustrator's most difficult tool—takes patience and practice. Once you become comfortable using it, refer to Chapter 11 to learn how to reshape the resulting paths. If you find the Pen tool to be too difficult to use, remember that you can create shapes using other methods. For example, you can draw simple geometric shapes (Chapter 6) and then combine them (Chapter 25), or if you prefer to draw in a freehand style, use the Pencil along with the Live Paint Bucket tool (Chapter 13).

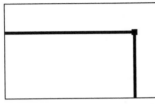

1 *This **corner** point joins two **straight** segments, and has **no** direction handles.*

2 *A **smooth** point always has a pair of direction handles that move in **tandem.** This is a smooth curve.*

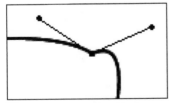

3 *This **corner** point has direction handles that move **independently.** This is a nonsmooth curve.*

Drawing with the Pen tool

The **Pen** tool creates precise curved and straight segments connected by anchor points. If you click with the Pen tool, you'll create corner points and straight segments without direction handles **1**. If you drag with the Pen tool, you'll create smooth points and curve segments with direction handles **2**. You can also create corner points that join nonsmooth curves with this tool **3**. The distance and direction in which you drag the mouse control the shape of the resulting curve segment.

In the instructions on the following pages, you'll learn how to draw straight segments, smooth curves, and nonsmooth curves. Once you master all three techniques, you'll naturally combine them without really thinking about it as you draw your artwork. Drag-drag-click, drag, click-click-drag…

©DANIEL PELAVIN

Before learning how to draw curves, practice clicking with the Pen tool to create an open or closed **polygon**.

To draw a polygon with the Pen tool:

1. If the current fill choice is a solid color, gradient, or pattern (not None) your Pen path will be filled as soon as you create the first three points. To create segments that appear as lines only, choose a stroke color and a fill of None now or at any time after drawing a path.

2. Choose the **Pen** tool (P).

3. Click to create the first anchor point, then click to create the second anchor point. A straight segment will now connect the two points.

4. Click to create additional anchor points. They will be also be connected by straight segments.

   ➤ You can use smart guides to position points and segments as you draw them (Cmd-U/Ctrl-U) 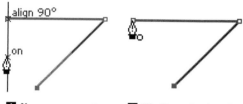.

5. To complete the shape as an **open** path:

   Click the Pen tool or any other **tool** on the Tools panel.
   or
   Cmd-click/Ctrl-click outside the new shape to deselect it.
   or
   Choose Select > **Deselect** (Cmd-Shift-A/ Ctrl-Shift-A).

   Or to complete the shape as a **closed** path, position the Pen pointer over the **starting point** (a small circle will appear next to the pointer), and click on it **2**–**3**.

   ➤ Hold down Shift while clicking with the Pen tool to draw segments at increments of 45°.

   ➤ If the artboard starts to fill up with extraneous points, use the Object > Path > Clean Up command (check only the Delete: Stray Points option).

1 *You can use **smart guides** to align points as you create them.*

2 *The Pen tool pointer is positioned over the starting point to **close** a new shape.*

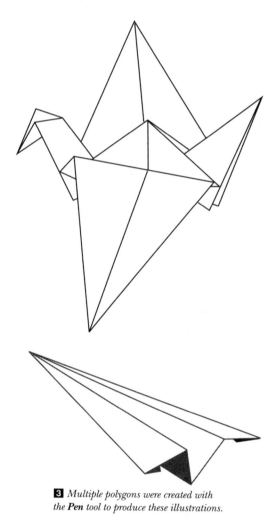

3 *Multiple polygons were created with the **Pen** tool to produce these illustrations.*

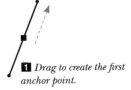

1 *Drag to create the first anchor point.*

2 *Release and reposition the mouse, then drag in the direction you want the curve to follow.*

3 *Continue to reposition and drag the mouse.*

4 *Continue to reposition and drag.*

Follow these instructions to create **smooth curves** with the **Pen** tool. Smooth anchor points that connect curve segments always have a pair of direction handles that move in tandem; the longer the direction handles, the steeper or wider the curves. You can practice drawing curves by converting curved objects to guides (see page 98) and then tracing the guide lines.

To draw curves with the Pen tool:

1. Choose the **Pen** tool (P). *Optional:* Turn on Smart Guides (Cmd-U/Ctrl-U).

2. **Drag** (don't click) to create the first anchor point **1**. The angle of the pair of direction handles that you create will be determined by the direction in which you drag.

3. **Release** the mouse, **move** it away from the last anchor point, then drag a short distance in the direction you want the curve to follow to create a second anchor point **2**. A curve segment will connect the first and second anchor points, and the next pair of direction handles will appear. The shape of the curve segment will be defined by the length and direction in which you drag the mouse.

   ➤ To produce smooth, symmetrical curves, place the points at the beginning and end of each curve rather than at the middle. You can use smart guides to position the points.

4. Drag to create additional anchor points and direction handles **3**–**4**. The points will be connected by curve segments.

   (Continued on the following page)

5. To complete the object as an **open** path:

Choose a different **tool**.
or
Cmd-click/Ctrl-click away from the new object to deselect it.
or
Choose Select > **Deselect** (Cmd-Shift-A/Ctrl-Shift-A).

Or to complete the object as a **closed** path, position the Pen pointer over the starting point—a small loop will appear next to the pointer. Drag, then release the mouse. (If Text Label Hints is on in Preferences > Smart Guides & Slices, the word "anchor" will also appear.)

➤ The fewer the anchor points, the smoother the shape. Too many anchor points will produce bumpy curves. Try to make your direction handles relatively short at first—you can always lengthen them later.

➤ You can reshape any curves you create (see Chapter 11).

Adjust points as you draw a path

➤ If the last anchor point you created was a smooth point (two direction handles) and you want to **convert** it to a **corner** point (one direction handle), click it with the Pen tool, release and reposition the mouse, then continue to draw.

➤ If the last point you created was a corner point and you want to **add** a **direction handle** to it, position the Pen tool pointer over it, then drag. A direction handle will appear. Release and reposition the mouse, then continue to draw.

➤ To **move** a point as you create it, keep the mouse button down, hold down the Spacebar, then to move a corner point, drag the point, or to move a smooth point, drag the direction handle. Release and reposition the mouse, then continue to draw.

Be smart with your pen

To display temporary angle lines that align to existing points as you click or drag with the Pen tool 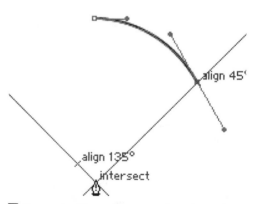, check **Construction Guides** in Preferences > Smart Guides & Slices, and turn on **Smart Guides** (Cmd-U/Ctrl-U).

©DANIEL PELAVIN

1 *Use **smart guides** to align new anchor points with existing, unselected anchor points.*

1 *Drag to create the first anchor point.*

2 *Release the mouse, reposition it, then drag to create a second anchor point.*

3 *Option-drag/Alt-drag from the last anchor point in the direction you want the new curve to follow. Both direction handles are now on the same side of the curve segment.*

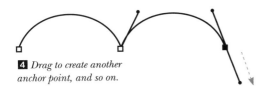

4 *Drag to create another anchor point, and so on.*

©DANIEL PELAVIN

Converting points

You can use the Pen tool to create corner points that join nonsmooth curves; the latter are segments that curve on the same side of an anchor point (as opposed to segments that curve on both sides of a smooth anchor point). If you move one direction handle that's connected to a corner point, only the curve on that side of the point will change shape. Smooth points and corner points can be combined in the same path, of course. You can **convert smooth points** into **corner points** (or vice versa) as you draw them (instructions below) or after you draw them (instructions on the next page).

To convert smooth points into corner points as you draw them:

1. Choose the **Pen** tool (P).

2. **Drag** to create the first anchor point **1**.

3. **Release** the mouse, **move** it away from the last anchor point, then drag to create a second anchor point **2**. A curve segment will connect the first and second anchor points, and a second pair of direction handles will appear. The shape of the curve segment will be determined by the length and direction in which you drag.

4. Position the pointer over the last anchor point, **Option-drag/Alt-drag** from that point to drag one direction handle independently, release and reposition the mouse, then continue to drag in the direction you want the curve to follow **3**.
   or
   Click the **last** anchor point to remove one of the direction handles from that point.

5. Repeat the last two steps to draw more anchor points and curves **4**.

6. To close the shape:
   Drag on the starting point to keep it as a **smooth** point.
   or
   Click the starting point to **convert** it to a **corner** point with one direction handle.

To convert points on an existing path:

Method 1 (Control panel buttons) NEW!

1. Choose the **Direct Selection** tool (A).

2. Click the point that you want to convert.

3. On the Control panel, click the **Convert Selected Anchor Points to Smooth** button or the **Convert Selected Anchor Points to Corner** button.

➤ To choose preferences for the display of anchor points and handles, see page 367. To make it easier to locate anchor points, check Highlight Anchors on Mouse Over.

Method 2 (Convert Anchor Point tool)

1. Choose the **Convert Anchor Point** tool (Shift-C).

2. To help you locate the anchor points easily, turn on **Smart Guides** (Cmd-U/Ctrl-U) and check **Text Label Hints** in Preferences > Smart Guides & Slices.

3. Drag new direction handles from a **corner point** to convert it to a smooth point 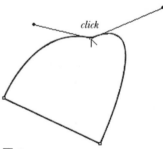.
   or
   To convert a **smooth point** to a corner point with a nonsmooth curve, rotate a **direction handle** from the point so it forms a V shape with the other direction handle .
   or
   Click a **smooth point** to convert it to a corner point with no direction handles **3**–**4**.

4. Repeat the last step to convert other anchor points.

➤ To turn the Pen tool to a temporary Convert Anchor Point tool, hold down Option/Alt. To turn the Pen tool temporarily to the last-used selection tool, hold down Cmd/Ctrl.

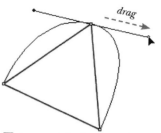

1 A **corner** point is converted to a **smooth** point.

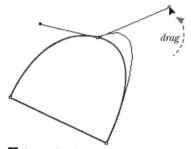

2 A **smooth** point is converted to a **corner** point, producing a **nonsmooth** curve.

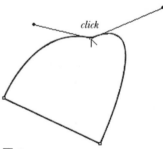

3 A **nonsmooth** curve is converted to a **corner** point (no direction handles).

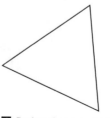

4 Back to the original triangle

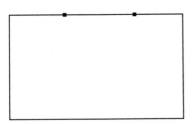

1 *Click to add two anchor points along the top segment, dividing it into thirds.*

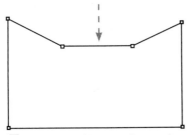

2 *Drag the middle segment downward.*

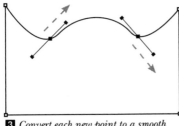

3 *Convert each new point to a smooth point.*

Exercise

Convert a rectangle into a costume mask

The outer part of the face mask

1. Choose the **Rectangle** tool ▣ (M), choose a fill of None and a 1-pt. black stroke, then draw a rectangle. Keep it selected.

2. Choose the **Direct Selection** tool (A).

3. Choose the **Pen** tool ♙ (P), and make sure Disable Auto Add/Delete is unchecked in Preferences (Cmd-K/Ctrl-K) > General.

4. Click to add 2 anchor points on the top segment of the rectangle, dividing it into thirds **1**.

5. Cmd-drag/Ctrl-drag the segment between the new points downward **2**.

6. Option-drag/Alt-drag the new point on the left upward and to the right to convert it into a smooth point, and Option-drag/Alt-drag the new point on the right downward and to the right **3**.

7. Cmd-click/Ctrl-click the point in the bottom left corner, then click the **Convert Selected Anchor Points to Smooth** button on the Control panel. Do the same thing for the point in the bottom right corner **4**.

8. Click to add a point in the middle of the bottommost segment.

9. Hold down Cmd/Ctrl, click the new middle point, then drag it slightly upward **5**.

(Continued on the following page)

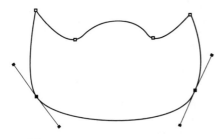

4 *Convert the bottom corner points into smooth points.*

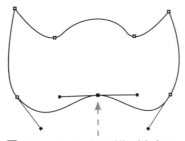

5 *Add a point in the middle of the bottom segment, then drag the new point upward.*

Exercise: Pen Tool

The eye holes

1. Choose the **Ellipse** tool (L), ⬭ move the pointer inside the existing shape, then draw a small ellipse for an eye hole .

2. Choose the **Direct Selection** tool (A). 🔺 Deselect, click the leftmost anchor point of the ellipse, then drag it upward to form an eye shape 2.

3. Click the bottommost anchor point of the ellipse, then drag the left handle of that point to the left to widen the bottom segment 3.

4. Click the top middle point of the ellipse, then drag the right handle of that point upward and to the right to widen the top right segment 4.

5. With the **Selection** tool (V), 🔺 move the ellipse to the left side of the mask shape, and keep it selected.

6. Choose the **Reflect** tool (O). 🔁

7. Option-click/Alt-click the center of the face mask. In the dialog box, check Preview, click Vertical, then click Copy 5.

8. Use the **Selection** tool to marquee all three shapes, fill the shapes with a color, and keep them selected.

9. To create a compound shape, click the **Subtract from Shape Area** button 🔲 on the Pathfinder panel. The eye holes, which now cut through the face mask 6, can be modified with the Direct Selection tool.

1 Create a small ellipse for the eye holes.

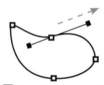

2 Drag the leftmost anchor point upward with the Direct Selection tool.

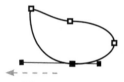

3 Drag the left direction handle of the bottommost anchor point to the left.

4 Drag the right handle of the top middle anchor point upward and to the right.

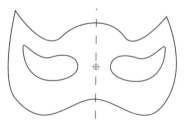

5 To create the second eye hole, Option-click/Alt-click in the center of the mask shape with the Reflect tool. Check Preview, click Vertical, then click Copy.

6 All the shapes were selected and made into a compound shape, and a fill color was applied to the compound shape. A gray rectangle is visible behind the mask, which proves that the eye holes are transparent.

Exercise: Pen Tool

In this important chapter you'll learn how to create top-level layers and sublayers; edit groups; delete layers and objects; select layer listings; select objects via the Layers panel; restack, duplicate, lock/unlock, and hide/show layers; collect objects onto a new layer; release objects to layers; and finally, merge and flatten layers.

Show/hide
layer, sublayer, group, or object

Lock/unlock
layer, sublayer, group, or object

Target *object or group to apply or edit appearances*

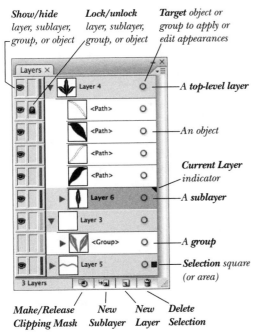

— *A top-level layer*

— *An object*

Current Layer
indicator

— *A sublayer*

— *A group*

— **Selection** *square (or area)*

Make/Release
Clipping Mask

New
Sublayer

New
Layer

Delete
Selection

1 *The objects in this document are nested within top-level layers and sublayers, at various stacking levels.*

2 *The Layers panel for this artwork is shown above.*

The Layers panel
What the panel is used for

Until now (unless you snuck ahead to this chapter!), you've been creating objects on a single, default layer that was created automatically when you created your document, and each new path was stacked above the last one automatically. In this chapter, you'll learn how to purposely change the stacking order of objects via the Layers panel 🔘 (F7). With a document open, click the Layer 1 arrowhead on the Layers panel to expand the list of objects on that layer. Layer 1 is called a **top-level layer**, meaning it's not nested within another layer **1**–**2**.

You can add as many layers as you like to a document, available memory permitting, and you can also create **sublayers** (nested layers) within any top-level layer. The actual objects that make up your artwork—paths, type, images, etc.—are nested within one or more top-level layers, or in groups or sublayers within top-level layers. When you create an object, it appears on the currently selected layer, but it can be moved to a different layer at any time, either individually or by restacking the whole layer or sublayer the object resides in.

The Layers panel also has other important functions beyond restacking! You can use it to select; target (for appearance changes); show or hide; and lock or unlock any layer, sublayer, group, or individual object.

(Continued on the following page)

Object names on the Layers panel

By default, each new vector object you create is listed as <Path> on the Layers panel; each placed raster image or rasterized object is listed as <Image> or by the name of the image file; each **symbol** is listed by the name of that symbol (e.g., "Blue Flower"); and each **type** object is listed by the first few characters in the object (e.g., "The planting season has begun" might be shortened to "The plan"). Similarly, object groups are listed by such names as Live Paint Group, Compound Path, etc.

You may say "Whoa!" when you first see the number of listings on the Layers panel. Once you get used to working with it, though, you may become enamored of its clean, logical design, as we are, and enjoy how easy it makes even simple tasks, such as selecting or locking objects.

➤ Double-click an object or layer name to assign a custom name to it. We suggest leaving the word "group" or "path" in the name to make it easy to identify.

You can choose different **Layers panel options** for each document.

To choose Layers panel options:

1. Choose **Panel Options** from the bottom of the Layers panel menu. The Layers Panel Options dialog box opens **1**.

2. Leave **Show Layers Only** unchecked; otherwise the panel will list only top-level layers and sublayers, not individual objects.

3. For the size of the layer and object thumbnails, click a **Row Size:** Small (12 pixels), Medium (20 pixels), or Large (32 pixels). Or click Other and enter a custom size (12–100 pixels).

4. Check which **Thumbnails** you want the panel to display: Layers, Groups, or Objects. If you check Top Level Only, thumbnails will display for top-level layers but not for sublayers.

5. Click OK **2**.

One catchall name

In this book, we refer to paths, images, and text objects collectively as **objects**. If we need to refer to one of these categories individually for some reason, we will.

1 *Via the **Layers Panel Options** dialog box, you can customize the **Layers** panel for each file.*

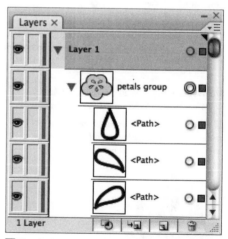

2 *For the Layers panel in our document, we chose a custom **Row Size** (Other: 40 pixels) and turned Thumbnails off for Layers.*

Creating a top-level layer quickly

To insert a new top-level layer in the **topmost** position on the panel, regardless of which layer name (listing) is currently selected, Cmd-click/Ctrl-click the New Layer button at the bottom of the Layers panel.

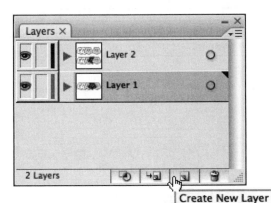

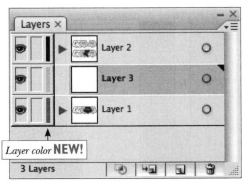

1 Click a layer, then Option-click/Alt-click the **New Layer** button. Choose options for, or rename, the new layer via the Layer Options dialog box.

2 The **new layer** (Layer 3) appears above Layer 1.

Creating layers

In these instructions, you'll learn how to create the granddaddy of layers—**top-level layers.**

To create a new top-level layer:

Method 1 (quick, no options)

1. On the **Layers** panel (F7), click the name of the top-level layer that you want the new layer to appear above.

2. To create a layer without choosing options for it, click the **New Layer** button at the bottom of the panel. Illustrator will assign to the new layer the next number in order and the next available color, in order, as listed on the Color menu in the Layer Options dialog box.

Method 2 (choose options)

1. On the **Layers** panel (F7), click the name of the top-level layer that you want the new layer to appear above **1**.

2. Option-click/Alt-click the **New Layer** button. The Layer Options dialog box opens.

3. Do any of the following:

   Change the layer **Name.**

   Via the **Color** menu, choose a different color for the selection border of objects on the layer, and to be used as the layer color on the Layers panel. Colors are assigned to new layers in the order in which they appear on this menu. If the fill or stroke colors of objects on the layer are similar to the selection border colors, making it hard to figure out which is which, see if choosing a different selection color helps.

   Choose other layer options (see the sidebar on page 205).

4. Click OK **2**.

➤ Objects always reside in a top-level layer or sublayer (or in a group in either of the above)—they can't float around by themselves.

➤ Layers and sublayers are numbered in the order in which they're created, regardless of their position in the stacking order or how far in they're indented.

Once you become accustomed to adding and using top-level layers, you're ready for the next level of intricacy: **sublayers.** Every sublayer is nested within (indented under) either a top-level layer or another sublayer. If you create a new object or group of objects while a sublayer is selected, the new object or group will be nested within that sublayer. You don't necessarily have to create or use sublayers, but you may find them to be helpful for keeping the panel organized.

By default, every sublayer has the same generic name: "Layer," but as with layers, you can rename them to make them easier to identify (e.g., "inner pieces" or "order form" or "tyrannosaurus").

To create a sublayer:

1. On the **Layers** panel ● (F7), click the top-level layer (or sublayer) name that you want the new sublayer to appear within.

2. To create a new sublayer without choosing options for it, click the **New Sublayer** button 🔾 **1**–**2**.

   or

   To choose options as you create a new sublayer, Option-click/Alt-click the **New Sublayer** button. In the Layer Options dialog box, enter a Name, check or uncheck any of the options (see the sidebar on page 205), then click OK.

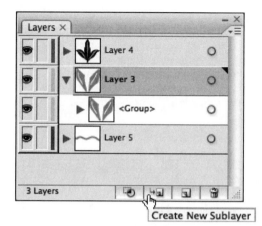

1 *Click a layer name, then click the **New Sublayer** button.*

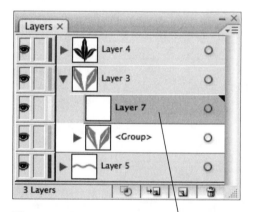

2 *A new sublayer name (in this case, Layer 7) appears within Layer 3.*

Deleting layers and objects

You know how to make 'em. Now you need to learn how to **get rid of** 'em.

Beware! If you delete a top-level layer or sublayer, all the objects on that layer will be removed from the document.

To delete a layer, sublayer, group, or object:

1. On the **Layers** panel, 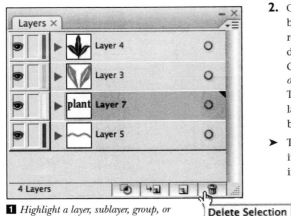 click the layer, sublayer, group, or object that you want to delete, or Cmd-click/Ctrl-click multiple items. You can click multiple items at the same indent level (e.g., all top-level layers), but not items from different indent levels (e.g., not a top-level layer with individual objects nested in a different top-level layer).

2. Click the **Delete Selection** button at the bottom of the Layers panel **1**. If any objects reside on the layer or sublayer that you're deleting, an alert dialog box will appear. Click Yes.
   or
   To bypass the prompt, drag the highlighted layers or objects over the **Delete Selection** button.

➤ To retrieve a deleted layer and the objects it contained, use the Undo command immediately.

1 *Highlight a layer, sublayer, group, or object, then click the* **Delete Selection** *button.*

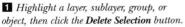

Delete Selection

Selecting Layers panel listings

If you want to control where a new (or pasted) object will be positioned within the overall stacking order of a document, you need to click the name of a top-level layer, sublayer, group, or object on the Layers panel before you start pasting or drawing.

If you select an object, the **listing** (name) for its top-level layer or sublayer becomes selected automatically, but the converse isn't true: simply clicking a top-level layer or sublayer listing won't cause objects to become selected in the document window. Selecting objects via the Layers panel is a separate step (see pages 200–202), and targeting items for appearance attributes is yet another step (see the sidebar on page 200). Think of selecting layer listings as a layer management technique, and selecting the objects themselves (making the anchor points, and possibly the bounding box, appear) as an essential first step in the editing process.

Before creating a new object or placing an image into your artwork, bear the following in mind:

➤ If you click a **top-level** layer listing but not a sublayer or group, and then create or place an object, the new object will be listed at the top of the top-level layer.

➤ If you click a **sublayer** listing (but no objects are selected), then create or place a new object, the new object will appear on that sublayer. Or if you click a **group** listing, the new object will appear just above the group.

➤ If you select an **object** and then create or place a new object, the new object will appear in the same layer or sublayer as the selected object, outside any group.

To select a layer, sublayer, group, or object listing:

Click a top-level layer, sublayer, group, or object **name** (or the area just to the right of the name)—not the selection area at the far right side of the panel. The Current Layer indicator (triangle) **1** will move to the layer that the item you clicked resides in.

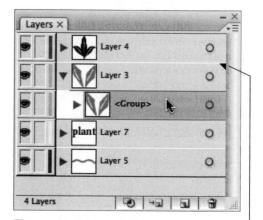

1 *A group is clicked, and the **Current Layer** indicator moves to the layer that group resides in.*

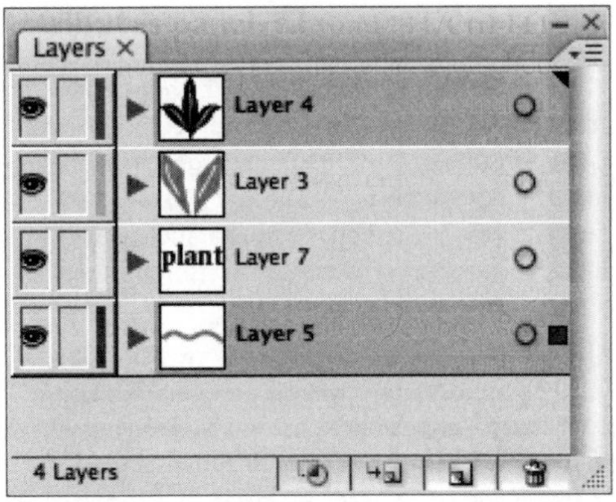

1 *Two noncontiguous top-level layers **listings** are selected.*

If you select **multiple layer listings** (layers, sub-layers, groups, or objects), you can restack them on the panel en masse, or apply the same layer options to them. Here, too, there are a few rules to remember:

➤ You can select multiple **sublayer** listings within the same top-level layer, provided they're at the same nesting level, but you can't select multiple sublayer listings on different top-level layers.

➤ You can select multiple listings of the same category (e.g., multiple top-level layers) and nesting level, but you can't select multiple item listings on different nesting levels (e.g., not both top-level layers and sublayers).

➤ You can select multiple **object** listings (such as paths and type) in the same top-level layer, but not multiple object listings on different top-level layers.

To select multiple layer listings:

1. On the **Layers** panel (F7), click the name of a top-level layer, sublayer, or object.

2. Shift-click the name of another layer, sub-layer, or object. The items you clicked and any items of a similar kind between them will become highlighted.
or
Cmd-click/Ctrl-click other noncontiguous top-level layer, sublayer, or object **names** **1**.

➤ Cmd-click/Ctrl-click to deselect any individual listings when multiple listings are selected.

➤ Although you can click multiple layers, only one top-level layer or sublayer will have a Current Layer indicator.

Select Multiple Layers Panel Listings

Selecting objects via the Layers panel

In Chapter 7, you learned how to select objects by using a variety of selection tools and Select menu commands. You can also use the **Layers panel** to **select** paths or groups—that is, make the anchor points visible in the document window to ready them for editing or reshaping.

To select all the objects in a layer:

Click the **selection area** **1** for a top-level layer or sublayer at the far right side of the Layers panel. A colored selection square will appear for every sublayer, group, and object on that layer, and every object on the layer, regardless of its indent level, will become selected in the document window (the bounding box will also appear, if that feature is on) **2**. In addition, unless the items are in a group, the target circle for each path and group will become selected.

➤ To deselect an individual object, expand the top-level layer or sublayer list for that object, then Shift-click the object's selection square.

To deselect all the objects in a layer:

Shift-click the **selection square** for the layer you want to deselect objects on. All the objects in the layer will be deselected, including any objects in any sublayers or groups on that layer.

Circle or square?

If you click the target circle ○ on the right side of the Layers panel for a **group** or **object,** or click the selection area to the right of the target circle, the object or group becomes selected and targeted and the item is listed on the Appearance panel. (To learn about applying appearance attributes, see Chapter 20.)

If you click the **selection area** for a top-level layer, all the objects on the layer become selected and targeted for appearance changes, and the item name (e.g., "Path") is listed on the Appearance panel. If you click the **target circle** for a top-level layer, all the objects on the layer become selected, but only the top-level layer is targeted; "Layer" becomes the Appearance panel listing.

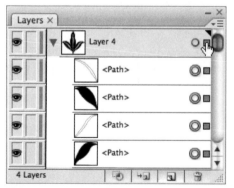

1 *Click the **selection area** for a layer to select all the paths and groups on that layer. The selection squares appear (in the color that's been assigned to that layer).*

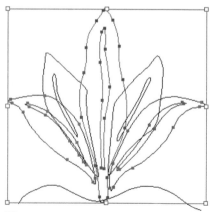

2 *All the paths and path groups on Layer 4 became selected in the document window.*

Locating a listing on the Layers panel

When the number of listings on the Layers panel grows long, it can be hard to locate a particular item. Organizing listings into sublayers can help, as does the Locate Object command. With the Selection tool, select the object in the document window whose listing you want to find, then choose **Locate Object** from the Layers panel menu. The list for the object's layer will expand and a selection square will appear for that item. (If "Locate Layer" appears on the panel menu instead of "Locate Object," choose Panel Options from the panel menu and uncheck Show Layers Only; the Locate Object command will become available.)

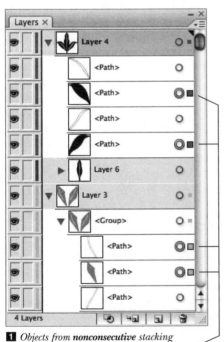

1 *Objects from **nonconsecutive** stacking levels are **selected** (note the selection squares).*

To select an object via the Layers panel:

1. Make sure the top-level layer, sublayer, or group list for the object that you want to select on the Layers panel is expanded.

2. At the far right side of the panel, click the **selection area** or **target circle** for the object you want to select.

Using the **Layers** panel, you can **select multiple groups** or **objects** on different—even nonconsecutive—top-level layers or sublayers.

To select multiple objects on different layers:

Method 1 (Shift-clicking)

On the Layers panel, make sure the names of all the nested objects that you want to select are visible (expand any layer or group lists, if necessary). Click the **selection area** or **target circle** for any object, then Shift-click any other individual groups or objects that you want to add to the selection **1**. The items don't have to be listed consecutively.

Method 2 (dragging)

Option-drag/Alt-drag upward or downward through a series of consecutive top-level or sublayer **listings** (the names, not the selection areas) to select all the objects on those layers.

➤ To deselect any selected object individually, Shift-click its selection square or target circle.

On pages 84–85, you learned how to create, isolate, add a new object to, and ungroup a group. Here, you'll learn how to select objects in a group.

To select a whole group via the Layers panel:

1. *Optional:* To put the group in isolation mode, double-click it with the Selection tool (V) **1**. *Note:* Double Click to Isolate must be checked in Preferences > General.

2. To select all the objects in the group (including any groups nested inside it), click the **selection area** or **target circle** ⬭ for the group listing on the right side of the Layers panel **2**.

➤ To select a whole group manually in non-isolation mode, click an object in the group with the Selection tool (V). To select an object in a group (or individual anchor points or segments), use the Direct Selection tool (A). To make the bounding box around a selected group visible, choose View > Show Bounding Box.

To select multiple objects in a group:

1. Deselect all (Cmd-Shift-A/Ctrl-Shift-A).

2. The group can be in isolation mode for this method, or not. Expand the group list on the Layers panel, then Shift-click the **selection area** or **target circle** ⬭ at the far right side of the panel for each object in the group that you want to select. (Shift-click it again to deselect any item.)

   or

   With the group in isolation mode, choose the **Selection** tool, click an object, then Shift-click additional objects. (Shift-click any item again to deselect it.)

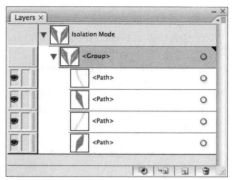

1 *When a group is in* **isolation mode**, *the Layers panel lists only the group and its objects. The figure below shows the same group listing in nonisolation mode.*

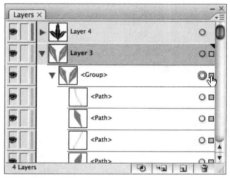

2 *To* **select** *all the objects in a group, expand the group list, then click the selection area or target circle for the group.*

Cut and Paste

To paste an object directly in front of or directly behind another object, drag the object to the desired location in the artwork, choose Edit > Cut (Cmd-X/Ctrl-X), select another object, then choose Edit > **Paste in Front** (Cmd-F/Ctrl-F) or **Paste in Back** (Cmd-B/Ctrl-B). The object will arrive in the same horizontal and vertical (*x/y*) position from which it was cut. *Note:* If this doesn't work the way you expect, undo, uncheck Paste Remembers Layers on the Layers panel menu, then paste again.

➤ You can use any of the paste commands to copy an object between Illustrator documents, or even simpler, drag and drop the object between files (see pages 92–93).

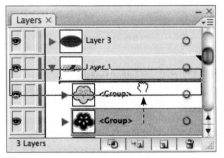

1 *Drag a layer listing upward or downward to change its stacking position. Here the mouse is being released at the same indent level, and within the same top-level layer.*

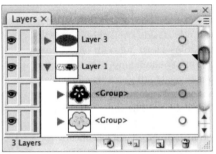

2 *The dark flower <Group> is now in front of the lighter flower <Group>.*

Restacking objects and layers

The order of objects (and layers) on the Layers panel matches the front-to-back order of objects (and layers) in the artwork. If you move a group or object to a different **stacking position** within the same layer, move a group or object to a different top-level layer or sublayer, or move a whole top-level layer or sublayer upward or downward on the list, the artwork will redraw accordingly. You can restack objects and layers by dragging or by using a command.

Note: On page 85, you learned how to add a new object to a group. Follow these instructions if you want to move an existing object into (or out of) a group.

To restack a layer, group, or object by dragging:

Drag a top-level layer, sublayer, group, or object upward or downward on the Layers panel (the pointer turns into a hand icon). Release the mouse **between** layers or objects to keep the object at the same indent level (say, to keep a group within the same top-level layer) **1**–**2**. Or to move an object to a different group or layer, release the mouse when the large **black arrowheads** point to the desired group or layer **3**–**4**. The document will redraw to reflect the new stacking position.

Beware! If you move an object that's part of a group or clipping mask to a different top-level layer, the object will be released from the group or mask.

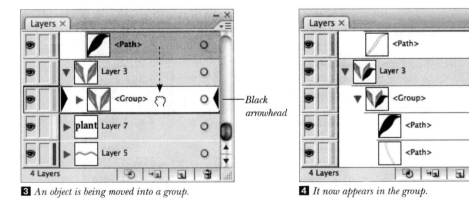

3 *An object is being moved into a group.*

Black arrowhead

4 *It now appears in the group.*

When a document contains many objects on many layers, it can be cumbersome to expand and collapse layers just to restack an object. The **Send to Current Layer** command, discussed below, is faster.

To move an object to a layer via a command:

1. With the **Selection** tool (V), select one or more objects.

2. On the Layers panel, click the layer you want to move the selected object(s) to.

3. Right-click/Ctrl-click in the document window and choose Arrange > **Send to Current Layer** (or choose the command from the Object > Arrange submenu).

➤ To reverse the current order of layers, groups, and objects on the Layers panel, Cmd-click/ Ctrl-click noncontiguous items (or click, then Shift-click a series of contiguous items), then choose Reverse Order from the Layers panel menu.

Duplicating layers and objects

Duplicate objects appear in the same x/y location as (directly on top of) the originals. If you duplicate a layer or sublayer, the word "copy" will appear in the duplicate name.

To duplicate a layer, sublayer, or object:

On the Layers panel, click the layer, sublayer, or object that you want to duplicate, then choose **Duplicate** "[layer or object name]" from the Layers panel menu.

or

Drag a layer, sublayer, or object listing over the **New Layer** button 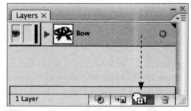 **1**–**2**.

or

Click the selection area for a sublayer, group, or object (expand the listing, if necessary), then Option-drag/Alt-drag the **selection square** upward or downward to the desired top-level layer or sublayer **3**–**4**. You can copy an object within a group or layer using this method.

1 *To duplicate a layer, sublayer, group, or object, drag it over the New Layer button (note the plus sign).*

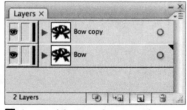

2 *A copy of the "Bow" layer is made.*

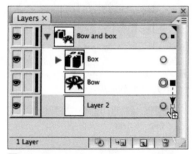

3 *To copy an object, Option-drag/Alt-drag its selection square.*

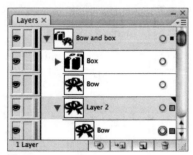

4 *A copy of the Bow object appears in Layer 2.*

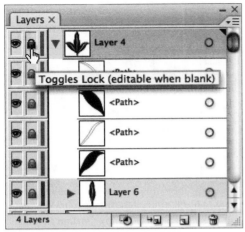

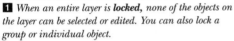

1 *When an entire layer is **locked,** none of the objects on the layer can be selected or edited. You can also lock a group or individual object.*

One-stop shopping for layer options

Via the **Layer Options** dialog box, you can choose multiple options for a layer or object. Options you choose for a top-level layer apply to all sublayers, groups, and objects that reside in the layer.

Double-click a top-level layer or sublayer on the Layers panel; or select multiple layer or sublayer listings, then choose **Options for Selection** from the panel menu. In the Layer Options dialog box, you can change the **Name,** and check or uncheck any options, such as **Lock, Show, Print,** or **Preview** (Preview view). Nonprintable layers are listed in italics on the Layers panel. You can also choose a different **Color** to be used for selections on that layer and for identification on the Layers panel. **NEW!** If the current selection color is similar to colors in the artwork, try choosing a contrasting selection color.

➤ The Template option, together with the Dim Images To option, makes a layer uneditable and dimmed—the first step if you're going to trace a placed image or object manually. For fast, automatic tracing, see Chapter 12.

➤ You can also double-click a group or object and change the Name, Lock, and Show options in a simpler dialog box.

Locking layers and objects

Locked objects can't be selected or modified, but they do remain visible. When a whole layer is locked, none of the objects on that layer are editable. When you save, close, and reopen a file that contains locked objects, the objects remain locked.

To lock or unlock layers or objects:

On the Layers panel, click in the **edit** (second) column for a layer **1**, sublayer, group, or object. The padlock icon 🔒 will appear. Click the icon to unlock.

or

To lock multiple layers, sublayers, groups, or objects, drag upward or downward in the **edit** column. Drag back over the padlock icons to unlock.

or

Option-click/Alt-click in the **edit** column for a top-level layer to lock or unlock all the other top-level layers except the one you click on.

➤ If you lock an object and then lock its top-level layer, but later decide to unlock the object, you have to unlock the top-level layer first.

➤ To lock layers via a command, select the layer listings that you want to keep unlocked, then lock all the other layers by choosing Lock Others from the Layers panel menu.

➤ To make a layer unprintable, hide it by clicking the visibility icon; hidden layers can't be printed, exported, or edited. Another option is to uncheck Print in the Layer Options dialog box; in this case, the layer won't print, but it can be exported and edited, and will remain visible.

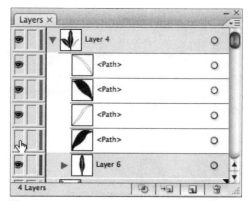

Hiding layers and objects

When you hide the objects you're not working on, you reduce the complexity of the artboard, as well as reap the benefit of a faster screen redraw. You can hide a top-level layer with all its nested layers, hide a group, or hide any individual object. Hidden objects don't print and are invisible in both Outline and Preview views. When you save, close, and reopen your file, hidden objects stay hidden.

To hide or show layers or objects:

Note: If you want to show an object, but its top-level layer is hidden, you must show its top-level layer first.

Click the visibility icon 👁 for a top-level layer, sublayer, group, or object **1**–**2**. To redisplay what was hidden, click in the visibility column.
or
Drag upward or downward in the visibility column to hide multiple, consecutive top-level layers, sublayers, groups, or objects. To redisplay what was hidden, drag again.
or
Display all layers, then **Option-click/Alt-click** the visibility column 👁 to hide or show all the top-level layers except the one you click on.

➤ To hide layers via a command, make sure all layers are visible (choose Show All Layers from the Layers panel menu if they're not), click the top-level layer or layers that you want to keep visible, then choose Hide Others from the Layers panel menu.

1 *You can hide/show individual* **objects** *or* **groups**...

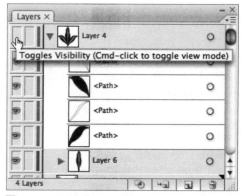

2 *...or hide whole* **layers.**

Changing layer views

If you change the **view** for a top-level layer, all nested layers and objects within the layer will display in that view:

Display layer in Outline view when document is in Preview view	Cmd-click/Ctrl-click the visibility icon 👁; Cmd-click/Ctrl-click the visibility icon 👁 again to redisplay the layer in Preview view
Display all layers in Preview view	Choose Preview All Layers from the Layers panel menu
Display all layers but one in Outline view	Cmd-Option-click/Ctrl-Alt-click the visibility icon 👁 for a top-level layer; repeat to redisplay all layers in Preview view

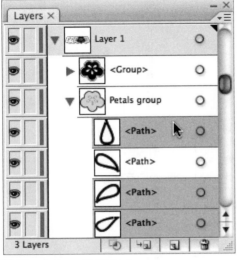

1 *Three paths are **highlighted**.*

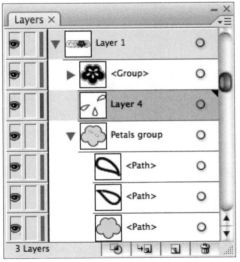

2 *The **Collect in New Layer** command gathered the three highlighted paths into a new sublayer (Layer 4). Note that the new sublayer doesn't have an expand triangle; we'd have to click the selection area or another layer to make it appear.*

Collecting objects in a new layer

The **Collect in New Layer** command moves all the currently highlighted top-level layers, sublayers, groups, or objects into a brand new layer.

To move layers, sublayers, groups, or objects to a new layer:

1. Cmd-click/Ctrl-click the listings for the layers, groups, or objects that you want to gather together **1**. They must all be at the same indent level (e.g., all objects from the same sublayer or on consecutive sublayers). Don't click the selection area.

2. From the Layers panel menu, choose **Collect in New Layer.** Sublayers, groups, or objects will be nested inside a new sublayer within the same top-level layer **2**, and top-level layers will be nested as sublayers within a new top-level layer.

➤ Quirky bug: To make the expand triangle appear for the new layer for the first time, you have to click the selection area or another layer.

Releasing objects to layers

The **Release to Layers** commands disperse all objects or groups that are nested within the currently selected top-level layer listing onto new, separate layers within the same layer. This command is useful when preparing an Illustrator file for an animation program.

To use Illustrator artwork as the contents of an object or frame animation, ungroup any groups and expand any appearances or blends, then use one of the Release to Layers commands to release the objects to individual layers. In the animation program, you'll then be able to convert the layers from the placed file into separate objects or into a sequence. *Note:* If you're going to export your artwork to Flash, use the SWF Options dialog box in Illustrator instead, which lets you control how layers and blends will import into Flash (see pages 408–409).

Read step 2 carefully before deciding which command to use.

To move objects to new, separate layers:

1. On the Layers panel, click a top-level layer, sublayer, or group (not an object) **1**.

2. From the Layers panel menu, choose:

   Release to Layers (Sequence) 2. Each object within the selected layer or group listing will be nested in its own new layer within the original layer. The original stacking order of the objects will be preserved.
   or
   If you're going to build a cumulative frame animation sequence in another application by adding objects in succession, choose **Release to Layers (Build) 3**. The bottommost layer will contain only the bottommost object; the next layer above that will contain the bottommost object plus the next object above it; the next layer above that will contain the two previous objects plus the next object above it, and so on.

➤ If you release a layer or sublayer that contains a clipping mask that you created via the Layers panel, the clipping mask will remain in effect.

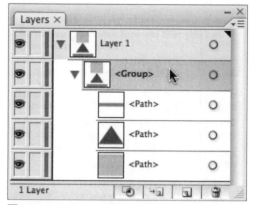

1 *A **group** listing is selected on the Layers panel.*

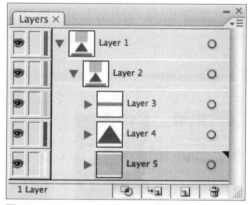

2 *We could choose the **Release to Layers (Sequence)** command...*

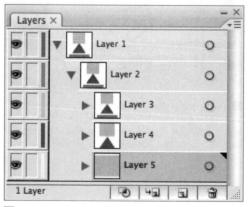

3 *...or the **Release to Layers (Build)** command.*

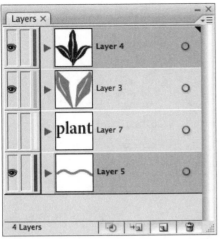

1 *Select the layers, sublayers, groups, or objects that you want to merge.*

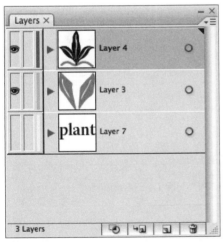

2 *The **Merge Selected** command merged the two selected layers into one.*

➤ If you release a layer or group that contains a scatter brush, the brush object will remain as a single <Path>. If you click just the object listing that contains the brush and release it to layers, each object in the scatter brush will be moved to a separate layer; the original scatter brush path will be preserved.

Merging layers and groups

If the number of layers and sublayers on the Layers panel gets unwieldly, you can consolidate them at any time via the **Merge Selected** command. Unlike the Flatten Artwork command, which flattens a whole document (see the next page), the Merge Selected command merges just the two or more listings that you select.

You can also merge two or more groups, or merge a group with a sublayer, provided they're both on the same top-level layer. In the latter case, the objects will be ungrouped and placed on the sublayer. You can't merge an object with another object.

Note: To preserve a copy of your file, with its layers intact, use File > Save As before applying the Merge Selected command.

To merge layers, sublayers, or groups:

1. As you Cmd-click/Ctrl-click the listings for two or more layers, sublayers, or groups, click last of all on the listing that you want to merge the selected items into **1**. You can merge locked and/or hidden layers.

2. Choose **Merge Selected** from the Layers panel menu **2**.

➤ If you created a clipping mask for a layer via the Layers panel that you want to preserve, select that layer last and merge the other layers into it.

Flattening artwork

The **Flatten Artwork** command reduces a document to one top-level layer, with sublayers and groups nested inside it. Objects remain fully editable. If your document contains any hidden top-level layers when you choose this command, you can opt via an alert dialog box to keep the hidden artwork (click No), or allow the hidden layers to be discarded (click Yes).

Note: If you want to preserve a copy of your file, with its layers intact, use File > Save As before applying the Flatten Artwork command.

To flatten artwork:

1. Redisplay any hidden top-level layers that you want to keep **1**.

2. By default, if no layers are selected, the Flatten Artwork command merges all the currently visible layers into whichever top-level layer has the Current Layer indicator. To flatten the document into a layer of your choice, click it now.

3. Choose **Flatten Artwork** from the Layers panel menu. If the document contains artwork on hidden layers, an alert dialog box will appear **2**–**3**. Click Yes to discard the hidden artwork or click No to preserve it; both options produce a flattened file. (You can undo this command.)

➤ If you click a layer that contains appearances before choosing the Flatten Artwork command, those appearances will be applied to all the objects in your document.

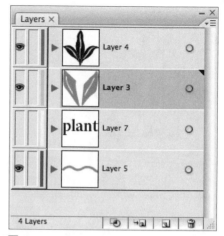

1 *One of the layers in this file is hidden and contains artwork, so an alert dialog box will appear when we choose the* **Flatten Artwork** *command.*

2 *It's always nice to get a second chance.*

3 *We clicked Yes, so the* **Flatten Artwork** *command flattened the artwork into the selected layer (Layer 3) and discarded the hidden layer.*

Flatten Artwork

This chapter is an introduction to Illustrator's type tools. First you'll learn how to create point type, type in a rectangle, area type (inside an object), and type along a path. Then you'll learn how to rotate type, import type from another application, thread type between objects, copy type and a type object, and convert type into graphic outlines. In the next chapter, you'll learn how to select type and change its typographic attributes.

The Type tool creates point type or type inside a rectangle.

1 *Type created with the **Type** tool*

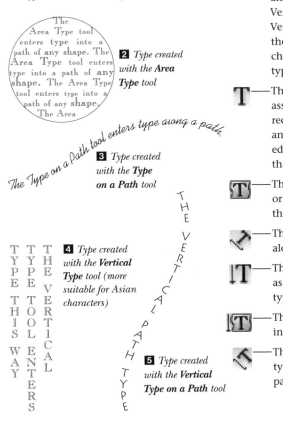

2 *Type created with the **Area Type** tool*

3 *Type created with the **Type on a Path** tool*

4 *Type created with the **Vertical Type** tool (more suitable for Asian characters)*

5 *Type created with the **Vertical Type on a Path** tool*

The type tools

There are three **horizontal** type tools: the Type tool, Area Type tool, and Type on a Path tool; and three equivalent **vertical** type tools: the Vertical Type tool, Vertical Area Type tool, and Vertical Type on a Path tool. Although some of their functions overlap, each tool has unique characteristics for producing a particular kind of type object.

The Type tool creates a block of type that isn't associated with a path **1**. You can also draw a rectangle with it and enter type inside the rectangle, or you can use it to enter type along the edge of an open path or inside a closed path. It's the most versatile of all the type tools.

The **Area Type** tool creates type inside an open or closed path. Lines of type that are created with this tool automatically wrap inside the path **2**.

The **Type on a Path** tool creates a line of type along the outer edge of an open or closed path **3**.

The **Vertical Type** tool has the same function as the Type tool, except that it creates vertical type **4**.

The **Vertical Area Type** tool creates vertical type inside an open or closed path.

The **Vertical Type on a Path** tool creates vertical type along the outer edge of an open or closed path **5**.

Creating point type

Point type stands by itself — it's neither inside an object nor along a path. This kind of type is appropriate for small amounts of text that stand independently, such as headlines, titles, button names, and the like.

To create point type:

1. Choose the **Type** tool (T) **T** or **Vertical Type** tool. **IT**

2. Click a blank area of the artboard where you want the type to start (don't click an object). A flashing insertion marker will appear.

3. Enter type. Press Return/Enter each time you want to start a new line **1**.

4. Choose a **selection** tool on the Tools panel (don't use a keyboard shortcut to select the tool), then click outside the type block to deselect it.

   or

   Click the **type** tool again to complete the type block and start another one.

➤ To align separate blocks of point type, use the align buttons on the Control panel or the Align panel (see pages 95–96).

➤ If you open a file containing text from a non-CS version of Illustrator into CS3, an alert dialog box will appear, offering you choices for updating the older, legacy text.

Choose type attributes before?

If you want to choose character and paragraph attributes for your type before creating it, you can choose from a variety of settings on the **Character** and **Paragraph** panels; or choose font, point size, and paragraph alignment settings from the **Control** panel; or even click a paragraph style on the **Paragraph Styles** panel. You'll learn about these panels in depth in the next chapter.

Recolor after?

When you enter type inside an object or along a path, a fill and stroke of None is applied to the object automatically. After entering type, if you want to apply fill and/or stroke colors to the type **object**, deselect it, click the edge of the object with the Direct Selection tool, then choose a color. To recolor the **type** itself, select it first with a type tool or a selection tool.

I DON'T KNOW THE KEY TO SUCCESS, BUT THE KEY TO FAILURE IS TRYING TO PLEASE EVERYBODY.

Bill Cosby

1 *Point type created with the **Type** tool*

No going back

Once you place type inside or along a graphic object, it becomes a **type object**; it can be converted back into a graphic object only via the Undo command. To preserve the original graphic object, Option-drag/Alt-drag it to copy it, then use the copy as a type object. You can't enter type into a compound path, a mask object, a mesh object, or a blend, nor can you make a compound path from a type object. If you create type on a path that has a brush stroke, the brush stroke will be removed.

> 'It spoils people's clothes to squeeze under a gate; the proper way to get in, is to climb down a pear tree.'
>
> **Beatrix Potter**

1 *Drag with the **Type** tool to create a rectangle, then enter type. To see the edges of the rectangle, choose Outline view or use smart guides with the Object Highlighting option.*

```
A  C
P  L
E  I
A  M
R  B
   
T  D
R  O
E  W
E  N
.  .
   .
```

'It spoils
people's
clothes to
squeeze
under a
gate; the
proper
way to
get in,
is to climb
down a
pear tree.'

2 *Drag with the **Vertical Type** tool, then enter type. The type will flow from top to bottom and from right to left.*

3 *After reshaping a type rectangle using the **Direct Selection** tool*

Creating type in a rectangle

In the instructions below, you'll draw a **rectangle**, then enter type into it. On the next page, you'll learn how to enter type inside an existing object of any shape.

To create type in a rectangle:

1. Choose the **Type** tool (T) **T** or **Vertical Type** tool. **T**

2. Drag to create a rectangle (or Shift-drag to draw a square). When you release the mouse, a flashing insertion marker will appear.

3. Enter type **1**–**2**. The type will wrap automatically to fit into the rectangle. Press Return/Enter only when you need to create a new paragraph.

4. Choose a **selection** tool on the Tools panel (don't use a keyboard shortcut to select the tool), then click outside the type block to deselect it.
   or
   To keep the **type** tool selected so you can create other separate type rectangles, hold down Cmd/Ctrl (to access the last-used selection tool temporarily), click outside the type block to deselect it, release Cmd/Ctrl, then drag to start the next type block. You can also complete a type object by clicking the type tool.

   Note: If the overflow symbol appears on the edge of the rectangle (a tiny red + in a square), it means the rectangle isn't large enough to display all the type. If you want to reveal the hidden type, deselect the rectangle, then reshape it using the Direct Selection tool. You can use smart guides (with Object Highlighting) to locate the edge of the rectangle. The type will reflow to fit the new shape **3**. Another option is to thread the overflow type into another object, which we show you how to do on page 219.

➤ To create vertical type with the Type tool or horizontal type with the Vertical Type tool, hold down Shift, start dragging to create a rectangle, release Shift, then continue dragging to complete the rectangle; enter text.

Type in a Rectangle

Creating area type

When you use the **Area Type** or **Vertical Area Type** tool to place type inside a path of any shape or inside an open path, the object is converted to a type object.

To enter type inside an object:

1. *Optional:* Drag-copy the object if you want to preserve the original.

2. To enter type in a closed path, choose the **Area Type** tool ⊤, **Vertical Area Type** tool ⊤, or either one of the **Type** tools (**T** or **IT**). To enter type inside an open path, choose either one of the Area Type tools.

3. Click precisely on the edge of the path. A flashing insertion marker will appear, and any fill or stroke on the object will be removed. The object will now be listed as <Type> (not <Path>) on the Layers panel.

4. Enter type in the path, or copy and paste text from a text-editing application into the path. The text will stay inside the object and conform to its shape **1**–**2**. Vertical area type flows from top to bottom and from right to left.

   ➤ To make the type fit well inside the object, choose a small point size, and on the Paragraph panel, turn on hyphenation and click one of the Justify alignment buttons.

5. Choose a **selection** tool, then click outside the type object to deselect it.
   or
   To keep the **type** tool selected (so as to enter type in another object), Cmd-click/Ctrl-click away from the type block to deselect it, release Cmd/Ctrl, then click the next type object; or click again on the tool that you used to enter the type.

   ➤ The Area Type Options, which control the position of type inside a type object, are discussed on pages 247–248.

discussed on pages 247–248.

Switcheroo

To rotate **vertical** area type characters, select only the characters that you want to convert. On the Control panel, click the word Character, then from the Character panel menu, choose Standard Vertical Roman Alignment to uncheck that option. (To rotate horizontal or vertical type characters on a custom angle, see page 217.)

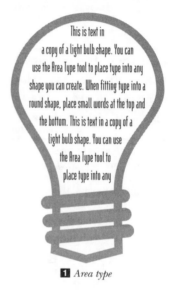

This is text in a copy of a light bulb shape. You can use the Area Type tool to place type into any shape you can create. When fitting type into a round shape, place small words at the top and the bottom. This is text in a copy of a light bulb shape. You can use the Area Type tool to place type into any

1 *Area type*

The kiss of memory made pictures of love and light against the wall. Here was peace. She pulled in her horizon like a great fish-net. Pulled it from around the waist of the world and draped it over her shoulder. So much of life in its meshes! She called in her soul to come and see.
ZORA NEALE HURSTON

2 *Type in a circle*

Area Type

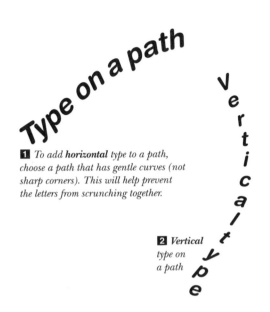

1 *To add **horizontal** type to a path, choose a path that has gentle curves (not sharp corners). This will help prevent the letters from scrunching together.*

2 *Vertical type on a path*

These icons appear next to the pointer when it's moved over a bracket on a selected type path:

Center bracket

Left bracket **Right bracket**

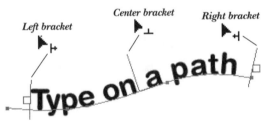

3 *The left, center, or right brackets are visible when **path type** is selected with the **Selection** or **Direct Selection** tool.*

4 *The **left bracket** is being dragged to the right.*

5 *The type has been moved to the right.*

Creating path type

Follow these instructions to place type along the inner or outer **edge** of a **path**. Type can't be placed on both sides of the same path, but it can be moved from one side to the other once you create it.

To place type along an object's path:

1. Choose the **Type on a Path** ⬩ or **Vertical Type on a Path** tool ⬩, then click the edge of a closed path. Or choose the **Type** T or **Vertical Type** IT tool, then click an open path. The path can be selected, but it doesn't have to be.

2. When the flashing insertion marker appears, enter type. Don't press Return/Enter. The type will appear along the edge of the object, and the object will now have a fill and stroke of None **1**–**2**.

3. Choose a **selection** tool (or hold down Cmd/Ctrl), then click outside the type object to deselect it.
    or
    If you want to use the same tool on another path, click the tool again.

To reposition type on a path:

1. Choose the **Selection** tool ⬩ (V) or **Direct Selection** ⬩ tool (A).

2. Click on the type. Center, left, and right brackets will appear **3**.

3. As you do any of the following, be sure to drag the bracket (the vertical bar)—not the little square! If your tool switches to a type tool, choose a selection tool and try again.

    Drag the **center** bracket to the left or right to reposition the type block along the path.

    Drag the **left** bracket **4**–**5** to reposition the starting point of the type on the path. Or drag the **right** bracket back across the existing type; this will shorten the amount of type that's visible on the path and may produce a type overflow. (For right-aligned type, do the opposite of the above.)

    To **flip** the type to the other side of an open path, drag the center bracket across to the other side of the path.

You can change the shape, orientation, and alignment of type on a path quickly via the **Type on a Path Options** dialog box. These settings are editable and reversible.

To apply options to path type:

1. Choose the **Selection** tool, then click type on a path (the more curvy the path, the more obvious the change in options will be).

2. Choose Type > Type on a Path > **Type on a Path Options.** The Type on a Path Options dialog box opens (**1**, next page).

3. Check Preview.

4. Do any of the following:

   From the **Effect** pop-up menu, choose **Rainbow, Skew, 3D Ribbon, Stair Step,** or **Gravity** **1**.

   Choose **Align to Path: Ascender, Descender, Center,** or **Baseline** to specify which part of the text will touch the path (**2**, next page).

   Check (or uncheck) **Flip.**

   Choose or enter a new letter **Spacing** value (–36 to 36). To avoid a text reflow, we recommend either leaving this option at the default value of 0 or changing it in very small increments.

5. Click OK. If you want to change or reverse any of the settings you've chosen, reselect the object and reopen the dialog box.

➤ Individual type effects can also be applied via the Type > Type on a Path submenu.

Rainbow effect

Skew effect

3D Ribbon effect

Stair Step effect

Gravity effect

1 *The* **Type on a Path** *effects change the shape and spacing of characters on a path.*

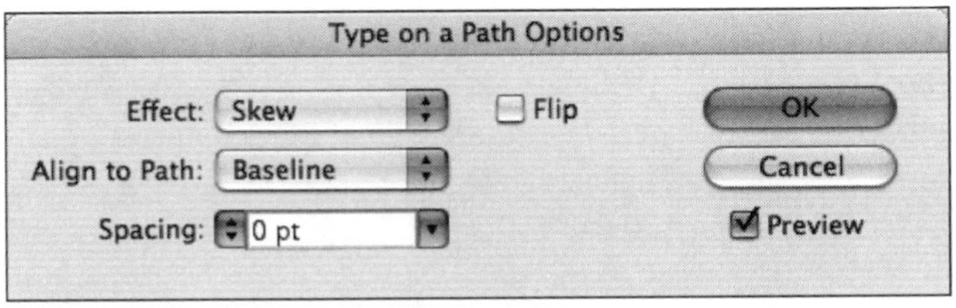

Type on a Path Options

Effect: Skew

Align to Path: Baseline

Spacing: 0 pt

☐ Flip

OK

Cancel

☑ Preview

1 *Use the* **Type on a Path Options** *dialog box to choose effect, alignment, orientation, and spacing options for type on a path.*

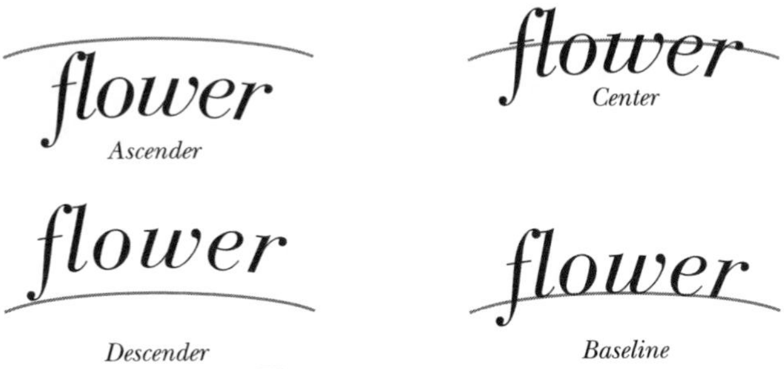

flower
Ascender

flower
Center

flower
Descender

flower
Baseline

2 *Align to Path options*

wild world

3 *The original type*

4 *Some characters in these words were rotated individually (using different rotation values).*

5 *The kerning was adjusted.*

Rotating type

To rotate type characters on a custom angle:

1. Select the type object with the Selection tool, or select a type character or characters with a type tool.

2. On the Character panel **A** (Cmd-T/Ctrl-T), choose or enter a positive or negative **Character Rotation** value ✿ **3**–**4**.

➤ After rotating type, you may need to adjust the spacing between the characters **5** (see page 232).

To make a whole horizontal type block vertical, or vice versa:

1. Choose the **Selection** tool, ↖ then click a type block.

2. Choose Type > Type Orientation > **Horizontal** or **Vertical**.

Importing text

Using the **Place** command, you can **import text files** in the following formats into an Illustrator document: plain text, or ASCII format (with the filename suffix .txt); Rich Text Format (.rtf); or Microsoft Word format (.doc or .docx). The text will appear in a new rectangle.

Note: To put text onto or into a custom path, first place it by following the instructions on this page, then copy and paste it onto or into the path (see "To move type from one object to another" on page 221).

To import text:

1. Choose File > **Place.** The Place dialog box opens.

2. Locate and click the text file that you want to import, then click **Place.**

3. For a Microsoft Word or RTF file, the Microsoft Word Options dialog box will open 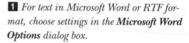. For a plain text format file, the Text Import Options dialog box will open **2**.

Decide which options you want to include. For Microsoft Word or RTF text, if you want to preserve any text styling, be sure to leave Remove Text Formatting unchecked. The plain text format (called Text Only in Microsoft Word) removes formatting and styling.

4. Click OK. The imported text will appear in a rectangle **3**. To restyle it, see the next chaper. To thread overflow type, see the next page.

➤ To create columns and rows of type, see pages 247–248.

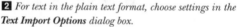

1 *For text in Microsoft Word or RTF format, choose settings in the* **Microsoft Word Options** *dialog box.*

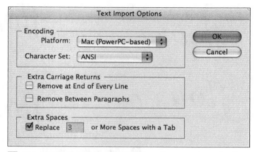

2 *For text in the plain text format, choose settings in the* **Text Import Options** *dialog box.*

May the day come (soon perhaps) when I'll flee to the woods on an island in Oceania, there to live on ecstasy, calm, and art. With a new family by my side, far from this European scramble for money. There, in Tahiti, in the silence of the beautiful tropical nights, I will be able to listen to the soft murmuring music of the movements of my heart in amorous harmony with the mysterious beings around me. Free at last, without financial worries and able to love, sing, and die. *Paul Gauguin*

3 **Placed** *text appears in a rectangle.*

Import Text

In port

Here was peace. She pulled in her horizon like a great fish-net. Pulled it from around the waist of the world and draped it over her

Out port

1 *To thread text, first click the **Out** port with the Selection tool...*

Here was peace. She pulled in her horizon like a great fish-net. Pulled it from around the waist of the world and draped it over her

2 *...then drag (or click) elsewhere with the **Loaded Text** pointer.*

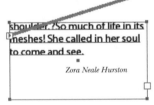

Here was peace. She pulled in her horizon like a great fish-net. Pulled it from around the waist of the world and draped it over her

shoulder. ?So much of life in its meshes! She called in her soul to come and see.

Zora Neale Hurston

3 *The overflow type spills from the first object into the second, in the direction shown by the **thread** arrowheads.*

Not all is copied

If you click to create a **duplicate** of a type object (step 4 on this page), only the object's shape will be copied, not its fill and stroke attributes or area type options. To copy the attributes afterward, choose the Direct Selection tool, click the edge of the duplicate object, choose the Eyedropper tool (I), then click the background of the original text object. Before you click with the Eyedropper, make sure the pointer doesn't have a little "t."

Threading type

Before we explore threading, the process of linking overflow text between text objects, consider this simple solution: If your type object is almost — but not quite — large enough to display all the type on or inside it, you can enlarge the object to reveal the hidden type by doing either of the following:

➤ Click the type block with the **Selection** tool, then drag a handle on its **bounding box** (choose View > Show Bounding Box if the box isn't visible).

➤ Select only the rectangle — not the type — with the **Direct Selection** tool (turn on Smart Guides with Object Highlighting or put the file into Outline view to locate the rectangle), then **Shift-drag** a segment.

If your type overfloweth, you can spill, or **thread**, it into a different object or into a copy of the same object. Text can be threaded between path objects and area type objects.

To thread overflow type to another object:

1. Choose the **Selection** tool (V).

2. Select the original type object.

3. Click the **Out** port ⊞ on the selected object. The pointer will turn into a Loaded Text pointer ⊞ **1**.

4. To create a **new** object for the overflow text, either click where you want a duplicate of the currently selected text object to appear, or drag to create a rectangular type object **2**–**3**.
or
Position the pointer over an **existing** object — the pointer will change to ⊞ — then click the object's path. A fill and stroke of None will be applied to the path.

Overflow type from the first object will flow into the second one.

5. Deselect the objects.

➤ If you double-click an Out port with the Selection tool, a linked copy of the text object will be created automatically.

Thread Type

If you're curious to see what's threaded to what, you can **display** the **text threads**.

To display text threads:

Select a linked type object. If the thread lines aren't visible, choose View > **Show Text Threads** (Cmd-Shift-Y/Ctrl-Shift-Y). *Note:* The stacking order of type objects on the Layers panel has no impact on how text flows from one object to another.

When you **unthread two objects,** you break the chain and the overflow text gets sucked back into the first object of the two. Both objects are preserved.

To unthread two type objects:

1. Choose the **Selection** tool (V), then click a threaded type object.

2. Double-click the object's **In** port or **Out** port **1**–**2**.
   or
   Click an **In** port or **Out** port, move the pointer slightly (the Unthread cursor displays), then click the port again to cut the thread.

Follow these instructions if you want to keep the remaining links intact as you **release one object** from a **thread**. The type will reflow.

To release an object from a thread and preserve the remaining threads:

1. Choose the **Selection** tool (V), then click the type object to be released **3**.

2. To unthread the object but also preserve it, choose Type > Threaded Text > **Release Selection 4**.
   or
   To unthread the type object by deleting it, press **Delete/Backspace.**

➤ To disconnect threaded objects from one another but keep the type where it is, click a threaded type object with the Selection tool, then choose Type > Threaded Text > Remove Threading.

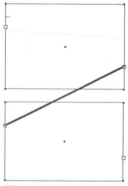

1 *When the Out port is double-clicked…*

2 *…that type object becomes* ***unthreaded.***

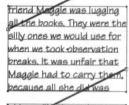

3 *The middle type object is selected…*

4 *…and then* ***released*** *from the thread.*

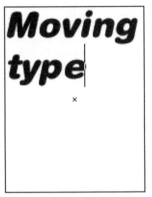

1 *Point type is **selected**, put onto the Clipboard via Edit > **Cut**...*

2 *...and then **pasted** into a rectangle.*

Copying and moving type

To **copy** or **move type** with or without its object, you can use the Clipboard, a temporary storage area in memory. The Clipboard commands are Cut, Copy, and Paste. (You can also copy a type object by using the methods discussed on pages 92–93.) You can copy type between Illustrator files, or from an Illustrator file to a Photoshop file.

To copy type and its object between files:

1. Choose the **Selection** tool (V).

2. Click the type you want to copy, or click the edge of the type object.

3. Choose Edit > **Copy** (Cmd-C/Ctrl-C).

4. Click in another Illustrator document window, then choose Edit > **Paste** (Cmd-V/Ctrl-V). The type and its object will appear.
   or
   Click in a Photoshop document window, choose Edit > **Paste** (Cmd-V/Ctrl-V), click **Smart Object**, then click OK. The type and object will appear as imagery on a new Smart Object layer (see page 415).

➤ If you copy a threaded text object, only that object and the text it contains will be copied.

To move type from one object to another:

1. Choose the **Type** tool **T** or **Vertical Type** !T tool.

2. Select (drag across) the type that you want to move **1**. Or to move all the text in a thread, click in one of the objects, then choose Select > **All** (Cmd-A/Ctrl-A).

3. Choose Edit > **Cut** (Cmd-X/Ctrl-X). The object you cut the type from will remain a type object.

4. Cmd-click/Ctrl-click the object you want to paste into, then click the edge of the object. A blinking insertion marker will appear. (Or to create path type, Option-click/Alt-click the object).
   or
   Drag to create a type rectangle.

5. Choose Edit > **Paste** (Cmd-V/Ctrl-V) **2**.

221

Creating type outlines

The **Create Outlines** command converts each character in a type object into a separate graphic object. As outlines, the paths can then be reshaped, used in a compound or as a mask, or filled with a gradient or mesh, like nontype objects.

Before proceeding, a word of caution: once type is converted into outlines, unless you undo the conversion immediately, you won't be able to change the font, apply other typographic attributes, or convert the outlines back into type. For this reason, we recommend converting a duplicate of a type object instead of the original.

To create type outlines:

1. Create type using any type tool, and duplicate it, if desired. All the characters in the type object or on the path will be converted, so enter only the text that you want to convert.

2. Choose the **Selection** tool (V).

3. If the type isn't already selected, click a character or the baseline.

4. Choose Type > **Create Outlines** (Cmd-Shift-O/Ctrl-Shift-O) **1**–**3**. Or Control-click/right-click the object and choose Create Outlines from the context menu.

   The fill and stroke attributes and any appearances from the original characters will be applied to the outlines. If the type was on or in an object, the object will be preserved as a separate entity—unless it had a stroke and fill of None, in which case it will be deleted.

   You can now reshape the points and segments on each object (see Chapter 11).

➤ Type characters become separate compound paths when converted to outlines. If any of the characters you convert had an interior shape (known as a "counter")—as in an "A" or a "P"—those outer and inner shapes will also form a compound path. To release the compound into separate objects, choose Object > Compound Path > Release. To reassemble the parts at any time into a compound path, select them, then choose Object > Compound Path > Make.

Let the converter beware

For creating **custom characters,** such as logos, the Create Outlines command is invaluable; plus, outlines can be printed from any application without printer fonts. However, we don't recommend using this command on small type, for the following reasons. First, it removes the hinting information that preserves character shapes for printing; second, because outline shapes are slightly heavier than their nonoutline counterparts, the characters will be less legible (especially if a stroke color is applied to them); and third, outlines increase the file size.

1 *The original type*

2 *The type is converted into **outlines**.*

3 *The outlines were reshaped in the areas indicated by the arrows, and filled with a gradient.*

Type Outlines

Don't space out!

If you press the Spacebar to access a temporary Hand tool when your cursor is in a type block (a type tool is selected), you'll end up adding spaces to your text instead of moving the artwork in the window. Worse yet, if type is selected, you'll end up replacing your text with spaces. Instead, to access a temporary Hand tool, press Cmd/Ctrl, then add the Spacebar, move the mouse, release Cmd/Ctrl, then drag with the Spacebar still held down. Practice until you get the hang of it.

And another thing: When editing type, keep track of the pointer. If it's in a panel field, you'll edit panel values instead of your type!

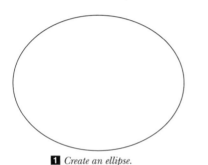

1 *Create an ellipse.*

2 *Create path type at the top of the inner ellipse. The ellipse will have a stroke of None.*

Exercise

Putting type on both sides of an ellipse, and having all of it read vertically, requires creating two ellipses.

Type on an ellipse
Type on the top

1. Choose File > Document Setup > **Artboard** (Cmd-Option-P/Ctrl-Alt-P), choose Units: **Inches,** then click OK.

2. Using the Control panel, make the fill color None and the stroke color black.

3. Choose the **Ellipse** tool (L), then click on the artboard (don't drag). The Ellipse dialog box opens.

4. Enter "3.6" in the **Width** field, enter "2.8" in the **Height** field, then click OK **1**.

5. Double-click the **Scale** tool. Enter "70" in the **Uniform: Scale** field, then click **Copy**. Deselect.

6. Choose the **Type on a Path** tool.

7. On the Control panel, click **Character** to open the Character panel, enter "24" in the **Size** field and "150" in the **Horizontal Scale** field, and choose a font.

8. Click the top of the inner ellipse, then type the desired text (*"type on top,"* in our example) **2**.

9. Click the **Selection** tool, then drag the center bracket (it's near the bottom of the circle) along the outside of the ellipse to reposition the type. Be aware that the left and right brackets are practically on top of each other near the starting point of the type. Don't move the left bracket over the right bracket, or you may cause a text overflow. If you like, you can move the right bracket slightly away from the left bracket.

Type on the bottom

1. With the smaller ellipse selected, double-click the **Selection** tool. In the Move dialog box, enter "0" in the Horizontal field and "–0.1" in the **Vertical** field, then click **Copy**.

(Continued on the following page)

2. Drag the center bracket into the copy of the ellipse (which should still be selected). The type will now be positioned on the inside of the ellipse **1**.

3. Double-click the bottom type with the Selection tool (the Type tool will be chosen automatically), select the type, enter the desired text, then click the Selection tool.

Click the type on the bottom to reveal the center bracket, then move the center bracket to center the type **2**.

4. On the **Layers** panel, ⬤ click and then Shift-click the selection area of each type object to select both of them.

5. *Optional:* To recolor the type, apply a fill color and a stroke of None to the selected type objects.

6. Choose Type > Type on a Path > **Gravity** to slant the type for better orientation on the ellipse. (The Rainbow options would work better on a circle.)

7. Choose Object > **Group** (Cmd-G/Ctrl-G). (To recolor either ellipse path now, you would need to select it first with the Direct Selection tool.)

8. *Optional:* To produce the artwork as shown in **3**, choose the Ellipse tool (L), click to the left of center of the current type objects, enter "1" for the Width and ".75" for the Height, then click OK. Choose the Selection tool (V), then drag the new ellipse into the center of the type objects. On the Control panel, click the Style thumbnail, then from the Graphic Styles Libraries menu on the Graphic Styles panel, choose Type Effects. On the library panel that opens, click the Neon graphic style. (To learn more about graphic styles, see Chapter 20.)

➤ With no type selected, set the Horizontal Scale on the Character panel back to zero to prevent the scale value from being applied to subsequently created type.

➤ To select either one of the type blocks, click its selection area on the Layers panel; or select it manually (use smart guides).

1 *Use the Move dialog box to copy the type object, then drag the center bracket into the ellipse.*

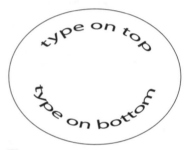

2 *Select the type on the bottom of the ellipse and type the words that you want to appear there. Center the type at the bottom of its ellipse.*

3 *For the inner circle, we created another ellipse and applied the Neon graphic style. You could create a graphic or import an image instead.*

Exercise: Type on an Ellipse

STYLE & EDIT TYPE

In this chapter, you'll learn how to select type for editing. Then you'll learn how to use the Character and Control panels to apply typographic attributes, such as a font, point size, and leading; the Glyphs and OpenType panels to insert special characters; the Paragraph panel to apply paragraph formats, such as alignment and indentation; and the Paragraph Styles and Character Styles panels to apply collections of attributes quickly. At the end of the chapter, you'll choose area type options, hang punctuation, set tabs, wrap type around an object, and perform a few practice exercises.

Selecting type

Before you can modify type, you have to select it. On the next two pages, we'll show you how to select type with these tools:

➤ The **Selection** tool selects both the type and its object **1**.

➤ The **Direct Selection** tool can be used to select just the type object, or both the type object and the type **2**.

➤ The **type** tools can be used to select only the type, not the type object **3**.

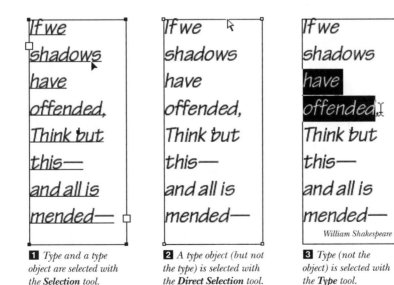

1 *Type and a type object are selected with the **Selection** tool.*

2 *A type object (but not the type) is selected with the **Direct Selection** tool.*

3 *Type (not the object) is selected with the **Type** tool.*

Use the selection method described below if you're going to move, transform, restyle, or recolor **all the type** in or on a type object. To reshape or recolor a type object (not the type), use the first selection method on the next page instead. Or to edit, restyle, or recolor just some of the type in a block, use the second selection method on the next page.

To select type and its object:

1. Choose the **Selection** tool (V).

2. Turn on **smart guides** (Cmd-U/Ctrl-U), and make sure Object Highlighting is on in Preferences > Smart Guides & Slices.

3. For **area** type (inside an object):

   If the object has a fill (other than None), you can click anywhere on the object: the fill, a character, the baseline, or the outer path. Otherwise, click the type **1** or, using smart guides with Object Highlighting on, click the path of the type object **2**–**3**.

   For **point** or **path** type:

   Click on the type, or, for path type, you can also click the path **4**. If the bounding box is visible (View > Show Bounding Box), you'll also see a bounding box around the object.

➤ If you select a threaded type object, all the other objects in the connecting thread will also become selected (see page 219).

➤ To change the paint attributes of type, use the Color panel (see the sidebar on page 212).

➤ To move, scale, rotate, shear, or reflect type, use either a command on the Object > Transform submenu or a transform tool.

Quick-select a type tool

If you double-click a type character in a type object with the Selection or Direct Selection tool, the **Type** tool (or Vertical Type tool) will become selected automatically and an insertion point will appear where you clicked.

Appearances and type

You might find the relationship between type color and appearances to be confusing at first. If you select a type object with the **Selection** tool, "Type" will be listed at the top of the Appearance panel and "Characters" will be listed as an attribute.

If you highlight text characters using a **type** tool or if you double-click the word "**Characters**" on the Appearance panel, the Stroke and Fill attributes for those characters will be listed on the panel. If you want to redisplay the attributes for the type object, click the word "**Type**." To learn more about the Appearance panel, see Chapter 20. To work with type color and appearances, see pages 266–267, and also page 341.

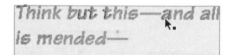

1 *To select type and its object, click right on the* **type** *(in this illustration, smart guides are on)…*

2 *…or click the* **path** *of the type object.*

3 *The* **type** *and* **type object** *are selected.*

4 *Point type is selected.*

Insert or delete

To **add** characters to an existing type block, choose a type tool, click to create an insertion point, then start typing.

To **delete** one character at a time, choose a type tool, click to the right of the character you want to delete, then press Delete/Backspace. Or to delete multiple characters, select them with a type tool first, then press Delete/Backspace.

Think but this—and all is mended—

1 *The **type object** is selected; the type is not.*

Think but this— and all is mended—

2 *The type object is reshaped and recolored.*

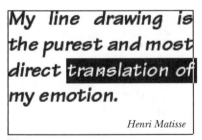

My line drawing is the purest and most direct translation of my emotion.

Henri Matisse

3 ***Two words*** *are selected.*

Use this selection method if you want to recolor or reshape just the **type object.**

To select a type object but not the type:

1. Choose the **Direct Selection** tool (A).

2. Click the **edge** of an area or path type object **1**. Use smart guides (with Object Highlighting on) to assist you. Now modifications you make will affect only the type object—not the type **2**.

Use this selection method to select only the **type**—not the object—so you can edit the text or change its character, paragraph, or paint attributes.

To select type but not its object:

1. Choose any **type** tool.

2. For horizontal type, drag horizontally with the I-beam cursor to select and highlight a **word** or a **line** of type **3**. For vertical type, drag vertically.
   or
   For horizontal type, drag vertically to select whole **lines** of type. For vertical type, drag horizontally to select lines.
   or
   Double-click to select a **word.**
   or
   Triple-click to select a **paragraph.**
   or
   Click in the text block, then choose Select > **All** (Cmd-A/Ctrl-A) to select all the type in the block or on the path, plus any other type that it's threaded to.
   or
   Click to start a **selection**, then Shift-click where you want it to stop. (Shift-click again, if desired, to extend the selection.)

3. After modifying the type:
   Click **in** the type block to create a new insertion point for further editing.
   or
   Cmd-click/Ctrl-click **outside** the type object to deselect it.

➤ If you recolor type with smart guides on and text characters highlighted, choose a selection tool afterward so you can see how the new color looks.

Character, Paragraph, Control Panels

The Character, Paragraph, and Control panels

In this section, we'll show you how to use the Character, Paragraph, and Control panels to apply type attributes. Later in this chapter, we'll show you how to use the Character Styles and Paragraph Styles panels to apply a collection of attributes. First, a brief introduction to the panels.

To modify font, style, point size, kerning, leading, and tracking values for one or more selected text characters, you'll use the **Character** panel A **1** (press Cmd-T/Ctrl-T to open the panel, or if a type object is selected, click Character on the Control panel). To access horizontal scale, baseline shift, vertical scale, character rotation, underline, strike-through, and language options, choose Show Options from the panel menu or click the up/down arrow ⇕ on the panel tab twice.

To modify paragraph attributes, such as alignment and indentation, use the **Paragraph** panel ¶ **2** (press Cmd-Option-T/Ctrl-Alt-T, or if a type object is selected, click Paragraph on the Control panel). To access the Space Before Paragraph, Space After Paragraph, and hyphenation options, choose Show Options from the panel menu or click the up/down arrow ⇕ on the panel tab twice.

You can also use the **Control** panel to change the font, point size, and alignment of type.

To summarize what you learned on the previous two pages: to change the paragraph attributes of all the text in a type object or on a path, select the object or path with the Selection tool; or to change the attributes of one or more consecutive paragraphs, select them with a type tool. (A discussion of the options that affect whole paragraphs begins on page 240; on that page, you'll also learn how to create paragraph breaks and soft returns.)

➤ When a type tool and type are selected, point size, font, and tracking info about the type is listed on the Info panel. ⓘ

1 On the **Character** panel, as on other panels, you can use tool tips to identify unfamiliar features.

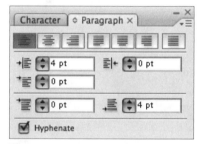

2 Options on the **Paragraph** panel affect whole paragraphs, not individual characters.

Panel shortcuts

You can use these shortcuts when entering values on the Character and Paragraph panels:

Apply value and highlight **next** field	Tab
Apply value and highlight **previous** field	Shift-Tab
Apply value and **exit** panel	Return/Enter
Highlight the **Font** field on the Character panel	Cmd-Option-Shift-M/ Ctrl-Alt-Shift-M

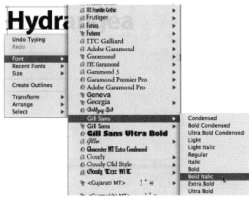

1 *Select the type you want to modify, then choose a **font** from the context menu.*

Hydrangea

2 *The **font** and **font style** were changed from Myriad Pro Bold to Gill Sans Bold Italic.*

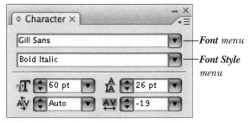

3 *The font options on the Character **panel***

4 *The **Font** and **Font Style** options are also available on the **Control** panel.*

> You must learn to be <u>still</u> in the midst of activity and to be vibrantly ~~alive~~ in repose.
> — *Indira Gandhi*

5 *You may also find an occasional use for **underline** and **strikethrough** type styling.*

Changing fonts

To change fonts:

1. Choose any **type** tool, then select the type you want to modify.
   or
   Choose the **Selection** tool, then click the type object.

2. Control-click/right-click the type and choose a font from the **Font** submenu **1**–**2** or **Recent Fonts** submenu on the context menu.
   or
   On the **Character** panel **3** or the **Control** panel **4**, choose a font from the **Font** menu and a style from the **Font Style** menu.

➤ To choose a font by typing a name, in the Mac OS, press Cmd-Option-Shift-M to select the Font field on the Character panel quickly, or in Windows, click the Font field. Start typing the first few characters of the desired font name and, when the name appears, press Tab. Next, for a style other than Roman (or Regular), start typing the style name in the Font Style field, then press Return/Enter. The name or style with the closest spelling match will appear in the field.

➤ To have font families display in the actual typeface (WYSIWYG) on the Font menu on the Character panel, Control panel, and context menu for type, go to Preferences > Type, check Font Preview, and choose Small, Medium, or Large for the Size.

If you create Web page mock-ups, you might find a use for the **underline** feature.

To apply underline or strikethrough styling:

1. Choose a **type** tool, then select the type you want to apply the underline or strikethrough styling to.

2. On the Character panel (with full options displaying), click the **T** button for **underlining**, or the **T** button for **strikethrough** styling **5**. (Click the same button again to remove the styling.)

229

Changing the point size

To change the point size:

1. Choose any **type** tool, then highlight the type you want to modify.
   or
   Choose the **Selection** tool (V), then click the type object.

2. On the **Character** panel  or the **Control** panel, enter a point size in the **Font Size** field 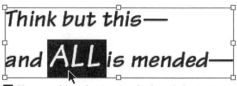; you don't need to reenter the unit of measure. You can also choose a preset size from the Font Size menu; or click the up or down arrow; or click in the Font Size field, then press the up or down arrow on the keyboard.

   ➤ If the selected type contains more than one point size, the Font Size field will be blank, but the new size you enter or choose will apply to all selected type. If you're using the Character panel, you can press Return/Enter to apply the new value and exit the panel, or press Tab to apply the value and highlight the next field.
   or
   Hold down **Cmd-Shift/Ctrl-Shift** and press > to enlarge the point size or < to reduce it . The type will scale according to the current Size/Leading value in Preferences > Type; the default increment is 2 pt. Hold Cmd-Option-Shift/Ctrl-Alt-Shift and press > or < to change the point size by 5 times the current Size/Leading value.
   or
   Control-click/right-click the type and choose a preset size from the **Size** submenu on the context menu. (Choosing Other from the context menu highlights the Font Size field on the Character panel.)

Scaling type interactively

To scale point or path type by **dragging,** select it first with the Selection tool, and make sure the bounding box is visible (if it's not, press Cmd-Shift-B/Ctrl-Shift-B. Drag a handle on the box, or Shift-drag to scale the type proportionally ▮.

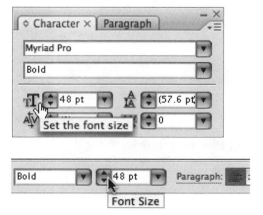

▮ *To scale type proportionally, Shift-drag a handle on its bounding box.*

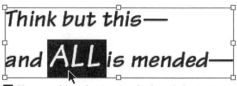

▮ *On the Character or Control panel, enter the desired Font Size, or click the up or down arrow, or choose a preset size from the menu.*

▮ *You can also scale type via a keyboard shortcut.*

1 *On the **Character** panel, enter a **Leading** value, or click the up or down arrow, or choose a preset value from the menu.*

How can one conceive
of a one-party system in
a country that has over
200 varieties of cheese?

— *Charles de Gaulle*

2 *12-pt. type, 18-pt. loose leading*

How can one conceive
of a one-party system in
a country that has over
200 varieties of cheese?

— *Charles de Gaulle*

3 *12-pt. type; 13-pt. tight leading*

Changing leading

Leading, the distance from baseline to baseline between lines of type, is traditionally measured in points. Each line of type can have a different leading value. (To adjust the spacing between paragraphs, see page 242.)

Note: To change the vertical spacing in vertical type, change the horizontal tracking (see the next page). In vertical type, leading controls the horizontal spacing between vertical columns.

To change leading via the Character panel:

1. Select horizontal type:

Click anywhere in a type block with the Selection tool to change the leading of the entire **block**.

or

Select an entire paragraph with a type tool (triple-click in the paragraph) to change the leading of all the lines in the **paragraph**.

or

Select (drag across) an entire line with a type tool, including any spaces at the end, to change the leading of just that **line**.

2. On the **Character** panel, [A] enter a **Leading** value (press Return/Enter or Tab to apply it) **1**–**3**; or choose a preset leading value from the Leading menu; or click the up or down arrow. If you choose Auto from the menu, the leading will be calculated as a percentage of the largest type size on each line. The Auto Leading value can be changed from the default of 120% via the Justification dialog box, which opens from the Paragraph panel menu.

To change leading via the keyboard:

1. Select the type you want to modify, as per step 1, above.

2. Option-press/Alt-press the **up arrow** on the keyboard to decrease the leading or the **down arrow** to increase it by the Size/Leading increment, which is set in Preferences > Type (the default is 2 pt.).

Hold down Cmd-Option/Ctrl-Alt as you press an arrow to change the leading by 5 times the current Size/Leading increment.

Change Leading

Applying kerning and tracking

Kerning is the addition or removal of space between **pairs** of adjacent characters. Kerning values for specific character pairs (e.g., an uppercase "T" next to a lowercase "a") are built into all fonts. The built-in kerning values are usually suitable for small text, such as body type, but not for large type, such as headlines and logos. You can remedy any awkward spacing in large type by applying manual kerning values. To kern a pair of characters, insert the cursor between them first.

Tracking is the simultaneous adjustment of the space between each of **three or more** characters. On occasion, you might apply tracking to a whole line of type, or on a very rare occasion, to a whole paragraph. To apply tracking, you'll highlight some type using a type tool first, or select an entire type block with a selection tool.

To apply manual kerning or tracking:

1. Zoom in on the type that you want to apply kerning or tracking to. Choose a **type** tool, then click to create an insertion point between two characters for kerning, or highlight a range of text for tracking.
or
To track (not kern) all the type in an object, choose the **Selection** tool, then click the object.

2. In the **Kerning** or **Tracking** area on the Character panel **A** **1**, enter a positive value to add space between the characters or a negative value to remove space, then press Return/Enter or Tab **2**–**4**; or choose a preset kerning or tracking amount from the menu; or click the up or down arrow.
or
Hold down Option/Alt and press the right **arrow** on the keyboard to add space between letters or the left arrow to remove space. Space will be added or subtracted by the current Tracking value in Preferences > Type. To kern or track by a larger increment, hold down Cmd-Option/Ctrl-Alt and press an arrow.

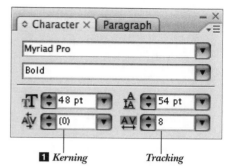

1 *Kerning*   *Tracking*

Simone

2 *The original type has no manual kerning or tracking.*

Simone

3 *Space between the first two characters was removed via **kerning**.*

Simone

4 *And space between the last five characters was removed via **tracking**.*

Auto vs. Optical kerning

Illustrator offers a choice of two types of automatic (nonmanual) kerning. The "all-purpose" default method, **Auto** kerning (or "metrics" kerning), is applied to new or imported text based on the information that is built into each font for kern pairs (such as To, Ta, We, Wo, Yo).

For fonts that have less than adequate or no built-in kerning, or for a line that contains multiple typefaces or point sizes, choose **Optical** for the type from the Kerning menu on the Character panel, and see if you like the results. Illustrator will adjust the spacing between adjacent characters as it sees fit.

FIT HEADLINE

1 *The original characters are selected.*

FIT HEADLINE

2 *The **Fit Headline** command added space between characters to fit type to the edges of its object.*

Spacing and scaling defaults

To change the horizontal word or letter spacing for justified paragraphs, choose **Justification** from the Paragraph panel menu, then in the Justification dialog box, change the Minimum, Desired, or Maximum **Word Spacing** or **Letter Spacing** values **3**–**5**. The Desired setting also affects nonjustified paragraphs. (Tip: try reducing the word spacing for large type.) Glyph Scaling (50%–200%) affects the width of all characters.

OCEAN
Body more immaculate than a wave,
salt washing away its own line,
and the brilliant bird
flying without ground roots.

4 *Loose **letter** spacing*

➤ Tracking/kerning changes the vertical spacing of characters in vertical type.

➤ To undo manual kerning for selected characters (or with your cursor between a pair of characters), reset the Kerning value in the Character panel to 0 (zero).

The **Fit Headline** command uses tracking to fit a one-line paragraph of horizontal or vertical area type to the edges of its object.

To fit type to its container:

1. Choose any type tool.

2. Select or click in a single-line paragraph of area type (not a line within a larger paragraph).

3. Choose Type > **Fit Headline** **1**–**2**.

➤ If you scale a type object that you applied the Fit Headline command to, you'll need to reapply the Fit Headline command afterward.

OCEAN
Body more immaculate than a wave,
salt washing away its own line,
and the brilliant bird
flying without ground roots. *Pablo Neruda*

3 *Normal **word** and **letter** spacing*

OCEAN
Body more immaculate than a wave,
salt washing away its own line,
and the brilliant bird
flying without ground roots.

5 *Tight **word** spacing*

Horizontal scaling

You can use the **Horizontal Scale** command to make type wider (extended) or narrower (condensed), or use the **Vertical Scale** command to make it taller or shorter. The default scale value is 100%. An important caveat: Regular or Roman style characters that are altered via the Horizontal or Vertical Scale command tend to look distorted, whereas typefaces that are narrow or wide by design, such as Helvetica Narrow or Univers Extended, have more pleasing and balanced proportions. That being said, if you want to "fake" a condensed or extended typeface, do as follows (by just a few percentage points!).

To scale type horizontally and/or vertically:

Make sure the full **Character** panel is displayed (click the up/down arrow ▲▼ on the panel tab, if necessary). Select the type that you want to modify, then change the **Horizontal** or **Vertical Scale** value (1 to 10,000%!) **1**–**2**. You can also choose a preset value from the menu or click the up or down arrow.

or

To scale point or path type manually **3**, select it using the **Selection** tool (V),▶ then drag a side handle on the bounding box without holding down Shift.

or

To scale a selected type block by a percentage, double-click the Scale tool,⬚ change the **Non-Uniform: Horizontal** or **Vertical** value, then click OK.

Back we go!

To restore normal scaling:

1. Select the type you want to restore normal scaling to.

2. Press Cmd-Shift-X/Ctrl-Shift-X.
   or
   Choose 100% from the **Horizontal Scale** and **Vertical Scale** menus on the **Character** panel.

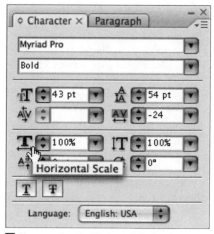

1 *You can alter the **Horizontal Scale** of type separately from the **Vertical Scale**.*

DANIELLA
Normal scaling (100%)

DANIELLA
75% horizontal scale

DANIELLA
125% horizontal scale

2 *Via the **Horizontal Scale** feature, you can dramatically alter the shape and weight of your type characters.*

3 *You can also **scale** path type manually by dragging a handle on its **bounding box**.*

Scale Type

Option in dialog box	Keyboard	Smart punctuation
ff, fi, ffi Ligatures	ff, fi, ffi	ff, fi, ffi
ff, fl, ffl Ligatures	ff, fl, ffl	ff, fl, ffl
Smart Quotes	' "	' " " '
Smart Spaces (one space after a period)	. T	. T
En (dashes)	--	–
Em Dashes	---	—
Ellipses	...	...
Expert Fractions	1/2	½

1 *Check* **Replace Punctuation** *options in the* **Smart Punctuation** *dialog box.*

Using smart punctuation

The **Smart Punctuation** command converts applicable text to professional typesetting characters in all fonts except OpenType fonts. If you want to set yourself apart from the amateurs, remember to use this feature!

To create smart punctuation:

1. To change all the type in your document, don't select anything; or with a type tool, select the text that you want to smart-punctuate.

2. Choose Type > **Smart Punctuation**.

3. Check any of the **Replace Punctuation** boxes **1** (see also the sidebar at left).

4. Click **Replace In: Selected Text Only** if you selected text for step 1; otherwise click **Entire Document**.

5. *Optional:* Check Report Results to have a list of your changes appear onscreen after you click OK.

6. Click OK **2**–**3**.

To specify a quotation marks style for future type:

1. Choose File > **Document Setup** (Cmd-Option-P/Ctrl-Alt-P).

2. Choose **Type** from the topmost menu, then choose the **Language** the text will be typeset in; the correct Double Quotes and Single Quotes marks for that language will display (or choose the desired styles from the menus). Also be sure to check **Use Typographers Quotes**.

Smart Punctuation

"We are living in a world today where lemonade is made from artificial flavors and furniture polish is made from real lemons."

--Alfred E. Newman

2 *Dumb punctuation: Straight quotation marks, double hyphens instead of dashes, and no ligatures. Bad, bad, bad.*

"We are living in a world today where lemonade is made from artificial flavors and furniture polish is made from real lemons."

–Alfred E. Newman

3 *Smart punctuation: Smart quotation marks, a single dash, and ligatures (the "fi" in "artificial" and the "fl" in "flavors"). To hang punctuation, see page 249.*

Inserting alternate glyphs

Fonts in the **OpenType** format, which was developed jointly by Adobe and Microsoft, can be used both in Macintosh and Windows to prevent font substitution and text reflow problems when transferring files between platforms. Illustrator CS3 supplies you with some OpenType font families. Of those, the fonts with "Pro" in the name have an expanded character set **1**.

The OpenType format also allows for a wide range of stylistic variations, called **glyphs,** for any given character in a specific font (sounds like something out of *The Hobbit!*). For each individual character in an OpenType font, you can choose from an assortment of alternate glyphs, such as ligatures, swashes, titling characters, stylistic alternates, ordinals, and fractions. Alternate glyphs can be inserted **manually** by using the **Glyphs** panel (see below) or automatically by using the OpenType panel (see the next page). The Glyphs panel isn't just used for OpenType fonts, though—you can use this panel to locate and insert characters in any font.

To replace or insert a glyph using the Glyphs panel:

1. Choose a **type** tool, then select a character or click in the text to insert the text cursor.

2. Open the **Glyphs** panel *Aa* (choose Glyphs from the Type menu or the Window > Type submenu). If you selected a character in the previous step, it will be highlighted on the panel.

3. *Optional:* Choose a different font and font style from the menus at the bottom of the panel.

4. From the **Show** menu **2**, choose a category of glyphs to be displayed on the panel: **Alternates for Current Selection, Entire Font,** or one of the specific categories **3**. The choices will vary depending on the current font and whether you selected a character or created an insertion point.

5. Double-click the glyph that you want to insert or replace the selected character with;

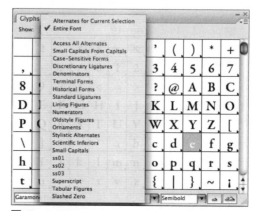

1 When **Font Preview** is checked in Preferences > Type, this symbol *O* appears next to **OpenType** ("Pro") font names on the font menus.

2 Via the **Show** menu, choose the type of glyphs you want to display on the **Glyphs** panel.

3 In this **Glyphs** panel, the letter "e" is highlighted and **Alternates for Current Selection** is chosen on the **Show** menu.

Glyphs Panel

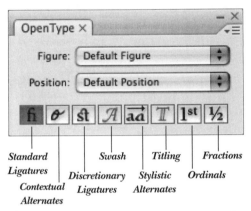

1 *This **Glyphs** panel is displaying a mini menu of alternate choices for the currently highlighted glyph.*

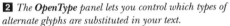

2 *The **OpenType** panel lets you control which types of alternate glyphs are substituted in your text.*

Standard
Ligatures

Swash

Titling

Fractions

Contextual
Alternates

Discretionary
Ligatures

Stylistic
Alternates

Ordinals

4 *The **OpenType** panel inserts alternate characters like these.*

or if the square containing the currently highlighted glyph has a mini arrowhead in the lower right corner, click the arrowhead and choose a glyph from the menu **1**. The chosen glyph will appear in your text.

➤ Click the Zoom Out or Zoom In button in the lower right corner of the Glyphs panel to change the display size of the glyphs on the panel.

Using the OpenType panel, you can decide ahead of time or for existing text whether alternate **glyphs** will be substituted for standard characters **automatically**, where applicable. For example, you can choose to have a glyph for a properly formatted fraction be inserted automatically whenever you type 1/2 or 1/4. Other available options, as shown on the Open Type panel **2**, include ligature glyphs for specific letter pairs (such as ff, ffl, and st) and swash, titling, and other special characters.

To specify or insert alternate glyphs via the OpenType panel:

1. Display the **OpenType** panel
   (Cmd-Option-Shift-T/Ctrl-Alt-Shift-T).

2. To change **existing** text, either select a text object to change all appropriate text occurrences in the object, or select specific text to limit changes to that text.
   or
   To specify alternate glyph options for **future** text to be entered in an OpenType font, deselect all type.

3. Click any of the available buttons on the panel **3**–**4**.

➤ For the Figure menu on the OpenType panel, see "Type > Choose a number style in OpenType fonts" in Illustrator Help.

Available

Selected

Not available

3 *The buttons on the **OpenType** panel have three **states**.*

OpenType Panel

To produce fractions:

1. Select a type object to change all applicable numerals (e.g., 1/2, 2/3, 3/4) in the object.
   or
   Select specific text that contains numerals, to limit the change to just that text.

2. Make sure an OpenType font is chosen for the numerals you want to restyle.

3. Click the **Fractions** button ½ on the **OpenType** panel. If the font used in the selected text contains glyphs for numerators, superscripts, denominators, or subscripts, the appropriate glyphs will appear in your text **1**–**2**.

The **Change Case** commands change selected text to all UPPERCASE, lowercase, Title Case, or Sentence case.

To change case:

1. With a type tool, select the text you want to modify.

2. Choose Type > Change Case > **UPPERCASE;** **lowercase; Title Case** (the first character in each word is uppercase, the other characters are lowercase); or **Sentence case** (only the first character in each sentence is uppercase).

➤ Some fonts, such as Lithos and Castellar, don't contain any lowercase characters.

1/2 4/5

1 *These* **standard** *numerals were entered with slashes in the Adobe Garamond Pro font.*

½ ⅘

2 *Here the same numerals and slashes are reformatted as proper* **fractions,** *which look much better!*

Fractions; Change Case

Your favorite composer

On the Paragraph panel menu, you have a choice of two line-composer options for selected type, or for future type when no type is selected:

Adobe Every-line Composer (the option we strongly prefer) examines all the lines within a paragraph and adjusts line lengths and endings to optimize the appearance of the overall paragraph.

Adobe Single-line Composer adjusts line breaks and hyphenation one line at a time, without regard to other lines or the overall paragraph.

➤ Always look over hyphenated text, and if necessary, correct any awkward breaks manually.

Gimme no break

To prevent a particular word from breaking at the end of a line, such as a compound word (e.g., "Single-line"), to reunite an awkwardly hyphenated word (e.g., "sex-tuplet"), or to keep related words together (e.g., "New York City"), select the word or words, then choose **No Break** from the Character panel menu.

1 Use the **Hyphenation** dialog box to set parameters for auto hyphenation.

```
AN
OVER-
ABUN-
DANCE
OF HY-
PHENS
MAKES    2
FOR TIR-
ING
READ-
ING.
```

Applying hyphenation
To choose hyphenation options:

1. Auto hyphenation affects only currently selected or subsequently created text. If you want to hyphenate existing text, select it with a type tool or selection tool now.

2. On the **Paragraph** panel ¶ with full options showing, check **Hyphenate.**

3. To choose hyphenation options, choose **Hyphenation** from the Paragraph panel menu. The Hyphenation Options dialog box opens **1**. Check Preview.

4. In the **Words Longer Than [ ] Letters** field, enter the minimum number of characters a word must contain in order to be hyphenated (3–25). We use a value of 6 or 7.

   In the **After First [ ] Letters** field, enter the minimum number of characters that can precede a hyphen (we use a value of 3).

   In the **Before Last [ ] Letters** field, enter the minimum number of characters that can be carried over to the next line following a hyphen (we use a value of 3 here, too).

   In the **Hyphen Limit** field, enter the maximum allowable number of hyphens in a row (0–25). More than 2 hyphens in a row can make the text hard to read, and looks ugly **2**.

   Another approach is to just move the slider toward **Better Spacing** or **Fewer Hyphens,** until you're satistfed with the way the line breaks look in your text.

   Finally, decide whether you want Illustrator to **Hyphenate Capitalized Words.**

5. *Optional:* When using Adobe Single-line Composer (see the sidebar at left), you can also limit the amount of hyphenation via the Hyphenation Zone value. A value of 0 permits all hyphenation; a positive value represents the distance from the right margin within which hyphenation isn't allowable.

6. Click OK.

➤ In Preferences > Hyphenation, you can enter hyphenation exceptions, specify how particular words are to be hyphenated, and confirm the default language for hyphenation.

Hyphenation

Changing paragraph alignment

Before you learn how to apply alignment, indentation values, and other paragraph formats, you need to know what a paragraph is, at least as far as Illustrator is concerned. To start a new paragraph as you enter a block of text (or to create a paragraph break where your cursor is inserted in existing text), press Return/Enter. Every paragraph ends with one of these hard returns. To reveal the nonprinting symbols for line breaks, paragraphs, and spaces, choose Type > Show Hidden Characters (Cmd-Option-I/Ctrl-Alt-I).

➤ To create a line break (soft return) within a paragraph in nontabular text, to bring text down to the next line, press Shift-Return.

To change paragraph alignment:

1. Choose a **type** tool, then click in a paragraph or drag through a series of paragraphs.
   or
   Choose a **selection** tool, then select a type object.

2. On the **Paragraph** panel ¶ (Cmd-Option-T/ Ctrl-Alt-T, or click Paragraph on the Control panel), click an **alignment** button **1**–**2**. The first three alignment options (Align left, Align center, and Align right) are also available as buttons on the **Control** panel.
   or
   Use one of the keyboard **shortcuts** listed in the sidebar on this page.

➤ Don't bother applying any of the justify alignment options to point type (type that's not in an object or block). Such objects don't have edges, so there's nothing for the type to justify to.

Paragraph alignment shortcuts

Align left	Cmd-Shift-L/Ctrl-Shift-L
Align center	Cmd-Shift-C/Ctrl-Shift-C
Align right	Cmd-Shift-R/Ctrl-Shift-R
Justify with last line aligned left	Cmd-Shift-J/Ctrl-Shift-J
Justify all lines	Cmd-Shift-F/Ctrl-Shift-F

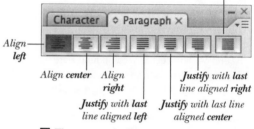

1 *The paragraph alignment options*

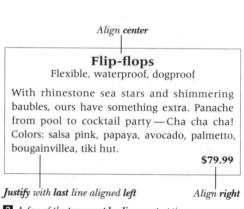

Align center

Flip-flops
Flexible, waterproof, dogproof

With rhinestone sea stars and shimmering baubles, ours have something extra. Panache from pool to cocktail party—Cha cha cha! Colors: salsa pink, papaya, avocado, palmetto, bougainvillea, tiki hut.

$79.99

Justify with last line aligned left　　　　*Align right*

2 *A few of the paragraph alignment options*

Paragraph Alignment

What to select

If you want to change paragraph attributes for all the text in a type object or on a path, select the object or path with the **Selection** tool.

To edit a paragraph or series of paragraphs, select just those paragraphs with a **type** tool.

Left Indent

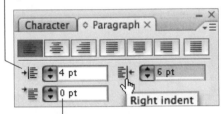

First-Line Left Indent

1 *If you forget which Indent field on the Paragraph panel is which, rest the mouse over an icon, and let the tool tip remind you.*

Changing paragraph indentation

You can apply left and first-line **indentation** values to area type and point type, and also apply a right indentation value to area type.

To change paragraph indentation:

1. Choose a **type** tool, then select the paragraph(s) you want to modify or click to create an insertion point in a single paragraph.
   or
   Choose a **selection** tool, then select a type object.

2. On the **Paragraph** panel: ¶
   Change the **Left Indent** and/or **Right Indent** value, then press Return/Enter or Tab **1**–**2**, or click the up or down arrow. Note that these values also affect any lines that follow a soft return.
   or
   To indent only the first line of each paragraph, enter a positive **First-Line Left Indent** value.

➤ To create a hanging indent **3**, enter a negative value in the First-Line Left Indent field.

The Mock Turtle sighed deeply, and began, in a voice choked with sobs, to sing this: —

    Beautiful Soup, so rich and green,
    Waiting in a hot tureen!
    Who for such dainties would not stoop?
    Soup of the evening, beautiful Soup!
    Soup of the evening, beautiful Soup!
        Beau — ootiful Soo-oop!
        Beau — ootiful Soo-oop!
    Soo — oop of the e — e — evening,
    Beautiful, beautiful Soup!

            — *Lewis Carroll*

2 *Left* indentation

BENE.: Pray thee, sweet Mistress Margaret, deserve well at my hands by helping me to the speech of Beatrice.

MARG.: Will you then write me a sonnet in praise of my beauty?

BENE.: In so high a style, Margaret, that no man living shall come over it; for, in most comely truth, thou deservest it.

MARG.: To have no man come over me? Why, shall I always keep below stairs?

BENE.: Thy wit is as quick as the greyhound's mouth; it catches.

          —William Shakespeare

3 *Hanging indents*

Inter-paragraph spacing

Use the **Space Before Paragraph** field or the **Space After Paragraph** field on the Paragraph panel to add or subtract space between paragraphs. (To adjust the spacing between lines of type within a paragraph, use leading, which is discussed on page 231.)

To adjust the spacing between paragraphs:

1. Select the type to be modified. To modify the space before only one paragraph in a type block, select the paragraph with a **type** tool. To change all the type in an object, select the object with the **Selection** tool.

2. In the **Space Before Paragraph** or **Space After Paragraph** field on the extended Paragraph panel **1**, ¶ enter a positive value to move paragraphs farther apart or a negative value to move them closer together (press Return/ Enter or Tab to apply) **2**, or click the up or down arrow.

➤ Keep in mind that the Space Before Paragraph value combines with the Space After Paragraph value from the paragraph above, so you could wind up with more space between paragraphs than you intend. For consistency, make one value a positive number and the other value zero.

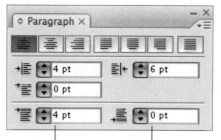

Space Before Paragraph   Space After Paragraph

1 *Use one of these 2 options to adjust the spacing between paragraphs.*

DEM DAR
BEVERLY HILLS

DIRTY LITTLE SOCKS

DON'T PLUNK MY
HEART STRINGS

COOL, CALM,
COLLECTIBLES

BEHIND THESE HAZY
EYES

LOSE CONTROL...
AND WEIGHT, TOO!

2 *The* **Space Before Paragraph** *values were increased for these paragraphs to add space above them.*

Inter-Paragraph Spacing

This **ahimsa** is the basis of the search for truth. ❦ I am realizing every day that the search is vain unless it is founded on **ahimsa** as the basis. ❦ It is quite proper to resist and attack a system, but to resist and attack its author is tantamount to resisting and attacking **oneself.** ❦ For we are all tarred with the same brush, and are children of one and the same Creator, and as such the divine powers within us are infinite. ❦ To slight a single human being is to slight those divine powers, and thus to harm not only that being but with him the whole **world.** ❦

Mohandas K. Gandhi

1 *Paragraph style*   **2** *Character styles*

3 *The Character Styles and Paragraph Styles panel group*

Character and paragraph styles

Now that you know how to style type manually by using the Character and Paragraph panels, you're ready to learn how to create and apply character and paragraph styles, which accomplish the same thing with much less sweat.

Paragraph **1** styles include paragraph formats, such as leading and indentation, as well as character attributes, such as font and point size. When you click a paragraph style, all currently selected paragraphs are reformatted with the attributes in that style.

Character styles contain only character attributes, and are normally used to emphasize or reformat selected characters or words within a paragraph (such as bullets, or boldfaced or italicized words), not whole paragraphs **2**. Character styles are applied in addition to paragraph styles—they're the icing on the cake.

To make light work of typesetting, and also to ensure consistency within a document and among related documents, we urge you to use styles. You'll create, modify, and apply them via the **Character Styles** and **Paragraph Styles** panels **3**.

To create or edit a character or paragraph style:

1. Choose Window > Type > **Character Styles** 🅐 or **Paragraph Styles** 🔲 (Window > Type submenu).

2. The easiest way to create a **new** style is to select some text in your document (with a type tool) that contains the attributes you want saved in the style, then Option-click/ Alt-click the **New Style** button 🔲 at the bottom of the Character or Paragraph Styles panel. If this is your first foray into styles, we recommend creating a paragraph style first.

or

To **edit** an existing style, deselect all, then double-click the style name on the panel. Or if text is selected, to prevent it from being restyled, Cmd-Option/Ctrl-Alt double-click the name of the style you want to edit.

(Continued on the following page)

Character and Paragraph Styles

3. An options dialog box will open for the chosen style type. For a new style, change the default **Style Name** to a more descriptive name for the type of formatting that it contains (such as "Subheads" or "Body Indent").

4. The dialog box has several option sets; to access a set, click a category on the left side. If you selected text in step 2, settings will already be chosen in some of the option sets. Check **Preview** to preview the chosen options in any currently selected text. Display any option set to choose attributes for the current style:

(Click **General** at any time to display a list of the current settings for all the categories **1**.)

Click **Basic Character Formats** to choose basic character attributes, such as font, point size, kerning, leading, and tracking.

Click **Advanced Character Formats** to choose scaling, baseline shift, and rotation values.

Click **Character Color,** click the Fill or Stroke box, then choose a fill and/or stroke color for the type. Colors from the Swatches panel will be listed here (nonglobal colors first, then global colors). For the stroke, you can also choose a Weight.

Click **OpenType Features** to choose options to be applied when OpenType fonts are used.

Checking an option here is equivalent to clicking a button on the OpenType panel.

5. In the Paragraph Style Options dialog box, you can also choose settings in the **Indents and Spacing**, **Tabs**, **Composition** (Composer), **Hyphenation**, and **Justification** option sets.

6. Click OK. To apply styles, see the next page. If you edited a style, all text that's linked to that style will update accordingly.

➤ Click Reset Panel in a style options dialog box to clear all the settings in the current option set. A few nonnumeric options can be reset to a blank state (no value or effect) by choosing "(Ignore)" from the individual menu.

➤ A dash/green fill in a check box means that option won't override any attributes that were applied manually to the text.

➤ Another way to edit an existing style is by redefining it; see the next page.

➤ You can also create a new style by duplicating an existing style and then choosing new attributes for the duplicate. To duplicate a style, click the style name, then choose Duplicate Character Style or Paragraph Style from the respective panel menu; or drag a style over the New Style button. You can't duplicate either of the Normal styles.

1 *The **General** options set of the **Paragraph Style Options** dialog box lists all the attributes in the current style. In the other option sets, you can edit the style.*

What if...

If you unintentionally apply a character style to a whole type object and then apply a paragraph style, only the formats from the paragraph style will be applied, not the character attributes, and the paragraph style name won't display a "+." To force a paragraph style to completely override a character style, select the type object, then click **[Normal Character Style]** on the Character Styles panel.

Two kinds of overrides

When you Option-click/Alt-click a paragraph style to remove manual overrides, remember that to remove overrides from a character style, you'll have to Option-click/Alt-click that style, too.

GEORGES BRAQUE (1882–1963)

THERE IS ONLY ONE VALUABLE THING IN ART: THE THING YOU CANNOT EXPLAIN.

REPORTED IN **SATURDAY REVIEW,** MAY 28, 1966

1 *Type styled with paragraph styles*   *Type styled with character styles*

GEORGES BRAQUE (1882–1963)

THERE IS ONLY ONE **VALUABLE** THING IN ART: THE THING YOU CANNOT EXPLAIN.

REPORTED IN **SATURDAY REVIEW,** MAY 28, 1966

2 *The boldfacing in the word "valuable" was applied manually, and so is considered an* **override.**

GEORGES BRAQUE (1882–1963)

THERE IS ONLY ONE VALUABLE THING IN ART: THE THING YOU CANNOT EXPLAIN.

REPORTED IN **SATURDAY REVIEW,** MAY 28, 1966

3 *Option-clicking/Alt-clicking the paragraph style for the main paragraph on the Paragraph Styles panel* **removed** *the boldfacing (override).*

To apply a type style:

1. For **paragraph** styling, select a type object or select some paragraphs in a type object.

For **character** styling, select some text (but not a whole object).

2. Click a style name on the **Paragraph Styles** or **Character Styles** panel **1**.

Note: If the text doesn't adopt the attributes of the style sheet, follow the next set of instructions.

➤ To choose a style for text before you type it, deselect all, click a style name on the Paragraph panel, then create your text.

A + (plus) sign after a style name on the Character Styles or Paragraph Styles panel signifies that some text in the selected type was styled **manually** after a style was assigned to it; that is, the text attributes no longer match the exact attributes as defined in the applied style. This manual styling is called an **override.**

Follow these instructions if you need to **clear** any **overrides** in your text. The text will readopt the character attributes as defined in the style.

To remove overrides from styled text:

1. Select the characters or paragraphs that contain overrides to be removed **2**–**3**. Or to "fix" the whole object, select the object but not any characters.

2. Option-click/Alt-click a name on the Character Styles or Paragraph Styles panel. The manually applied attributes in your text will disappear, and the + sign will disappear from the style name on the panel (see also the sidebar on this page).

To redefine a type style:

1. Select a word or paragraph that has been assigned the style you want to edit (the style name will become selected on the panel), and change any of the paragraph and/or character attributes manually.

2. Choose **Redefine Character Style** from the Character Styles panel menu or **Redefine Paragraph Style** from the Paragraph Styles panel menu. The style will update to reflect the custom styling in the selected text.

Character and Paragraph Styles

When you **delete** a **paragraph** or **character style**, the text attributes don't change in the document — the text merely ceases to be associated with the style.

To delete a character or paragraph style:

1. Deselect all.

2. Click a style name (or Cmd-click/Ctrl-click multiple style names) on the Character Styles or Paragraph Styles panel, then click the **Delete Selected Styles** button. 🗑
or
Drag a style name over the **Delete Selected Styles** button.

3. If the style is currently applied to text in your document, an alert dialog box will appear; click Yes.

➤ You can't delete the Normal Paragraph Style or Normal Character Style.

➤ To delete all unused styles in the current document (styles that aren't assigned to any text in your document), choose Select All Unused from the panel menu, then click the Delete Selected Styles button.

You can **load paragraph** and **character styles** from one file to another. If you're working on a series of documents for the same client, this is a good way to keep your type styling consistent.

To load type styles from another Illustrator document:

1. From the Character Styles or Paragraph Styles panel menu, choose one of the following:

Load Character Styles.

Load Paragraph Styles.

Load All Styles to load both character and paragraph styles.

2. In the Select a File to Import dialog box, locate and double-click the desired Illustrator document name; or click the document name, then click Open. *Note:* If an incoming style bears the same name as a style in the current document, it won't be loaded.

Choosing area type options

Using the **Area Type Options** dialog box, you can change the inset spacing between area type and the edge of its type object, reposition the first line of type in a type object, or divide a type block into columns and/or rows.

To choose area type options:

1. Select an area type object with a selection tool or type tool **1**.

2. Choose Type > **Area Type Options.** The Area Type Options dialog box opens **2**.

3. Check Preview.

4. In the Offset area, choose an **Inset Spacing** value for the space between the type and the type object.

5. To control the distance between the first line of text and the top edge of the object, choose a **First Baseline** option:

   Ascent to have the top of the tallest characters touch the top of the object.

   Cap Height to have uppercase letters touch the top of the object.

   Leading to make the distance between the first baseline of text and the top of the object equal to the leading value.

   x Height to have the top of the "x" character in the current font touch the top of the object.

Em Box Height to have the top of the em box in Asian fonts touch the top of the object.

Fixed, then enter a Min value for the location of the baseline of the first line of text.

Legacy to use the method from previous versions of Illustrator.

Also, enter a minimum baseline offset value in the **Min** field. Illustrator will use either this minimum value or the **First Baseline** option value, whichever is greater.

6. To arrange text in linked rows and/or columns:

   Enter the total **Width** and total **Height** of the entire type object (read about the Fixed option below).

   Next, in the **Rows** and **Columns** areas, click an up or down arrow or enter values in the fields to choose:

   The total **Number** of rows and columns to be produced.

   The **Span** for the height of each row and the width of each column. With **Fixed** checked, if you scale the type object, columns will be

   (Continued on the following page)

Hey! diddle, diddle,
The cat and the fiddle,
The cow jumped over the moon;
The little dog laugh'd
To see such sport,
And the dish ran away with the spoon.

1 *The original text object*

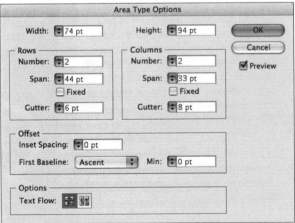

2 *Use the **Area Type Options** dialog box to reposition type within an object or to arrange type into columns and/or rows.*

Area Type Options

added or deleted as needed, but the row or column span won't change. With this option unchecked, the row or column span will change to fit a newly scaled object, but no new rows or columns will be added.

The **Gutter** (space) between the rows and the columns. If you check **Fixed** and change the Gutter value, the overall width or height will change but not the span; if you uncheck Fixed and change the Gutter value, the span will change but not the width or height.

7. Click one of the two **Text Flow** buttons to control the direction of the text flow—from row to row or from column to column.

8. Click OK **1**.

➤ If you select an area type object and then reopen the Area Type Options dialog box, the current settings for that type object will display and can be edited.

Baseline-shifting type

Via the **Baseline Shift** feature, you can shift characters upward or downward from the baseline, or for path type, from a path.

To shift type from its baseline:

1. Select the type you want to shift **2**.

2. On on the **Control** panel **A** (with full options displaying), enter a positive **Baseline Shift** value to shift characters upward or a negative value to shift them downward **3**–**5**; or choose a preset value from the menu; or click the up or down arrow.
   or
   Option-Shift-press/Alt-Shift-press the **up arrow** on the keyboard to shift the characters upward or the **down arrow** to shift them downward as per the current Baseline Shift increment in Preferences > Type. Cmd-Option-Shift-press/Ctrl-Alt-Shift-press an arrow to shift by 5 times that increment.

➤ To insert superscript and subscript characters in an OpenType font, use the OpenType panel.

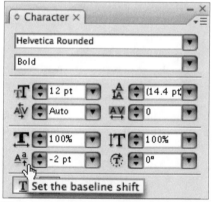

Hey! diddle, diddle, The cat and the fiddle,

To see such sport,

The cow jumped over the moon; The little dog laugh'd

And the dish ran away with the spoon.

1 *The object is converted into two **rows** and two **columns**. The arrows show the direction of the text flow.*

2 *Path type, Baseline Shift 0*

3 *The **Baseline Shift** feature lets you shift selected characters upward or downward.*

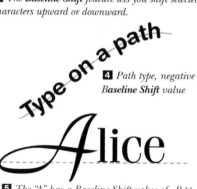

4 *Path type, negative Baseline Shift value*

5 *The "A" has a Baseline Shift value of −9 pt.*

"Dining is and always was a great artistic opportunity."

—*Frank Lloyd Wright*

1 *Let it hang out, with Roman Hanging Punctuation*

Out of hiding

To display the tab characters that are hidden in your text, along with other nonprinting characters, such as hard (paragraph) returns, soft returns, and spaces, choose Type > **Show Hidden Characters** (Cmd-Option-I/Ctrl-Alt-I). Tab characters display as right-pointing arrows. The nonprinting characters display in the color that's assigned to the layer the objects reside in **2**. Choose the command again at any time to turn off the display.

→	Front.9 →	Back.9 →	Total¶
Vijay →	34 →	34 →	68¶
Phil →	38 →	44 →	82¶
Ernie →	34 →	38 →	72¶
Tiger →	35 →	38 →	73¶

2 *This text is aligned using **custom tab stops,** as shown by the hidden characters.*

Hanging punctuation

The **Roman Hanging Punctuation** command, mimicking a traditional typesetting technique, forces punctuation marks that fall at the beginning and/or end of a line of area type to hang partially or fully outside the type block. Single and double quotation marks, hyphens, periods, and commas hang outside the margins; asterisks, ellipses, en and em dashes, colons, semicolons, and tildes hang halfway outside the margins.

To hang punctuation:

1. With a **type** tool, select a paragraph in an area type object; or with a **selection** tool, select the whole object. Or to enable the feature for future type objects, deselect all.

2. From the **Paragraph** panel menu, choose **Roman Hanging Punctuation 1**.

➤ For a more pleasing alignment of letters, such as the letter "W," "O," or "A" (not punctuation), at the beginning and/or end of lines in a whole type object, select the object, then choose Type > Optical Margin Alignment. Some characters may shift slightly outside the block, but they'll still print.

Setting tabs

To align columns of text correctly, you must use **tabs**—not spaces. The default tab stops are half an inch apart. After inserting tabs in your text, as per the instructions below, you can use the Tabs panel to add or change the alignment type or location of the tab markers, or add an optional leader character (such as a repeating period, for a table of contents).

To insert tabs into text:

1. Press Tab **once** as you **input** copy, before typing each new column. The cursor will jump to the next default tab stop.
   or
   To add a tab to **existing** text, click just to the left of the text that is to start a new column, then press Tab (once!). The text will move to the next default tab stop.

2. To customize the tabs (usually necessary), follow the instructions on the next page.

To set or modify custom tab stops:

I. Choose the **Selection** tool, then click a text object.
or
Choose a **type** tool and select some text.

2. Display the **Tabs** panel 📰 (Window > Type > Tabs or Cmd-Shift-T/Ctrl-Shift-T).

3. If the panel isn't docked, click the **Position Panel Above Text** button 🔓 to align the tabs ruler with the left and right margins of the selected text for horizontal type, or the top and bottom margins for vertical type.

4. Do any of the following:

Click just above the Tabs panel ruler to **insert** a new marker (the selected text will align to that stop) **1**, then click a tab **alignment** button in the top left corner of the panel. Repeat to insert more markers. You can change the alignment of any marker at any time; simply Option-click/Alt-click a tab marker to cycle through the alignment types.

To **delete** a marker, drag it off the ruler. Or Cmd-drag/Ctrl-drag to delete a marker and all markers to its right.

To **move** a tab marker, drag it to the left or right, or enter an exact location in the X field for horizontal type, or the Y field for vertical type. Cmd-drag/Ctrl-drag a marker to move that marker and all the markers to its right by the same amount.

5. *Optional:* Click a tab marker in the ruler, then enter a character (or up to 8 charac-

ters), such as a period, in the **Leader** field; that character will be repeated in your text **2**. The style of the leader characters can be changed only manually in the text or via a character style.

6. *Optional:* For the Decimal-Justified tab alignment option, you can enter a character in the **Align On** field for numerals to align to **3**. Unlike the Leader option, you must enter the Align On characters in your text.

➤ To create a series of tab stops that are equidistant from one another, click one marker, then choose Repeat Tab from the panel menu. *Beware!* This command deletes all existing markers to the right of the one you clicked, then inserts the new ones.

➤ The Tabs panel ruler units display in the increment currently chosen in File > Document Setup (Artboard: Units).

➤ Choose Snap to Unit from the Tabs panel menu to have tab markers snap to the nearest ruler tick mark as you insert or move them. Shift-drag a marker to turn the snap feature on or off temporarily (the opposite of the current Snap to Unit state).

2 *The two **Leader** characters used here are a period and a space.*

3 *The **Align On** character is a period.*

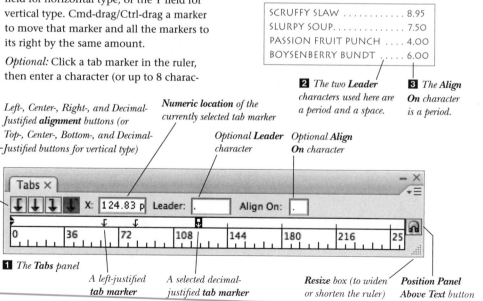

*Left-, Center-, Right-, and Decimal-Justified **alignment** buttons (or Top-, Center-, Bottom-, and Decimal-Justified buttons for vertical type)*

***Numeric location** of the currently selected tab marker*

*Optional **Leader** character*

*Optional **Align On** character*

1 *The **Tabs** panel*

*A left-justified **tab marker***

*A selected decimal-justified **tab marker***

***Resize** box (to widen or shorten the ruler)*

***Position Panel Above Text** button*

Just picture a large sparrow cage made of bamboo grillwork and having a coconut-thatch roof, divided off into two parts by the curtains from my old studio. One of the makes a bedroom, with very little light, so as to keep it cool. The other part, with a large window up high, is my studio. On the floor, some mats and my old Persian rug; and I've decorated the rest with fabrics, trinkets, and drawings. *Paul Gauguin*

1 *Select the object that the area type is going to wrap around.*

2 *In the **Text Wrap Options** dialog box, enter an Offset value and check Preview.*

Just picture a large sparrow cage made of bamboo grillwork and having a coconut-thatch roof, divided off into two parts by the curtains from my old studio. One of the two parts makes a bedroom, with very little light, so as to keep it cool. The other part, with a large window up high, is my studio. On the floor, some mats and my old Persian rug; and I've decorated the rest with fabrics, trinkets, and drawings. *Paul Gauguin*

3 *Now the type is **wrapping** around the palm tree.*

Creating special effects with type

Type can **wrap** around an Illustrator path, an Illustrator type object, or a placed bitmap image.

To wrap type around an object:

1. Create area type (type inside an object). For the cleanest wrap, choose one of the justify alignment options for the type.

2. Follow this instruction carefully, or the wrap won't work: Make sure the object that the type is going to wrap around (we'll call it the "wrap object") is in **front** of the type to be wrapped around it, in the **same** top-level layer, sublayer, or group. You can use the Layers panel to restack the wrap object, if necessary. It can be a vector object or a bitmap (placed) image that contains transparency.

3. Select the wrap object **1** (click its selection area on the Layers panel).

4. Choose Object > Text Wrap > **Make.** If an alert dialog box appears, click OK.

5. Choose Object > Text Wrap > **Text Wrap Options.** In the dialog box **2**, click Preview, then enter or choose an Offset value for the distance between the wrap object and any type that wraps around it (start with just a few points). If the wrap object is a placed image, the type will wrap around opaque or partially opaque pixels in the image.

6. Click OK **3**. Try moving the wrap object slightly; the text will rewrap around it.

➤ To prevent a text object from being affected by the wrap object, via the Layers panel, move it above the wrap object or to a different top-level layer.

➤ To modify the options for an existing wrap object, select it, then choose Object > Text Wrap > Text Wrap Options to reopen the dialog box.

➤ The Invert Wrap option forces the text to wrap inside the path instead of outside it.

To release a text wrap:

1. Select the wrap object (not the type).

2. Choose Object > Text Wrap > **Release.**

Text Wrap

Exercise

A **drop shadow** that you create using the following method (unlike the Effect > Drop Shadow command) will be an independent vector object, and can be modified with effects, the transform tools, and other techniques.

Create a shadow for point type

1. Create **point** type.

2. *Optional:* Select the type, then apply some positive tracking (Option-right arrow/Alt-right arrow).

3. With the Selection tool, select the type.

4. Apply a dark fill color and a stroke of None.

5. Option-drag/Alt-drag the type block slightly to the right and downward. Release the mouse, then release Option/Alt.

6. With the copy of the type block still selected, lighten its shade.

7. On the **Layers** panel, ◆ drag the copy of the type below the original **1**, and make sure it still has a selection square.

8. Choose Effect > Stylize (on the upper part of the menu) > **Feather,** check Preview, choose a Radius value (try a low value), click OK, and then, via the **Transparency** panel, ◎ lower the shadow transparency.

Slant the shadow

1. Make sure the shadow object is still selected (use the Layers panel).

2. Choose the Selection tool. Drag the top center handle downward a bit to shorten the type **2**.

3. Double-click the **Shear** tool ✐ (on the Scale tool pop-out menu).

4. Enter "45" in the **Shear Angle** field, click **Axis: Horizontal,** then click OK.

5. Use the arrow keys to move the baseline of the shadow text so it aligns with the baseline of the original text **3**.

> ### A different slant
>
> Use the Layers panel to select the shadow object, choose the Free Transform tool, then vertically **scale** or **shear** the object by moving its top center handle. Or to **reflect** the shadow block with the same tool, drag the top center handle downward all the way across the object.

Reflect the shadow

1. Select the shadow type.

2. Double-click the **Reflect** tool 🔁 (on the Rotate tool pop-out menu), click **Axis: Horizontal,** then click OK.

3. Move the two blocks of type together so their baselines and the characters meet **4**.

1 *Create a shadow, then stack it below the original type via the Layers panel.*

2 *Shorten the shadow by dragging the top center handle on its bounding box.*

3 *Slant the shadow using the **Shear** tool.*

4 *Reflect the shadow using the **Reflect** tool.*

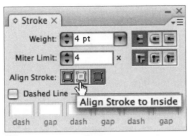

1 *Click an **Align Stroke** button on the **Stroke** panel to reposition a stroke on its path.*

2 *The Appearance panel is listing 4 strokes that were applied to a type object.*

3 *The type object is finished.*

Exercises

We'll show you three different ways to embellish type. This will be a good introduction to the Appearance panel, which you'll learn more about in Chapter 20.

Add multiple strokes to a character

1. Create and color a type character in a font of your choosing, approximately 200 pt. in size.

2. Click the type object with the Selection tool (V) and choose Type > **Create Outlines** (Cmd-Shift-O/Ctrl-Shift-O). Keep the object selected.

3. On the **Appearance** panel, double-click Contents, click the **Fill** listing, then apply a gradient fill.

4. *Optional:* Choose the **Gradient** tool, then drag vertically to position the gradient within the type shape.

5. Click the **Stroke** listing (Appearance panel).

6. On the **Control** panel, click the Stroke thumbnail and apply a stroke color. Click Stroke, choose a Weight of 4 pt., then click the **Align Stroke: To Inside** button **1**.

7. Drag the Stroke listing on the Appearance panel over the **Duplicate Selected Item** button. Apply a new color to the lower Stroke listing. On the **Stroke** panel, click the **Align Stroke: To Center** button.

8. Duplicate the lower Stroke listing again, apply a new stroke color, then click the **Align Stroke: to Outside** button.

9. Finally, duplicate the bottommost Stroke listing, and apply a new stroke color, this time in a 7-pt. width **2**–**3**.

Create type with a rough fill area

1. Create a type character, approximately 180 pt. in size. On the **Layers** panel, click the target circle to target the type object.

2. From the **Appearance** panel menu, choose **Add New Fill**. A Stroke and a Fill listing will now display on the panel.

3. Click the **Fill** listing. Choose Effect > Distort & Transform > **Roughen**. Click Relative, set the Size to 5 and the Detail to 4; click OK.

(Continued on the following page)

Exercise: Multiple Strokes on Type; Rough Fill

4. On the Appearance panel, click the **Stroke** listing. Via the Control panel, apply a 1-pt. stroke and choose a light stroke color.

5. Drag the **Stroke** listing over the Duplicate Selected Item button. To the lower Stroke listing, apply a new stroke color, 7-pt. width.

6. Double-click the **Characters** appearance listing, then set both the Stroke and Fill listings to a color of None 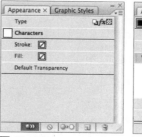.

7. Click the **Type** appearance listing to view appearance attributes for the type object.

8. To make the fill and stroke colors blend with any underlying objects, click the Fill listing, then via the **Transparency** panel, change the blend mode to Overlay or lower the Opacity .

1 The **Appearance** panel with Characters selected

2 The **Appearance** panel for the finished type object

Create an embossed letter

1. Create a type character, approximately 180 pt. in size. Click the type object with the Selection tool and choose Type > **Create Outlines** (Cmd-Shift-O/Ctrl-Shift-O).

2. Apply a medium-tone fill color to the selected object.

3. Choose the **Rectangle** tool (M), and drag a rectangle that covers the type object (it should have the same fill color).

4. On the **Layers** panel, drag the rectangle Path below the Group listing for the type outline, and expand the group listing.

5. Click the Compound Path name and choose **Duplicate "<Compound Path>"** from the panel menu. Repeat to create another duplicate .

6. Click the selection area for the bottommost **Compound Path**, then apply a dark fill color. Press the left arrow on the keyboard three times to move the object.

7. Click the selection area for the middle **Compound Path**, then apply a white fill color. Press the right arrow on the keyboard three times to move the object.

The dark and white type shapes should now look like dark and light edges behind the topmost type shape 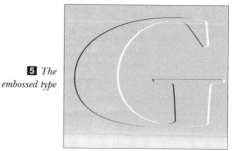.

3 The "rough" fill

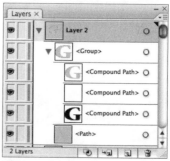

4 The Layers panel shows the three objects that make up the embossed type.

5 The embossed type

Exercise: Embossed Letter

ACQUIRE 19

In this chapter you'll learn how to get images into an Illustrator document via the Open and Place commands; learn how to work with the Links and Control panels to edit, replace, locate, update, relink, and convert linked images; and also learn how to drag and drop images between applications.

1 *This image was imported into an Illustrator file via the Place command, then a type layer was added.*

Acquiring images

In Illustrator, you can open or import objects or images from other applications in a variety of formats, and incorporate them into your overall design. For instance, you could layer path type over a bitmap image for a book jacket or poster, or use a graphic as part of a logo or product label.

Methods for acquiring images from other applications include the Open command, the Place command, and drag-and-drop. Your method of choice will depend on which file formats are available for saving the file in its original application and how you're planning to use the imagery in Illustrator.

When you open a document from another drawing (vector) application via the **Open** command, a new Illustrator file is created, and the acquired objects can be manipulated using Illustrator tools and commands. When you open a bitmap image by using the Open command, the image isn't converted into separate vector objects, but rather is embedded in a new file as an object in its own box.

Via the **Place** command, you can link or embed images into an existing Illustrator file. For print output, the recommended formats for linked images—EPS, TIFF, and PDF—preserve the color, detail, and resolution of the original image **1**. If you place a layered Photoshop (PSD) file into Illustrator, you can choose, via a dialog box, to have it appear as a single flattened object or as separate objects on separate layers.

You can also acquire images quickly by using the **drag-and-drop** method: simply drag an image from one Illustrator window into another or from a window in another application, such as Photoshop, into your Illustrator document, and a duplicate image appears in the target file automatically.

A bitmap image that you acquire in Illustrator via the Open, Place, or drag-and-drop method can be moved, placed on a different layer, masked, modified using any transformation tool, or modified using raster (bitmap) filters. All three methods preserve the resolution of the original image.

(The Clipboard commands—Cut, Copy, and Paste—are discussed on page 93.)

Using the Open command

A list of some of the file formats that you can open in Illustrator appears in the sidebar at right.

To use the Open command:

1. In Illustrator, choose File > **Open** (Cmd-O/ Ctrl-O). The Open dialog box opens. In the Mac OS, choose **Enable: All Documents** to list files in all formats, or to make life simpler, choose **All Readable Documents** to dim the files in formats that Illustrator can't read. In Windows, you can filter out files via the **Files of Type** menu, or choose **All Formats** (the default setting) to display files in all formats. Double-click a file name; or locate and click a file name, then click **Open.**

   or

   In Bridge, click a thumbnail, then choose File > Open With > **Adobe Illustrator CS3.**

2. If you're opening a multipage PDF, the Open PDF dialog box opens **1**. Check Preview, click an arrow to locate the desired page (or enter the desired page number in the field), then click OK. Respond to any alert dialog boxes that appear (see the sidebar on the following page).

   If you're opening a Photoshop file that contains layers or layer comps, the **Photoshop Import Options** dialog box opens. See pages 258–259.

➤ If you open an EPS file that contains a clipping path, the image will be nested in a group on the Layers panel, with the path directly above it. To move or reshape the path, click the selection area for the path on the Layers panel, and use the Direct Selection tool. If you delete or hide the selected clipping path, the entire image will become visible. To release the clipping path at any time, click the selection area for the clipping path on the Layers panel, then choose Object > Clipping Mask > Release.

➤ To preserve the editability of appearances and text in an Adobe PDF file, use the Open command (above), not the Place command.

File formats

The native Illustrator formats that you can open in Illustrator CS3

Illustrator (ai) versions 1.0 through CS3, Illustrator .ait, Illustrator EPS, and Adobe PDF.

Other formats that you can open or place into Illustrator CS3

Raster (bitmap) formats: BMP, GIF, JPEG, JPEG2000, PCX, PDF, PIXAR, PNG, PSD, TGA, and TIFF.

Graphics (vector) formats: CGM; CorelDRAW versions 5 through 10; DWG (AutoCAD drawing and export); EMF; FreeHand (up to version 11); PDF; PICT; SVG; SVGZ; and WMF. Illustrator can't open Macromedia Flash SWF files.

Text formats: Plain text (TXT), RTF, and MS Word (up to version 2004 in Macintosh and version 2007 in Windows).

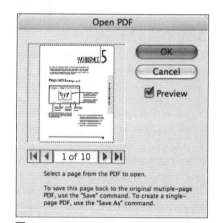

1 *For a **multipage PDF,** navigate to the page you want to open.*

Deciphering the alert dialogs

When opening or placing an image into Illustrator, you may encounter any of these alert dialog boxes:

Illustrator PDF: Warnings lists missing fonts and/or objects that have been reinterpreted. Click OK to accept the substitutions (or click Cancel) **1**.

Convert Color Mode lets you decide which color mode to use when an imported file contains objects in both CMYK and RGB color modes **2**.

Embedded Profile Mismatch and **Missing Profile** let you decide how to color-manage an imported image that does or does not contain an embedded color profile **3**–**4**.

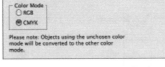

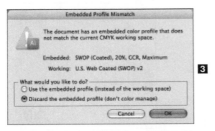

Using the Place command

After importing a file into an Illustrator document via the **Place** command, you can move it to a different location on the artboard; restack it within the same layer; move it to a different layer; mask, transform, or modify it using effects or filters; or change its opacity or blending mode. For a list of "place-able" file formats, see the sidebar on the previous page.

To place an image into an Illustrator document:

1. Open an Illustrator file, and click the layer you want the image to appear on.

2. In Illustrator, choose File > **Place**, then click a file to be placed. Check **Link** to place a screen version of the image into your Illustrator document, with a link to the original image file (Illustrator won't color-manage the image). The original image file won't be affected by your edits in Illustrator, but in order for it to print properly, the original file must be available on your hard disk (read more about linking on pages 260–263). Or uncheck Link to **embed** a copy of the actual image into the Illustrator file, in which case Illustrator will color-manage the image. Embedding increases the storage size of the Illustrator file. Click **Place.**
   or
   In Bridge, click a thumbnail, then choose File > Place > **In Illustrator.** The image will be linked automatically.

   If you're placing a Photoshop file that contains layers, the Photoshop Import Options dialog box opens. See the next page.

➤ Check Template in the Place dialog box to place a dimmed version of the image on a template layer for tracing.

➤ In Preview view, a selected, linked image will have an X on top of it, in the color of the current layer.

Choosing Photoshop import options

Importing a single-layer image

If you import a single-layer Photoshop image via the Open or Place command, it will be listed on the Layers panel by its file name on the currently active layer and no dialog box will open (if an alert appears, see the sidebar on the previous page). No clipping mask will be generated by Illustrator, but any Photoshop clipping path will remain in effect and will be listed by the name that was assigned to it in Photoshop.

Importing a multilayer image

If you use the Place command (with Link unchecked) or the Open command to import a Photoshop file that contains layers or layer comps, the **Photoshop Import Options** dialog box opens 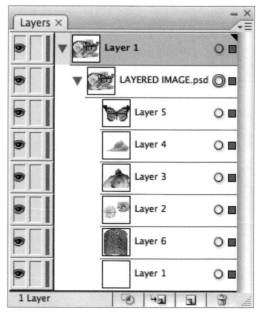. The options are described below.

Check **Show Preview** to display a thumbnail preview of the image.

Importing layer comps

Choose from the **Layer Comp** menu to import a layer comp. Any comments entered in Photoshop for the chosen comp will display in the **Comments** window. (The Layer Comp menu will be blank if the Photoshop file doesn't contain any layer comps.) If you need to import additional layer comps from the same Photoshop image, you'll have to choose the Place command again for each one.

If the image contains layer comps and you checked Link in the Place dialog box, you can choose **When Updating Link: Keep Layer Visibility Overrides** to preserve the layer visibility (hide/show) state the layers were in when you originally placed the image and ignore any subsequent visibility changes made in Photoshop; or choose **Use Photoshop's Layer Visibility** to apply any subsequent layer visibility changes made in Photoshop.

Importing Photoshop layers

If you unchecked the Link option in the Place dialog box, you now have the option to keep or flatten the layers. If you click **Convert Photoshop Layers to Objects**, each object will be nested within an image group within the current layer **2**. Transparency levels, blending

1 *The **Photoshop Import Options** dialog box opens if you place a Photoshop image with the **Link** option **unchecked**.*

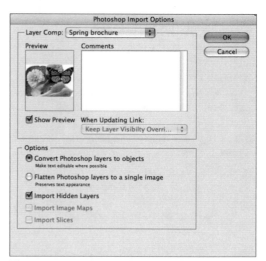

2 *When you check **Convert Photoshop Layers to Objects**, each Photoshop layer becomes a separate Illustrator object, nested within an image group.*

modes, layer masks, and vector masks will be preserved, will be listed as editable appearances (see page 269), and will be targeted to the appropriate converted object in Illustrator. Layer sets will be preserved; any vector mask will remain in effect and will be listed as a clipping path; and plain type will remain editable, if possible (see the second to last paragraph on this page). Any clipping path that was saved with the Photoshop file will remain in effect and will be listed at the top of the nested objects. Each converted layer from the Photoshop file will be listed as a separate item on the Links panel, but any imagery outside the original canvas area will be trimmed.

If you click **Flatten Photoshop Layers to a Single Image**, a flattened version of the image will be nested within the current layer. All transparency levels, blending modes, and layer mask effects will be applied to the flattened image, but those attributes won't be listed as editable appearances in Illustrator. Any clipping path saved with the Photoshop file will remain in effect and will be listed above the nested image within a group.

Check **Import Hidden Layers, Import Image Maps**, and/or **Import Slices**, if available (and if desired), to import those elements with the file.

Linked files are flattened automatically (that is, the Convert Photoshop Layers to Objects option is dimmed).

➤ If you open or place (with the Link option unchecked) a layered Photoshop image into Illustrator and you click Convert Photoshop Layers to Objects in the Photoshop Import Options dialog box, the Background from the Photoshop file will become one of the nested objects within Illustrator, and will be opaque. You can change its opacity, hide it, or delete it via the Layers panel in Illustrator.

Other Photoshop issues

In Photoshop, the position of **adjustment layers** in the layer stack affects how image layers are converted into objects when the file is placed and embedded (not linked) into Illustrator. Any layers above an adjustment layer in the Photoshop file will be converted to separate objects in Illustrator. Any layers below an adjustment layer in the Photoshop file will be flattened along with the adjustment layer into one object in Illustrator. You can delete or hide adjustment layers in Photoshop before placing the image into Illustrator.

When placing or opening a Photoshop **EPS** file, any Photoshop shape layers will become a clipping set in Illustrator, editable text will become a compound path, and all other Photoshop layers will be flattened into one object below the shape layer(s). In contrast, each layer from a Photoshop **PSD** file will be converted to a separate object layer.

If you place a Photoshop file that contains **editable type** into Illustrator (with the Link option unchecked) and click Convert Photoshop Layers to Objects, the type objects will remain editable, provided the type layer in Photoshop was neither warped nor had any effects applied to it. If you want to import a type layer as vector outlines instead, in Photoshop, use Layer > Type > Convert to Shape, save the file, then open the file in Illustrator via the Open or Place command.

If the current layer in a Photoshop file contains pixels that extend outside the live **canvas area**, those pixels will be dropped when you import it into Illustrator, no matter which method you use—drag-and-drop, place, or open. Before acquiring an image from Photoshop, make sure the pixels that you want to import are visible within the live canvas area in the original file.

Photoshop Import Options, Issues

Managing linked images

To keep your Illustrator files from becoming too large, you can link the images you import instead of embedding them. A screen version of each image will act as a placeholder in your document, but the actual image will remain separate from the Illustrator file. To link a file, use the File > Place command with the Link option checked.

The **Links** panel **1** lets you and your output service provider keep track of imported files. The panel lists all the linked and embedded files in your Illustrator document and puts a number of useful controls at your fingertips. For example, you can open a linked image in its orginal application via the **Edit Original** button (discussed below), and update a revised file in Illustrator via the Update Link button (see page 262).

Some of the same commands are also available on the **Control** panel when a linked image is selected in your document **2**–**4**. In fact, you can open a temporary Links panel by clicking Linked File or Image on the Control panel.**NEW!**

To edit a linked image in its original application:

1. On the **Links** panel, click the image name, then click the **Edit Original** button.
   or
   Click the image in the document window, then click **Edit Original** on the **Control** panel.

   The application in which the linked image was created will launch, if it isn't already open, and the image will open.

2. Make your edits, resave the file, then return to Illustrator. If an alert dialog box appears **5**, click Yes. The linked image will update in your document.

➤ In Preferences > File Handling & Clipboard, you can choose preferences for linked images. For example, via the Update Links menu, you can specify whether linked images will update automatically when modified in their original application (see page 375).

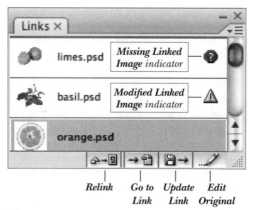

| Relink | Go to Link | Update Link | Edit Original |

1 *The **Links** panel lets you keep track of, replace, and embed your linked files.*

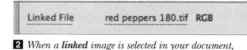

2 *When a **linked** image is selected in your document, you can click Linked File on the Control panel to open a temporary Links panel, or click the image name to access Links panel commands.*

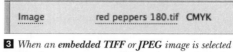

3 *When an **embedded TIFF** or **JPEG** image is selected in your document, you can click Image on the Control panel to open a temporary Links panel, or click the image name to access Links panel commands.*

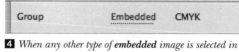

4 *When any other type of **embedded** image is selected in your document, you can click Embedded on the Control panel to access Links panel commands.*

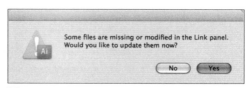

5 *This prompt appears if you edit a linked file in its original application via the **Edit Original** button.*

Linked versus embedded images

A **linked** image will be listed on the Layers panel as <Linked File> (or, for a PSD file, as the file name) within the currently active layer. Any clipping path in the original file will be applied, but it won't have a listing on the Layers panel.

An **embedded** TIFF or JPEG image will be listed on the Layers panel as an image object on the current layer; a file in another format will be nested within a group. If a clipping path is included, it will be active and will be listed on the Layers panel as such, above the image object.

➤ Photoshop filters (on the Filter menu) can be applied only to embedded images and aren't editable, whereas Photoshop effects (on the Effect menu) can be applied to both linked and embedded images and remain editable.

➤ You can apply Transparency panel settings to, or transform (move, rotate, shear, or reflect), linked and embedded images.

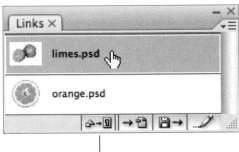

1 *Click the linked image that you want to replace, then click the* **Relink** *button.*

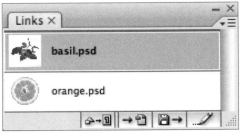

2 *The "limes.psd" image is* **replaced** *with "basil.psd."*

If you **replace** one **placed image** with another, any transformations that you applied to the image in Illustrator, such as scaling or rotation, will be applied to the replacement automatically.

To replace a linked or embedded image:

1. On the **Links** panel, click the name of the file that you want to replace, then click the **Relink** button ⟨⟩⟶▣ at the bottom of the Links panel **1**. The Place dialog box opens.
or
Click the image in the document window, then click the image name or Embedded on the Control panel **NEW!** and choose **Relink** from the menu.

2. Locate the replacement file, then click **Place 2**.

➤ To replace a placed image another way, select it in the document window, choose File > Place, locate the replacement image, check the Replace option, then click Place.

The **Go To Link** command locates a placed image for you and selects and centers it in the document window.

To go to a linked or embedded image:

On the **Links** panel, click an image name, then click the **Go to Link** button ⟶▣ at the bottom of the panel.
or
Click the image in the document window, then click the image name or Embedded on the Control panel **NEW!** and choose **Go to Link** from the menu.

➤ To locate a linked image in Bridge, click the image name on the Links panel, then choose Reveal in Bridge from the panel menu.

➤ When you shrink (scale down) a linked or embedded image in Illustrator, its resolution increases accordingly; enlarge it and its resolution decreases.

Replace, Select Image

If this icon ⚠ appears on the Links panel, it means the original file has been **modified** and that link is outdated. To **update** a linked file that's been modified, follow the instructions below. You'll also need to update a linked file if you edit it via the Edit Original button and Manually is chosen on the Update Links menu in Preferences > File Handling & Clipboard. (If the setting is Automatically, the image will be updated automatically; if the setting is Ask When Modified, an alert will appear, giving you the option to update the file or not.)

To update a modified linked image:

1. Click the name of the modified image ⚠ on the Links panel.

2. Click the **Update Link** button 💾➜ at the bottom of the panel.
   or
   Click the image in the document window, then click the image name on the Control panel and choose **Update Link** from the menu.

To view information about a file:

1. On the **Links** panel, double-click the listing for a linked or embedded file.
   or
   Click the image in the document window, then click the image name on the Control panel and choose **Link Information.**

2. A dialog box listing information about the image, such as its file format, location, size, modifications, and transform information will appear. Click OK.

➤ To see metadata (information) about a linked file, such as keywords, copyright info, IPTC contact, content, image, and status info, click the file on the Links panel, then choose Link File Info from the panel menu.

To locate or replace images upon opening a file:

An alert dialog box will appear if you move an image file from its original location after linking it to an Illustrator file, and then reopen the Illustrator file **1**. Do one of the following:

To locate the missing image, click **Repair**, locate the file, then click Replace. (The Repair button displays only if Enable Version Cue is checked in Preferences > File Handling & Clipboard.)

To substitute another file for the missing one, click **Replace**, locate a replacement file, then click Replace.

If you click **Ignore**, the linked image won't display, but a question mark icon will display for that file on the Links panel and its bounding box will still be visible in the Illustrator file in Outline view or, if smart guides are on, when the cursor passes over the bounding box. To completely break the link and prevent any alert prompts from appearing in the future, delete the bounding box and resave the file.

Optional: Check Apply to All to have the button you click apply to all missing images.

Choosing Links panel display options

To change the size of the thumbnail images on the Links panel, choose **Panel Options** from the panel menu, click the preferred size, then click OK.

To change the order of files as listed on the panel, from the panel menu choose **Sort by Name** (alphabetical order), **Sort by Kind** (file format), or **Sort by Status** (missing, then modified, then embedded, then fully linked). To sort only selected links, Cmd-click/Ctrl-click the file names first.

To control which types of links display on the Links panel, choose **Show All, Show Missing, Show Modified,** or **Show Embedded** from the panel menu.

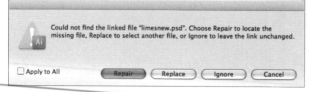

1 *If Illustrator detects that a **linked** file is **missing** when you open a document, this alert will appear.*

1 *Use the **Placement Options** dialog box to choose options for a placed image.*

2 *Click an image name on the Links panel, then choose **Embed Image** from the panel menu.*

Embedded files have this icon

3 *Note that the file name is listed for embedded TIFF, GIF, JPEG, and flattened PSD files, but not for embedded files in other formats.*

Via the **Placement Options** dialog box, you can control how any replacement image fits into its bounding box.

To choose placement options for a linked image:

1. Click a linked image in the document window, then on the **Control** panel, click the image name and choose **Placement Options.**
   or
   On the **Links** panel, click a linked image, then choose **Placement Options** from the panel menu.
   The Placement Options dialog box opens **1**.

2. Choose a **Preserve** option, then study the thumbnails and read the description to learn how the image will be affected.

3. *Optional:* For an option other than Transforms or Bounds, you can click a point on the **Alignment** icon. The artwork will be aligned to that point on the bounding box. To prevent the artwork from overlapping the bounding box, you can check **Clip to Bounding Box.**

4. Click OK.

The **Embed Image** command changes a file's status from linked to embedded, which increases the file size.

To change a file's status from linked to embedded:

On the **Links** panel, click the name of the image that you want to embed **2**, then choose **Embed Image** from the Links panel menu **3**.
   or
Click the image in the document window, then click **Embedded** on the Control panel.**NEW!**

When you embed a multilayer Photoshop image, the Photoshop Import Options dialog box opens. See pages 258–259.

➤ Object > Rasterize also converts a selected linked image into an embedded one, whereas Effect > Rasterize does not.

➤ To convert a single-layer embedded image into a linked image, click the image, then click the Relink button on the Links panel.

Placement Options; Embed Linked File

Using drag-and-drop

Drag-and-drop is a quick method for duplicating images between applications or files; the copy is made automatically. You can drag and drop objects between Illustrator documents or between Illustrator and Adobe GoLive, Adobe InDesign, or any other drag-aware application, and you can drag and drop a selection or layer from Photoshop to Illustrator, as per the instructions below.

Note: To acquire a Photoshop image for print output, instead of using the drag-and-drop method, we prefer to convert the image to CMYK Color mode in Photoshop, save it in the Photoshop PSD format, then acquire it via the Place command in Illustrator. Just our humble opinion.

To drag and drop an image from Photoshop to Illustrator:

1. In Photoshop, select some pixels or click a layer.

2. Open an Illustrator file.

3. In Photoshop, choose the **Move** tool (V), then drag the selection or layer into the Illustrator document window; a copy of the image appears.

   The selection or layer will be embedded at the resolution of the original image. In the Mac OS, the image will be nested within a new <Group> in the currently active layer; in Windows, it will be listed as <Image>. *Note:* If the image is very large, Illustrator will divide it into multiple horizontal segments, which will appear on separate layers.

➤ The drag-and-drop method doesn't use the Clipboard.

➤ The opacity of the Photoshop selection or layer will become 100%, regardless of its original opacity (it may appear lighter if its original opacity was below 100%). You can lower the transparency in Illustrator, if desired. Photoshop blending modes are ignored.

➤ Layer masks and vector masks from Photoshop will be applied to the image (meaning the image will be clipped), and then will be discarded. Any clipping paths in the Photoshop file will be ignored. In the Mac OS, a generic clipping path (based on the dimensions of the Photoshop selection or layer) will appear within the image group, but can be deleted without affecting the image. You can create a clipping mask in Illustrator to mask the image.

➤ If you drag and drop a selection or layer (even editable type or a shape layer) from Photoshop with the Move tool, it will become rasterized, if it isn't already. Any transparent pixels will become opaque white. If you drag and drop a selected path (or vector mask) from Photoshop to Illustrator with the Path Selection tool, it will become a compound path in Illustrator, and won't be rasterized. Another option is to copy a path from Photoshop and paste it into Illustrator, in which case the Paste Options dialog box opens. Click Paste As: Compound Shape (fully editable) or Compound Path (faster); the Compound Shape option is recommended for multiple or overlapping paths.

To drag and drop an image into Illustrator from Bridge:

1. In Bridge, click an image thumbnail.

2. To **link** the image, drag the thumbnail into an Illustrator document window.
   or
   To **embed** the image, Shift-drag the thumbnail into an Illustrator document window.

APPEARANCES & GRAPHIC STYLES

20

In this chapter, you'll learn how to apply, edit, copy, and remove appearance attributes (strokes, fills, effects, and transparency settings) via the Appearance panel. You'll also learn how to to apply appearance attributes collectively as graphic styles via the Graphic Styles panel; create, duplicate, edit, move, merge, delete, unlink from, and expand graphic styles; and save graphic styles to libraries for easy access.

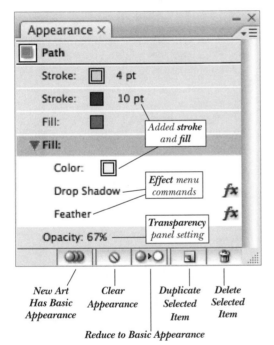

New Art Has Basic Appearance   Clear Appearance   Duplicate Selected Item   Delete Selected Item

Reduce to Basic Appearance

1 *Use the* **Appearance** *panel to apply, edit, restack, or remove* **appearance attributes** *from a layer, sublayer, group, object, or graphic style. This screen capture shows the appearance attributes for a selected path.*

Applying appearance attributes

Using the **Appearance** panel ◉ **1**, you can not only apply multiple fills and strokes to the same object (beyond the basic fill and stroke), but you can also apply a different opacity level, blending mode, or Effect menu command to each fill or stroke. Settings applied in this manner are called appearance attributes.

Because appearance attributes change only how an object looks, not its actual underlying path, you can save, close, and reopen a document and still be able to edit or remove the appearance attributes in the saved file. When an object is selected, its appearance attributes are listed on the Appearance panel. You can also use the panel to edit, restack, and remove appearance attributes. Appearance attributes add flexibility—but also some complexity—to object editing.

You can either apply appearance attributes to individual objects one by one, or target a whole top-level layer or group for appearance changes. In the latter case, the appearance attributes that you choose will apply to all the objects nested within the targeted layer or group. For example, if you target a layer and then modify its opacity or blending mode, all objects nested within that layer will adopt that opacity or blending mode. To edit an attribute at any time, simply retarget the layer. When an object contains appearance

(Continued on the following page)

Apply Appearance Attributes

attributes, its listing has a gray **target circle** on the Layers panel **1**.

When you **apply appearance attributes,** your object adopts a new look that can be modified or removed at any time, even after you save, close, and reopen the file.

To apply appearance attributes:

1. In the document window, select the object you want to apply appearance attributes to.
or
On the **Layers** panel, click the target circle for a layer, group, or object. A ring will appear around the circle, indicating it's now an active target. If you click the target circle for a layer, all the objects on the layer will become selected, and the word "Layer" will appear at the top of the Appearance panel.

2. Show the **Appearance** panel (Shift-F6).

3. For a targeted object, do any of the following:

   Click **Stroke**, then modify the stroke color via the Color or Swatches panel; or the stroke width or other settings via the Stroke panel; or the brush stroke via the Brushes panel (add or edit a brush stroke); or the stroke and brush attributes via the Control panel.

   Click **Fill**, then modify the fill via the Color, Swatches, Control, Gradient, or Transparency panel.

4. For a targeted object, group, or layer, do any of the following:

   Double-click **Default Transparency** (or the current transparency appearance attribute), then on the Transparency panel, change the Opacity value and/or blending mode.

   Choose a command from the **Effect** menu (for starters, try applying an effect on the Distort & Transform or Stylize submenu), modify the dialog box settings, then click OK. The Effect command will be listed on the Appearance panel. (You'll learn about effects in the next chapter.)

➤ Whenever possible, choose appearance commands from the Effect menu instead of the

Targeting layers correctly

Although both selecting and targeting cause objects to become selected in your document, they're not interchangeable operations when you're working with whole layers. If you **target** a top-level layer by clicking its target circle and then apply appearance attributes (e.g., fill color, Effect menu command, Transparency panel settings), those attributes will be applied to, and listed on, the Appearance panel for the layer as a whole.

If you click the **selection** area for a top-level layer instead of the target circle and then apply appearance attributes, those attributes will be applied separately to each object or group in that layer, not to the layer as a whole. In this case, you won't see an itemized list of appearance attributes on the Appearance panel; you'll just see the generic words "Mixed Appearances" at the top of the panel. Nor will the appearance attributes be listed if you subsequently target the layer.

Selecting and targeting do work interchangeably for an object or group. That is, clicking the selection area or target circle on the Layers panel for an object or group both selects and targets that entity.

*This layer is **active** but **not targeted,** and it doesn't contain any appearance attributes.*

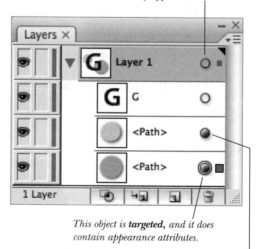

*This object is **targeted,** and it does contain appearance attributes.*

1 *This path object contains **appearance attributes,** but it isn't currently targeted.*

1 *The **Appearance** panel below lists the attributes for the type in this illustration.*

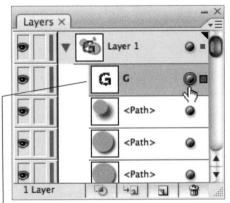

*This **targeted** object (a type character) is nested within a layer.*

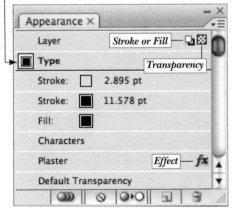

2 *The **Appearance** panel is listing the attributes for **Type**, the currently targeted object. (The layer the path resides in has its own appearance attributes, but they're not currently displayed.)*

Filter menu. Filter menu commands alter an object permanently, whereas Effect menu commands, because they're vector effects, can be reedited or removed at any time without changing the object permanently.

➤ To view (and to modify) the existing appearance attributes for an object, group, or layer, click the gray target circle, then look at the Appearance panel. To untarget an object, group, or layer, Shift-click the gray circle.

Deciphering the Appearance panel

Depending on what entity (object, group, or layer) is currently targeted and what attributes are applied to them, you may see one or more of these icons in the upper portion of the Appearance panel:

➤ Additional **stroke** and/or **fill** attributes 🗗

➤ **Transparency panel** settings ▨

➤ **Effects** *fx*

The name for the currently targeted entity (e.g., Layer, Group, or Path) is listed in boldface at the top of the Appearance panel. Note that if the selected object happens to be type, the word "Type" will appear instead of the word "Path." The same holds true for an image ("Image"), a symbol ("Symbol"), or a compound shape ("Compound Shape")—you get the idea.

If an object is targeted and that object is nested within a layer and/or group to which appearance attributes have been applied, a "Layer" and/or "Group" listing will also appear above the "Path" listing at the top of the Appearance panel **1**–**2**. If a layer or group is targeted, a "Contents" listing will also appear on the Appearance panel. (Yes, it can be confusing!)

To apply multiple stroke or fill attributes:

1. Target an object, group, or layer **1**.

2. From the Appearance panel menu, choose **Add New Fill** (Cmd-/; Ctrl-/) or **Add New Stroke** (Cmd-Option-/; Ctrl-Alt-/).
   or
   Click an existing Stroke or Fill listing on the Appearance panel, then click the **Duplicate Selected Item** button ⬓ at the bottom of the panel **2**.

3. A second **Stroke** or **Fill** attribute will appear on the panel **3**–**4**. Click the new listing, then modify its attributes so it differs from the original (or modify the original listing instead). In any case, make sure narrower strokes are stacked above wider ones; if the narrower strokes are on the bottom, you won't be able to see them. You can drag a listing upward or downward. Similarly, apply opacity and blending modes to the upper fill attributes, not to the lower ones.

➤ By changing the stacking position of a stroke or fill listing, you can change how the object looks. For example, if you drag a Stroke listing below a Fill listing and then lower the opacity of the Fill listing, the stroke (if it's fairly wide) will be visible below the semi-transparent fill.

To choose appearance options for future objects:

If the **New Art Has Basic Appearance** command on the Appearance panel menu has a check mark or you click the **New Art Has Basic Appearance** button ⬡ at the bottom of the panel, subsequently created objects will have just one fill and one stroke. With this option unchecked in either location, the appearance attributes currently displayed on the panel will apply automatically to new objects you create.

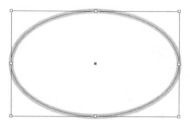

1 *Target* an object. This ellipse has a gray stroke and a fill of None.

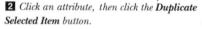

2 *Click an attribute, then click the **Duplicate Selected Item** button.*

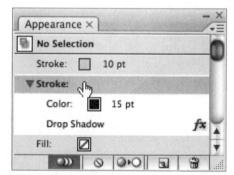

3 *Edit the **duplicate** attribute.*

4 *The color was changed, the width of the duplicate stroke was increased, and the Drop Shadow effect was applied.*

Apply Strokes and Fills; New Art Setting

1 *A path is **targeted** via the **Layers** panel.*

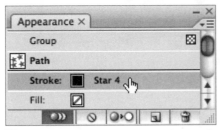

2 *We clicked the Stroke listing on the Appearance panel, then applied the "Star 4" scatter brush to the path.*

![Appearance panel]

3 *The brush is listed for the Stroke attribute on the* **Appearance** *panel.*

Editing appearance attributes

Aside from merely listing appearance attributes, the Appearance panel can also be used to open panels and dialog boxes for previously applied appearance attributes (e.g., effects, strokes, fills) for **editing**.

To edit appearance attributes:

1. In the document window, select the **object** whose appearance attributes you want to modify.
   or
   On the Layers panel, click the gray **target** circle for a layer, group, or object **1**.

2. On the **Appearance** panel, double-click any appearance listing (e.g., an effect or the transparency setting) to open a related dialog box or show a related panel. If there are multiple fill or stroke attributes, be careful to click the listing you want to modify.

3. Make the desired edits (see steps 3 and 4 on page 266). If you apply a brush stroke **2**, the brush name will be listed on the panel **3**. You can double-click the brush name to open the Stroke Options dialog box.

   Note: If a Stroke or Fill listing has an expand/collapse arrow, and you expand the list, you'll see attributes that belong only to that listing. For example, if you change the opacity or blending mode (Transparency panel) or apply an Effect menu command, that edit will apply only to (and will be listed under) the currently selected stroke or fill—not to the whole object.

➤ If you select a type object with the Selection tool, "Type" will be listed at the top of the Appearance panel and "Characters" will be listed as an attribute. If you select text characters using a type tool or if you double-click the word "Characters" on the Appearance panel, the attributes for those characters will be listed (and can be edited). To redisplay the attributes for the type object, click the word "Type."

Edit Appearance Attributes

Removing appearance attributes

To remove an appearance attribute:

1. Target a layer, group, or object.

2. On the **Appearance** panel, ⚫ click the attribute you want to remove.

3. Click the **Delete Selected Item** button 🗑 at the bottom of the panel.

➤ The sole remaining Fill and Stroke appearance attributes can't be removed. Clicking the Delete Selected Item button 🗑 for either of these appearance attributes will produce a fill or stroke of None.

To remove a brush stroke from a stroke attribute:

1. Target a layer, group, or object.

2. Show the Brushes panel (F5), 🖌 then click the **Remove Brush Stroke** button ✖ on the panel. The result will be a stroke in the same color as the former brush stroke.
   or
   Click the **Stroke** attribute on the Appearance panel, ⚫ then click the **Delete Selected Item** button 🗑 at the bottom of the panel. The stroke either reverts to None or is deleted.

To remove all appearance attributes from an item:

1. Target an object, layer, sublayer, or group .

2. To remove all the appearance attributes and apply a stroke and fill of None, click the **Clear Appearance** button ⊘ at the bottom of the Appearance panel (for type, the fill color will become black).
   or
   To remove all the appearance attributes except the basic stroke and fill, click the **Reduce to Basic Appearance** button ⚫▸⚫ at the bottom of the Appearance panel **2**.

➤ If you target a layer or group, the Clear... and Reduce... commands will remove only attributes that were applied to the layer or group, not ones that were applied directly to nested paths within the layer or group. To remove attributes from a nested path, you have to retarget that path.

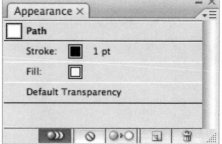

1 *Target a layer, group, or object, then click the **Reduce to Basic Appearance** button at the bottom of the Appearance panel.*

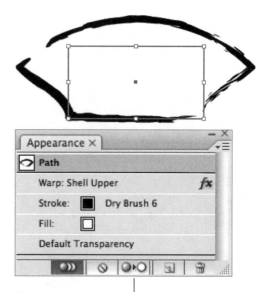

2 *All the appearance attributes (Warp and brush stroke, in this case) were **removed** from the object.*

Remove Appearance Attributes

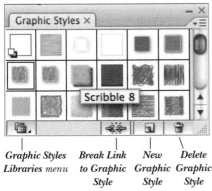

Graphic Styles | Break Link | New | Delete
Libraries *menu* | to Graphic | Graphic | Graphic
| Style | Style | Style

1 *The Graphic Styles panel*

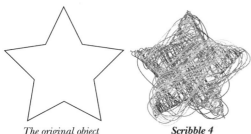

The original object | *Scribble 4*

RGB Denim | **Motion Trail Long**

RGB Cartoon Shading | *Scribble 6*

2 *We applied a few Illustrator **graphic styles** to an object, just to give you an inkling of what styles can do.*

Applying graphic styles

A **graphic style** is a collection of appearance attributes that can be applied to an object, group, or layer. Any appearance attributes that you could apply to an object can also be saved in a graphic style, such as solid colors, gradients, and patterns; Stroke panel attributes (weight, dashes, etc.); Transparency panel settings; and effects.

To create, save, or apply a graphic style, you'll use the **Graphic Styles** panel ![icon] (Shift-F5 or, for a temporary panel, click the style thumbnail or arrowhead on the Control panel) **1**–**2**. The attributes within each graphic style are listed on, and are edited via, the Appearance panel.

There are several compelling reasons to work with graphic styles:

➤ By applying a graphic style, you can quickly apply many attributes at once.

➤ Like appearance attributes, graphic styles change the way an object looks without changing its underlying path. You can remove a graphic style from an object at any time and, if desired, apply a different style.

➤ If you edit a graphic style, the style will update on any objects that it's linked to.

If you're wondering if graphic styles are similar to paragraph and character styles, you're right, except for one significant difference. If you modify an attribute directly on an object that a graphic style is linked to, that modification breaks the link between the object and the style. In other words, if you subsequently edit that graphic style, it won't update on the object.

Graphic styles can be applied to layers, sublayers, groups, or objects. When applied to a layer or group, a graphic style will be assigned to all the objects in that layer or group, as well as to any objects that you may subsequently add to it.

Apply Graphic Styles

If you **apply** a **graphic style** to a layer or group, that style will be applied to all the current and subsequently created objects in that layer or group. It will remain associated with the objects that it's applied to unless you deliberately break the link (see page 278).

To apply a graphic style:

1. With the **Selection** tool (V), select an object or objects in the document window.

or

On the **Layers** panel, ● click the target circle for an object, layer, sublayer, or group **1**–**2**.

Remember, for a top-level layer, selecting and targeting have different functions! (See the sidebar on page 266.)

2. Display the **Graphic Styles** panel.

3. Click a style name or thumbnail on the panel **3**–**5**. The name of the graphic style that's linked to the currently selected object, group, or layer will be listed at the top of the Appearance panel.

➤ To access graphic styles in other libraries, see page 277.

➤ To change the view for the Graphic Styles panel, from the panel menu, choose Thumbnail View, Small List View, or Large List View.

➤ Graphic styles can also be applied to symbol instances by using the Symbol Styler tool (see pages 362–363).

➤ You can also apply a style by dragging from the Graphic Styles panel over an unselected object in the document window.

➤ You can apply a graphic style to a layer or group, and another graphic style to individual objects nested within that layer or group.

1 *The original text object*

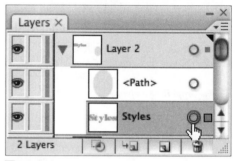

2 *Use the **Layers** panel to **target** the text object for an appearance change.*

3 *Click a swatch on the **Graphic Styles** panel ("Powder Puff" is a custom style).*

4 *The **graphic style** appears on the object.*

5 *A graphic style was applied to this **group** of buttons.*

Apply Graphic Style

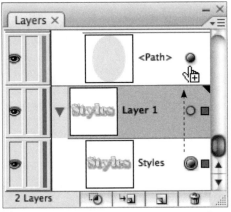

1 *Appearance attributes are copied from one path ("Styles") to another (<Path>.)*

Blends and appearances

If you blend objects that contain different **appearance** attributes (e.g., fills, strokes, most effects and filters), those attributes will be in full force in the original objects and will have sequentially less intensity in the intermediate blend steps **3**. The Object > Blend > Make command automatically nests blend objects on a <Blend> sublayer.

If you blend objects that contain different **blending modes,** the mode for the topmost object will be applied to all the intermediate blend steps.

On the Layers panel, <Blend> sublayers have a gray target circle, indicating that an appearance attribute is applied to the objects. Also, the **Knockout Group** option is checked on the Transparency panel by default to prevent the blend steps from blending with or showing through one another when a blend object has an opacity below 100% or has a blending mode other than Normal. Uncheck Knockout Group if you want to allow the blend steps to show through or blend with one another. If the blend objects have an opacity below 100% or a blending mode other than Normal—whether Knockout Group is on or off—objects behind the blend will be visible.

To attach appearance attributes to, and view the Transparency panel options for, an entire blend, click the target circle for the <Blend> sublayer on the Layers panel first, or select the blend in the document window with the Selection tool.

Copying appearance attributes
To copy appearance attributes from one object or layer to another:

Option-drag/Alt-drag the target circle on the **Layers** panel from the item that you want to copy onto the target circle for another layer, group, or object **1**.
or
Choose the Selection tool (V), click an object whose graphic style or appearance attributes you want to copy, then drag the square thumbnail from the uppermost left corner of the **Appearance** panel over an unselected object **2**.

➤ To move (not copy) appearance attributes from one item to another, drag a target circle from one layer, group, or object to another without holding down any keys. The appearance attributes will be removed from the original layer, group, or object.

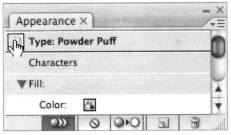

2 *Drag the thumbnail from the **Appearance** panel over an object.*

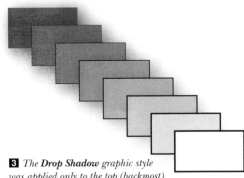

3 *The **Drop Shadow** graphic style was applied only to the top (backmost) rectangle. The attributes from the style fade gradually to the bottom rectangle.*

Copy Appearance Attributes

Creating graphic styles

There are two ways to create a **new graphic style:** You can either create a graphic style from an existing object or duplicate an existing graphic style and then modify the duplicate. The first method will probably feel the most natural and intuitive, especially if you're going to experiment with various settings for the new style.

1 *Click the object that contains the attributes you want to* ***save*** *as a graphic style.*

To create a graphic style from an object:

1. Target an object that has the attributes you want to save as a graphic style. If desired, use the Appearance panel to apply other attributes you want the style to contain **1**.

2. On the **Graphic Styles** panel, Option-click/Alt-click the **New Graphic Style** button, enter a name for the style in the Graphic Style Options dialog box, then click OK **2**. The new style will appear as the last listing or thumbnail on the panel **3**.

or

Drag the thumbnail from the uppermost left corner of the Appearance panel onto the Graphic Styles panel, or with the Selection tool, drag the object onto the Graphic Styles panel. Double-click the new style swatch, type a suitable name for it, then click OK.

To duplicate a graphic style:

1. On the **Graphic Styles** panel, click the style swatch or name that you want to duplicate, then click the **New Graphic Style** button (or drag the swatch over the button). If it's the first duplicate of that style, the numeral "1" will be appended to the existing style name.

2. Double-click the duplicate style to open the Graphic Style Options dialog box, type a name for the style, then click OK.

3. You can click the duplicate graphic style swatch or name, then view a listing of the attributes it contains on the Appearance panel. Edit the style, as per the instructions on the following page.

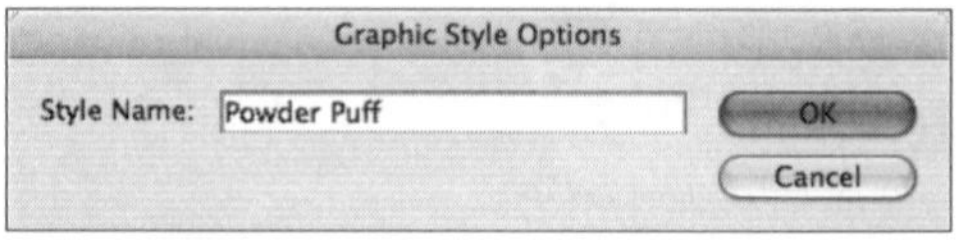

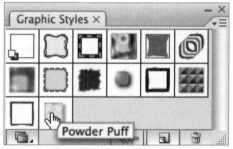

2 *Enter a* ***Style Name*** *for the new graphic style.*

3 *The new swatch appears at the bottom of the Graphic Styles panel.*

1 *Start by **applying** the graphic style that you want to edit to an object.*

2 *Edit the style on the object, by way of the **Appearance** panel.*

3 *The style updates on the **Graphic Styles** panel.*

Editing graphic styles

Beware! If you **edit** a **graphic style**, the changes will apply to any objects that it's linked to. If you don't want this to happen, duplicate the style (follow the instructions on the previous page), then edit the duplicate instead.

To edit a graphic style:

1. Apply the graphic style to be edited to an object, so you'll be able to preview your edits **1**.

2. Via the **Appearance** panel, ● edit or restack the existing appearance attributes or add new attributes **2**.

3. From the Appearance panel menu, choose **Redefine Graphic Style** "[style name]."
   or
   Option-drag/Alt-drag the object thumbnail from the uppermost left corner of the Appearance panel over the original swatch on the **Graphic Styles** panel.

   Regardless of which method you use, the style swatch will update to reflect the modifications **3**, and any objects to which the style is linked will update automatically **4**.

➤ While editing a graphic style, be careful not to click other styled objects or graphic style swatches, or your current appearance settings will be lost.

4 *The graphic style also **updates** automatically on any other objects that it's linked to.*

Edit Graphic Style

Merging graphic styles

If you have **two graphic styles** whose attributes you want to combine, you can **merge** them into one new (additional) style without changing the original swatches.

To merge graphic styles:

1. Cmd-click/Ctrl-click two or more style swatches or names on the Graphic Styles panel **1**.

2. Choose **Merge Graphic Styles** from the Graphic Styles panel menu. The Graphic Style Options dialog box opens **2**.

3. Enter a name for the new merged style, then click OK. The new style will appear as the last listing or thumbnail on the panel **3**.

➤ When you merge graphic styles, the order of attributes on the Appearance panel for the new style matches the order of attributes in the styles that you selected for merging, but the result may need adjusting. For example, if you merge graphic styles that contain fully opaque fills, only the topmost fill will be visible. To change the result, edit the opacity and/or blending mode of the fill attributes, or restack them (and thus change the order in which they're applied).

Deleting graphic styles

If you **delete** a **graphic style** that's linked to any objects in your document, the attributes from the style will remain on the objects, but the objects won't update if you edit the style.

To delete a style from the Graphic Styles panel:

1. On the Graphic Styles panel, click the style you want to remove, or Cmd-click/Ctrl-click multiple styles.

2. Click the **Delete Graphic Style** button on the panel.
   or
   Choose **Delete Graphic Style** from the Graphic Styles panel menu.

3. Click **Yes** in the alert dialog box.

➤ Oops! Change your mind? Choose Undo.

1 *Cmd/Ctrl click two styles, then choose* **Merge Graphic Styles** *from the Graphic Styles panel menu.*

2 *Enter a* **name** *for the new* **merged** *style.*

3 *The new* **style** *appears on the panel.*

Using graphic style libraries

To use graphic styles from other libraries:

1. From the **Graphic Styles Libraries** menu at the bottom of the Graphic Styles panel, choose a library name. **NEW!** A separate library panel opens 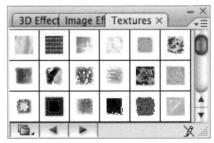.

2. To add a style to the Graphic Styles panel by styling an object, **select** an object, then click a style thumbnail in the library. Or drag a style thumbnail from the library over any object, selected or not. The style you selected will appear on the Graphic Styles panel.

   or

   To add a style to the Graphic Styles panel without styling an object, **deselect** all, then click a style thumbnail in the library.

   or

   To add **multiple** styles, click, then Shift-click consecutive styles or Cmd-click/Ctrl-click multiple styles on the library panel, then choose **Add to Graphic Styles** from the library panel menu.

3. To browse through another library, choose another library name from the Graphic Styles Libraries menu; or scroll through the available libraries in alphabetical order by clicking the **Load Prevous Graphic Styles Library** button ◀ or **Load Next Graphic Styles Library** button ▶ at the bottom of the Graphic Styles panel. **NEW!**

➤ If you apply a graphic style that contains a brush stroke to an object, and that brush isn't already present on the document's Brushes panel, it will be added to the Brushes panel.

By **saving graphic styles** to **custom libraries**, you'll be able to load them onto the Graphic Styles panel for use in any document. You can organize and name your libraries in any way that makes sense to you, such as by theme, client name, or project name.

To save a graphic styles library:

1. Make sure the Graphic Styles panel contains only the styles you want to save in a library.

2. *Optional:* To remove all the styles from the Graphic Styles panel that aren't currently being used in the document, choose Select All Unused from the Graphic Styles panel menu, click the Delete Graphic Style button 🗑 on the panel, then click Yes in the alert dialog box.

3. From the **Graphic Styles Libraries** menu at the bottom of the Graphic Styles panel, choose **Save Graphic Styles**. **NEW!** The Save Graphic Styles as Library dialog box opens.

4. Type a name for the library in the Save As field, then click Save. Keep the default location, which in the Mac OS is /Users/[user name]/Library/Application Support/Adobe/Adobe Illustrator CS3/Graphic Styles; and in Windows, C:\Documents and Settings\[user name]\Application Data\Adobe\Adobe Illustrator CS3 Settings\Graphic Styles.

5. The new library will be listed on, and can be opened from, the **User Defined** submenu on the Graphic Styles Libraries menu (bottom of the Graphic Styles panel).

1 *Graphic style libraries load onto a separate panel from the Graphic Styles panel.*

Breaking the link to a graphic style

If you **break the link** between an object and a graphic style and then subsequently edit the style, logically, the style won't update on that object.

To break the link to a graphic style:

1. Choose the **Selection** tool (V), then select an object or objects in the document window, or click the target circle for an object on the Layers panel.

   or

   If the style was applied to a group or layer, click the **target** circle for that layer, sublayer, or group on the **Layers** panel.

2. Click the **Break Link to Graphic Style** button at the bottom of the Graphic Styles panel.

   or

   Change any **appearance** attribute for the selected item or items (e.g., apply a different fill color, stroke settings, pattern, gradient, transparency settings, or effect).

   Note that the graphic style name is no longer listed at the top of the Appearance panel for the selected item.

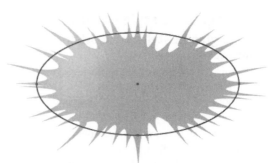

1 *Select an object that contains **appearance attributes**.*

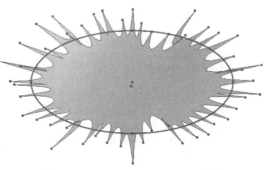

2 *The object's appearances are expanded.*

Expanding attributes

When you **expand** an object's **appearance attributes**, the paths that were used to create the attributes become (dozens of!) separate objects, and can be edited individually. This command comes in handy when you need to export files to other applications that can't read appearance attributes per se.

To expand an object's appearance attributes:

1. Select an object that contains the appearance attributes (or graphic style) that you want to expand **1**.

2. Choose Object > **Expand Appearance 2**. On the Layers panel, you'll now see a new <Group> (or a nested series of groups) containing the original object and the effects and appearance attributes, which will be listed either as individual paths or as images.

EFFECTS & FILTERS 21

In this chapter, after learning the differences between filters and effects, you'll learn how to apply them directly and via a graphic style; explore a few effects and fiilters in depth; rasterize an object to prepare it for filters; and use the Filter Gallery and Effect Gallery.

Effect	
Apply Sumi-e	⇧⌘E
Sumi-e...	⌥⇧⌘E
Document Raster Effects Settings...	
Illustrator Effects	
3D	▶
Convert to Shape	▶
Distort & Transform	▶
Path	▶
Pathfinder	▶
Rasterize...	
Stylize	▶
SVG Filters	▶
Warp	▶
Photoshop Effects	
Effect Gallery...	
Artistic	▶
Blur	▶
Brush Strokes	▶
Distort	▶
Pixelate	▶
Sharpen	▶
Sketch	▶
Stylize	▶
Texture	▶
Video	▶

1 *The* **Effect** *menu has two sections:* ***Illustrator Effects*** *(vector effects plus a few raster effects) on the top, and* ***Photoshop Effects*** *(raster effects) on the bottom.*

Effects and filters: An overview

Effects and **filters** apply distortion, texture, color adjustment, artistic, shape, and stylistic changes to objects and images, with results ranging from subtle to marked. Many of the filters on the Filter menu have matching counterparts on the Effect menu **1**. In fact, the Filter and Effect menus are so interdependent that settings used for a command on one menu become the settings for its counterpart on the other menu.

There are significant differences between effects and filters, however, in terms of the kind of objects they can be applied to and whether the results are editable after the command is applied. We'll address some of those differences next.

Using effects...

Filter menu commands change the path of the underlying object and aren't editable, whereas **effects** change only the **appearance** of an object—not its underlying path—and are fully **editable.** Because they can be edited or deleted at any time without permanently affecting the object they're applied to (and without affecting other effects or appearance attributes on the same object), effects lend themselves to experimentation. What's more, if you reshape the underlying object's path, the effects adjust

(Continued on the following page)

accordingly. In other words, unlike filters, effects are live.

All the **Illustrator effects** (on the top part of the Effect menu) are vector, and they output as vectors. Exceptions are Drop Shadow, Inner Glow, Outer Glow, and Feather on the Effect > Stylize submenu, which are rasterized (converted from vector to raster) on output. Some Illustrator effects have counterparts on the Filter menu, such as Drop Shadow and Roughen, but many are exclusive to the Effect menu, such as Feather and Convert to Shape.

All the **Photoshop effects** (on the bottom part of the Effect menu) are raster, meaning they're rasterized on output even when exported to a vector format such as SWF. All the Photoshop effects have counterparts on the Filter menu.

Both Illustrator effects and Photoshop effects can be applied to editable type (you don't have to convert the type to outlines), and the type will remain editable.

Like object attributes, effects are listed on the **Appearance** panel for each object they're applied to **1**. If you apply an effect to a **targeted** layer, sublayer, or group, it will apply automatically to all the current and future objects on the targeted entity.

Furthermore, because effects are appearance attributes (are listed on the Appearance panel), they can be saved in and applied via **graphic styles**, and can be edited at any time.

➤ To intensify the results of a Photoshop effect on a vector object, apply an effect such as Feather or Inner or Outer Glow first to add variation to the fill color.

...versus using filters

Unlike effects, Filter menu commands (**1**, next page) alter an object's actual path. Vector filters for path objects are found in the Illustrator Filters (upper) portion of the menu.

Photoshop filters for embedded bitmap images and rasterized objects are on the bottom portion of the Filter menu. Some of them introduce randomness or distortion; others, such as the Artistic, Brush Strokes, Sketch, and Texture filters, produce a hand-rendered look.

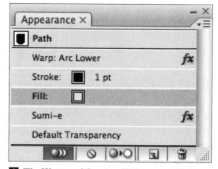

1 *The Warp and Sumi-e effects were applied to a path, as listed on the **Appearance** panel.*

Choosing raster settings

All the Photoshop Effects, along with the Stylize > Drop Shadow, Inner Glow, Outer Glow, and Feather effects, are rasterized upon output. But how do you control the rasterization process? Choose Effect > **Document Raster Effects Settings,** then choose Color Model, Resolution, Background treatment, and other options **2**. These settings also control how a raster effect looks in your Illustrator document. For a more detailed explanation of these settings, see page 290.

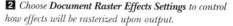

2 *Choose **Document Raster Effects Settings** to control how effects will be rasterized upon output.*

Reapply filter or effect quickly

Reapply **last effect** using the same settings (no dialog box opens) — Cmd-Shift-E / Ctrl-Shift-E

Reopen **Effect Gallery** or last effects dialog box — Cmd-Option-Shift-E / Ctrl-Alt-Shift-E

Reapply **last filter** using the same settings (no dialog box opens) — Cmd-E / Ctrl-E

Reopen **Filter Gallery** or last filter dialog box — Cmd-Option-E / Ctrl-Alt-E

Filter

Apply Last Filter	⌘E
Last Filter	⌥⌘E
Illustrator Filters	
Colors	▶
Create	▶
Distort	▶
Stylize	▶
Photoshop Filters	
Filter Gallery...	
Artistic	▶
Blur	▶
Brush Strokes	▶
Distort	▶
Pixelate	▶
Sharpen	▶
Sketch	▶
Stylize	▶
Texture	▶
Video	▶

1 *The* **Filter** *menu*

Roughen

Options
Size: `25` %
⊙ Relative   ○ Absolute
Detail: `10` /in

OK
Cancel
☑ Preview

Points
○ Smooth   ⊙ Corner

2 *To monitor changes in the document window, check* **Preview** *(if available) in an effect or filter dialog box.*

Applying filters and effects

To apply a filter or an effect, target a layer, group, or object, then choose a command from a submenu on the Filter or Effect menu (your document can be in CMYK or RGB color mode **NEW!**).

An **individual** dialog box opens when you open a filter under Filter > Illustrator Filters; under Effect > Illustrator Effects; or from the Blur, Pixelate, Sharpen, or Video submenu on the Filter or Effect menu. To learn more about applying Illustrator effects, see the next page.

When you choose any other Photoshop filter or Photoshop effect, the **Filter Gallery** or **Effect Gallery** opens, respectively. You can also choose Filter > Filter Gallery or Effect > Effect Gallery to open that gallery (see pages 292–294).

Many vector filter and effect dialog boxes have a **Preview** option that lets you preview the results in your document as you choose settings **2**. If you enter a value in a field, press Tab to update the preview.

➤ You can apply filters to embedded bitmap images, but not to linked images. You can apply effects to embedded bitmap images, or to the embedded preview of a linked image (not to the linked image itself).

➤ You can install and use plug-in filters from third-party developers in Illustrator.

Applying Illustrator effects

In the instructions below, you'll **apply** an **Illustrator effect** directly to a layer, sublayer, group, or object. In the instructions on the next page, you'll learn how to add to, or edit an effect in, a graphic style.

To apply an effect:

1. On the **Layers** panel (F7), 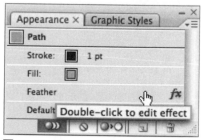 click the **target** circle for a layer, sublayer, group, or object **1**. The target circle should have a double border.

   or

   To limit the effect to just an object's stroke or fill, select the object, then click the **Stroke** or **Fill** listing on the **Appearance** panel.

2. Choose an **Illustrator effect** from the top portion of the Effect menu.

3. Check Preview (if available) to preview the effect as you choose options, then choose options **2**.

4. Click OK **3**. If you applied the effect to just a stroke or fill, the effect will be nested within the Stroke or Fill listing on the Appearance panel.

To edit an applied effect:

1. On the Layers panel (F7), **target** the layer, sublayer, group, or object that the effect you want to edit is applied to.

   or

   If you applied the effect to just an object's stroke or fill, select the object, then expand the **Stroke** or **Fill** listing on the Appearance panel.

2. Double-click the effect listing on the **Appearance** panel **4**. The effect dialog box reopens.

3. Make the desired adjustments, then click OK.

1 *The original object*

2 *A value is chosen in the **Feather** effect dialog box.*

3 *The **Feather** effect is applied.*

4 *Double-click an effect listing on the **Appearance** panel to **edit** that attribute.*

1 *Click a style on the **Graphic Styles** panel. (The Scribble 5 effect is in the Scribble Effects library.)*

2 *To edit an effect, double-click the effect name or icon on the **Appearance** panel.*

From effect to graphic style

To save all the attributes currently listed on the Appearance panel as a graphic style, click the **New Graphic Style** button on the **Graphic Styles** panel, or drag the square thumbnail from the upper left corner of the Appearance panel to the Graphic Styles panel (separate the panels first).

Using effects in graphic styles

Graphic styles let you apply multiple attributes at once, including effects. You can **edit** any effect that was used in a style, and **add effects** to a **style**. To learn more about graphic styles, see pages 271–278.

To add an effect to or edit an effect in a graphic style:

1. Click a style name or swatch on the **Graphic Styles** panel ⬛ (access it via the Control panel, if you wish) **1**, or select an object that uses that graphic style so you can preview your edits. The style name will appear at the top of the Appearance panel.

2. To **add** an effect to the selected graphic style, choose an Illustrator effect from the Effect menu, choose options (check Preview if you selected an object in the previous step), then click OK.
   or
   To **edit** an existing effect, double-click the effect name or icon on the Appearance panel, choose options, then click OK **2**.

3. From the Appearance panel menu, ⬤ choose **Redefine Graphic Style** "[style name]" to update the style.

You can **remove** an **effect** from a layer, object, or style as easily as you can add one.

To remove an effect from a layer, object, or graphic style:

1. On the **Layers** panel, ⬛ target the layer, sublayer, group, or object that contains the effect you want to remove.
   or
   On the **Graphic Styles** panel, ⬛ click the graphic style name or swatch that contains the effect you want to remove.

2. On the Appearance panel, ⬤ click the effect name or icon, then click the **Delete Selected Item** button 🗑 on the Appearance panel (or drag the effect name over the button).

3. If you're removing an effect from a style, choose **Redefine Graphic Style** "[style name]" from the Appearance panel menu to update the style.

Effects in Graphic Styles

A few Illustrator effects and filters up close

The effects discussed in this section are found only on the upper part of the Effects menu; they don't have counterparts on the Filter menu.

To apply Pathfinder effects

The commands on the **Effect > Pathfinder** sub-menu are like the commands on the Pathfinder panel (see pages 327–328), except for the following important differences **1**:

➤ The Pathfinder effects modify an object's appearance but not its actual path.

➤ You can delete a Pathfinder appearance attribute at any time.

➤ The effects don't create compound shapes.

➤ The Divide, Trim, and Merge effects don't break up overlapping areas into separate objects. To create separate objects, use the Divide, Trim, or Merge button on the Pathfinder panel.

Next, a few **guidelines** for **applying Pathfinder effects:**

➤ Before applying a Pathfinder effect, collect the objects to which you want to apply the effect into a **sublayer** or **group**, then target the sublayer or group (be sure to target — not select).

➤ Via the Layers panel, you can **move** objects into or out of a group that a Pathfinder effect is applied to.

➤ Pathfinder effects can be included in a **graphic style** (see the previous page).

➤ Pathfinder effects can be **removed** at any time (see the previous page).

➤ To **replace** a Pathfinder effect in a targeted group (with a convenient preview), double-click a Pathfinder effect listing on the Appearance panel to open the Pathfinder Options dialog box, then choose a Pathfinder option from the Operation menu.

➤ If you **expand** a Pathfinder effect by choosing Object > Expand Appearance, the result will be a path shape, a compound path, or an image.

1 *The **Pathfinder** commands can be applied as effects via the **Effect** menu.*

It's a hard mix

To simulate overprinting, target a group or layer that contains two or more objects that overlap one another, at least partially (they can be type objects), then choose Effect > **Pathfinder** > **Hard Mix.** The highest CMYK or RGB values from the objects will be mixed in areas where they overlap. The greater the difference between the original colors, the more marked the result.

1 *The original object*

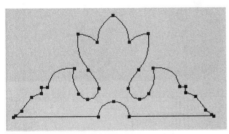

2 *Choose shape and scale options in the **Shape Options** dialog box.*

3 *The **Convert to Shape** > **Rectangle** effect was applied to this object. As you can see, it didn't change the underlying path.*

In these instructions, you'll use a **Convert to Shape** effect to change an object's silhouette to a rectangle, rounded rectangle, or ellipse without altering the actual underlying path.

To apply a Convert to Shape effect:

1. Select or target an object or objects in the document window or via the Layers panel **1**.

2. Choose Effect > Convert to Shape > **Rectangle, Rounded Rectangle,** or **Ellipse.** The Shape Options dialog box opens **2**. (You can also choose one of the 3 shapes from the Shape menu in the dialog box.)

3. Check Preview.

4. Click **Absolute,** then enter the total desired **Width** and **Height** values for the shape's appearance.
or
Click **Relative,** then enter the **Extra Width** or **Extra Height** if you want the shape to be larger or smaller than the actual path (enter a positive or negative value).

5. For the Rounded Rectangle shape, you can also change the **Corner Radius** value.

6. Click OK **3**–**4**.

➤ To simply round off sharp corners on an object without converting its shape, use Effect > Stylize > Round Corners.

4 *The **Rectangle** effect is listed on the Appearance panel.*

Keeping up with appearances

Appearances, such as effects or extra fill attributes, can be applied to a whole type object but not to individual type characters. That's why the Appearance panel displays a list of attributes when a whole type object is selected, and the original fill and stroke colors if you double-click the "Characters" listing on the panel or select the type with a type tool. Confusing? Just keep track of the name next to the thumbnail at the top of the Appearance panel. If it says **Characters,** your edits will affect selected characters; if it says **Type,** your edits will affect all the type in the object.

The **Inner Glow** effect spreads a color from the edge of an object inward; the **Outer Glow** effect spreads a color from the edge of an object outward.

To apply the Inner Glow or Outer Glow effect:

1. Select or target a layer, sublayer, group, or object **1**.

2. Choose Effect > Stylize > **Inner Glow** or **Outer Glow.**

3. In the Inner Glow or Outer Glow dialog box, check Preview **2**.

4. Do any of the following:

Click the **Color** square next to the Mode menu, then choose a different glow color (it can be a spot color).

Choose a blending **Mode** for the glow color.

Choose an **Opacity** for the glow color.

Click the **Blur** arrowhead, then move the slider slowly to adjust how far the glow extends inward or outward. The higher the Blur value, the wider the glow.

For the Inner Glow effect, click **Center** to have the glow spread outward from the center of the object, or **Edge** to have the glow spread inward from the edge of the object toward the center.

5. Click OK **3**–**5**.

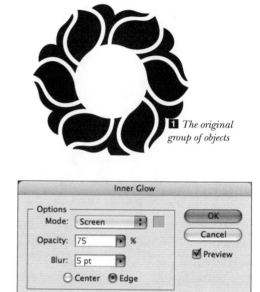

1 *The original group of objects*

2 *Options are chosen in the **Inner Glow** dialog box.*

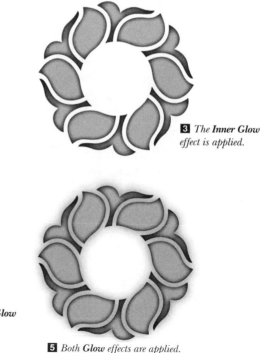

3 *The **Inner Glow** effect is applied.*

4 *The **Outer Glow** effect is applied.*

5 *Both **Glow** effects are applied.*

1 *The original object*

2 *Choose Scribble Options.*

3 *Scribble filter,*
Settings: Moiré

4 *Scribble filter,*
Settings: Sketch

The **Scribble** effect makes an object's fill and stroke look as though they were drawn with a felt-tip marker or pen.

To apply the Scribble effect:

1. Select a path object or objects, or type **1**.

2. Choose Effect > Stylize > **Scribble**. The Scribble Options dialog box opens **2**.

3. Check Preview. As a start, choose a preset from the **Settings** menu. Follow the remaining steps if you want to choose custom settings for the preset; otherwise, click OK.

4. Enter an **Angle** value or rotate the dial to change the angle of the sketch lines.

5. Drag the **Path Overlap** slider toward Outside to allow the sketch lines to extend beyond the edge of the path, or toward Inside to keep them inside the path. Choose a high **Variation** value to produce random variations in line lengths and a wilder, more haphazard look, or a low Variation for more uniform lengths.

6. For the **Line Options** sliders, do any of the following:

Change the **Stroke Width** for the lines.

Change the **Curviness** value to control whether the lines angle more sharply or loop more loosely where they change direction. The **Variation** slider controls the degree of random variation in these direction changes.

Change the **Spacing** value to cluster sketch lines more tightly or to spread them apart. The **Variation** slider controls the degree of random variation in the spacing.

7. Click OK **3**–**4**. Scribble will become an effect listing on the Appearance panel. Double-click the listing at any time to edit the effect.

➤ If you make Scribble setting changes and then choose a preset from the Settings menu, your custom settings will be deleted. Unfortunately, you can't save your settings as a preset.

Scribble Effect

Three Illustrator filters and effects up close

The **Drop Shadow** command creates soft, naturalistic shadows and can be applied as a filter or as an effect. The filter creates a new shadow image layer, separate from the original object, and has a Create Separate Shadows option that nests the object and the shadow image into a new group on the Layers panel.

Unlike the filter, the Drop Shadow effect has a Preview option and becomes an appearance on the original object. You can double-click the Drop Shadow listing on the Appearance panel and change the settings, including the shadow color, at any time.

To apply the Drop Shadow effect or filter:

1. Select one or more path objects or editable type.

2. Choose **Filter** > Stylize > **Drop Shadow** or **Effect** > Stylize > **Drop Shadow.** The Drop Shadow dialog box opens **1**. If you chose the command from the Effect menu, check Preview.

3. Do the following:

   Choose a blending **Mode.**

   Choose an **Opacity** value for the shadow.

   Enter an **X Offset** for the horizontal distance between the object and the shadow and a **Y Offset** for the vertical distance between the object and the shadow.

   Enter a **Blur** value (0–144 pt) for the width of the shadow.

   Optional: Click Color, click the color square, then choose a different shadow color from the Color Picker (it can be a spot color), then click OK. Or click Darkness, then enter a percentage of black to be added to the shadow.

4. *Optional:* If you're using the filter (not the effect), you can check Create Separate Shadows to make the shadow a separate layer in a new group, nested with the object it's applied to.

5. Click OK **2**–**3**.

1 *Sometimes we're satisfied with the default **Drop Shadow** settings (shown above); at other times we might change the Opacity or Blur value.*

2 *The **Drop Shadow** effect is applied to editable type.*

3 *The **Drop Shadow** effect is applied (as well as the Feather effect).*

1 *The original object*

2 *The Roughen dialog box*

The **Roughen** filter and effect add anchor points and then move them, with the result being an object that looks more hand-drawn.

To apply the Roughen effect or filter:

1. Select a path object or objects **1**. If you like, also choose View > Hide Edges (Cmd-H/Ctrl-H) to make it easier to preview the result.

2. Choose Effect > Distort & Transform > **Roughen,** or Filter > Distort > **Roughen.** The Roughen dialog box opens **2**. Check Preview.

3. Click **Relative** to move points by a percentage of the object's size, or **Absolute** to move points by a specific amount, then choose a **Size** amount to specify how far the object's anchor points may move. To preserve the object's overall shape, choose a very low Size amount.

4. Choose a **Detail** amount for the number of points to be added to each inch of the path segments.

5. Click **Smooth** to produce curves, or click **Corner** to produce pointy angles.

6. Click OK **3**.

3 *After applying the **Roughen** filter (or eyeing a dog!)*

The **Twist** effect and filter twist an object's outer shape but not its fill. You can twist a single object or twist multiple objects together.

To apply the Twist effect or filter:

1. Select a path object or objects **4**.

2. Choose Effect > Distort & Transform > **Twist,** or Filter > Distort > **Twist.** The Twist dialog box opens.

3. Enter a positive **Angle** (press Tab) to twirl the path(s) clockwise or a negative value to twirl it counterclockwise (–360 to 360).

4. Click OK **5**.

4 *The original object*

5 *After applying the **Twist** effect*

Roughen, Twist

Rasterizing objects

The **Rasterize** command converts vector objects to bitmap images. If you choose the RGB Color Model in the Rasterize dialog box, you'll be able to apply any of the Photoshop filters to the resulting object. (Photoshop effects can be applied to vector objects, so there's no need to rasterize them—at least for that reason).

To rasterize a path object:

1. Select a path object or objects, or target them on the Layers panel.

2. Choose Object > **Rasterize.** The Rasterize dialog box opens.

3. Choose a **Color Model** for the object. Depending on the current document color mode, you can choose **CMYK** for print output (few Photoshop filters and effects will be available for the object); **RGB** for video or onscreen output (all Photoshop filters and effects will be available); **Grayscale** (all Photoshop filters and effects will be available); or **Bitmap** for only black-and-white or black-and-transparent (no Photoshop filters or effects will be available).

4. For **Resolution,** choose **Screen** for Web or video output, **Medium** for desktop printers, or **High** for commercial printing; or enter

a resolution in the **Other** field; or click **Use Document Raster Effects Resolution** to use the global resolution settings as specified in Effect > Document Raster Effects Settings.

5. Click **Background: White** to make any transparent areas in the object opaque white, or **Transparent** to make the background transparent (see the sidebar on this page).

6. For **Options:**

Choose **Anti-aliasing: Art Optimized (Supersampling)** to have Illustrator soften the edges of the rasterized shape, but keep in mind that this option could make type or thin lines look blurry. For type objects, **Type Optimized (Hinted)** is a better option. If you choose **None,** edges will be jagged.

To add pixels around the object to allow for effects or filters that extend beyond the object, enter an **Add [ ] Around Object** value.

Check **Preserve Spot Colors** to preserve spot colors that are applied to the object. **NEW!**

7. Click OK.

➤ If you rasterize an object that contains a pattern fill and you want to preserve any transparency in the pattern, in the Rasterize dialog box, click Background: Transparent and choose Anti-aliasing: Art Optimized.

➤ Although you can also rasterize an object via a reversible and editable effect, and the Object menu command discussed here is permanent, if you're going to apply Photoshop filters to the object, you must use the command.

Transparent vs. clipping mask options

Both the Background: Transparent and Create Clipping Mask options in the Rasterize dialog box remove an object's background, but with different results. The **Transparent** option creates an alpha channel in order to remove the background. Any appearances or transparency (blending mode and opacity) settings are removed, without changing how the object looks. The **Create Clipping Mask** option creates a clipping path around the image. Any existing appearance attributes are applied to the mask, and any transparency reverts to Normal mode and 100% opacity. If you click the Transparent option, you don't need to check Create Clipping Mask.

1 *The original image*

2 *Choose settings in the **Object Mosaic** dialog box.*

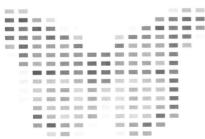

3 *The **Object Mosaic** filter is applied.*

4 *The **Object Mosaic** filter is applied to the original image, this time with spacing between the tiles.*

An Illustrator filter up close

The **Object Mosaic** filter breaks up a raster image into a grid of little squares; each square is a separate object that can be moved or recolored individually. (There's no effect version of this filter.)

To apply the Object Mosaic filter:

1. Select a rasterized object or an embedded bitmap image **1**.

2. Choose Filter > Create > **Object Mosaic**. The Object Mosaic dialog box opens **2**.

3. *Optional :*

    Change the **New Size: Width** and/or **Height** values. If you want to enter dimensions in percentages relative to the original, check Resize Using Percentages at the bottom of the dialog box; the Width and Height fields will switch to percentage values.
    or
    Enter a **New Size: Width** (or **Height**), click Constrain Ratio: Width (or Height) under Options to lock in that dimension, then click Use Ratio to have Illustrator automatically calculate the second dimension proportionate to the object's original dimensions.

4. Enter the desired **Number of Tiles** to fill the **Width** and **Height** dimensions.

5. *Optional:* To add spacing between the tiles, enter Tile Spacing: Width and Height values.

6. *Optional:* Illustrator will apply the Object Mosaic filter to a copy of a bitmap image (stacked above the original). Check Delete Raster to delete the original image; uncheck to keep it.

7. Click **Result: Color** or **Gray**.

8. Click OK **3**–**4**. The mosaic object will be listed as a new group on the Layers panel.

Object Mosaic Filter

291

Using the Filter or Effect Gallery

The **Filter Gallery** or **Effect Gallery** lets you access all the Photoshop filters or Photoshop effects in one place. In the Filter Gallery (not the Effect Gallery), you can also preview multiple filters, show/hide individual previews, and change the sequence in which they're applied. As you try out multiple filters—whether solo or in combination—let your creative juices flow!

To use the Filter or Effect Gallery:

1. Select a rasterized object, an embedded image, or editable or outline type.

2. Choose Filter > **Filter Gallery** or Effect > **Effect Gallery** or choose any individual Photoshop filter or Photoshop effect from either menu (except from the Pixelate, Blur, Sharpen, or Video submenu). The gallery opens (**1**, next page).

3. If you chose an individual filter or effect, that effect thumbnail will be highlighted in the dialog box. To choose a different filter or effect in the dialog box, in the middle panel, click an arrowhead/chevron to expand one of the six categories, then click a thumbnail.

4. Choose settings for the chosen filter or effect in the right panel. You can change the zoom level for the preview via the zoom buttons or menu, and you can move the preview in the window.

5. *In the Filter Gallery, you can also do any of the following:*

   To apply an additional filter, click the **New Effect Layer** button,▣ click another filter thumbnail in any category (or choose from the menu on the right side of the dialog box), then choose settings. The previewed filters are listed in the bottom right of the dialog box, with the most recently chosen filter at the top of the list.

   To **replace** a filter, keep the existing name selected on the scroll list, click a new thumbnail, and choose settings.

   To **hide** a filter preview, click the visibility (eye) icon on the scroll list; click again to redisplay it. Hidden filters won't be applied to the selected object.

   To change the **sequence** in which the filters are applied, drag an effect name upward or downward on the list. A different sequence will produce a different result in the document.

   To **remove** the currently selected filter from the list, click the Delete Effect Layer button.🗑

6. For some effects and filters, such as Artistic > Rough Pastels or Underpainting, you can choose a texture type from the **Texture** menu (**1**, page 294). Move the Scaling slider to scale the pattern, and move the Relief slider, if there is one, to adjust the depth and prominence of the texture on the surface of the image.

7. Click OK (**2**–**5**, page 294).

➤ In the Filter Gallery, hold down Cmd/Ctrl and click Default (the Cancel button becomes a Default button) to remove any added filters from the scroll list and restore the default settings. Hold down Option/Alt and click Reset to restore the settings that were in place when you opened the dialog box.

➤ In addition to the Photoshop filters, you can apply most of the Edit > Edit Colors commands and all the Filter > Illustrator Filters to a rasterized object or embedded image.

Filter, Effect Gallery

To **move** the image in the **preview** window, use the scroll bars or arrows or drag the preview image.

Click the arrowhead/chevron to hide the **middle panel** and expand the preview window to two panels wide; click it again to redisplay the middle panel.

Choose a different filter or effect from this menu.

Choose **settings** for the selected filter or effect.

Filter Gallery

Click the **Zoom Out** or **Zoom In** button, or choose a **zoom level** from the menu.

Click the visibility column to **hide** or **show** the preview for that filter, and thereby disable or enable it.

Click the **New Effect Layer** button to preview an additional filter.

1 The **Filter Gallery** has three panels: an image **preview** on the left; filter **thumbnails** in categories in the middle; and **settings** and a list of **previewed filters** on the right.

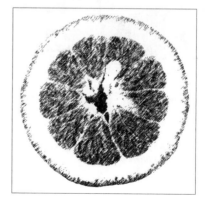

1 *Some filters and effects (such as Glass, shown here) have a **Texture** menu.*

Three Photoshop effects

2 *The original placed bitmap image*

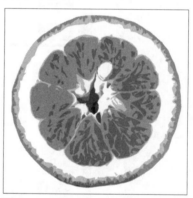

3 *The Artistic > **Cutout** effect*

4 *The Distort > **Ocean Ripple** effect*

5 *The Sketch > **Graphic Pen** effect*

Apply Texture; Photoshop Effects

BRASHES 22

In this chapter, you'll learn how to use the Paintbrush tool; embellish path edges with Calligraphic, Scatter, and Art brushes; create and edit custom brushes; modify existing brush strokes; remove brush strokes from existing paths; create and access brush libraries; and add, duplicate, and delete brushes from the Brushes panel.

Calligraphic brushes

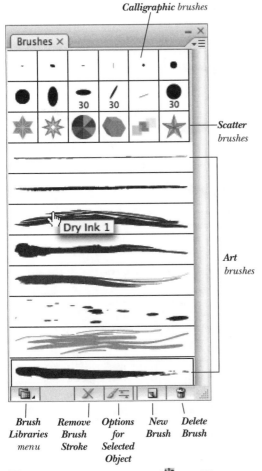

Scatter brushes

Art brushes

Brush	Remove	Options	New	Delete
Libraries	Brush	for	Brush	Brush
menu	**Stroke**	Selected		
		Object		

1 *To open or close the* **Brushes** *panel,* press **F5**. *Or to open a temporary Brushes panel, click the brush thumbnail or arrowhead on the* **Control** *panel.*

Using brushes

Illustrator's **brushes** let you draw variable, free-hand brush strokes or apply a texture, pattern, or shapes to a path with all the advantages of vector graphics—small file sizes, resizability, and crisp output.

The brushes come in four flavors: **Scatter, Calligraphic, Art,** and **Pattern,*** and they're stored on and accessed from the **Brushes** panel (F5) **1**. (The default Brushes panel contains only a small handful of the available brushes; we'll show you how to add more.)

To apply a brush stroke, you can either choose the Paintbrush tool and a brush and draw a shape right off the bat with a brush stroke built into it, or you can apply a brush stroke to an existing path of any kind. To change the contour of a brush stroke, you reshape the path it's attached to (see Chapter 11).

Brushes are also live, so if you edit a brush that's being used in your document, you'll be given the option via an alert dialog box to update the paths that use that brush. You can also create your own brushes from objects in your artwork or via an options dialog box.

To start, you'll grab the Paintbrush tool, click a brush on the Brushes panel, and draw some shapes, as per the instructions on the next page.

*To learn about Pattern brushes, see Illustrator Help.

Brushes

Using the Paintbrush tool

If you use a stylus and a pressure-sensitive tablet, the **Paintbrush** tool will respond to pressure. The harder you press on the tablet, the wider the resulting shape or stroke.

To draw with the Paintbrush tool:

1. Choose the **Paintbrush** tool (B), and choose a fill color of None.

2. Show the **Brushes** panel (press F5, or click the Brush thumbnail or arrowhead on the Control panel); then click any type of brush on the panel.

3. To draw open paths, draw freehand lines **1**–**2**. Or to draw a closed path, drag to draw the path, then Option-drag/Alt-drag to close it (release Option/Alt last).

Preferences you choose for the **Paintbrush** tool affect only future (not existing) brush strokes.

To choose preferences for the Paintbrush tool:

1. Double-click the **Paintbrush** tool (or choose the tool, then press Return/Enter) to open its preferences dialog box.

2. Choose a **Fidelity** value (0.5–20 pixels) **3**. A low Fidelity setting produces many anchor points and paths that accurately follow the movement of your mouse; a high setting produces fewer anchor points and smoother, but less accurate, paths.

3. Choose a **Smoothness** value (0–100%). The higher the Smoothness, the fewer the irregularities in the path.

4. Check any of the following **Options:**

   Fill New Brush Strokes to have new paths you draw (open or closed) fill with the current fill color automatically.

   Keep Selected to have paths stay selected after you draw them (for immediate reshaping with the same tool).

   Edit Selected Paths, and choose a range (2–20 pixels) within which the tool can reshape selected paths (see page 141).

5. Click OK.

1 *This drawing was created using the **Paintbrush** tool and various brushes.*

2 *These strokes were drawn with the Paintbrush tool and an **Art** brush.*

3 *Choose settings for the **Paintbrush** in its own preferences dialog box.*

Paintbrush Tool

Scale strokes?

If you scale an object that has a brush stroke and **Scale Strokes & Effects** is checked in the Scale dialog box (double-click the Scale tool) or in Preferences (Cmd-K/Ctrl-K) > General, the brush stroke will scale accordingly. With this option unchecked, a brush stroke will stay the same size when you scale an object.

Applying brushes

You'll learn how to create and modify Scatter, Calligraphic, and Art brushes later in this chapter. But first, you need to learn how to **apply** a **brush** to an existing **path**.

To apply a brush to a path:

1. Display the **Brushes** panel. 🖫

2. Select a path of any kind with any selection tool ▮, then **click** a brush on the Brushes panel ▮–▮. You can apply a brush to type **NEW!** or a type path.
   or
   Drag a brush from the Brushes panel onto a path or type (the object doesn't have to be selected). Release the mouse when the pointer is over the object.

➤ To select all the paths in your document that have brush strokes, choose Select > Object > Brush Strokes. If you then click a brush on the Brushes panel, it will be applied to all the selected objects.

➤ What's the difference between Pattern and Scatter brushes? For a Scatter brush you can specify a degree of randomness for the size, spacing, and scatter variables; not so for a Pattern brush. Pattern brushes contain up to 5 tiles (Side, Outer Corner, Inner Corner, Start, and End), which enable the strokes to fit tightly on a path. Unlike Scatter brushes, Pattern brushes are useful for creating borders or frames.

▮ *Select a path...*

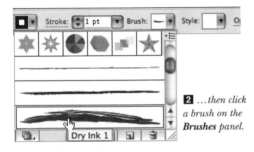
▮ *...then click a brush on the* **Brushes** *panel.*

▮ *The* **Calligraphic** *brush we chose appears on the path.*

▮ *An* **Art** *brush stroke*

▮ *A* **Scatter** *brush stroke*

▮ *Another* **Scatter** *brush stroke (made from 5 birds)*

▮ *A* **Pattern** *brush stroke*

Using the Brushes panel

Once you open a brush library, you can apply a brush from that library directly to any path, or you can add brushes from the **library** to the **Brushes panel**, in which case they'll save with your document.

Furthermore, you can use any brush from a library as the starting point for creating a custom brush. After adding it to your document's Brushes panel, you can duplicate it, if desired, and then customize it to your liking.

To add brushes from other libraries:

1. From the **Brush Libraries** menu 🗔 at the bottom of the Brushes panel, choose a library name.**NEW!**

2. Deselect all the objects in your document (Cmd-Shift-A/Ctrl-Shift-A).

3. **Click** a brush in the library; it will appear on the Brushes panel.
or
Click, then Shift-click, a consecutive series of brushes in the library, then choose **Add to Brushes** from the library menu **1**–**2**.
or
Drag a brush directly from the library onto any object in the document window (the object doesn't have to be selected). The brush stroke will appear on the object and the brush will appear on the Brushes panel.

➤ To delete brushes from the Brushes panel, see page 308.

➤ To close a panel group, click the close box (x) on the gray bar. To close just one library in a group, click the close box on the library tab.

Be persistent

Normally, open libraries don't reopen when you relaunch Illustrator, which can be irritating if you want to keep a library readily accessible. To force a particular library to reopen when you relaunch the program, choose **Persistent** from the library menu. To save brushes with your document, follow the instructions at left.

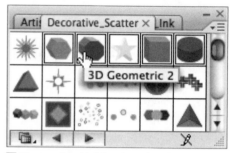

1 *To append multiple brushes, select them, then choose **Add to Brushes** from the library menu.*

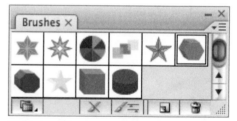

2 *The brushes appear on the **Brushes** panel in the current document.*

Which type are they?

Type	Library
Calligraphic	Artistic_Calligraphic
Scatter	Arrows_Special, Arrows_Standard, Artistic_Ink, Decorative_Scatter
Art	Arrows_Standard; all the "Artistic" libraries except _Calligraphic; Decorative_Banners and Seals; Decorative_Text Dividers
Pattern	All the "Borders" libraries

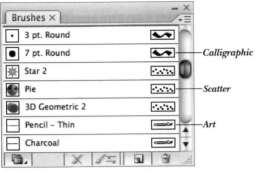

1 When the Brushes panel is in **List** view, each brush type has a unique icon.

2 The original object has a **brush stroke**.

3 The brush stroke is **removed** from the object.

4 The original object has a **brush stroke**.

5 The **Expand Appearance** command converted the brush stroke into an object, which is now separate from the original path (we ungrouped the stroke and object and moved them apart for you to see).

To choose display options for the Brushes panel:

From the **Brushes** panel menu:

Choose **List View** to have a small thumbnail, the brush name, and an icon for the brush type (Calligraphic, Scatter, Art, or Pattern) display for each brush on the panel **1**; or **Thumbnail View** to display larger thumbnails with no name or icon.

To control which **brush types** (categories) display on the panel, choose "Show [brush type]" to check or uncheck that option.

➤ You can drag any brush upward or downward on the panel to a different location within its category. To move multiple brushes, select them first (click, then Shift-click consecutive brushes). *Note:* You can't do this if you open a temporary Brushes panel via the Control panel.

Removing brush strokes

When you **remove a brush stroke** from a path, you're left with a plain vanilla path.

To remove a brush stroke from an object:

1. Select the object or objects from which you want to remove a brush stroke **2**.

2. Click the **Remove Brush Stroke** button at the bottom of the Brushes panel **3**.

Expanding brush strokes

When you **expand a brush stroke**, it's converted into editable outlined paths (objects in the shape of the former brush strokes) that you can reshape as you would normal paths. The stroke will no longer be live, though, so you won't be able to replace it via the Brushes panel or edit it by editing the brush.

To expand a brush stroke into outlined paths:

1. Select an object that has a brush stroke **4**.

2. Choose Object > **Expand Appearance**. The brush stroke is now a separate object or objects **5**, nested (or double- or triple-nested) in a group sublayer on the Layers panel.

CHAPTER 22

Next, we'll show you how to modify Scatter, Calligraphic, and Art brushes.

Creating and editing Scatter brushes

Objects from a **Scatter** brush are placed evenly or randomly along the contour of a path. You can create a Scatter brush from an open or closed path, type character, type outline, blend, or compound path, but not from a gradient, bitmap image (placed or rasterized), mesh, or clipping mask.

To create or edit a Scatter brush:

1. To create a new brush, select one or more objects **1**, then click the **New Brush** button **⊡** on the Brushes panel. The New Brush dialog box opens. Click **New Scatter Brush**, then click OK.
   or
   To modify an existing brush, deselect, then **double-click** a Scatter brush on the Brushes panel. (Or click a Scatter brush, then choose Brush Options from the panel menu.)

2. The Scatter Brush Options dialog box opens **2**. If you're creating a new brush, enter a new name; or to edit an existing brush, leave the name as is.

3. Check Preview (available only for existing brushes) to view changes on any paths where the brush is currently in use.

4. For **Size**, **Spacing**, **Scatter**, and **Rotation**, choose one of the following variations from the menu:

   Fixed to use a single fixed value.

   Random, then move the sliders (or enter different values in the two fields) to define a range within which that property can vary.

   If you're using a graphics tablet, choose **Pressure, Stylus Wheel, Tilt, Bearing, or Rotation.** Move the sliders (or enter different values in the two fields) to define a range within which that property can respond to stylus pressure. Light pressure uses the minimum property value from the left field; heavy pressure uses the maximum property value from the right field.

Creating brush variations

To create a variation of an existing brush of any type, **duplicate** it first by following the instructions on page 305. To create a variation of a brush in a library, add the brush to the Brushes panel, then duplicate it.

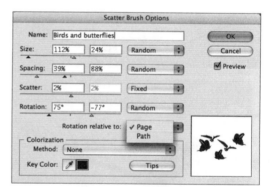

DIANE MARGOLIN

1 *The original objects*

2 *The Preview option will be available in the* **Scatter Brush Options** *dialog box if the brush in question is currently in use in your document.*

Create, Edit Scatter Brush

1 *The new **Scatter brush** is applied to a path.*

2 *This is the same **Scatter brush** after the **Size** sliders were moved apart (Random setting).*

3 *This prompt will appear if you **modify** a **brush** that's currently in use on objects in your file.*

4 *The "Confetti" Scatter brush, from the Decorative_ Scatter brush library is applied to a path.*

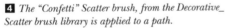

5 *The **Size, Spacing,** and **Rotation** values were raised via the Scatter Brush Options dialog box.*

The following is a description of the **properties:**

Size controls the size of the scatter objects.

Spacing controls the spacing between the scatter objects.

Scatter controls the distance between the objects and the path. When Fixed is chosen as the Scatter setting, a positive value places all the objects on one side of the path, and a negative value places all the objects on the opposite side of the path. The further the Scatter value is from 0%, the less closely the objects will adhere to the path shape.

Rotation controls how much the scatter objects can rotate relative to the page or the path. Choose **Page** or **Path** from the **Rotation Relative To** menu for the axis of rotation.

5. For the **Colorization** options, see the sidebar on page 305.

6. Click OK **1**–**2**. If the brush is in use in the document, an alert dialog box will appear **3**. Click **Apply to Strokes** to update those objects with the revised brush, or click **Leave Strokes** to leave the existing objects unchanged.

➤ Shift-drag a slider in the Scatter Brush Options dialog box to move its counterpart gradually along with it. Option-drag/Alt-drag a slider to simultaneously move the slider and its counterpart toward or away from each other from the center.

➤ To orient the scatter objects uniformly along a path, set Scatter and Rotation to Fixed, set Scatter to 0°, and choose Rotation Relative To: Path **4**–**5**.

➤ To create a scatter brush from type, with the Selection tool, select a type object that contains just a single character.

Creating and editing Calligraphic brushes

Calligraphic brush strokes vary in thickness as you draw, as in traditional calligraphy.

To create or edit a Calligraphic brush:

1. To create a new Calligraphic brush, click the **New Brush** button ⬛ on the Brushes panel. The New Brush dialog box opens. Click **New Calligraphic Brush**, then click OK.
   or
   To modify an existing brush, deselect all objects, then **double-click** a Calligraphic brush on the Brushes panel ■.

2. The Calligraphic Brush Options dialog box opens ②. If you're creating a new brush, enter a new name; or to edit an existing brush, leave the name as is.

3. Check Preview (available only for existing brushes) to view changes on any paths where the brush is in use. The brush shape will also preview in the dialog box.

4. For **Angle**, **Roundness**, and **Diameter**, choose one of the following variations from the menu:

   Fixed to keep the value constant.

   Random, then move the Variation slider to define a range within which that brush

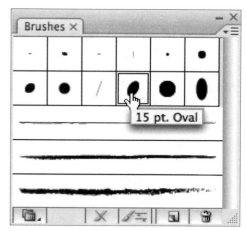

■ *Double-click a **Calligraphic** brush on the Brushes panel.*

Create, Edit Calligraphic Brush

② *Use the **Calligraphic Brush Options** dialog box to adjust the settings for a new or existing brush of that type.*

1 *The original object*

2 *This alert dialog box will appear if you modify a brush that's currently in use.*

3 *The brush Angle and Diameter were edited in the Calligraphic Brush Options dialog box, then **Apply to Strokes** was clicked when the prompt appeared, which caused the brush strokes to update on the object.*

attribute value can vary. A stroke can range between the value specified for angle, roundness, or diameter, plus or minus the Variation value. For example, a 50° angle with a Random Variation value of 10 could have an angle anywhere between 40° and 60°.

If you're using a graphics tablet, choose **Pressure, Stylus Wheel, Tilt, Bearing,** or **Rotation.** Move the Variation slider to define a range within which the brush attribute can respond to pressure from a stylus. Light pressure produces a brush attribute based on the angle, roundness, or diameter value minus the Variation value; heavy pressure produces a brush attribute based on the specified value plus the Variation value.

5. Enter an **Angle** (–180˚ to 180˚) or drag the gray arrowhead in the preview box to control the thickness of the horizontals and verticals in the stroke. A 0° angle will produce a thin horizontal stroke and a thick vertical stroke; a 90° angle will produce the opposite result.

6. Enter a **Roundness** value (0–100%), or reshape the tip by dragging either black dot inward or outward on the ellipse.

7. For the brush size, enter a **Diameter** value (0–1296 pt.) or drag the slider.

8. Click OK. If the brush is already in use in the document, an alert dialog box will appear **1**–**2**. Click **Apply to Strokes** to update the existing strokes with the revised brush **3**, or click **Leave Strokes** to leave the existing strokes unchanged.

Create, Edit Calligraphic Brush

Creating and editing Art brushes

An **Art brush** can be made from one or more objects (even a compound path), but not from a gradient, mask, mesh, editable type, or bitmap image. When applied to a path, an Art brush stroke will conform to the path. If you reshape the path, the Art brush stroke will stretch or bend to fit the new path contour (fun!).

To create or edit an Art brush:

1. To create a new brush, select one or more objects , then click the **New Brush** button ⬛ on the Brushes panel. The New Brush dialog box opens. Click **New Art Brush**, then click OK.

   or

   To modify an existing brush, deselect all objects, then **double-click** the brush on the Brushes panel. Or click an Art brush, then choose **Brush Options** from the panel menu.

2. The Art Brush Options dialog box opens **2**. If you're creating a new brush, enter a new name; to edit an existing brush, leave the name as is.

3. Check Preview (available only for existing brushes) to view changes on any paths where the brush is in use.

4. Click a **Direction** button to control the orientation of the object on the path. The object will be drawn in the direction the arrow is pointing. The direction will be more obvious for objects that have a distinct or recognizable orientation, such as type outlines, or an object, such as a tree or building.

5. Enter a **Size: Width** to scale the brush. Check **Proportional** to preserve the proportions of the original object as you scale it.

6. *Optional:* Check Flip Along to reverse the object on the path (from left to right) and/or check Flip Across to reverse the object across the path (up to down).

7. Choose a **Colorization** option (see the sidebar on the following page).

8. Click OK **3**–**4**.

➤ To edit an art brush manually, see page 306.

1 *To create an Art brush, select an object (or objects).*

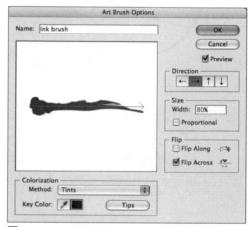

2 *Use the Art Brush Options dialog box to choose settings for a new or existing brush.*

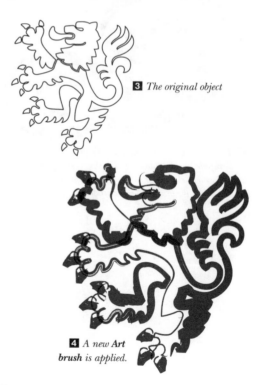

3 *The original object*

4 *A new Art brush is applied.*

Create, Edit Art Brush

The Colorization options

To change how a brush applies color, from the **Colorization: Method** menu in the Brush Options dialog box for any brush type except Calligraphic, you can choose from the options listed below. You can also recolor an existing brush stroke via the same menu; see page 307.

None to leave the colors unchanged.

Tints to change black areas in the brush stroke to the current stroke color at 100% and non-black areas to tints of the current stroke color. White areas stay white. Use for grayscale or spot colors.

Tints and Shades to change colors in the brush stroke to tints of the current stroke color. Black and white areas stay the same.

Hue Shift to apply the current stroke color to areas that contain the most prominent color (called the "key" color) and to change other colors in the brush stroke to related hues. Use for multicolored brushes.

If you're editing the brush itself (not a brush stroke), you can click the **Key Color** eyedropper, then click a color in the preview area of the dialog box to change the key color.

To learn more about colorization, click **Tips** in the Scatter Brush or Art Brush Options dialog box **1**.

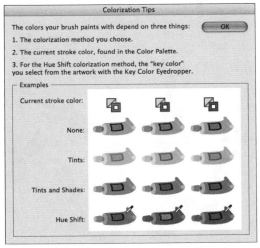

1 *Click* **Tips** *in in the Scatter Brush or Art Brush Options dialog box to open this* **Colorization Tips** *dialog box.*

Duplicating brushes

Using the **Duplicate Brush** command, you can create a variation of an existing brush—a slimmer or fatter version, for example.

To duplicate a brush:

1. Deselect all objects, then click the brush you want to duplicate **2**. (To create a variation from a brush in a library, add the brush to the Brushes panel first.)

2. Choose **Duplicate Brush** from the panel menu. The word "copy" will be appended to the brush name **3**. To modify the brush, see the individual instructions for that brush type earlier in this chapter.

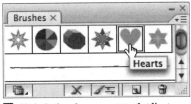

2 *Click the brush you want to* **duplicate.**

3 *The duplicate brush appears after the last brush icon in its category.*

Duplicate Brush

Editing brushes manually

On the previous page you learned how to edit
a brush via its options dialog box. Here you'll
learn how to **edit** a **brush manually**.

To edit a Scatter or Art brush manually:

1. Deselect all objects (Cmd-Shift-A/
Ctrl-Shift-A), then drag a brush from the
Brushes panel 🖌 onto a blank area of the
artboard **1**–**2**.

2. Do any of the following:

To recolor or transform the entire brush,
select it first using the Selection tool, then
perform your edits.

To isolate a group for editing, choose the
Selection tool, then double-click the group.*
When you're done editing, double-click out-
side the group to exit isolation mode.

To recolor or transform individual objects
within the brush, select them first, using the
Direct Selection tool or the Layers panel.

3. With the Selection tool (V), select the modified brush object or objects. Start dragging
them onto the Brushes panel, hold down
Option/Alt when you pass over the Brushes
panel, then release the mouse when the
pointer is over the original brush icon and
the icon has a highlight border **3**.
or
To make the object(s) into a new, separate
brush, drag it (or them) onto the panel
without holding down Option/Alt. The New
Brush dialog box opens. Click New Scatter
Brush or New Art Brush, then click OK.

4. The Scatter Brush Options or Art Brush
Options dialog box opens. Click OK.

5. If the brush is currently in use on paths in
the file, an alert dialog box will appear. Click
Apply to Strokes to update the paths with
the revised brush **4**, or click **Leave Strokes**
to leave them be.

*Double Click to Isolate must be checked in Preferences >
General.*

1 *The original scatter brush is applied to a path.*

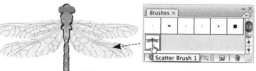

2 *Drag a brush from the Brushes
panel to the artboard.*

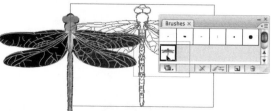

3 *Edit the brush object(s) manually,
then Option-drag/Alt-drag it over the
original brush on the Brushes panel.*

4 *The brush updates on the path.*

Edit Brush Manually

Select an object or objects on which the brush is being used.

*The **brush stroke** is altered on the **object.***

Editing brush strokes on objects

If you edit a brush, all objects on which that brush is in use will update to reflect your changes. If you want to **edit** a **brush stroke** on an individual **object** or objects without editing the brush itself, follow these instructions instead.

To change the stroke options for an individual object:

1. Select one or more objects to which the same brush is currently applied ▮.

2. If you want to recolor the brush stroke, choose a stroke color now.

3. Click the **Options of Selected Object** button ✐ on the Brushes panel. The Stroke Options dialog box opens.

4. Check Preview.

5. For a **Calligraphic** brush stroke, follow steps 4–7 on pages 302–303; for an **Art** brush stroke, follow steps 4–7 on page 304; or for a **Scatter** brush stroke, follow step 4 starting on page 300.

6. From the **Colorization** menu (not available for Calligraphic brushes), choose:

   None to leave the colors unchanged.

   Tints to change black areas in the brush stroke to the stroke color at 100% and non-black areas to tints of the current stroke color. White areas stay white.

   Tints and Shades to change colors in the brush stroke to tints of the current stroke color. Black and white stay the same.

   Hue Shift to apply the current stroke color to areas containing the most prominent color (the key color) and to change other colors in the brush stroke to related hues.

   Click Tips if you want to see an illustration of the **Colorization** options.

7. Click OK ▮. Only the selected object or objects will change, not the brush on the Brushes panel.

➤ To restore the original brush stroke to the object, select the object, click the Remove Brush Stroke button ✖ on the Brushes panel, then click the original brush.

Edit Brush Stroke on Object

307

Creating brush libraries

By **saving brushes** in a **library**, you'll be able to find them easily and use them in any file.

To create a brush library:

1. Create brushes in a document, or move them from other libraries to the Brushes panel in the current document.

2. From the **Brush Libraries** menu ![icon] at the bottom of the Brushes panel,**NEW!** choose **Save Brushes.** The Save Brushes as Library dialog box opens.

3. Enter a name. In the Mac OS, keep the default location, Users/[user name]/Library/Application Support/Adobe/Adobe Illustrator CS3/Brushes. In Windows, keep the default location, C:\Documents and Settings\[user name]\Application Data\Adobe\Adobe Illustrator CS3 Settings\Brushes.

4. Click Save. The library should now be listed on, and can be opened from, the **User Defined** submenu on the Brush Libraries menu (at the bottom of the Brushes panel).

Deleting brushes

When you **delete** a **brush** that's being used in your document, you can choose whether to expand or remove the brush strokes.

To delete a brush from the Brushes panel:

1. Deselect all objects in your document.

2. On the Brushes panel, click the **brush** you want to delete.
   or
   To delete all the brushes that aren't being used in the file, choose **Select All Unused** from the Brushes panel menu.

3. Click the **Delete Brush** button ![icon] on the Brushes panel. An alert dialog box appears.

4. If the brush is not currently in use in the document, click Yes **1**. If the brush is in use in the document, click **Expand Strokes** **2** to expand the brush strokes (they'll be converted into standard paths and will no longer be live), or click **Remove Strokes** to remove them from the objects.

➤ To restore a deleted brush to the Brushes panel, choose Undo immediately. Or if the brush is in a library, you can add it again to the Brushes panel (see page 298).

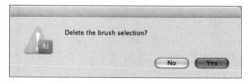

1 *This alert dialog box will appear if you* **delete** *a* **brush** *that* **isn't in use** *in the document.*

2 *This alert dialog box will appear if the brush you're deleting* **is in use** *in the document.*

In this chapter, you'll learn how to use the Blend command and the Blend tool to create live (editable), multistep color and shape progressions between two or more objects. You'll also change blend options for, edit, reverse the objects in, replace the spine in, and release a blend, and perform an easy practice exercise.

Process or spot?

➤ If you blend an object that contains a **process** color with an object that contains a **spot** color, the intermediate objects will be painted with **process** colors.

➤ If the objects you blend contain different **spot** colors, the intermediate objects will be painted with **process** colors.

➤ If the objects you blend contain different **tints** of the **same spot** color, the intermediate objects will be painted with graduated **tints** of that spot color. To blend between a spot color and white, change the white fill to 0% of the spot color.

Daniel Pelavin
blended two
lines *to create the shading on this lighthouse.*

©DANIEL PELAVIN

Blends are live!

Both the **Make Blend** command and the **Blend** tool create a multistep color and shape progression between two or more objects. Using the Blend tool, you can control which parts of the objects Illustrator uses to calculate the blend, whereas the Make Blend command controls this function automatically.

Although you can't alter the transitional objects in a blend directly, the whole blend will update instantly if you edit the original blend objects or reshape or replace the nonprinting spine that the objects adhere to. You can also select a blend and change the number of steps (transitional objects) it contains, as well as transform, recolor, or move any of the original objects.

When you create blends, bear in mind the following:

➤ You can blend similar shapes or nonmatching shapes, and they can have different fill and stroke attributes or brush strokes.

➤ You can blend editable type, gradients, or blends, but not mesh objects.

➤ You can blend open paths, closed paths, or a combination thereof.

➤ You can blend symbol instances, but to prevent printing errors, we don't recommend blending symbol sets.

Note: To blend just the colors between objects— not the shapes, use a blend command on the Edit > Edit Colors submenu (see page 120).

Blending objects via a command
To blend objects via a command:

1. Position two or more objects or groups in your artwork, allowing room for the transitional shapes that will be created between them, and select all the objects using the Selection tool, Lasso tool, or Layers panel **1**. These will be referred to as the "blend objects."

   ➤ For your first try, you could blend two different sizes of the same object, with the same or different fill colors but no stroke colors.

2. Choose Object > Blend > **Make** (Cmd-Option-B/Ctrl-Alt-B) **2**–**4**.

3. To edit the blend, read the instructions on the next three pages.

   If you don't like the blend, you can Undo it, or you can release it (instructions below).

   For tips on preventing banding in a printed blend, see page 313.

Releasing a blend
To release a blend:

1. Select the blend.

2. Choose Object > Blend > **Release** (Cmd-Option-Shift-B/Ctrl-Alt-Shift-B). The original objects and the path (spine) that the blend created will remain, but the transitional objects will be deleted.

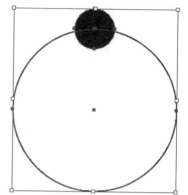

1 *The original two objects are a circle with a black fill and white stroke on top of a circle with a white fill and black stroke.*

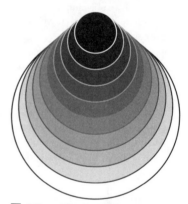

2 *Object > **Blend** > **Make** is applied to the original objects, with Spacing: **Specified Steps** (8) chosen in the Blend Options dialog box (see the following page).*

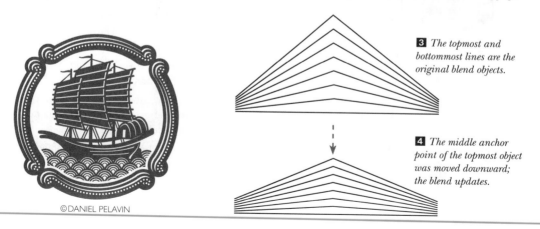

©DANIEL PELAVIN

3 *The topmost and bottommost lines are the original blend objects.*

4 *The middle anchor point of the topmost object was moved downward; the blend updates.*

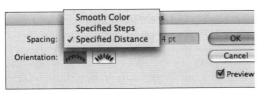

1 Use the **Blend Options** dialog box to choose **Spacing** and **Orientation** options for existing and future blends.

2 Spacing: **Smooth Color**

3 Spacing: **Specified Steps** (7)

4 Orientation: **Align to Page**

5 Orientation: **Align to Path**

Choosing blend options

If you change the settings in the **Blend Options** dialog box, the new settings will apply automatically to all currently selected and subsequently created blends.

To change the Blend Options:

1. *Optional:* Select an existing blend or blends.

2. Choose Object > Blend > **Blend Options.**
   or
   Double-click the **Blend** tool 🖫 (not the Gradient tool).

3. The Blend Options dialog box opens **1**. Check Preview (if you selected a blend).

4. From the **Spacing** menu, choose one of the following:

   Smooth Color to have Illustrator automatically calculate the necessary number of blend steps (transitional shapes) to produce smooth, nonbanding color transitions **2**. This option may take a moment to preview.

   Specified Steps, enter the desired number of transitional steps for the blend (1–1000), then press Tab to preview. This option creates distinct, discernible transition shapes **3**.

   Specified Distance, then enter the desired distance (.1–1000 pt.) between the transition shapes in the blend. This value won't affect the overall length of the blend.

5. Click an **Orientation** button (you may or may not see a change, depending on the orientation of the original objects):

   Align to Page ⊔ᵗᵗᵗ⁴ₙ to keep the blend objects perpendicular to the horizontal axis **4**.
   or
   Align to Path ⋙ₜₜₜₜ₄ to keep the blend objects perpendicular to the blend path **5**. (To replace the existing spine with a user-drawn spine, see page 315.)

6. Click OK.

Choose Blend Options

Editing blend objects

You can use any of the following methods to **edit a blend**. As you do so, the blend will update instantly **1**–**2**:

To **recolor, move,** or **transform** one of the original blend objects, select it with the Direct Selection tool, or double-click the blend with the Selection tool to isolate it.*
To perform a transformation, you can use the Free Transform tool, an individual transformation tool, or the object's bounding box. (To exit isolation mode, double-click a blank area of the artboard.)

Note: You can't select or edit the transitional objects individually—no way, no how.

To **recolor all** the objects in the blend, select it via the Selection tool or the Layers panel, then click the Recolor Artwork button ![icon] on the Control panel. In the Live Color dialog box, click the Edit tab and edit the colors using the color wheel and sliders. Click OK.

Apply a **stroke** color to the blend objects if you want the transitional shapes to be clearly delineated. Choose the Selection tool, click the blend, then choose a stroke color.

To **transform** the **entire** blend, select it with the Selection tool, then manipulate the bounding box or use a transformation tool.

To **reshape** the blend **path**, move one of the original objects with the Direct Selection tool or use any of the path-reshaping tools, such as the Reshape, Direct Selection, Add Anchor Point, or Convert Anchor Point tool.

➤ Effects and other appearance attributes can be applied to blend objects, either before or after the blend is created (see the sidebar on page 273). Ditto for brush strokes.

➤ To recolor a blend between symbols, use the Symbol Stainer tool on a selected instance (see pages 360–361).

Double Click to Isolate must be checked in Preferences > General.

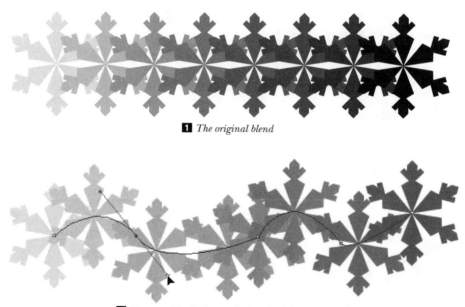

1 *The original blend*

2 *The same blend after **recoloring** the rightmost snowflake, **adding points** to the blend path, and **reshaping** the path*

Outputting blends

When creating blends using the Smooth Color option, Illustrator calculates the number of steps needed to output the blend smoothly from a high-resolution device based on the percentage differences between CMYK colors in the blend objects. To avoid banding (noticeable color strips) and printing errors, Adobe recommends the following:

➤ Create short blends (no wider than 7 inches).

➤ Use two or more process colors, and make sure two of their color components differ by 50% or more.

➤ Use relatively light colors; or if you must use dark colors, make the blend short. Avoid creating a blend between a dark color and white.

See "Printing gradients, meshes, and color blends" under "Printing" in Illustrator Help.

For a wider blend, you could try rasterizing it by using Object > Rasterize, then applying Filter > Blur > Smart Blur at low settings to soften the color transitions.

Reversing blend components

The **Reverse Front to Back** command changes the stacking order of the blend objects without changing their x/y locations.

To reverse the stacking position of objects in a blend:

1. Select a blend **1**.

2. Choose Object > Blend > **Reverse Front to Back 2**. The original and transitional objects will now be in reverse stacking order (what was originally the backmost object will now be the frontmost object, and vice versa).

The **Reverse Spine** command swaps the x/y location of all the blend objects without changing their stacking positions.

To reverse the location of objects in a blend:

1. Select a blend **1**.

2. Choose Object > Blend > **Reverse Spine**. The blend objects will swap locations **3**.

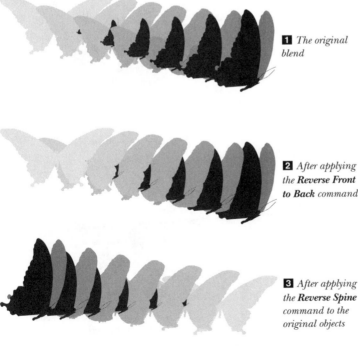

1 *The original blend*

2 *After applying the **Reverse Front to Back** command*

3 *After applying the **Reverse Spine** command to the original objects*

Using the Blend tool
To blend objects using the Blend tool:

1. Position two or more different-shaped open or closed paths, allowing room for the transitional shapes that will be created between them. You can apply different colors or gradients to each object.

2. Choose the **Blend** tool (W).

3. To let Illustrator decide which anchor points to use for the blend, click the **fill** of the first object (not the center point!).
   or
   If you want to control which anchor point will be used, click an **anchor point** on the first object **1**. The little square on the Blend tool pointer will change from hollow to filled when it's over an anchor point.

4. Click the fill or an anchor point on the next object **2**. If the path is open, click an endpoint. For the smoothest shape transitions, click corresponding points on all the objects (e.g., you could click the top left corner point of all the objects, but don't click the top left corner point of one object and the lower right corner point of another object). You can add points in advance so the objects have a similar number of points.

   The blend will appear **3**–**4**.

5. Repeat the previous step for any other objects that you want to include in the blend. The blend will update automatically!

6. To edit the blend, see the instructions on the previous three pages.

   If you don't like the blend, use Undo or choose Object > Blend > Release.

➤ If the original objects contain different pattern fills, the transitional shapes will be filled with the pattern in the topmost object.

1 *With the **Blend tool,** click the fill or an anchor point on one object...*

2 *...then click the fill or an anchor point on another object.*

3 *The blend appears.*

4 *This is the kind of mayhem that occurs if you click noncorresponding points.*

1 *The original user-drawn path and blend*

2 *The **Replace Spine** command is chosen, and the blend reshapes to the user-drawn path.*

Replacing the blend spine

You can use any path as a **replacement spine** for the original blend and transitional objects to adhere to, in lieu of the one that Illustrator created for you automatically.

To replace a blend spine:

1. Create a blend, then draw a separate path to become the new spine. The path can be closed or open, but an open one will probably work better. You could use the Arc tool to create a curve.

2. With the Selection tool or the Lasso tool, select both the blend and the path **1**.

3. Choose Object > Blend > **Replace Spine**. The blend will adhere to the new path **2**.

➤ To change the orientation of the blend objects relative to the path, select the blend, choose Object > Blend > Blend Options, then click whichever Orientation icon isn't currently highlighted (see the last two figures on page 311).

➤ If you release a blend that has a replacement spine, the path (turned spine) will have a stroke color of None. You can locate it in Outline view or by using smart guides with Object Highlighting.

Replace Spine

Exercise

Use a blend to apply shading

1. Select an object, then apply a fill color and a stroke color of None.

2. Double-click the **Scale** tool.

3. Click **Uniform**, enter a number between 60 and 80 in the **Scale** field, then click **Copy.**

4. With the copy still selected, choose a lighter or darker variation of the original fill color by clicking a variation on the **Color Guide** panel.

5. Make sure the smaller object is in front of the larger one, then select both objects with the Selection tool **1**.

6. Choose Object > Blend > **Make** (Cmd-Option-B/Ctrl-Alt-B) **2**, then deselect. If the resulting blend doesn't look smooth, select it, double-click the Blend tool, choose Smooth Color from the Spacing menu, then click OK.

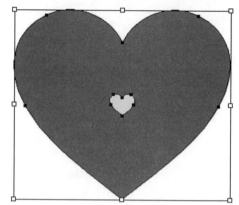

1 *Select two objects.*

1 *Object > Blend > Make is chosen.*

GRADIENTS | 24

A gradient fill is a gradual blend between two or more colors. In this chapter you'll learn how to fill an object or objects with a gradient; access gradient libraries; create and save gradients; edit a gradient using the Gradient panel; change the way a gradient fills an object or objects by using the Gradient tool; and expand a gradient into objects.

DANIEL PELAVIN

Blend or gradient?

A **blend** is made from two or more objects, with transitional shapes and colors between them.

A **gradient** is a smooth transition between two or more colors within an object, with no transitional shapes to other objects.

A **mesh** is an object with a flexible armature, to which you can apply multiple smoothly blended fill colors (see Illustrator Help).

Applying gradients

If you want to soften some abstract shapes or add shading or volume to realistic or geometric objects, **gradients** fit the bill. A gradient can consist of a simple transition between two colors—a starting and an ending color—or it can contain multiple colors. It can spread from one side of an object to another (linear); it can spread outward from the center of an object (radial); or it can be applied across a series of objects.

Illustrator supplies you with a set of predefined gradients, but you can also create custom gradients by using the **Gradient panel** (Cmd-F9/Ctrl-F9). For the instructions in this chapter, you'll also be using the Color and Swatches panels.

Once an object is filled with a gradient, you can use the **Gradient tool** to change the direction of the gradient or to change how gradually or abruptly each color transitions into the next.

You can apply any of the predefined gradients that ship with Illustrator or, even better, create your own. Follow these instructions to **apply** an **existing gradient** to an **object**. In the next set of instructions, you'll create your own gradients.

To fill an object with a gradient:

1. Select an object , then click a gradient swatch on the **Swatches** panel **2**–**3** (access it via the Control panel, if you like), or on any open gradient **library** (see "To access other gradient libraries," below).
or
Drag a gradient swatch from the **Swatches** panel, or from any open gradient **library** panel, or from the Gradient Fill box on the **Gradient** panel (Cmd-F9/Ctrl-F9) **4** over a selected or unselected object.

2. *Optional:* If you applied a Linear gradient, you can select the object and change the Angle on the Gradient panel.

➤ You can't apply a gradient to a stroke, but there is a workaround. Make the stroke the desired width, apply Object > Path > Outline Stroke to convert the stroke into a closed object (see page 329), select the new object, then apply a gradient.

➤ To fill type with a gradient, first convert it to outlines (Type > Create Outlines). Or select the type with the Selection tool, choose Add New Fill from the Appearance panel menu, then apply a gradient.

To access other gradient libraries:

1. From the **Gradients** submenu on the **Swatch Libraries** menu at the bottom of the Swatches panel, **NEW!** choose a library.

2. A separate library panel opens **5**. Click the gradient you want to use; it will appear at the bottom of the Swatches panel. Now that one gradient library is open, you can cycle through other libraries by clicking the **Load Next Swatch Library** or **Load Previous Swatch Library** button.

➤ User-defined libraries appear on, and can be chosen from, the User Defined submenu on the Swatch Libraries menu. To save a library of swatches, see page 117.

1 *The original object*

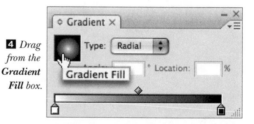

2 *Click a gradient on the* **Swatches** *panel.*

3 *The object is filled with a* **radial** *gradient.*

4 *Drag from the* **Gradient Fill** *box.*

5 *Gradient libraries open in a separate panel.*

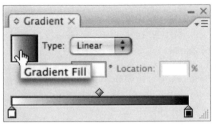

1 *Click the* **Gradient Fill** *box on the Gradient panel.*

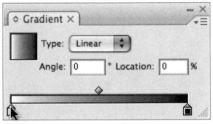

2 *Click, then choose a color for, the left and right* **color stops.**

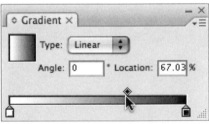

3 *Move the* **midpoint diamond** *to adjust the amount of each color.*

Back to the gradient

If a selected object has a solid-color or pattern fill, but it previously had a gradient fill, you can reapply the gradient by clicking the Gradient Fill box on the Gradient panel, or by clicking the Gradient button on the Toolbox, █ or by pressing "." (period).

Creating gradients

A **custom gradient** can contain all CMYK colors, all RGB process colors, tints of the same spot color, or multiple spot colors.

To create and save a two-color gradient:

1. *Optional:* Select an object or objects.

2. Display the full **Gradient** panel,█ with its options panel.

3. Click the **Gradient Fill** box on the Gradient panel **1**.

4. Drag a solid-color swatch from the **Swatches** panel ▦ over the left color stop on the Gradient panel.
   or
   Click the left color stop on the **Gradient** panel **2**. Then use the **Color** panel to mix a solid color; or Option-click/Alt-click a solid-color swatch on the **Swatches** panel.

5. Repeat the previous step to choose a solid color for the right color stop.

6. From the **Type** menu on the Gradient panel, choose **Radial** or **Linear.**

7. *Optional:* Move the midpoint diamond to the right to produce more of the starting color than the ending color, or to the left to produce more of the ending color than the starting color (this will be easier to see if you selected an object in step 1) **3**. Or click the diamond, then change the Location value.

8. *Optional:* For a Linear gradient, you can change the Angle.

9. If you select another object or swatch now, the new gradient will be lost—unless you save it (and then save your document). To save the gradient:

   Drag the Gradient Fill box from the Gradient panel onto the **Swatches** panel.
   or
   Click the Gradient Fill box on the Gradient panel, then Option-click/Alt-click the **New Swatch** button ▣ at the bottom of the Swatches panel.**NEW!**
   or

(Continued on the following page)

Create, Save Two-Color Gradient

To name the gradient as you save it, click the Gradient Fill box on the **Gradient** panel, click the **New Swatch** button on the Swatches panel, enter a name, then click OK.

➤ To swap the starting and ending colors or any other two colors in a radial or linear gradient, Option-drag/Alt-drag one stop on top of the other.

➤ To delete a gradient swatch from the Swatches panel, drag it over the Delete Swatch button.🗑

Editing gradients

It's hard to tell whether a gradient is going to look good until you see it in an object. Luckily, gradients are easy to edit. You can recolor, add, move, or remove color stops, move the midpoint diamonds to change the location of the color transitions, or change the gradient angle or type (from linear to radial, or vice versa) at any time.

You can either **edit** a **gradient** in an object and leave the swatch alone, or you can edit the gradient swatch, with or without recoloring any objects in which the gradient is being used. For steps 2–5, you can pick and choose which characteristics of the gradient you want to edit.

To edit a gradient:

1. Choose the **Selection** tool (V),▶ then click an object that contains the gradient you want to edit. For editable type, click the type, then click the Fill attribute on the Appearance panel that has a gradient icon.
or
On the **Swatches** panel, click the gradient swatch that you want to edit. In addition, you may also select any objects that contain that gradient.

You can do any or all of the following steps.

2. To change the color of a stop:

On the **Gradient** panel,■ click a stop that you want to recolor, then choose a color from the **Color** panel or Option-click/Alt-click a solid color on the **Swatches** panel.
or

Start from something

To use an **existing** gradient as a starting point for a **new** gradient, on the Swatches panel, drag a gradient over the New Swatch button (or click a predefined gradient in a library). Click the new swatch, then edit the gradient as per the instructions on this page.

Color-separating gradients

➤ To color-separate a gradient that changes from a spot color to white onto one plate, create a gradient with the spot color as the starting color and a **0%** tint of the **same spot color** as the ending color.

➤ If you're going to color-separate a gradient that contains **more than one** spot color, get some advice from your prepress specialist. He or she may tell you to assign a different screen angle to each color via the File > Print > Output option set (Convert All Spot Colors to Process should be unchecked). See page 385.

➤ To **convert** a spot color in a gradient to a **process** color, click the color stop on the Gradient panel, then on the Color panel, click the **Spot Color** button.◉ The color will convert to the current document color mode (RGB or CMYK). Repeat for the other color stops.

Edit Gradient

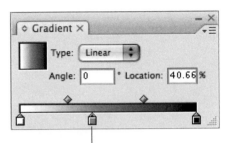

1 *Click below the slider to add a new color stop, then choose a color.*

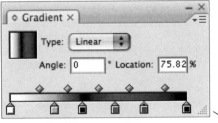

2 *Four shades of gray were **added** to this gradient.*

(You can drag from this corner to widen the panel.)

3 *These gradients contain **multiple colors**.*

Drag a solid-color swatch from the **Swatches** panel over a color stop on the Gradient panel.

3. To **add** a new color to the gradient:

On the **Gradient** panel, click below the gradient slider to add a color stop **1**, then use the **Color** panel to mix a color or Option-click/Alt-click a swatch on the **Swatches** panel.
or
Drag a solid-color swatch from the **Swatches** panel to the gradient slider (but not on top of an existing color stop) on the **Gradient** panel. A new color stop will be created.

Repeat, if desired, to add more colors **2**–**3**.

4. To change how **abruptly** a color spreads into adjacent colors, move the color stop to the left or right.

To adjust the **amount** of a color, move the midpoint diamond (located above the gradient slider) to the left or right.

To **duplicate** a color stop, Option-drag/Alt-drag it.

To **remove** a color stop, drag it downward out of the Gradient panel.

5. Choose a different gradient **Type** (Radial or Linear). For a Linear gradient, you can also change the **Angle**.

6. To **resave** your newly edited swatch, Option-drag/Alt-drag from the Gradient Fill box on the Gradient panel over the swatch on the Swatches panel.
or
To save your modified gradient as a **new** swatch instead of saving over the original, drag it to the Swatches panel without holding down Option/Alt.

7. Save your file.

Edit Gradient

Using the Gradient tool

You've already learned how to edit a gradient. Now you'll learn how to use the **Gradient tool** on an object to quickly change how abruptly the gradient colors blend, change the angle of a linear gradient, or change the location of the center in a radial gradient. On the next page, you'll learn how to use this tool to spread a gradient across multiple objects.

To use the Gradient tool:

1. Apply a gradient to an object , and keep the object selected.

2. Choose the **Gradient** tool (G).

3. Drag across the object in any direction, such as from right to left or diagonally.

   For abrupt **transitions** between colors, drag a short distance **2**–**3**, or for more gradual transitions across a wider span, drag a long distance.

   To **reverse** the order of the colors in a linear gradient, drag in the opposite direction.

   For a radial gradient, position the pointer where you want the **center** of the fill to be, then click or drag.

   ➤ You can start dragging or finish dragging with the pointer outside the object. In this case, the colors at the beginning or end of the gradient won't appear in the object.

4. If you don't like the results, drag in a different direction. Keep trying until you're satisfied with the results **4**. Note that the gradient swatch on the Swatches panel hasn't changed a bit, because you used the Gradient tool instead of the Gradient panel.

   ➤ If you use the Gradient tool on an object and then apply a different gradient of the same type (radial or linear) to the same object, the effect of the Gradient tool will be applied to the new gradient.

   ➤ To restore the original gradient to the object, select the object, then click the swatch on the Swatches panel.

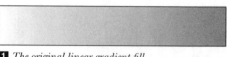

1 *The original linear gradient fill*

2 *The **Gradient** tool is dragged a short distance.*

3 *This is the result after using the Gradient tool as shown in the previous figure.*

4 *The same linear gradient fill looks different in these 3 objects, thanks to our use of the **Gradient** tool.*

Gradient Tool

To spread a gradient across multiple objects:

1. Select several objects, fill all of them with the same gradient **1**, and keep them selected.

2. Choose the **Gradient** tool (G).

3. Drag across all the objects in one pass **2**. Shift-drag to constrain the angle to a multiple of 45° (actually, to a multiple of the current Constrain Angle in Preferences > General).

➤ Once multiple objects are filled with the same gradient, don't combine them into a compound path. This could change how the gradient looks or cause a printing error.

1 *In the original gradient fill, the gradient starts **anew** in **each** type outline.*

2 *Because we dragged across all the objects using the **Gradient tool** (in the direction shown by the arrow), now the gradient starts in the **first** type outline and ends in the **last** one.*

BIRD BY DIANE MARGOLIN

1 *The original object contains a **linear** gradient.*

Expanding a gradient into objects

At some point you may have a need or desire to **expand** the colors in a gradient fill into individual objects. One practical reason for doing this might be to simplify a gradient fill that's causing a printing error.

To expand a standard gradient into separate objects:

1. Select an object that contains a gradient fill (not a mesh) **1**.

2. Choose Object > **Expand.** The Expand dialog box opens **2**.

3. Click **Expand Gradient to: Specify**, then enter the desired number of objects to be created. To print the expanded gradient successfully, this number must be high enough to produce smooth color transitions (say, over 100). To expand the gradient into obvious bands of color, enter a value below 20.

4. Click OK **3**. *Note:* The resulting number of objects may not match the specified number of objects if the original gradient contained too few colors.

➤ To expand a gradient using the last "Specify [ ] Objects" setting used without opening the dialog box, hold down Option/Alt as you choose Object > Expand.

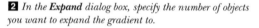

2 *In the **Expand** dialog box, specify the number of objects you want to expand the gradient to.*

3 *The **Expand** command converted the gradient into a series of separate rectangles in different shades, grouped together with a clipping mask.*

COMBINE PATHS 25

In this chapter, you'll first learn about the Shape Mode commands, which create editable compound shapes from multiple objects. Then you'll learn about the Pathfinder commands, which produce a flattened, closed object or compound path. And finally, you'll learn how to join two or more objects into a compound path via the Compound Path command, then add objects to, reverse an object's fill in, and release the compound path.

Shop and compare

For a comparison between compound shapes and compound paths, see page 330. Also, remember that you can recolor intersecting shapes in a Live Paint group without having to use any Pathfinder commands (see Chapter 13).

Add to — *Shape Area*   *Subtract from Shape Area*   *Intersect Shape Areas*   *Exclude Overlapping Shape Areas*

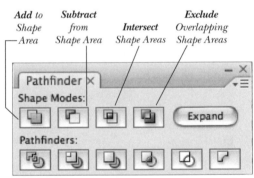

1 *The Shape Mode buttons on the Pathfinder panel produce compound shapes from two or more objects.*

©DANIEL PELAVIN

Applying Shape Mode commands

The **Shape Mode** commands **1** on the **Pathfinder** panel ▪ produce a compound shape from selected, overlapping objects. Like appearances, compound shapes are fully editable and reversible. On the Layers panel, the objects are nested individually under a Compound Shape listing, making it easy to select them for editing. If you move, restack, or reshape individual objects within a compound shape, the overall compound shape adjusts accordingly. And finally, if you release a compound shape, the original attributes are restored to the objects.

A few rules about Shape Modes to keep in mind:

➤ They can be applied to multiple paths, compound paths and shapes, blends, envelopes, editable or outline type, and to a Live Paint group in combination with other paths.

➤ They can't be applied to placed images, rasterized images, or mesh objects.

➤ They can't be applied to a single group, but they can be applied to a group in combination with other paths.

➤ Except for the Subtract from Shape Area command, which preserves the color attributes of the backmost selected object, the Shape Mode commands apply the color attributes of the topmost object and hide all other color attributes.

➤ The distort and warp effects remain visible; other effects are hidden.

To apply a Shape Mode command:

1. Select two or more overlapping objects.

2. On the **Pathfinder** panel, click one of the following **Shape Mode** buttons:

Add to Shape Area to join the outer edges of selected objects into one compound shape, hide the edges of interior objects, and close open paths (see also page 147) **1**.

Subtract from Shape Area to subtract the objects in front from the backmost object and preserve the paint attributes of the backmost object **2**.

Intersect Shape Areas to preserve areas that overlap and hide areas that don't **3**.

Exclude Overlapping Shape Areas to make areas where objects overlap transparent, and thereby reveal underlying objects **4**.

➤ You can copy a compound shape from Illustrator and paste it into Adobe Photoshop (click Shape Layer in the Paste dialog box). It will show up as multiple paths on a shape layer.

When you **expand** a **compound shape,** the result is a single path, unless the compound shape has interior cutouts, in which case the result is a compound path. Compare these results with those of the Release Compound Shape command, which is discussed on the next page.

To expand a compound shape:

1. Select the compound shape with the **Selection** tool (V).

2. Click the **Expand** button on the Pathfinder panel.

1 *The leaf is the topmost of the original objects.*

Add to Shape Area *joins the perimeter of all the objects.*

2 *The original objects*

Subtract from Shape Area *uses the front-most object like a cookie cutter on the object(s) behind it.*

3 *The original objects*

Intersect Shape Areas: *Only areas that originally overlapped other objects remain visible.*

4 *The original objects*

Exclude Overlapping Shape Areas: *Areas where the original objects overlapped become a cutout.*

Shape Mode Commands; Expand Compound

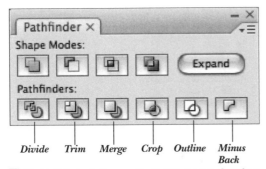

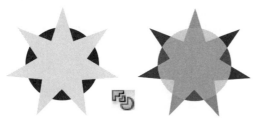

1 *The* **Pathfinder** *buttons on the* **Pathfinder** *panel produce separate closed paths or lines.*

2 *The original objects*

3 *The* **Divide** *command was applied, then the resulting shapes were recolored.*

Choosing Pathfinder options

To open the **Pathfinder Options** dialog box, from which you can choose preferences for the Pathfinder commands, choose Pathfinder Options from the Pathfinder panel menu:

➤ The higher the **Precision** value (.001–100 pt), the more precisely the commands are applied, and the longer they take to process.

➤ With **Remove Redundant Points** checked, duplicate anchor points in the same location will be deleted.

➤ With **Divide and Outline Will Remove Unpainted Artwork** checked, the Divide and Outline commands will delete any overlapping areas of selected paths that have a fill of None.

When you **release** a **compound shape**, the objects' original attributes are restored.

To release a compound shape:

1. Select the compound shape with the **Selection** tool (V).

2. Choose **Release Compound Shape** from the Pathfinder panel menu.

Applying the Pathfinder commands

The **Pathfinder** commands divide, trim, merge, crop, outline, or subtract areas where selected paths overlap to produce separate, nonoverlapping closed paths or lines. Object colors and appearances are preserved, and the resulting paths are put into a group. The Pathfinder commands can be applied via the Pathfinder panel (discussed here) **1** or as removable effects (see page 284).

Keep these guidelines in mind when applying the Pathfinder commands:

➤ The original objects can't be restored after applying a Pathfinder command, except by choosing Undo, so duplicate your objects first!

➤ We recommend applying the Pathfinder commands to closed paths, as Illustrator may take the liberty of closing open paths for you as it performs the command. To close a path, see page 329.

➤ Pathfinder commands can be applied to objects that contain a pattern fill, brush stroke, or applied effect.

➤ To apply a Pathfinder command to type, convert the type to outlines first.

To apply a Pathfinder command:

1. Select two or more overlapping objects.

2. Click one of the Pathfinder buttons on the **Pathfinder** panel:

   Divide: Each overlapping area becomes a separate, nonoverlapping object **2**–**3**.

   ➤ After applying the Divide command, deselect all the objects, choose the Direct

(Continued on the following page)

Release Compound; Pathfinder Commands

Pathfinder Commands

Selection tool, click any of the objects, then do any of the following: apply new fill colors or effects; apply a fill of None; lower an object's transparency; or remove an object to create a cutout effect.

Trim: The frontmost object shape is preserved; sections of objects behind and overlapping it are deleted **1**. Adjacent or overlapping objects of the same color or shade remain separate (unlike the results from the Merge command). Stroke colors are deleted, unless they contain effects.

Merge: Adjacent or overlapping objects with the same fill attributes are united **2**. Stroke colors are deleted, unless they contain effects.

Crop: Areas of objects that extend beyond the edges of the frontmost object are cropped away, and the frontmost object loses its fill and stroke **3**. Stroke colors are removed (unless effects were applied to the original strokes). Crop works like a clipping mask, but in this case, you can't restore the original objects except by choosing Undo.

Outline: All the objects turn into 0-pt. strokes, and the original fill colors are applied as stroke colors **4**. Transparency settings are preserved; fill colors are removed. The resulting strokes can be transformed, reshaped, and recolored individually.

Minus Back: Objects in back are subtracted from the frontmost object, leaving only portions of the frontmost object **5**. The paint attributes and appearances of the frontmost object are applied to the new path. The objects must overlap (at least partially) for this command to produce a result.

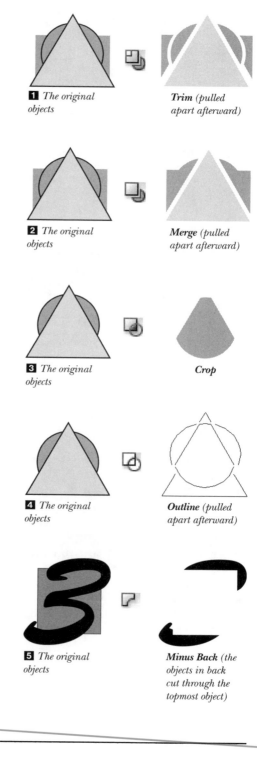

1 *The original objects* — *Trim (pulled apart afterward)*

2 *The original objects* — *Merge (pulled apart afterward)*

3 *The original objects* — *Crop*

4 *The original objects* — *Outline (pulled apart afterward)*

5 *The original objects* — *Minus Back (the objects in back cut through the topmost object)*

Pathfinder shortcuts

Apply **last-used Pathfinder** command to selected objects	Cmd-4/Ctrl-4
Turn **Shape Mode** command into a **Pathfinder** command	Option-click/Alt-click the button

1 *Select an object that has a stroke in the desired weight (this object has gradient fill and a stroke color).*

2 *The **Outline Stroke** command converted the stroke into a compound path. We selected the outer ring, applied a gradient fill, then dragged downward with the Gradient tool to make the ring contrast better with the inner circle.*

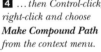
3 *Place smaller objects on top of a larger object, make sure all the objects are selected,...*

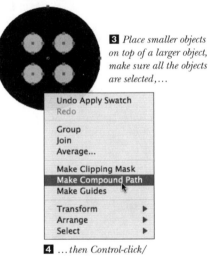
4 *...then Control-click/ right-click and choose **Make Compound Path** from the context menu.*

Instead of letting a Pathfinder command close any open paths for you, you can use the **Outline Stroke** command to turn the stroke on a path into a filled object first. You can also use this command to convert a line or a stroke into a closed path so it can then be filled with a gradient, or to prepare it for trapping.

To convert a stroke or an open path into a filled object:

1. Select an object that has a stroke in the desired weight **1**.

2. Choose Object > Path > **Outline Stroke.** The new object **2** will be the same width as the original stroke, and the original fill color, if any, will be preserved as a separate object (select it with the Direct Selection tool).

Creating compound paths

The **Make Compound Path** command joins two or more objects into one object. A transparent hole is created where the objects originally overlapped, through which shapes or patterns behind the object are revealed. Regardless of their original paint attributes, all the objects in a compound path are painted with the attributes of the backmost object, and form one unit. A compound path can be released at any time, and the original object shapes are fully restored.

To create a compound path:

1. Arrange the objects you want to make see-through in front of a larger shape **3**. Closed paths work best, and they may have brush strokes.

2. Select all the objects.

3. Choose Object > Compound Path > **Make** (Cmd-8/Ctrl-8).
   or
   If the objects aren't grouped, you can Control-click/right-click on the artboard and choose **Make Compound Path** from the context menu **4**.

(Continued on the following page)

Outline Stroke; Create Compound Path

329

The frontmost objects will cut through the backmost object like a cookie cutter **1**–**2**. A Compound Path listing will appear on the Layers panel; the original objects will no longer be listed separately. (Compound shapes, in contrast, are preserved as individual objects within a Compound Shape listing on the Layers panel.)

The fill and stroke attributes of the backmost object will be applied to areas of objects that overlap it or that extend beyond its edges.

If the see-through holes don't result, follow the second set of instructions on the next page.

➤ All objects in a compound path are placed onto the layer of the frontmost object.

➤ To avoid printing errors, don't make compound paths from very complex shapes or create a lot of compound paths in one file.

1 *The objects are converted into a* **compound path.**

2 *We placed an object containing a pattern behind the compound path, and applied a white stroke to the compound path.*

How compound shapes...	...differ from compound paths,	and how they're alike
Subpaths are nested as **separate** objects within a **Compound Shape** listing on the Layers panel.	Subpaths become part of one **Compound Path** object.	Select or transform a whole compound shape or whole compound path with the **Selection** tool.
Click with the **Direct Selection** tool to select a whole subpath within a compound shape.	**Option-click/Alt-click** with the **Direct Selection** tool to select a whole subpath within a compound path.	**Reshape** any subpath within a compound shape or compound path by the usual methods (e.g., add, delete, or move points).
There are **four** Shape Mode buttons to choose from. And after a compound shape is created, Shape Mode commands can also be applied to individual objects within it.	There is only **one** kind of compound path: Overlapping areas are subtracted from the backmost object, period.	
The **Release Compound Shape** command restores the original objects and their appearances.	Released objects adopt the appearances of the **compound path**, not their original appearances.	A **stroke** applied to a compound shape or compound path will appear on the outer edge of the overall shape and on any interior cutout shapes.

1 *Two objects are selected in the original* **compound path.**

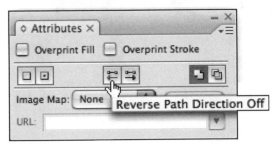

2 *Click the* **Reverse Path Direction On** *or* **Reverse Path Direction Off** *button on the* **Attributes** *panel.*

3 *The color of the two selected holes is reversed.*

To add an object to a compound path:

1. Move the object you want to add in front of the compound path. (If it's in the back, its attributes will be applied to the compound path.) Using the Selection tool or the Lasso tool, select both the compound path and the object you want to add to it.

2. Choose Object > Compound Path > **Make** (Cmd-8/Ctrl-8).

You can remove the fill color of any shape in a compound path, and thereby make the object transparent, or vice versa, by flipping the **Reverse Path Direction** switch on the Attributes panel.

To reverse an object's fill in a compound path:

1. Deselect the compound path.

2. Choose the **Direct Selection** tool (A).

3. Click the edge of the object in the compound path that you want to reverse the color of **1**.

4. Show the **Attributes** panel 🔲 (Cmd-F11/ Ctrl-F11).

5. Click the **Reverse Path Direction Off** button 🔁 or **Reverse Path Direction On** button 🔁 — whichever button isn't currently highlighted **2**–**3**.

   Note: If the Reverse Path Direction buttons aren't available, you have selected the whole compound path. Select only one object in the compound and try again.

Add to, Reverse Fill in Compound Path

331

You can **release** a **compound path** back to its individual objects at any time.

To release a compound path:

1. Select the compound path .

2. Control-click/right-click the artboard and choose **Release Compound Path** from the context menu.
   or
   Choose Object > Compound Path > **Release** (Cmd-Option-Shift-8/Ctrl-Alt-Shift-8).

   All the objects will be selected and will be painted with the attributes, effects, and appearances from the compound path—not their original, precompound appearances . You can use smart guides (with Object Highlighting on) to figure out which shape is which.

➤ All the released objects will be nested within the same top-level layer that the compound path resided in.

➤ The Type > Create Outlines command always produces a compound path. If the original character had a counter (interior shape, such as in the letters P, A, R, or D) and you release the compound path, the counter will be a separate path and will have the same paint attributes and appearances as the outer part of the letterform **3**–**4**.

1 *Click a compound path.*

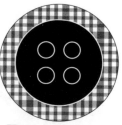

2 *The **compound path** is **released,** so the holes are no longer transparent.*

3 *Type outlines (a compound path)*

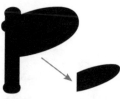

4 *The **compound path** is **released** into separate objects. (We moved the counter of the "P.")*

*The holes in the center of this **compound path** by Daniel Pelavin were originally separate paths.*

CLIPPING MASKS | 26

In this chapter you'll learn how to create a clipping set, in which a masking object crops objects or images below it, like a picture frame.

The rectangular masking object is masking (cropping) parts of objects that extend beyond its border. Together, the objects form what is called a **clipping set**.

The **masking** object   A **masked** object

The same image in **Outline** view

Using clipping sets

In Illustrator, a clipping path works like a picture frame or mat, clipping objects outside its borders and revealing only the objects within. The masked objects can be moved, restacked, reshaped, or repainted. A clipping path and the objects it's masking are referred to collectively as a **clipping set**.

To create a clipping set:

1. Arrange the object or objects to be masked **1**. They can be grouped, or not. To avoid a printing error, don't use very intricate objects.

2. Put the masking object (called the **clipping path**) in front of the objects it will be masking. If you need to restack it, on the Layers panel, drag its name upward on the list. It can be an open or closed path, editable type, or a compound shape, and it can have a brush stroke (in the latter case, the path itself — not the brush stroke — will do the clipping).

3. Choose the Selection tool (V).

4. Select the clipping path and the object or objects behind it that are to be masked.

5. Control-click/right-click and choose **Make Clipping Mask.**
   or
   Choose Object > Clipping Mask > **Make** (Cmd-7/Ctrl-7) **2**.

   The clipping path will now have a stroke and fill of None, and all the objects will remain selected. The words "<Clipping Path>" (underlined) will appear on the Layers panel (unless editable type was used as the clipping path, in which case the type characters will be underlined instead). Also, the clipping path and masked objects will be moved into a clipping set <Group> in the top-level layer of the original clipping path.

➤ If you use File > Export to export your Illustrator file in the Photoshop (psd) format, a clipping set in a layer or within a group will export as a layer group with a vector mask, and the mask will clip all the objects in the group.

Click the button

The **Make/Release Clipping Mask** button at the bottom of the Layers panel clips *all* the objects and groups on the currently active layer, sublayer, or group (whether objects are selected or not), using the topmost object of the layer or group as the clipping path. If a layer is active, the resulting clipping set won't be in a group. The instructions for using clipping sets in this chapter also apply to clipping sets made using the Layers panel, but instead of working with a group you'll be working with a layer.

1 *Two objects are selected: a standard type character and a placed raster image.*

2 *After choosing Object > **Clipping Mask** > Make*

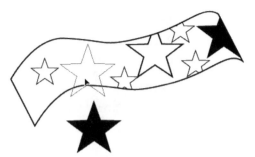

1 *The object to be **added** (the star) is moved over the clipping set (the banner).*

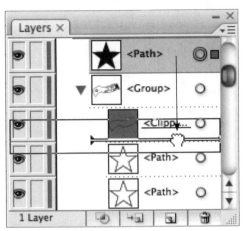

2 *The black star (<Path>) is moved downward into the clipping set <Group>.*

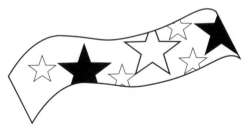

3 *The second black star is now part of the **clipping set**.*

A **clipping set** contains a clipping path and the objects it's masking.

To select a whole clipping set:

On the **Layers** panel ⬡ (F7), click the selection area for the clipping set (group or layer).
or
For a clipping set <Group>, choose the **Selection** tool (V), then click the clipping path or one of the masked objects in the document window.

To select an individual clipping path or masked object:

On the **Layers** panel, click the selection area for the clipping path or a masked object.
or
Choose the Direct Selection tool (A), then click the clipping path or a masked object in the **document** window. You can use smart guides to help you locate the objects (with Object Highlighting on in Preferences > Smart Guides & Slices).
or
Choose the Selection (V) or Direct Selection (A) tool, select any object in the clipping set, then click the **Edit Clipping Path** button 🔲 on the Control panel to select the clipping path, or click the **Edit Contents** button 🔲 to select all the masked objects.**NEW!**

➤ To select all the clipping masks in a document (except any type characters that are being used as a clipping mask), deselect all, then choose Select > Object > Clipping Masks.

To add an object to a clipping set:

1. Choose the **Selection** tool (V).

2. In the document window, move the object to be added over the clipping set **1**.

3. On the Layers panel, expand the list for the clipping set <Group> or layer.

4. Drag the name of the object to be added to the set upward or downward into the <Group> **2** or layer, to the desired stacking position **3**.

Here is a simple recap of the basic technique for **restacking** objects via the Layers panel (see also page 203).

To restack a masked object within its clipping set:

On the **Layers** panel (F7), drag the object name upward or downward to a new position within its group or layer **1**–**4**.

To copy an object in a clipping set:

1. On the Layers panel, click the selection area for the object you want to copy.

2. Option-drag/Alt-drag the selection square upward or downward, and release it somewhere within the same clipping set <Group> or layer.

3. The copy will be in the same x/y location as the original object, so you'll need to reposition it (use the Selection or Direct Selection tool).

➤ By clicking in the edit column on the Layers panel, you can lock or unlock any object within a clipping set or lock or unlock a whole set.

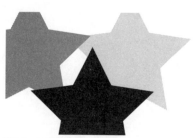

1 *In this **clipping set**, a rectangle was used as a clipping mask.*

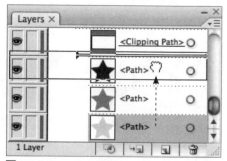

2 *The lightest star <Path> is **dragged upward**...*

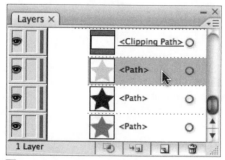

3 *...to the **top** of the clipping set.*

4 *Now the lightest star is in **front** of the other objects in the clipping set.*

Restack, Copy Masked Object

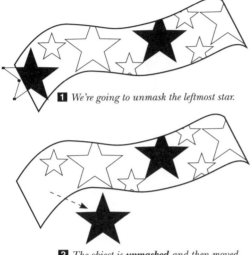

1 *We're going to unmask the leftmost star.*

2 *The object is **unmasked** and then moved.*

3 *The original clipping mask*

4 *A black **fill** was applied to the clipping mask object and the masked objects were recolored.*

5 *The original clipping mask object (zebra) and masked objects (stripes)*

6 *The **recolored** clipping mask object, and the masked objects*

To take an **object out** of a **clipping set**, all you have to do is drag it outside its group or top-level layer on the Layers panel.

To take an object out of a clipping set:

1. Expand the clipping set list on the Layers panel.

2. On the Layers panel, drag the nested object upward or downward out of the group or layer **1**–**2**.

➤ To take an object out of a clipping set and also delete it from the document, select it, then press Delete/Backspace. Adios.

To recolor a clipping path:

1. Select the <Clipping Path> by clicking its selection area on the Layers panel.

2. Apply colors as you would to any object **3**–**6**. The stroke and fill will be listed as attributes on the Appearance panel. The fill will be visible only if there are gaps between the masked objects.

➤ Don't apply a brush stroke to a clipping path; it won't be visible.

Take Object Out of Set; Recolor Clipping Path

337

If you **release** a **clipping set,** the complete, original objects will redisplay, and the former clipping path will be listed as a standard path on the Layers panel. The former clipping path will have a stroke and fill of None (unless you applied a color to it while it was a clipping path).

If you created the clipping set via Object > Clipping Mask, you can use Method 1 or 2 below to release it; if you created the clipping set via the Layers panel, use only Method 2.

To release a clipping set:

Method 1 (command)

1. With the **Selection** tool (V), click any part of the clipping set .
   or
   On the **Layers** panel, ☚ click the selection area for the clipping set <Group>.

2. Control-click/right-click in the document window and choose **Release Clipping Mask,** or choose Object > Clipping Mask > **Release** (Cmd-Option-7/Ctrl-Alt-7) 2. The <Group> listing for the clipping set will disappear from the Layers panel.

Method 2 (Layers panel)

1. On the Layers panel (F7), click the name of the layer or group that contains a clipping set.

2. Click the **Make/Release Clipping Mask** button ☚ at the bottom of the Layers panel. If you release a clipping set that was in a group, the released objects will remain in the group.

➤ If you create a clipping set via the Layers panel button, you won't be able to select the whole set with the Selection tool; you have to use the Layers panel.

1 *The original* **clipping set**

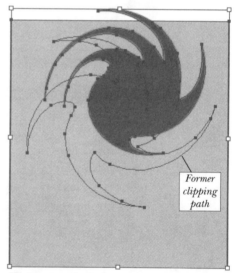

Former clipping path

2 *After choosing the* **Release Clipping Mask** *command.*

TRANSPARENCY 27

In this chapter, you'll choose opacity levels and blending modes for objects via the Transparency panel to create an illusion of semitransparency.

Changing the opacity and blending mode

Study an object on your desk for a minute, such as a lamp or a beverage in a glass. You might say "The shade is white" when you describe it, but on closer inspection, you may notice that rather than being a dense, uniform color, it contains various permutations of white. And if the lamp is on and light is projecting through it, the shade will look semitransparent rather than opaque. Objects have different densities, depending on what type of material they're made of, and may look different depending on how much light is filtering through, or reflecting off, them.

Using Illustrator's **transparency** controls, you can add a touch of realism to your drawings. If you draw a window, for example, you can add a tinted, semisheer, diaphanous curtain on top of it. Draw some autumn leaves, and you could lower their opacity to make them look

semitransparent **1**. You can change the **opacity** of any kind of object, even editable type. You can also choose a **blending mode** for any object to control how its colors blend with the colors in the objects below it.

To change the opacity and blending mode of an object, you'll use the **Transparency** panel. To open it, press Cmd-Shift-F10/Ctrl-Shift-F10; or select an object or objects, then click Opacity on the Control panel.

The fine print: Exporting files that contain transparency to other applications requires choosing special options in the File > Export dialog boxes and in the Document Setup dialogs, but even with the correct settings chosen, such files can cause printing errors. See page 344 and pages 390–392.

1 *J.D. King applied different* **opacity** *percentages to objects in this illustration.*

The **Opacity** setting controls the transparency of an object; the **blending mode** controls how an object's colors are affected by the colors in underlying objects. Objects that you add to a group or layer adopt the transparency settings of that group or layer automatically.

To change the opacity or blending mode of an object, group, or layer:

1. Do one of the following:

   On the Layers panel 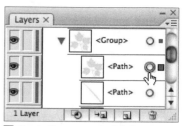 (F7), **select** (or click the target circle for) the object or image you want to choose opacity or blending mode settings for **1**.

   To edit the **appearance** of all the objects on a group or layer, click the target circle for the group or layer.

   Select an object or objects in the **document window.**

   Select some type **characters** with a type tool, or select a whole **type object** using the Selection tool. (To change the opacity of just the fill or stroke on type, see the second set of instructions on the next page.)

2. To change just the opacity, enter or choose an **Opacity** percentage (0–100%) on the Control panel.
   or
   To change the opacity and/or blending mode, click Opacity on the Control panel or press Cmd-Shift-F10/Ctrl-Shift-F10 to open the **Transparency** panel. A thumbnail for the selected or targeted layer, group, or object will display on the panel. Choose a different **blending mode** **2** from the menu and/or move the **Opacity** slider **3**.

1 *On the Layers panel, click the **target** circle for an object, group, or layer.*

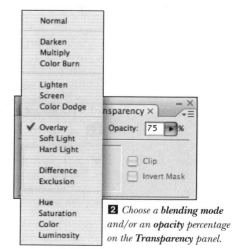

2 *Choose a **blending mode** and/or an **opacity** percentage on the **Transparency** panel.*

3 *The **opacity** of an **entire** type character is lowered to 29%.*

Change Opacity, Blending Mode

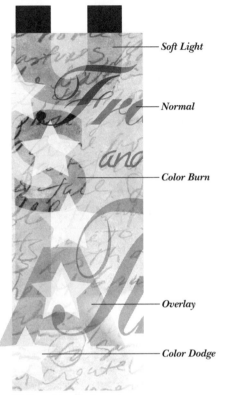

— *Soft Light*

— *Normal*

— *Color Burn*

— *Overlay*

— *Color Dodge*

1 *Type objects in front of an image object, with five different* **blending modes** *used*

2 *The* **Fill opacity** *of the type is lowered to 29%; the Stroke opacity is left at 100%.*

To change the opacity or blending mode of an object's fill or stroke:

1. On the Layers panel, click the target circle for an object. (For a type object, follow the next set of instructions instead.)

2. On the Appearance panel ◉ (Shift-F6), click **Fill** or **Stroke.**

3. On the Transparency or Control panel, move the **Opacity** slider or choose a **blending mode 1**. Attribute changes will be nested below the Fill or Stroke listing for the targeted object on the Appearance panel.

Before you can change the **opacity** of the **stroke** on **type** separately from the **fill**, or vice versa, you must either convert the type to outlines or, if you prefer to keep the type editable, follow these instructions.

To change the opacity or blending mode of the fill and stroke on type individually:

1. Select a type object using the Selection tool. You're going to add a fill and a stroke appearance, so make sure the type is large enough for both appearances to be visible.

2. From the Appearance panel menu, choose **Add New Fill.** A new fill and stroke are created.

3. Choose a fill color, then choose a stroke color and weight.

4. Double-click "Characters" on the Appearance panel. All the characters in the object, plus a type tool, will become selected.

5. Click "Fill" on the Appearance panel, then click the **Delete Selected Item** button 🗑 on the panel; do the same for the Stroke attribute. The fill and stroke are now None.

6. Click "Type" at the top of the Appearance panel.

7. Click the new Fill or Stroke attribute, and change the Opacity and/or blending mode via the Transparency panel **2**.

Controlling which objects the transparency settings affect

If you apply a blending mode to multiple selected objects, that mode will become an appearance for each object. In other words, the objects will blend with one another and with any underlying objects below them. Checking the **Isolate Blending** option, as per the instructions below, seals a collection of objects so the blending modes affect those objects, but not the objects below them.

Note: The Isolate Blending option has no effect on opacity settings; underlying objects will still show through objects that aren't fully opaque.

To restrict a blending mode to specific objects:

1. On the Layers panel 🌐 (F7), click the target circle for a group or layer that contains nested objects that you've applied a blending mode or modes to **1**.

2. On the Transparency panel, 🌐 check **Isolate Blending 2**. (If this option isn't visible, double-click the double arrowhead on the panel tab.) Nested objects within the targeted group or layer will blend with one another, but not with any underlying objects outside the layer or group.

    Note: To reverse the effect, retarget the group or layer, then uncheck Isolate Blending.

➤ Isolate Blending can also be used on individual objects that have overlapping strokes and/or fills. Each stroke or fill can be assigned a different blending mode.

➤ If Isolate Blending is checked for objects nested within a group or layer and you export the Illustrator file to Photoshop (via File > Export, with the Photoshop .psd format chosen), the group will be preserved as separate layers within a layer group and each layer will keep the blending mode setting that was assigned to it in Illustrator.

1 *The original objects include a placed image and a group of squares. The blending mode and opacity for each square interacts with **all** the underlying layers.*

2 *With **Isolate Blending** on for the group of squares, the blending modes affect only objects within the **group**. (Note that where the objects in the group don't overlap one another, you can still see through to the globe image below the group.)*

When to put it in neutral

Objects that have an opacity below 100% will show through one another, whether the **Knockout Group** icon is blank (unchecked) or neutral. Neutral is represented by a dash in Mac  and by a green square in Windows. If you choose the neutral setting for a group of objects nested within a larger group, the nested group will adopt the Knockout Group setting of the larger group.

1 *The Knockout Group option is off for the group of squares.*

2 *With the Knockout Group option on, the squares are no longer transparent to one another or blend with one another (but they still blend with the underlying image).*

3 *With Knockout Group off, the stroke is semitransparent, revealing the part of the object's fill that it straddles.*

4 *With Knockout Group on, the stroke knocks out the object's fill.*

The **Knockout Group** option on the Transparency panel controls whether objects nested in a group or layer will show through each other (knock out) where they overlap. This option affects only objects within the currently targeted group or layer.

To knock out objects:

1. Nest objects in the same group or layer and arrange them so they partially overlap one another. In order to see how the Knockout Group option works, to some or all of the nested objects, apply opacity values below 100% and/or different blending modes (other than Normal mode).

2. On the Layers panel (F7), target the group or layer that the objects are nested within **1**.

3. On the Transparency panel, keep clicking the **Knockout Group** box until a check mark displays **2**. With this option checked, objects won't show through each other, but you'll still be able to see through any semi-transparent objects to underlying objects.

Note: To turn off the Knockout Group option at any time, target the group or layer that the option is applied to, then keep clicking the Knockout Group box until the check mark disappears.

➤ Let's say you lower the opacity of a stroke attribute for an object or type outline via the Appearance panel. If you want the stroke to be opaque just where it overlaps the fill, select the object, click the Default Transparency listing on the Appearance panel, then check Knockout Group on the Transparency panel **3**–**4**.

Knockout Group

Using the transparency grid

Once you start working with semitransparent objects, you may find it hard to distinguish between objects that have a light but solid tint and those that are semitransparent. With the **transparency grid** on, you'll be able to see the gray and white checkerboard behind any objects that have an opacity below 100%.

To show/hide the transparency grid:

Choose View > **Show Transparency Grid** (Cmd-Shift-D/Ctrl-Shift-D) 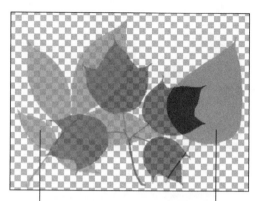. (To hide the grid, choose the command again or repeat the shortcut.)

You can change the **colors** or **size** of the **transparency grid** to make it contrast better with the colors in your artwork.

To choose preferences for the transparency grid:

1. Choose File > **Document Setup** (Cmd-Option-P/Ctrl-Alt-P). The Document Setup dialog box opens.

2. From the first menu, choose **Transparency.**

3. Choose a **Grid Size** of **Small, Medium,** or **Large.**

4. From the **Grid Colors** menu, choose **Light, Medium,** or **Dark** for a grayscale grid, or choose a preset color. (Or to choose custom grid colors, click the top color swatch, choose a color from the Colors dialog box, then click OK. Repeat for the second swatch.)

5. *Optional:* Check Simulate Colored Paper if you want objects and placed images in the document to look as though they're printed on colored paper. The object color will blend with the "colored paper"; the top color swatch is used as the paper color. Hide the transparency grid to see this effect.

6. Click OK.

Semitransparent object   *Light-colored, opaque object*

1 *With the **transparency grid** showing, you can easily see which objects are opaque and which are not.*

Selective flattening

For semitransparent, overlapping objects, the Object > **Flatten Transparency** command helps create a more printable file. It flattens (divides) the areas where objects overlap into separate, nonoverlapping objects **2**–**3**. The semitransparent look is preserved, but the transparency is no longer editable, so this should be done on a copy of your file when your artwork is finished (select the objects, then choose the command).

Unlike the Flatten Transparency command, the **Transparency Flattener** settings that you choose in File > Document Setup and in File > Print (Advanced panel) affect the whole document, not just selected objects. Read more about printing and exporting transparency on pages 390–392.

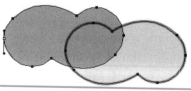

2 *The object on the left (in the back) has a fill color and a stroke of None; the object on the right has a semitranspar- ent fill and a stroke color.*

3 *The **Flatten Transparency** command yielded five objects from two. (We pulled them apart to demonstrate our point.)*

Transparency Grid

In this chapter you'll learn how to work with symbols — Illustrator objects that are stored on the Symbols panel and can be placed singly or in multiples in any document. You'll learn how to place symbol instances into a document, either by dragging or by using the Symbol Sprayer tool; edit those instances using the Symbol Shifter, Scruncher, Sizer, Spinner, Stainer, Screener, and Styler tools; and use the Symbols panel to create, rename, duplicate, edit, and delete symbols.

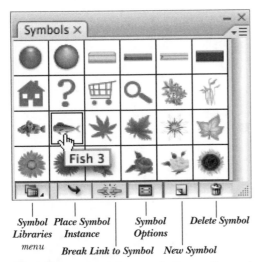

Symbol Libraries menu · Place Symbol Instance · Symbol Options · Delete Symbol · Break Link to Symbol · New Symbol

1 Use the **Symbols** panel to store, duplicate, replace, and delete symbols, and to place symbol instances.

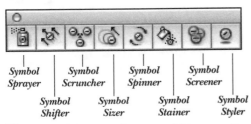

Symbol Sprayer · Symbol Scruncher · Symbol Spinner · Symbol Screener

Symbol Shifter · Symbol Sizer · Symbol Stainer · Symbol Styler

2 The **Symbol Sprayer** tool creates symbol instances; the other **symbolism** tools modify symbol instances in various ways.

Using the Symbols panel

Any object that you can create in Illustrator can be stored on the **Symbols** panel ♣ (Cmd-Shift-F11/Ctrl-Shift-F11) **1**. Symbols on the panel can be placed into any document. To place an **instance** of a symbol onto the artboard, you simply drag it out of the Symbols panel. To place multiple instances of a symbol, you drag with the **Symbol Sprayer** tool or hold the tool down in one spot. A collection of instances in the same bounding box is called a **symbol set.** With symbols, you can create complex art quickly and easily. Spray a tree symbol, spray a grass symbol, then spray a flower symbol to create a flowering forest meadow with just a few clicks of the mouse.

Using the other symbolism tools (**Symbol Shifter, Scruncher, Sizer, Spinner, Stainer, Screener,** and **Styler**) **2**, you can change the density, position, stacking order, size, rotation angle, transparency, or color tint of multiple symbol instances in a selected symbol set, while still maintaining the link to the original symbol. Because of this link, if you edit the original symbol, any instances of that symbol in the document will update automatically. Also, you can apply graphic styles, effects, and tranformations to individual instances or whole sets.

Another advantage of using symbols is that each time you create an instance, Illustrator uses the

(Continued on the following page)

original symbol instead of creating individual objects multiple times. For example, say you draw a boat, save it as a symbol in the Symbols panel, then drag with the Symbol Sprayer to create multiple instances in a symbol set. Even though 50 instances of the boat may appear in the symbol set, Illustrator defines the object in the document code only once. This speeds up printing and keeps the file size down. File size is especially critical when outputting to the Web in SVG (Scalable Vector Graphics) or Flash (swf) format. Because each symbol is defined only once in the exported SVG image or Flash animation, the size of the export file is kept small, and thus its download time is significantly reduced.

In these instructions, you'll create an **instance** of a **symbol** by dragging from the Symbols panel onto your artboard. To place many instances of a symbol quickly, it's much more efficient (and fun) to use the Symbol Sprayer tool (see page 350).

To begin with, you can use the default symbols on the Symbols panel. On the next page, you'll learn how to access other symbol libraries, and on page 348, you'll learn how to create your own symbols.

To create individual symbol instances:

I. Display the **Symbols** panel.

2. **Drag** a symbol from the Symbols panel onto the artboard **1**–**2**.
   or
   Click a symbol on the Symbols panel, then click the **Place Symbol Instance** button on the panel. The instance will appear in the center of the document window.

3. Repeat if you want to add more instances **3**. Each instance is automatically linked to the original symbol. To demonstrate this point, select an instance on the artboard, then look at the Symbols panel; the symbol will be selected on the panel automatically. You'll learn how to preserve or break this link later in this chapter.

➤ To duplicate an instance, Option-drag/Alt-drag it on the artboard as you would a non-symbol object.

1 *Drag a **symbol** from the **Symbols** panel...*

2 *...onto the **artboard**.*

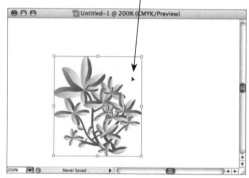

3 *This graphic was created by using symbols from the **Nature** library (shown on the next page).*

Create Symbol Instance

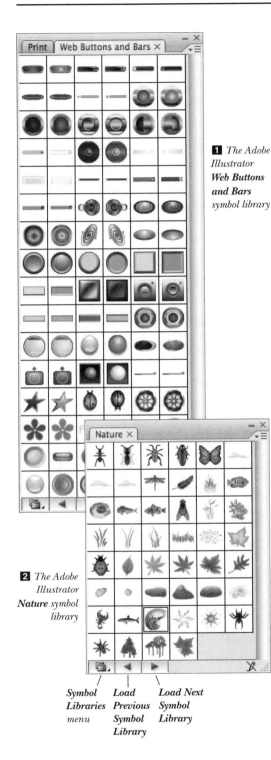

1 *The Adobe Illustrator* **Web Buttons and Bars** *symbol library*

2 *The Adobe Illustrator* **Nature** *symbol library*

Symbol Libraries menu

Load Previous Symbol Library

Load Next Symbol Library

Accessing the symbol libraries

Already bored with the default choices on the Symbols panel? It's time to explore the **Adobe symbol libraries.**

To use symbols from other libraries:

1. From the **Symbol Libraries** menu at the bottom of the Symbols panel, choose a library. **NEW!** When you create your own libraries, you'll be able to choose them from the User Defined submenu on the Symbol Libraries menu. **NEW!** A separate library panel opens **1**–**2**.

2. **Click** a symbol on the library panel; it will appear on the Symbols panel.
   or
   To add multiple symbols from the same library, click the first symbol in a series of consecutive symbols, then Shift-click the last one (or Cmd-click/Ctrl-click nonconsecutive symbols), then choose **Add to Symbols** from the library panel menu, or drag them to the Symbols panel.

3. To browse through another library, choose another library name from the Symbol Libraries menu; or scroll through the available libraries in alphabetical order by clicking the **Load Prevous Symbol Library** button or **Load Next Symbol Library** button at the bottom of the Symbols panel. **NEW!**

➤ If you drag a symbol from a library panel into your document, the symbol will appear on the Symbols panel automatically.

➤ To close a library panel, click the close button (x) on its tab. **NEW!**

➤ To change the Symbols panel display, from the Symbols panel menu, choose Thumbnail, Small List, or Large List View. Choose Sort by Name from the panel menu to sort the symbols alphabetically by name. You can also identify symbols by using tool tips.

Access Symbol Libraries

Replacing symbols

When you **replace** a **symbol** in a solo instance or in a symbol set with a different symbol, any transformations, transparency settings, or effects that were applied to the original instance or set also appear in the replacement symbols.

To replace one symbol with another in an instance:

1. With the **Selection** tool (V), click a symbol instance in your document 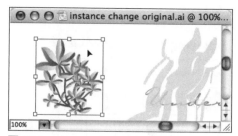.

2. On the Control panel, click the **Replace** thumbnail or arrowhead; a temporary Symbols panel opens.**NEW!** Click a replacement symbol 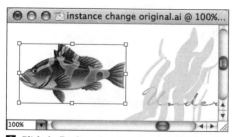.

When you apply a **replacement symbol** to a **set**, all instances in the set are replaced, even if they originated from different symbols.

To replace the symbols in a symbol set:

1. With the **Selection** tool (V), click a symbol set in your document.

2. Click a replacement symbol on the Symbols panel, then choose **Replace Symbol** on the panel menu.

Creating symbols

Now that you're acquainted with the Symbols panel, you're ready to **create** your own **symbols.** Any Illustrator object (or group of objects) can be made into a symbol: a path, compound path, mesh, embedded raster image, type—even another symbol. Within reason, that is. If you're going to use the Symbol Sprayer to spray a gazillion instances of a symbol, you'd be wise to use a symbol that's relatively simple.

Although the object that you make a symbol from can contain a brush stroke, blend, effect, graphic style, or other symbols, those attributes won't be editable in the symbol instances. You can, however, apply graphic styles to instances via the Symbol Styler tool (see pages 362–363).

To create a symbol from an object in your artwork:

1. Create one (or multiple objects or a group), scale it to the desired size, and keep it selected .

1 *Click an **instance** in your document.*

2 *Click the **Replace** thumbnail or arrowhead on the **Control** panel, then click a replacement symbol on the temporary **Symbols** panel that opens.*

3 *Drag an object or group from a document to the **Symbols** panel.*

2. Choose the **Selection** tool (V), then drag the object onto the **Symbols** panel or click the **New Symbol** button ▣ at the bottom of the panel. The Symbol Options dialog box opens ▣.**NEW!**

3. Click **Graphic**, then click OK ▣.

➤ For the Movie Clip option, **NEW!** see Drawing > Symbols > Create a symbol, in Illustrator Help.

➤ To create a new symbol using the current Symbol Options settings—but without naming it—select the object, then Option-click/Alt-click the New Symbol button on the panel.

1 *The Symbol Options dialog box opens. Enter a name and click Graphic.*

2 *The new symbol appears on the panel.*

Saving symbol libraries

If you **save** the **symbols** currently on the Symbols panel into a **library**, you'll be able to access them at any time.

To save a symbol library:

1. Make sure the Symbols panel contains only the symbols you want to save in a library, then choose **Save Symbols** from the Symbol Libraries menu at the bottom of the Symbols panel.**NEW!** The Save Symbols as Library dialog box opens.

2. Type a name for the library in the Save As field, keep the default location, then click **Save.**

3. To open the new library (or another custom library), from the **User Defined** submenu on the Symbol Libraries menu (bottom of the Symbols panel), choose a library.**NEW!** The library will open as a separate panel.

Deleting symbols

If you try to **delete** a **symbol** from the **Symbols** panel that's being used in your document, you'll have a choice, via alert dialog box, to expand or delete the instances.

To delete symbols from the Symbols panel:

1. Drag the symbol you want to delete over the **Delete Symbol** button 🗑 at the bottom of the Symbols panel.
or
Click a symbol on the Symbols panel, then click the **Delete Symbol** button 🗑 at the bottom of the panel.

2. If there are no instances of the deleted symbol in your document, click Yes in the alert dialog box. If the document does contain any instances of the symbol, a different alert dialog box appears. Click **Expand Instances** to expand the linked instances into nonsymbol objects, or click **Delete** Instances to delete the linked instances (or click Cancel to call the whole thing off).

For the remaining instructions in this chapter, we recommend that you open the tearoff toolbar for the symbolism tools **1**.

Using the Symbol Sprayer tool

The **Symbol Sprayer** tool sprays multiple instances of a symbol into a symbol **set**, and can also be used to delete instances from a set. You can choose from a slew of options for this tool, but first do a little spraying.

To create instances with the Symbol Sprayer tool:

1. Choose the **Symbol Sprayer** tool (Shift-S).
2. Click a symbol on the **Symbols** panel.
3. Click to create one instance per click, or click and hold or drag the mouse to create multiple instances quickly **2**. The instances will appear in a set (within a bounding box).
4. *Optional:* To put instances into a new set, Cmd-click/Ctrl-click outside the bounding box for the current set, then click, or click and hold or drag to create instances.

To delete instances from a symbol set:

1. Select a symbol set via a Selection tool or the Layers panel.
2. Click a **symbol** on the Symbols panel that is linked to the instances you want to delete, or deselect all symbols on the panel to remove any symbols from the set.
3. Choose the **Symbol Sprayer** tool. (You can't use a selection tool for this job.)
4. Option-click/Alt-click or Option-drag/Alt-drag inside the set.

To **add symbols** to an existing **set**, you must use the Symbol Sprayer tool (not the Place Symbol Instance button).

To add instances to a symbol set:

1. Select a symbol set via a Selection tool or the Layers panel.
2. Click a symbol on the Symbols panel. It can be a different symbol than those already in the set.
3. Use the **Symbol Sprayer** tool **3**.

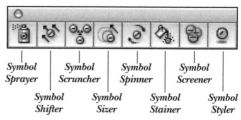

| Symbol | Symbol | Symbol | Symbol |
| Sprayer | Scruncher | Spinner | Screener |

| Symbol | Symbol | Symbol | Symbol |
| Shifter | Sizer | Stainer | Styler |

1 *The **symbolism** tools on the tearoff toolbar*

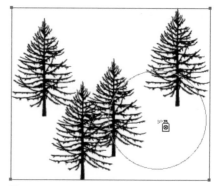

2 *Create a symbol set with the **Symbol Sprayer** tool.*

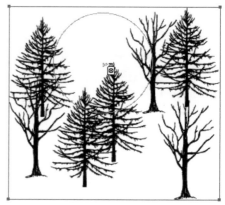

3 *To add instances of a **different** symbol to a set, select the set, choose the **Symbol Sprayer** tool, click a new symbol on the Symbols panel, then drag inside the set.*

Symbol Sprayer Tool

Symbolism Tools Options

Diameter: 222 pt | Method: User Defined

Intensity: 7 | Fixed

Symbol Set Density: 6

Scrunch: Average | Screen: Average

Size: Average | Stain: Average

Spin: Average | Style: Average

☑ Show Brush Size and Intensity

1 *Use the Symbolism Tools Options dialog box to choose global and individual properties for the symbolism tools.*

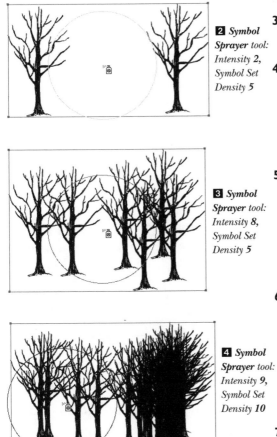

2 *Symbol Sprayer tool: Intensity 2, Symbol Set Density 5*

3 *Symbol Sprayer tool: Intensity 8, Symbol Set Density 5*

4 *Symbol Sprayer tool: Intensity 9, Symbol Set Density 10*

Choosing global properties

In the **Symbolism Tools Options** dialog box, you can choose global settings that apply to all the symbolism tools, as well as settings that apply just to individual tools. We'll discuss the global settings first.

To choose global properties for the symbolism tools:

1. If you're going to adjust the density for the Symbol Sprayer tool, you may want to select a symbol set in your document now. This way, you'll be able to preview changes with the dialog box open.

2. Double-click any symbolism tool. The Symbolism Tools Options dialog box opens **1**.

3. To specify a default size for all the symbolism tools, choose or enter a **Diameter** value (1–999 pt).

4. To adjust the rate at which the tools produce changes (or the sprayer creates instances), choose an **Intensity** value (1–10). The higher the Intensity, the quicker the changes. Or to have a stylus control this option instead, choose any option from the menu other than Fixed.

5. To specify how close instances will be to one another when applied with the Symbol Sprayer tool, choose a **Symbol Set Density** value (1–10) **2**–**4**. The higher the Symbol Set Density, the more tightly the instances will be packed within each set. Changes in this value will preview in any currently selected sets.

6. Check **Show Brush Size and Intensity** to have the current Diameter setting be reflected as a ring around the tool icon, and the Intensity setting be expressed as a shade on the ring of the brush cursor—black for high intensity, gray for medium intensity, and light gray for low intensity. With this option off, you'll see just a tool icon with no ring.

7. Click OK.

Global Symbolism Tool Options

Once you're acquainted with the basic behavior of the Symbol Sprayer tool, you can customize it by way of the **User Defined** options.

To choose options for the Symbol Sprayer tool:

1. Double-click the **Symbol Sprayer** tool (Shift-S). 🖼

   or

   Double-click a symbolism tool, then click the **Symbol Sprayer** button 🖼 in the Symbolism Tools Options dialog box.

2. Choose **Diameter, Intensity,** and **Symbol Set Density** settings **1** (see the previous page for definitions).

3. The **Scrunch, Size, Spin, Screen, Stain,** and **Style** menus define the properties for instances that the Symbol Sprayer tool creates. Choose **Average** from a property menu to have the tool add each new instance based on an average sampling of neighboring instances already in the set, within the diameter of the brush cursor. Or choose **User Defined** to add instances based on a predetermined value (see the sidebar).

   Note: The settings chosen from the six individual tool menus bear no relationship to the Method setting, which applies to the other symbolism tools.

4. Click OK.

User Defined defined

For each property of the **Symbol Sprayer** tool, you can choose Average or User Defined. If you choose **User Defined,** the properties will be based on the following variables:

Scrunch (density) and **Size** are based on the original symbol size.

Spin is based on the direction in which you move the mouse.

Screen is based on 100% opacity.

Stain is based on the current Fill color at a 100% tint.

Style is based on whichever graphic style is currently selected on the Graphic Styles panel.

Symbol Sprayer Tool Options

1 *The pop-up menus in the lower portion of the **Symbolism Tools Options** dialog box appear only when the **Symbol Sprayer** tool icon is selected.*

Quick diameter and intensity changes

When you use any symbolism tool, you can change the tool Diameter and Intensity without opening the options dialog box.

To **increase** the brush diameter, press or hold down] (right bracket). To **shrink** the diameter, press or hold down [(left bracket).

To **increase** the brush **intensity**, press or hold down Shift-] ; or to **decrease** the brush intensity, press or hold down Shift-[.

1 *A symbol instance is clicked.*

2 *We **enlarged** the instance, lowered its **opacity**, and applied the Drop Shadow **effect.***

Modifying symbol instances
To modify symbol instances:

Modifications that you make to an instance (or set of instances) affect neither the original symbol nor the link to it.

Using these methods, you can modify a solo instance or all the instances in a set:

➤ **Move** an instance or set with the Selection tool.

➤ Change the **opacity** or **blending mode** via the Transparency panel.

➤ **Transform** an instance or set by dragging the handles on its bounding box **1**–**2**.

➤ Apply **effects** or **graphic styles.** To modify an effect that you've applied to an instance or set, double-click the effect listing on the Appearance panel, then change the settings.

Note: You can recolor instances via the Symbol Stainer tool, but not via the Swatches, Color, or Color Guide panel.

You can also modify instances or sets by using the Symbol Shifter, Symbol Scruncher, Symbol Sizer, Symbol Spinner, Symbol Stainer, Symbol Screener, or Symbol Styler tool (see pages 356–363). Although these tools affect all the instances in a set, by positioning your pointer carefully, you can control where the tool has its greatest impact. The effect is strongest in the center of the brush diameter and diminishes gradually toward the edge. And the longer you hold the mouse button down, the stronger the effect.

➤ When you use a symbolism tool (such as the Symbol Shifter, Scruncher, or Sizer) to modify instances in a set, keep these two seemingly conflicting tendencies in mind: The tool will shift or scale the instances, while also trying to maintain the original set density. Yin and yang.

353

Duplicating symbols

Before you learn how to edit a symbol (not the instances), you may want to **duplicate** it.

To duplicate a symbol:

Drag a symbol over the **New Symbol** button at the bottom of the Symbols panel **1**–**2** (or click a symbol, then choose Duplicate Symbol from the panel menu). The duplicate symbol will appear after the last symbol on the panel.
or
Click a single instance on the artboard, then click **Duplicate** on the Control panel.**NEW!**

➤ To rename a symbol, click the symbol, choose Symbol Options from the panel menu, then change the name in the dialog box. If you're going to export your symbol artwork to Flash, you can assign names to individual instances. Click an instance, then enter a new name in the Instance Name field on the Control panel.**NEW!**

➤ You can rearrange the symbols on the panel by dragging any symbol thumbnail or listing to a new spot.

Editing symbols NEW!

In these instructions, you'll change the original symbol. *Beware!* When you edit a symbol, those changes are applied to any and all instances in the document that it's linked to. This makes for very efficient editing, but it can also wreak havoc on your design if you're not careful. And with the new methods for editing symbols in Illustrator CS3, your changes are applied more easily—and more quickly.

To edit a symbol: NEW!

1. **Double-click** a symbol on the Symbols panel **3**. A temporary instance of that symbol will appear in your document **4**.
or
Click a symbol instance in your document, click **Edit Symbol** on the Control panel, then click OK in the alert dialog box.

2. The instance (or temporary instance) should now be in isolation mode. Select and modify the object(s) as desired (**1**, next page).

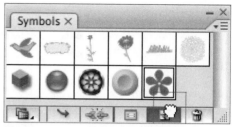

1 *Drag a symbol over the **New Symbol** button.*

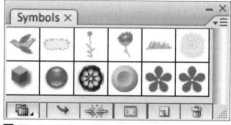

2 *The **duplicate** symbol appears on the panel.*

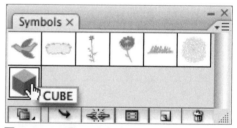

3 *Double-click a symbol on the **Symbols** panel.*

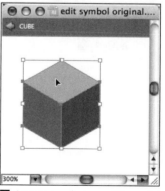

4 *A **temporary instance** of the symbol appears in the document window, in isolation mode.*

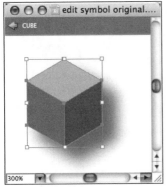

1 *Edit the temporary instance, then click the Exit Isolated Group button in the upper left corner of the window.*

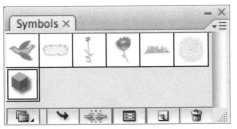

2 *The edits appear in the thumbnail on the Symbols panel (in this case, we added a drop shadow).*

3. To apply your edits to the **original** symbol, click the **Exit Isolated Group** button or gray bar at the top of the document window. The symbol will update on the Symbols panel **2**, and any instances that are currently linked to that symbol will update automatically to reflect your edits. Any transformations, effects, opacity values, etc. that were applied to those instances before the symbol was edited will be preserved.

To create a variation of an existing symbol:

1. Click a symbol instance in your document.

2. Click the **Break Link to Symbol** button on the Symbols panel.

3. Edit the object(s) or group.

4. Drag the object or group onto a blank area of the Symbols panel. The Symbol Options dialog box opens.

5. Enter a name, click **Type: Graphic**, then click OK.

➤ If you want to replace an existing symbol with your newly edited, nonsymbol object, Option-drag/Alt-drag the object over the symbol on the Symbols panel that you want to redefine (or select the object, click the symbol to be redefined on the panel, then choose Redefine Symbol from the panel menu). Any other instances that are linked to that symbol will update accordingly.

When you break the **link** between an instance and the original symbol, the instance is converted to a normal object or objects.

To break the link between an instance and the symbol:

1. Select a symbol instance in your document.

2. Click the **Break Link to Symbol** button at the bottom of the Symbols panel.
or
Click the **Break Link** button on the Control panel.**NEW!**

➤ To break the link between a whole symbol set and the original symbol(s), you must use the button on the Symbols panel.

Using the Symbol Shifter tool

Except for the Sprayer, all the symbolism tools —Symbol Shifter, Scruncher, Sizer, Spinner, Stainer, Screener, and Styler—let you modify attributes of a symbol instance or symbol set, such as the position, size, orientation, color, transparency, or graphic style, while preserving the link to the original symbol. We'll explore each tool individually.

➤ Remember, you can change the intensity and diameter of each tool via the shortcuts listed in the sidebar on page 353.

The **Symbol Shifter** tool has two functions. It either shifts instances in a set sideways, based on the direction you drag the cursor, or changes their stacking order (front-to-back position). Being able to bring instances forward or behind other instances is useful, say, in a set in which trees are obscuring some figures. You could use the Symbol Shifter tool to move the trees closer together to create a forest, then bring the figures forward, in front of the trees.

To use the Symbol Shifter tool:

I. Select a symbol set in your document.

2. Choose the **Symbol Shifter** tool.

3. Drag in the direction you want the instances to **shift**. The tool will try to preserve the current density and arrangement of instances as it performs its job.
or
Shift-click an instance to bring it in **front** of adjacent instances **1**–**2**.
or
Option-Shift/Alt-Shift click an instance to send it **behind** adjacent instances.

To choose options for the Symbol Shifter tool:

I. Double-click the **Symbol Shifter** tool.

2. Choose a brush **Diameter 3**.

3. Choose an **Intensity** value for the rate of shifting and thus the amount of space the tool creates between shifted instances.

4. Choose a **Symbol Set Density** value (see page 351).

5. Click OK.

Why aren't all the instances changing?

If a selected set contains instances from more than one symbol and one of those symbols happens to be selected on the Symbols panel, modifications made by a symbolism tool will be limited to only the instances from the currently selected symbol. If you want to modify instances of more than one type of symbol in a set, deselect all symbols by clicking an empty area of the Symbols panel first.

1 *The Symbol Shifter tool is used (with Shift held down, in this case) on this symbol set...*

2 *...to shift the plovers into a more naturalistic front-to-back order.*

Symbolism Tools Options		
Diameter: 222 pt	Method:	User Defined
Intensity: 8	Fixed	
Symbol Set Density: 6		

Hold down the Shift key to bring symbol instances forward.
Hold down the Shift+Option keys to send symbol instances backward.

3 *Options for the Symbol Shifter tool*

One method for all

The current choice on the **Method** pop-up menu in the Symbolism Tool Options dialog box applies to all the symbolism tools except the Symbol Sprayer and Symbol Shifter.

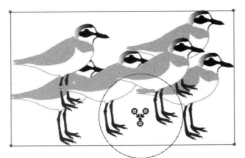

1 *Option-drag/Alt drag across a symbol set with the Symbol Scruncher tool.*

2 *The plovers were moved **apart**.*

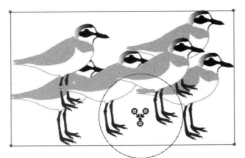

Symbolism Tools Options
Diameter: 41.18 pt · Method: Average
Intensity: 8 · Fixed
Symbol Set Density: 5 ·
Hold down the Option key to push symbol instances away from the cursor.
☑ Show Brush Size and Intensity

3 *Choose options for the **Symbol Scruncher** tool.*

Using the Symbol Scruncher tool

The **Symbol Scruncher** tool pulls symbol instances closer together or spreads them apart. A symbol set of clouds or fish, for example, could be contracted (scrunched) to bring the instances closer together or expanded to spread them out. You can either drag with the tool or hold the mouse button down in one spot.

To use the Symbol Scruncher tool:

1. Select a symbol set in your document.

2. Choose the **Symbol Scruncher** tool.

3. To move instances closer **together**, either click and hold in one spot or drag inside the set.
   or
   To push symbol instances **away** from one another, Option-click/Alt-click or Option-drag/Alt-drag **1**–**2**.

To choose options for the Symbol Scruncher tool:

1. Double-click the **Symbol Scruncher** tool.
   or
   To change the density in an existing set, click the set, then double-click the **Symbol Scruncher** tool.

2. Choose a brush **Diameter** and a **Symbol Set Density** value (see page 351) **3**.

3. Choose an **Intensity** value to control how much the tool changes the density and how quickly it produces the change.

4. Choose a **Method:**

   User Defined to gradually increase or decrease the amount of space between symbol instances based on how you click or drag.

   Average to make the spacing between instances more uniform based on an average of the existing density of instances. This method will produce a minor effect if the spacing is already averaged.

   Random to randomize the spacing between instances.

5. Click OK.

Symbol Scruncher Tool

Using the Symbol Sizer tool

The **Symbol Sizer** tool reduces or enlarges instances in a symbol set. Because the Symbol Sprayer tool can't create instances of variable size, the Symbol Sizer is useful for applying scale variations to an existing set of instances.

To use the Symbol Sizer tool:

1. Click a symbol set in your document.

2. Choose the **Symbol Sizer** tool.

3. Click on or drag over instances to **enlarge** them ∎.

   or

   Option-click/Alt-click or Option-drag/Alt-drag over instances to **shrink** them.

   The instances closest to the cursor will scale the most.

   Note: If very little happens when you use this tool, change the Method to User Defined or Random (see step 6, below).

To choose options for the Symbol Sizer tool:

1. Double-click the **Symbol Sizer** tool.

2. Choose brush **Diameter** and **Symbol Set Density** values ∎.

3. Choose an **Intensity** value for the rate and amount of scaling. The higher the Intensity, the wider the range of scale changes.

4. *Optional:* Check Proportional Resizing to resize instances without distorting them.

5. *Optional:* Check Resizing Affects Density to force instances to move away from one another when they're enlarged or move closer together when they're scaled down, while maintaining the current set density. With this option unchecked, instances may overlap more.

6. Choose one of these **Methods:**

   User Defined to gradually increase or scale the instances based on the way you click or drag.

   Average to make the instances more uniform in size. If the sizes are already near uniform, this method will produce little effect.

1 *These instances were **scaled** using the **Symbol Sizer** tool.*

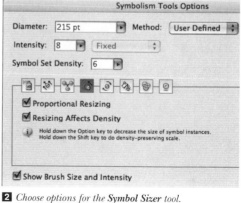

2 *Choose options for the **Symbol Sizer** tool.*

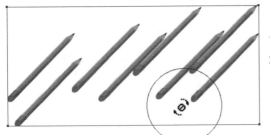

1 *The **Symbol Spinner** tool, with the **Random** Method chosen, is dragged across a symbol set.*

2 *The pencils are **rotated** randomly.*

3 *Choose options for the **Symbol Spinner** tool.*

Random to randomize scale changes within the brush diameter.

7. Click OK.

➤ With Average or Random chosen as the brush Method, Shift-click or Shift-drag to scale instances while maintaining (if possible) the current density.

Using the Symbol Spinner tool

The **Symbol Spinner** tool changes the orientation of instances within a symbol set.

To use the Symbol Spinner tool:

1. Click a symbol set in your document.

2. Choose the **Symbol Spinner** tool.

3. Drag a symbol instance or instances in the direction you want them to rotate, using the arrows as an orientation guide **1**–**2**. Clicking and holding has no effect.

➤ If the arrows are hard to see, change the selection color for the layer that the set resides in.

➤ The smaller the brush Diameter, the easier it will be to isolate individual symbol instances for rotation.

To choose options for the Symbol Spinner tool:

1. Double-click the **Symbol Spinner** tool.

2. Choose brush **Diameter** and **Symbol Set Density** values **3**.

3. Choose an **Intensity** value for the rate and amount the instances can be rotated. The higher the Intensity, the sharper the angles of rotation with the least amount of mouse action.

4. Choose a **Method:**

User Defined to rotate symbol instances in the direction the mouse is moved.

Average to gradually make the orientation of all instances within the brush diameter more uniform.

Random to randomize the orientation of instances.

5. Click OK.

Symbol Spinner Tool

Using the Symbol Stainer tool

Like the Colorization (Tints and Shades) option for brushes, the **Symbol Stainer** tool colorizes symbol instances. It recolors solid fills, patterns, and gradients with varied tints of the current fill color. You could use this tool to vary the shades of green in foliage, the shades of brown in buildings, etc.

Note: The Symbol Stainer tool increases the file size and diminishes performance, so don't use it if you're going to export your file in the Flash (swf) format or if system memory is a concern.

1 *The Symbol Stainer tool is dragged across a symbol set.*

To use the Symbol Stainer tool:

1. Select a symbol set in your document.
2. Choose the **Symbol Stainer** tool.
3. Choose a fill color to be used for staining.
4. **Click** an instance to apply a tint of the current fill color. Continue clicking to increase the amount of colorization, up to the maximum amount.

   or

   Drag across the symbol set to colorize any instances within the brush diameter **1**–**2**. Drag again to intensify the effect.

➤ Option-click/Alt-click or Option-drag/Alt-drag to decrease the amount of colorization and restore more of the original symbol color.

➤ Shift-click or Shift-drag to tint only instances that have already been stained.

To choose options for the Symbol Stainer tool:

1. Double-click the **Symbol Stainer** tool.
2. Choose brush **Diameter** and **Symbol Set Density** values **3**.
3. Choose an **Intensity** value for the rate and amount of tint the Stainer applies.
4. Chose a **Method:**

   User Defined to gradually tint symbol instances with the current fill color.

   Average to even out the amount of existing colorization among selected instances without applying a new tint.

2 *The fireworks are **tinted** gradually.*

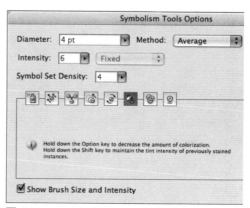
3 *Choose options for the **Symbol Stainer** tool.*

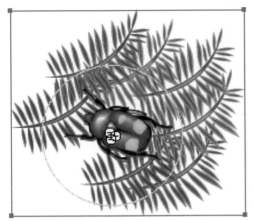

1 *With the* ***Symbol Screener*** *tool, the mouse is held down on an instance (the beetle).*

2 *The beetle is* ***screened***.

Symbolism Tools Options

Diameter: 2.78 in | Method: Average
Intensity: 8 | Fixed
Symbol Set Density: 5

ⓘ Hold down the Option key to decrease transparency.

☑ Show Brush Size and Intensity

3 *Choose options for the* ***Symbol Screener*** *tool.*

Random to randomize the colorization, for a more naturalistic effect.

5. Click OK.

Using the Symbol Screener tool

The **Symbol Screener** tool increases or decreases the opacity of instances within the brush diameter. Use this tool to fade instances and make them more transparent.

To use the Symbol Screener tool:

1. Select a symbol set in your document.

2. Choose the **Symbol Screener** tool.☺

3. Click and hold on or drag across instances to make them more **transparent 1**–**2**.
   or
   Option-click/Alt-click on or Option-drag/Alt-drag across instances to make them more **opaque.**

   Note: If nothing happens when you use this tool, change the Method to User Defined or Random (see step 4, below).

To choose options for the Symbol Screener tool:

1. Double-click the **Symbol Screener** tool.

2. Choose brush **Diameter** and **Symbol Set Density** values **3**.

3. Choose an **Intensity** value for the rate and amount of transparency that is applied. The higher the Intensity, the more quickly and intensely instances will fade or become more opaque.

4. Choose a **Method:**

   User Defined to have the transparency increase or decrease gradually.

   Average to make the amount of transparency among instances become more uniform within the diameter of the brush.

   Random to gradually introduce transparency in a random manner.

5. Click OK.

Symbol Styler Tool

Using the Symbol Styler tool

The **Symbol Styler** tool applies the graphic style that's currently selected on the Graphic Styles panel to instances in a set. By selecting different styles on the Graphic Styles panel, you can apply multiple styles to a symbol set. Logically, the tool can also be used to remove styling.

1 *Choose the* **Symbol Styler** *tool, then click a style on the* **Graphic Styles** *panel.*

To use the Symbol Styler tool:

1. Select a symbol set in your document.

2. Choose the **Symbol Styler** tool.

3. Click a graphic style on the **Graphic Styles** panel (you can access it via the Control panel) **1**. *Note:* Be sure to choose the symbolism tool first. If you choose a style while a nonsymbolism tool is selected, the style will be applied uniformly to the whole set.

4. Click and hold on or drag across an instance or instances to **apply** the selected style within the brush diameter **2** (and **1**, next page). The longer you hold the mouse down, the more intensely the style will be applied. Pause for the screen to redraw. This can take some time even on a fast machine.
   or
   Option-click/Alt-click or Option-drag/Alt-drag to **undo** the styling.

➤ Shift-click or Shift-drag to gradually apply the currently selected graphic style only to instances that have already been styled, while keeping any unstyled instances unchanged.

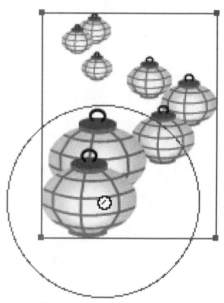

2 *An instance is clicked with the* **Symbol Styler** *tool.*

To choose Symbol Styler tool options:

1. Double-click the **Symbol Styler** tool.

2. Choose brush **Diameter** and **Symbol Set Density** values.

3. Choose an **Intensity** value for the rate and amount of attributes in a graphic style that are applied. The higher the Intensity, the more intense and quick the styling.

4. Choose a **Method:**

   User Defined to gradually increase or decrease the amount of styling.

   Average to even out the amount of styling already applied to instances within

362

1 *To produce this graphic, different **graphic styles** were applied to **different** instances. Compare with the figure on the previous page.*

the brush diameter, without applying new styling.

Random to apply styling gradually but randomly.

5. Click OK.

➤ If you want to view the attributes used in an applied graphic but you don't know which style was applied, click the symbol set, choose Object > Expand, check Fill and Stroke, then click OK. On the Layers panel, click the gray target circle for one of the expanded instances, then look at the appearance listings on the Appearance panel. Be sure to Undo to restore the symbol set.

Expanding symbol instances

Vis-a-vis symbols, the **Expand** command can be used for two different purposes. When applied to a symbol **set**, it breaks the set apart without disturbing the instances themselves or their link to the original symbol. The instances will be nested inside a group on the Layers panel.

When applied to an individual **instance** (not in a set), the Expand command breaks the link to the original symbol. The individual paths from the former instance will be nested inside a group on the Layers panel.

To expand an instance or a symbol set:

1. Select a symbol instance, multiple instances, or symbol set.

2. Choose Object > **Expand** (or choose Object > **Expand Appearance** if the instance has an effect applied to it).

3. Check **Object** and **Fill** █, then click OK.

4. If you expanded a symbol set █–█, you can now use the **Direct Selection** tool to move the individual instances apart, if desired, or double-click the group with the Selection tool to isolate it, then modify the instances. In either case, they'll remain linked to the original symbol.

   If you expanded an individual instance █–█, it will now be a group of paths, unlinked from the original symbol. To modify any individual path, select it via the Layers panel.

➤ If the artwork the symbol originated from contained any live appearances or effects, they'll be editable once you expand an individual instance of that symbol (not originally from a set). Use the Layers panel to target any individual path or group, and the Appearance panel to edit the effects. To use the edited object to redefine the symbol or to create a new symbol, see pages 354–355.

➤ If you use the Symbol Stainer tool on a symbol set and then expand the set, the instances affected by the tool will have a numeric listing on the Layers panel.

Select all instances

To select all the solo instances of a particular symbol in your document that don't belong to a set, click the symbol on the Symbols panel, then choose **Select All Instances** from the panel menu.

█ *Check* **Object** *and* **Fill** *in the* **Expand** *dialog box.*

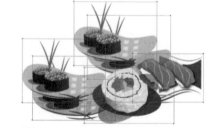

█ *The original symbol* **set**

█ *After using the* **Expand** *command*

█ *The original symbol* **instance**

█ *After using the* **Expand** *command and moving paths apart*

PREFERENCES 29

In this reference chapter, you'll learn how to choose default command, tool, and panel settings for current and future documents in the 11 panes of the Preferences dialog box: General, Selection & Anchor Display, Type, Units & Display Performance, Guides & Grid, Smart Guides & Slices, Hyphenation, Plug-ins & Scratch Disks, User Interface, File Handling & Clipboard, and Appearance of Black.

General Preferences

*To open this dialog box, choose Illustrator (Edit, in Windows) > Preferences > **General (Cmd-K/Ctrl-K).***

Keyboard Increment

This value is the distance (0–1296 pt.) a selected object moves when an arrow key is pressed on the keyboard. To move a selected object 10 times the current Keyboard Increment, press Shift-arrow.

Constrain Angle

This is the angle (–360 to 360°) for the x and y axes. The default setting is 0° (parallel to the edges of the document window). Tool operations, transformations, dialog box measurements, new objects, the grid, etc. are calculated relative to the current Constrain Angle (see also the sidebar on the next page).

Corner Radius

This value (0–1296 pt.) controls the amount of curvature in the corners of objects drawn with the Rounded Rectangle tool. 0 produces a right angle. Changing this value updates the Corner Radius field in the Rounded Rectangle dialog box, and vice versa.

Disable Auto Add/Delete

Checking this option disables the ability of the Pen tool to change to the Add Anchor Point tool when the pointer passes over a path segment, or to the Delete Anchor Point tool when the pointer passes over an anchor point.

(Continued on the following page)

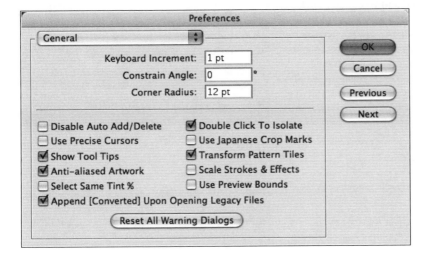

CHAPTER 29

Use Precise Cursors

When this option is checked, the drawing and editing tool pointers display as crosshairs instead of as the tool icon. To turn this option on temporarily for your tool when the preference is off, press Caps Lock.

Show Tool Tips

When this option is checked and you rest the pointer on a panel button, tool, swatch, icon, or other option, a short description of that feature pops up onscreen.

Anti-aliased Artwork

When this option is checked, edges of existing and future vector objects (not placed images) look smoother onscreen. It doesn't affect print output.

Select Same Tint %

When this option is checked, the Select > Same > Fill Color and Stroke Color commands select only objects with the same spot (not process) color and tint percentage as the currently selected object. When this option is off, the tint percentage is ignored as a criterion.

Append [Converted] Upon Opening Legacy Files

With this option checked, when opening a file that was created in Illustrator 10 or earlier, Illustrator appends the word "[Converted]" to the file name.

Double Click to Isolate NEW!

If this option is checked and you double-click a group of objects, the group will be put in isolation mode (other objects will become temporarily uneditable). If this option is unchecked and you want to put a group into isolation mode, select the group, then click the Isolate Selected Group button ⊞ on the Control panel.

Use Japanese Crop Marks

Check this box to use Japanese-style crop marks when printing separations. (You can preview this style via Object > Crop Area > Make or Filter > Create > Crop Marks.)

Transform Pattern Tiles

With this option checked, if you use a transformation tool on an object that contains a pattern, the pattern will also transform. You can also turn this option on or off for any individual transformation tool in its own dialog box, in the Move dialog box, or on the Transform panel menu.

Scale Strokes & Effects

Check this box to allow an object's stroke weight and appearances to be scaled when you scale an object by using its bounding box, the Scale tool, or the Free Transform tool. This option can also be turned on or off in the Scale dialog box or via the Transform panel menu.

Use Preview Bounds

If this option is checked, an object's stroke weight and any effects are factored in when an object's height and width dimensions are calculated or the Align panel is used. This option changes the dimensions of the bounding box.

Reset All Warning Dialogs

Click this button to allow warnings in which you checked "Don't Show Again" to redisplay when editing operations cause them to appear.

What the Constrain Angle affects

➤ Type objects

➤ Rectangle, Ellipse, and Graph tools **1**

➤ Some transformation tool dialog boxes (Scale, Reflect, and Shear, but not Rotate or Blend)

➤ Gradient tool and Pen tool (with Shift key down)

➤ Objects moved with Shift down or via an arrow key

➤ Grid

➤ Smart guides

➤ Info panel readouts

Note: To establish a Constrain Angle based on an object that was rotated using the Rotate tool, select the object, then enter the Angle readout ⊿ from the Info panel as the new Constrain Angle.

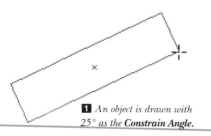

1 *An object is drawn with 25° as the* **Constrain Angle.**

> ## Getting to the preference panes
> After opening the Preferences dialog box (Cmd-K/Ctrl-K), choose a pane from the menu at the top of the dialog box or click Previous or Next. You can also get directly to a pane by choosing it from the Illustrator/Edit > Preferences submenu.

Selection & Anchor Display Preferences NEW!

Selection

Tolerance

Specify the range within which an anchor point will become selected when you click near it with the Direct Selection tool.

Object Selection by Path Only

With this option checked, in order to select an object with the Selection or Direct Selection tool, you must click a path segment or anchor point. With this option unchecked, you can select a filled object in Preview view by clicking the fill area with a selection tool.

Snap to Point

With this option checked, objects will snap to a nearby anchor point or guide, within the range of pixels that you specify in the adjacent field.

For the Pencil tool preferences, see page 163.

Anchor Point and Handle Display

Anchors

Choose a display style for anchor points: small selected and unselected points, large selected points and small unselected points, or large selected and unselected points.

Handles

Choose a display style for direction points on direction handles: small, large, or hollow.

Highlight Anchors on Mouse Over

If this option is checked and you move the Direct Selection tool over an anchor point, the point will become highlighted (enlarged). This makes it easier to locate points.

Show Handles When Multiple Anchors Are Selected

Check this option to permit the display of dual direction handles on multiple anchor points when selected with the Direct Selection tool, or uncheck this option to allow a pair of direction handles to display on only one selected point at a time.

Type Preferences

Size/Leading; Baseline Shift; Tracking
Selected text is modified by this increment each time a keyboard shortcut is executed for the respective command.

Type Object Selection by Path Only
With this option checked, to select type, you have to click right on a type path. With this option unchecked, you can select type by clicking with a selection tool anywhere on or near the type.

Show Asian Options
Check this option to access options for Chinese, Japanese, and Korean language characters on the Character panel, Paragraph panel, and Font menu.

Show Font Names in English
When this option is checked, Chinese, Japanese, or Korean font names display in English on the Font menus. When this option is unchecked, two-byte font names display in the native characters for the font.

Number of Recent Fonts
Choose the maximum number of recently chosen fonts (1–15) to be listed on the Type > Recent Fonts submenu.

Font Preview
Check this option to have font family names display in their actual fonts, for easy identification on the Type > Font menu, on the Character panel, and in the Find Font dialog box. Also choose a Size for the font display of Small, Medium, or Large.

Enable Missing Glyph Protection NEW!
Check this option to let Illustrator preserve a glyph that's being used in your artwork if you switch to a font that doesn't support that glyph.

Use Inline Input for Non-Latin Text NEW!
Check this option to be able to type non-Roman characters directly into Illustrator (rather than having to use a separate dialog box outside Illustrator).

Units & Display Performance Preferences

Units

General

This unit of measure is used for the rulers; dialog boxes; and Transform, Control, and Info panels in the current and future documents.

➤ For the current document, the Units chosen in File > Document Setup (under Artboard: Setup) override the Units chosen in this preference pane.

Stroke

This unit of measure is used on the Stroke panel and in the Stroke Weight field on the Control panel.

Type

This unit of measure is used on the Character and Paragraph panels. (We use points.)

Asian Type

This unit of measure is used for Asian type.

Numbers Without Units Are Points

If this option is checked and Picas is chosen for Units: General, when you enter a value in points in a field, the value won't be converted into picas. For example, if you enter "99," instead of being converted into "8p3," it will stay as "99."

Identify Objects By

When creating dynamic objects associated with variables, you can specify whether variables are assigned the Object Name or an XML ID number. Consult with your Web developer regarding this option.

Display Performance

Hand Tool

Drag the Hand Tool slider to the left toward Full Quality for better onscreen display as you move the artwork in the document window with the Hand tool; or move the slider to the right toward Faster Updates to move the artwork more quickly, but at a lower display quality.

Guides & Grid Preferences

Guides

Color

For Guides, choose a color from the Color menu; or choose Other or double-click the color square to open the Colors dialog box and mix a custom color.

Style

Choose a Style of Lines or Dots for the guides.

Grid

Color

For the Grid (View > Show Grid), choose a color from the Color menu; or choose Other or double-click the color square to open the System color picker and mix a custom color.

➤ If View > Snap to Grid is on, guides and objects will snap to gridlines as you create or move them.

Style

Choose a Style of Lines or Dots for the Grid. Subdivision lines don't display for the Dots Style.

Gridline every

Enter the distance between gridlines.

Subdivisions

Enter the number of subdivision lines **1**–**2** to be drawn between the darker gridlines when the Lines Style is chosen for the grid.

Grids in Back

Check Grids in Back (the default setting) to have the grid display behind all objects, or uncheck this option to have the grid display in front of all objects.

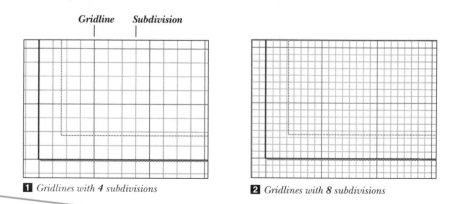

1 *Gridlines with 4 subdivisions*   **2** *Gridlines with 8 subdivisions*

Smart Guides & Slices Preferences

Display Options

Text Label Hints

Check this option to allow text labels to display as you pass the pointer over an object, anchor point, etc. **3**.

Construction Guides

Check this option to have angle lines display as you draw or drag an object **1**. Choose or create an angles set in the Angles area (see below).

Transform Tools

Check this option to have angle lines display as you transform an object via a transformation tool or via the object's bounding box **2**. Choose or create an angles set in the Angles area (see below).

Object Highlighting

Check this option to have an object's path display as you pass the pointer over it **3**. This is helpful for locating unpainted paths, such as clipping masks, or paths hidden behind other paths. Paths for which the visibility icon is off on the Layers panel won't become highlighted.

Angles

If smart guides are on and you drag an object, temporary lines will display on the angles designated in the fields. Choose a preset angles set from the Angles menu or enter custom angles in any or all of the fields (press Tab to update the preview). If you enter custom angles, "Custom Angles" will appear on the menu. If you switch from Custom Angles to a predefined set and then later switch back to Custom Angles, the last custom angles used will reappear in the fields.

Snapping Tolerance

This is the distance (0–10 pt) within which the pointer must be from an object for smart guides to display. The default value is 4 pt.

Note: To activate smart guides, choose View > Smart Guides (Cmd-U/Ctrl-U).

Slicing

Show Slice Numbers

Check this option to have slice numbers display onscreen (for Web graphics). From the **Line Color** menu, choose a color for those numbers and for the lines that surround each slice.

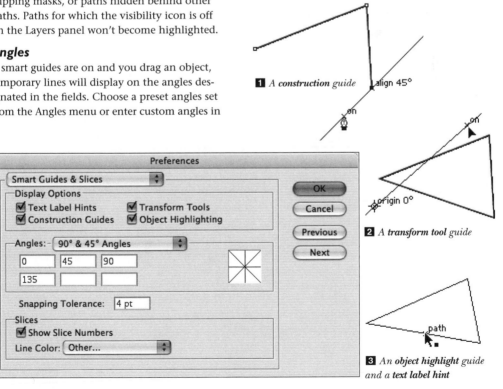

1 *A construction guide*

2 *A transform tool guide*

3 *An object highlight guide and a text label hint*

Hyphenation Preferences

Default Language

Choose the language dictionary for Illustrator
to refer to when it inserts hyphen breaks. (From
the Language menu on the Character panel, you
can choose a different hyphenation language
dictionary for the current document.)

Exceptions

Enter words that you want hyphenated in
a particular way. Type the word in the New
Entry field, inserting hyphens where you would
want them to appear (or enter a word with no
hyphens to prevent Illustrator from hyphenat-
ing it), then click Add. To remove a word from
the list, click it, then click Delete.

Plug-ins & Scratch Disks Preferences

Note: For changes made in this dialog box to take effect, you must quit/exit and relaunch Illustrator.

Additional Plug-ins Folder

The core and add-on plug-in files that come with Illustrator provide additional functionality to the main application, and are put in the Plug-ins folder inside the Adobe Illustrator CS3 folder automatically when you install the program.

If you have additional plug-ins that you want to use with Illustrator but want to keep in a separate folder, you must use this Preferences dialog box to tell Illustrator where that folder is located. Click Choose. In the New Additional Plug-ins Folder dialog box, locate and click the name of the desired plug-ins folder, then click Choose to exit. The new location will now be listed.

Scratch Disks

Primary

The Primary scratch disk is used as virtual memory when available RAM is insufficient for processing. Choose an available hard drive — preferably your largest and fastest — from the Primary menu. Startup is the default.

Secondary

As an optional step, choose an alternate Secondary hard drive to be used as extra virtual memory when needed. If you have only one hard drive, of course you can have only one scratch disk.

Preferences

Plug-ins & Scratch Disks

☑ Additional Plug-ins Folder

/Library/Application Support/Adobe/Plug-Ins   Choose...

OK
Cancel
Previous
Next

Scratch Disks

Primary: Startup

Secondary: None

Note: Changes will take effect the next time you start Illustrator.

Plug-ins & Scratch Disks Preferences

User Interface Preferences NEW!

Brightness
Choose a gray value, from Dark to Light, for the background of all the panels.

Auto-Collapse Icon Panels
With this option checked, if you expand a panel that was collapsed to an icon, then click away from the panel, the panel will collapse to an icon again automatically. With this option unchecked, an expanded panel will stay expanded.

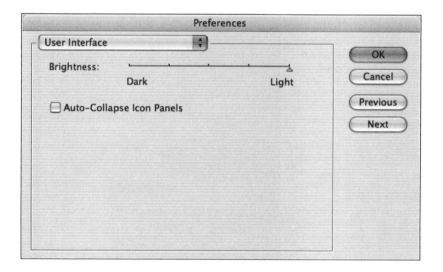

File Handling & Clipboard Preferences

Version Cue and Files

If you have the Adobe Creative Suite 3 installed (or someone on your network has the suite installed and has given you access to a shared project), and **Enable Version Cue** is checked, you'll be able to utilize the Adobe Version Cue Workspace features to control file security, organize files into private or shared projects, and search and review file information and file statuses among the suite applications, such as Dreamweaver and Photoshop. For more information, read the Adobe Version Cue section in Illustrator Help, the Help file

in Documentation > Adobe Bridge CS3, or the Version Cue CS3 folder on the Creative Suite 3 Content DVD.

If you're working with a lot of linked files, you can enhance performance by checking **Use Low Resolution Proxy for Linked EPS;** placed images will display as low-resolution bitmap proxies (screen previews, in plain English). With this preference unchecked, raster images will display at full resolution and vector objects will display in full color.

To specify how linked images are updated when the original files are modifed, from the **Update Links** menu, choose one of the following:

Automatically to have Illustrator update linked images automatically, with no dialog box opening, when you edit a file and then click back in Illustrator.

Manually to leave linked images unchanged when the original files are modified. You can update links at any time via the Links panel.

Ask When Modified to display a dialog box when the original files are modified. (In the dialog box, click Yes to update the linked image, or click No to leave it unchanged.)

Clipboard on Quit

The Clipboard can be used to transfer selections between Illustrator and other programs in the Adobe Creative Suite, such as Photoshop, Dreamweaver, and InDesign. When a selection is copied to the Clipboard, it's copied in the PDF and/or AICB format, depending on which of the following **Copy As** options you choose:

PDF preserves transparency information in the Clipboard contents and is designed for use with Adobe programs, such as Photoshop and InDesign.

AICB (no transparency support), a PostScript format, preserves the appearance of transparency through flattening (which breaks objects into smaller opaque objects). Click **Preserve Paths** to copy a selection as a set of detailed paths, or click **Preserve Appearance and Overprints** to preserve the appearance of the selection and any overprinting objects.

Note: If you check both PDF and AICB, the receiving application will choose between the two. Fills and effects will copy and paste more accurately, but the copying time will be longer and the memory requirements higher.

➤ If you're unable to paste a selection into Illustrator, try using drag-and-drop to acquire it instead.

➤ In the Mac OS, if you plan to drag and drop or copy and paste an Illustrator object that contains gradients, blends, patterns, or transparency into InDesign CS3, you must first uncheck the Copy as: AICB option and check the PDF option. InDesign won't read the PDF data if AICB data is also present. You can leave both options checked if you're going to drag or paste an Illustrator object with a solid, opaque fill.

Appearance of Black Preferences

Options for Black on RGB and Grayscale Devices

Sometimes printers use a combination of CMYK inks instead of 100K (black alone) to produce richer, more lustrous blacks. Options in this preference pane control whether blacks will be displayed onscreen and output using their actual values or as rich blacks. The examples of 100K Black and Rich Black as shown in the dialog box are exaggerated intentionally so you can compare them.

On Screen

Choose **Display All Blacks Accurately** to display blacks onscreen based on their actual values (pure CMYK black will display as dark gray), or choose **Display All Blacks as Rich Black** to display all blacks as rich black regardless of their actual CMYK values.

Printing/Exporting

Choose **Output All Blacks Accurately** to print blacks using their actual K or CMYK values on RGB and grayscale devices, or choose **Output All Blacks as Rich Black** to print blacks as a mixture of CMYK values (rich blacks) on RGB devices. This setting affects output data only, not values in the actual document. Output All Blacks as Rich Black produces the darkest possible black on an RGB printer.

Description

To learn about any option in the dialog box, rest the pointer on it with the mouse button up, and read the relevant information in the **Description** area.

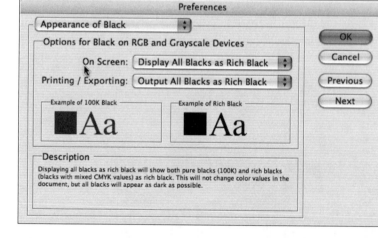

Resetting the preferences

To restore all the default Illustrator preferences, quit the program, then trash the Application preferences file. When you relaunch Illustrator, a new preferences file is created.

➤ In the Mac OS, delete /Users/[user name]/ Library/Preferences/Adobe Illustrator CS3 Settings/Adobe Illustrator Prefs.

➤ In Windows, delete C:\Documents and Settings\[user name]\Application Data\ Adobe\Adobe Illustrator CS3 Settings\AIPrefs.

Whatever you do, don't delete the whole Preferences folder! You need the other items in that folder to run other applications and utilities.

Although Illustrator objects are described and stored as mathematical commands, when printed, they're rendered as dots. The higher the resolution of the output device, the more smoothly and sharply the lines, curves, gradients, and continuous-tone images in your artwork are rendered. In this chapter you'll learn how to print a document on a black-and-white or composite color printer; tile an oversized document; specify bleeds and printer's marks; prepare a file for color separations; choose flatness settings; download fonts; print using color management; choose overprint options; create and edit presets; create crop marks; choose a resolution for effects; and use the Document Info panel.

CHARLES, NANCY STAHL

NORAH, NANCY STAHL

Print dialog box: General and Setup options

To access options in the **Print** dialog box, you'll click one of the 8 option set names. We'll show you how to print using basic settings first, then discuss a few of the option sets in depth.

To print to a black-and-white or color printer:

1. For a composite print on a desktop inkjet printer (all colors on one sheet), choose File > Document Color Mode > RGB Color; for a composite print on a desktop color laser printer, check your printer documentation for the correct document color mode; either color mode is fine for a grayscale printout.

2. Choose File > **Print** (Cmd-P/Ctrl-P). The Print dialog box opens (**1**, next page).

3. From the **Printer** menu, choose from the list of printers that are available in your system.

If you chose a PostScript printer, the **PPD** menu will display the default PPD (PostScript printer description) file for that printer. Or if your commercial printer supplied (and you installed) a custom PPD file for the chosen printer, choose it from the menu.

4. On the list of option sets on the left side of the dialog box, click **General**.

5. In the **Copies** field, enter the desired number of print copies.

For **Media**, from the **Size** menu, choose Defined by Driver or the desired paper size.

Click an **Orientation** button to print vertically or horizontally on the paper.

6. In the Options area, from the **Print Layers** menu, choose which layers will print:

Visible & Printable Layers to print only the visible layers for which the Print option is checked in the Layer Options dialog box. (To prevent any individual object from printing, you would have to uncheck the Print option for its layer before choosing File > Print.)

Visible Layers to print only those layers that have a visibility icon on the Layers panel.

All Layers to print all layers, regardless of the current Layers panel settings.

7. For scaling, click **Do Not Scale** to print the document at its current size, even if it exceeds the paper size; or **Fit to Page** to scale the document to fit the current paper size; or **Custom Scale,** then enter a Width or Height value to scale the document proportionally. (For nonproportional scaling, deselect the Constrain Proportions button,⃞ then enter separate Width and Height values.)

8. Click **Setup** on the list of option sets.

9. From the **Crop Artwork To** menu, choose Artboard.

10. *To change the position of your artwork on the paper, do any of the following (optional):*

Click a different point on the Placement icon to print the artwork relative to that part of the paper.

Enter Origin X and Origin Y values to specify the position of the upper left corner of the artwork on the paper.

Drag the artwork in the preview area (this actually repositions the page borders on the artboard). Only parts of the artwork that are visible in the preview area will print.

Leave the Tiling choice as Single Full Page. (If the document is large and has to be tiled onto multiple pieces of paper, see pages 380–381.)

11. Click **Print** to print the document; or to save the current settings with your document without printing, click Done, then save the file.

➤ Although you can access the dialog boxes for the system's printer driver from the Print dialog box by clicking the Page Setup or Printer button in the Mac OS, or the Setup button in Windows, to utilize the print capabilities of Illustrator as you output your file, Adobe recommends choosing all print settings from the Print dialog box instead.

Save your print settings!

Considering how many options you need to choose in the Print dialog box, why not save your settings as a preset so you don't have to reenter them each time you print to a particular output device? To create a print preset of the current print settings, click **Save Preset** at the bottom of the dialog box, enter a name for the preset, then click OK.

Saved presets can be chosen from the **Print Preset** menu at the top of the Print dialog box. To edit a print preset, see page 393.

List of option sets

Print preview area

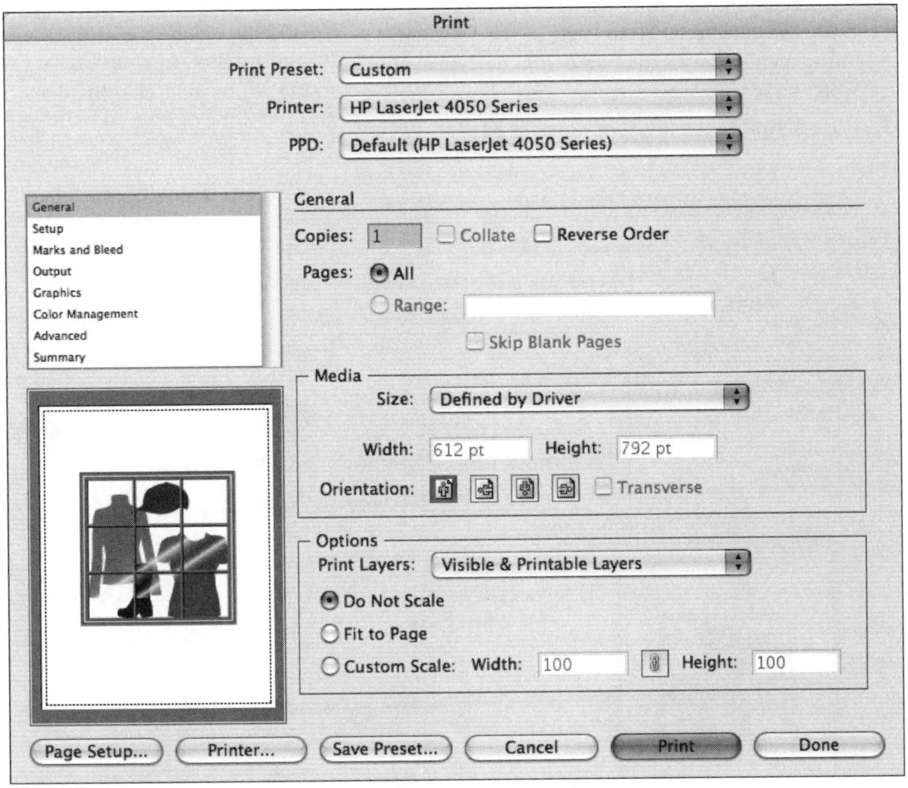

1 *From the General option set in the Print dialog box, choose basic print settings.*

In the remaining pages of this chapter, we'll explore the settings in the 8 option sets of the Print dialog box.

The **Setup** options control the position of the artwork on the printed page (you were introduced to this option set on page 378). Use these options to tile a large document onto multiple pages or, by defining a crop area, control which objects will print.

To print (tile) a document that's larger than the paper size:

1. Choose File > **Print** (Cmd-P/Ctrl-P), then click **General** on the list of option sets.

2. Choose **Media** (page) **Size** and **Orientation** settings, and under Options, click **Do Not Scale.** (Don't choose Fit to Page, or the Tiling menu that you'll choose from in step 5 won't be accessible.)

3. Click **Setup** on the list of option sets **1**.

4. From the **Crop Artwork To** menu:

   If all the objects to be printed lie within the artboard, choose **Artboard.**
   or
   If you want to print all the objects in the document, even objects that extend beyond the edge of the artboard, choose **Artwork Bounding Box.** A bounding box will surround all the objects in the document (see also the tiling option, step 5).
   or

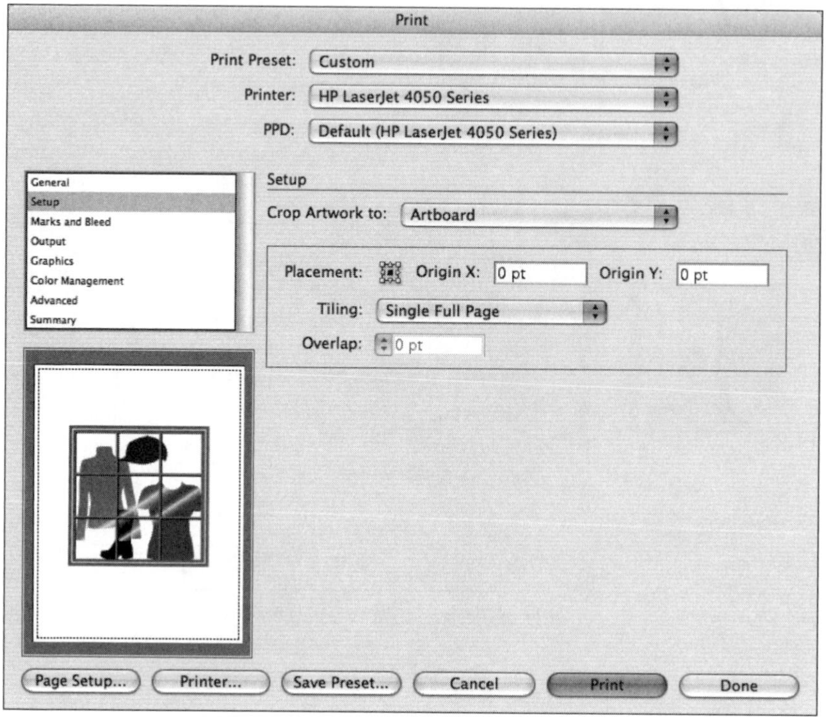

1 *Via the **Setup** option set in the **Print** dialog box, you can control the position of your artwork on the printed page.*

1 *This shows the* **Tile Imageable Areas,** *with the* **Crop Artwork To: Crop Area** *setting, as viewed in the preview area.*

If you've already defined a crop area in the document to limit which objects will print, choose **Crop Area 1**. To create a crop area, see page 395.

5. From the **Tiling** menu, choose:

   Tile Full Pages 2 to divide the artwork into whole pages, as per the printer media size.
   or
   Tile Imageable Areas 3 to divide the artwork into a grid of pages as per the printer media size.

6. *Optional:* Click a point on the Placement icon to position the artwork on that corresponding part of the paper or grid of pages; click the center point if you need to recenter the artwork.
   or
   Place the pointer over the preview area and drag to reposition the artwork on the grid of pages. Dragging the preview will reposition the page borders on the artboard (just as the Page tool does).

   If you chose Tile Full Pages from the Tiling menu, you can change the Overlap value for the amount of overlap between pages.

2 *This shows the* **Tile Full Pages** *setting, as viewed in the preview area.*

7. To print all the tiled pages, go back to the General option set, leave the **Pages: All** button chosen and check **Skip Blank Pages** to prevent any blank tiled pages from printing. Or to print select tiled pages, click **Range**, then enter the desired tile values as the range of pages in the field, separated by a hyphen.

8. Choose any other print settings. Click **Print** to print the document; or to save the current settings with the document without printing, click **Done**, then save your file.

3 *This shows the* **Tile Imageable Areas** *setting, as viewed in the preview area.*

> ## Printing slightly smaller
>
> A simple way to print a document that's slightly larger than the paper size in your printer is to reduce the output size. Go to the General option set in the Print dialog box, and in the Options area, click **Fit to Page**. With this option chosen, the Tiling menu options won't apply.

Tile Oversized Document

Marks and Bleed options

Use options in the **Marks and Bleed** set of the Print dialog box to create printer's marks at the edge of the printable area, or to set up bleed parameters for objects that extend beyond that area. Commercial printers use trim marks to trim the final printout, registration marks to align printing plates, and color bars to help them evaluate the print colors.

To include printer's marks in your printout:

1. Click **Marks and Bleed** on the list of option sets in the **Print** dialog box (**1**, next page).

2. Check Marks: **All Printer's Marks**, and leave checked (or uncheck) any of the following options:

    Trim Marks adds thin lines to designate where the printed pages are to be trimmed. The lines will align with the horizontal and vertical edges of the printable area, which is controlled by the current setting on the Crop Artwork To menu in the Setup option set.

    Registration Marks adds small circles outside each corner of the bounding box.

    Color Bars adds color swatches outside the printable area.

    Page Information adds a text label above the top edge of the printout, containing specs for the commercial printer.

3. Choose a printer mark style from the **Printer Mark Type** menu: Roman or Japanese.

4. Choose a thickness for trim marks from the **Trim Mark Weight** menu.

5. Enter or choose an **Offset** value (0–72 pt) for the distance between trim marks and the bounding box.

➤ The Crop Area tool creates nonprinting trim marks. To produce trim marks on the actual printout, check Trim Marks in the Print dialog box.

The **bleed** area is the area just outside the edge of a printed document. You can position objects in your artwork so they extend into the bleed area, thus ensuring that they'll print to the very edge of the final trimmed page. Ask your commercial printer what bleed values are appropriate for their specific printer.

To choose bleed values:

1. On the left side of the **Print** dialog box, click **Marks and Bleed.**

2. In the **Bleeds** area:

    For asymmetrical bleed values, deselect the link icon,▣ then enter **Top, Left, Bottom,** and **Right** values (0–1 inch, or 0–72 pt.). Enter a low bleed value to move the trim marks closer to the edges of the printed artwork, or a higher bleed value to move them farther away and thus print more of any objects that extend into the bleed area.

    Or click the link icon to activate it, then enter a single bleed value to be used for all four sides of the document.

3. Enter a Marks: **Offset** value greater than the bleed width to ensure that any printer's marks won't be obscured by the bleed objects. The Offset increases the distance between the printable page size and the trim marks but, like the Bleeds settings, doesn't change the printable page size.

    ➤ Make sure the output medium (paper size) is large enough to accommodate printer's marks and/or the bleed area.

4. Choose any other print settings, then click **Print** to print the document; or to save the current settings with the document without printing, click **Done,** then save your file.

1 Use the **Marks and Bleed** option set in the **Print** dialog box to choose printer's marks and set bleed values.

Output options

Settings in the **Output** option set of the Print dialog box are used primarily by prepress operators to produce color separations for commercial printing. (During color separation, each color prints to a separate plate or piece of film.) If you want to proof which colors in your artwork will output to which plate, you can choose the appropriate Output settings, then print your file to a color or grayscale printer. And finally, if you're using a composite printer (all colors on one sheet), in the Output option set, you can simply confirm that the correct printer is chosen on the Mode menu.

To output a composite print or color separations:

1. Make sure your file is in CMYK Color mode, choose File > **Print**, then click **Output** on the list of option sets **1**.

2. On the **Printer** menu, choose the PostScript color or grayscale printer that's available to your system.

Before choosing other settings (steps 3–6), ask your commercial printer for advice.

3. From the **Mode** menu:

   For color separations, choose **Separations (Host-Based)** to have Illustrator prepare the separation information and send the data to the printing device, or choose **In-RIP Separations** to have Illustrator send PostScript data to the printer's RIP* and have that device perform the separation. (Available options will vary depending on the type of printer you chose in step 2.)

4. Choose **Emulsion:** Up (Right Reading) or Down (Right Reading).

5. Choose **Image:** Positive or Negative.

6. From the **Printer Resolution** menu, choose the halftone screen ruling (lpi)/device resolution (dpi) that your commercial printer recommends.

   For more Output options, see the next page.

1 *Use the **Output** option set in the **Print** dialog box to choose settings for composite printing or color separations.*

*The RIP (short for "raster image processor") converts vector data into printable dots.

Overprinting

Normally, Illustrator automatically knocks out any color below an object so colors in the upper object won't mix with any underlying colors on press. If you check **Overprint Fill** and/or **Overprint Stroke** on the Attributes panel for a selected object, its fill and/or stroke colors will print on top of underlying colors instead. Where colors overlap, the inks will mix, producing a combination color. *Notes:* In RGB Color mode, only spot colors can be set to overprint. Colors overprint on a printing press but not on a PostScript composite color printer.

➤ To preview the current overprint settings, choose View > Overprint Preview **1**–**2**. "Overprint Preview" will be listed in the title bar of the document window.

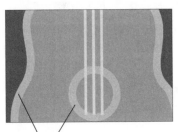

1 *The strokes on these two objects are set to* ***overprint.***

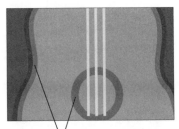

2 *With the* ***Overprint Preview*** *feature on, you can see how the ink from the overprinting strokes will mix with colors in underlying objects.*

If you choose a Separations option from the Mode menu in the Output option set, Illustrator will create and print a separate plate for each process and spot color used in the document. In the same option set, you can turn **printing** on or off for individual colors or convert individual spot colors into **process** colors.

To change the print setting for, or convert, individual colors:

1. Choose File > **Print**, click **Output** on the left side, then choose a separation Mode.

2. In the **Document Ink Options** area **3**, you'll see a listing for each color used in the document. For each process or spot color you don't want to print, click the printer icon 🖨 next to the color name. (Click again to redisplay the icon.)

3. Check **Convert All Spot Colors to Process** to convert all spot colors in the document to process colors.
   or
   For each spot color you want to convert to a process color, uncheck Convert All Spot Colors to Process, then click the **spot color** icon 🔘; the process color icon ▨ will appear in its place.

4. Choose other print settings, then click **Print**.

➤ Don't change the Frequency, Angle, or Dot Shape settings unless your commercial printer advises you to do so. (You can click Reset to Defaults at any time to restore all the default ink settings.)

➤ To allow black fills and strokes to overprint underlying colors, check Overprint Black in the Output option set (see also the sidebar on this page).

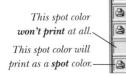

This spot color ***won't print*** *at all.*

This spot color will print as a ***spot color.***

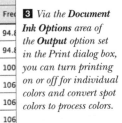

3 *Via the* ***Document Ink Options*** *area of the* ***Output*** *option set in the Print dialog box, you can turn printing on or off for individual colors and convert spot colors to process colors.*

Graphics options

The **Flatness** setting in the **Graphics** option set of the Print dialog box controls how precisely all the objects in a document print on a PostScript printer. If your document doesn't print, raise the Flatness setting, then try printing again.

To change the flatness setting for a file to facilitate printing:

1. Open the file that stubbornly refuses to print, choose File > **Print**, then click **Graphics** on the list of option sets (■, next page).

2. Check **Automatic** to let Illustrator choose an optimal Flatness value for the chosen printing device.

   or

   If you have encountered a printing error, under Paths, uncheck Automatic, drag the **Flatness** slider one or two notches to the right, then click Print. If the document prints, but with noticeably jagged curve segments, you raised the Flatness setting too much. Lower it slightly by dragging the slider back to the left, and print again.

   ➤ To see a numeric display (tool tip) of the current Flatness settings, rest the pointer on the slider.

To download fonts:

1. To manage how fonts are downloaded to the printer, open the Print dialog box, **Graphics** option set. From the **Download** menu in the **Fonts** area, choose one of these options:

   None to have no fonts download. This is the preferred setting when fonts are permanently stored in the printer.

   Subset to download only the characters (glyphs) used in the document.

   Complete to have all the fonts used in the document download at the beginning of the print job. This is effective when printing multiple pages that use the same fonts (Illustrator files are usually single pages, though).

2. Click **Print** to print the document; or to save your settings with the document without printing, click **Done**, then save the file.

Flatten versus flatness

On output, Illustrator flattens overlapping shapes automatically in order to preserve the look of transparency — an altogether different process from establishing a **Flatness** setting, which controls how precisely curve segments print. To arrive at this setting, Illustrator divides the printing device resolution by the output resolution. For any given printer, raising the Flatness value lowers the output resolution. The higher the Flatness value (or the lower the output resolution), the less precisely any curve segments in your artwork will print.

Graphics choices

Normally, you don't need to choose **PostScript®** LanguageLevel or **Data Format** options in the Print dialog box (Graphics option set), because Illustrator sets these options for you automatically, based on the chosen printer. However, if your printer supports more than one option in the above-mentioned categories, the settings become available, and you'll need to choose one (decisions, decisions!). Whenever possible, choose PostScript® LanguageLevel 3 because it contains the latest definitions for printing transparency and facilitates smooth shading to prevent banding in gradients.

1 *Use the **Graphics** option set in the **Print** dialog box to choose settings for outputting graphics and fonts.*

Print: Graphics Options

Color Management options

Use the **Color Management** option set of the Print dialog box to control how color conversion will be handled. *Note:* If you haven't learned about profiles and color settings yet, read Chapter 4 first.

To print using color management:

1. Choose File > **Print** (Cmd-P/Ctrl-P), then click **Color Management** on the list of option sets **1**.

2. Follow one of these two procedures:

   From the **Color Handling** menu, choose **Let Illustrator Determine Colors** (the preferred choice) to let Illustrator convert document colors to the printer gamut based on the chosen printer profile and send the converted data to the printer. The quality of the conversion depends on the accuracy of the chosen printer profile. From the **Printer Profile** menu, be sure to choose the appropriate ICC profile for your printer, ink, and paper. Click **Printer/Setup**, then locate and turn off color management for the printer driver.

   or

   From the **Color Handling** menu, choose **Let PostScript® Printer Determine Colors** to send the color data to the printer and let the printer convert the colors to its gamut. Click **Printer/Setup**, then locate and turn on color management for the printer driver if your printing device requires it.

3. If you chose Let PostScript® Printer Determine Colors, check **Preserve CMYK Numbers** to hold off any color conversion of the artwork until the color data reaches the printer. For RGB documents, Adobe recommends leaving the Preserve RGB Numbers option unchecked.

4. Leave the **Rendering Intent** on the default setting of Relative Colorimetric unless you or your output specialist have a specific reason to change it. For more about the intents, see page 58.

5. Choose other print options, then click **Print** to print the document; or to save the current settings with the document without printing, click **Done**, then save your file.

1 *Use the **Color Management** option set in the **Print** dialog box to control whether Illustrator or your PostScript printer will handle color conversions.*

Got a non-PostScript printer?

If your document contains complex objects (such as gradients, meshes, or soft-edged effects) and it generates a printing error from a non-PostScript or low-resolution printer, instead of printing the file as vectors, check **Print as Bitmap** in the Advanced option set in the Print dialog box. Note that the driver for the chosen printer controls whether this option is available, and most Macintosh printer drivers don't include it.

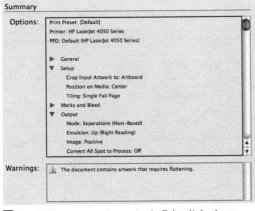

1 *Use the **Advanced** option set in the **Print** dialog box to choose overprint settings.*

2 *Use the **Summary** option set in the **Print** dialog box to see a listing of the current print settings.*

Advanced options

In the **Advanced** option set of the Print dialog box, you'll choose overprint options for fills and strokes for color separation or composite printing.

To choose overprint and flattening options for output:

1. On the left side of the **Print** dialog box (Cmd-P/Ctrl-P), click **Advanced**.

2. Choose an option from the **Overprints** menu **1**:

   Preserve to keep the file's overprint settings, for color separations.

   Discard to ignore a file's overprint settings when printing.

   Simulate to create the visual effect of overprinting on a composite printer, for proofing purposes.

   Note: The Overprints setting doesn't override the Overprint Fill or Stroke settings chosen in the Attributes option set.

3. To specify how transparent objects are flattened for printing, choose a preset from the **Preset** menu (see the sidebar on the next page), or click **Custom** to create and save a custom preset that saves with the file (see pages 391–392).

4. Choose other print settings, then click either Print or Done.

Summary options

In the **Summary** option set, you can read a summary of the current Print dialog box settings.

To view a summary of the current print settings:

1. On the left side of the **Print** dialog box, click **Summary** **2**.

2. Scroll down the **Options** window to view the settings, and read any alerts in the **Warnings** window.

3. *Optional:* Click Save Summary to save the current settings to a separate file.

Printing and exporting transparency

Transparency settings in objects, groups, or layers (blending modes other than Normal and opacity levels below 100%) are preserved when a document is saved in a native Adobe Illustrator format (CS through CS3) or the Adobe PDF format (Compatibility: Acrobat 5 or higher).

When you print a file that contains transparency settings, or export it in a nonnative format, Illustrator uses the current transparency flattener settings to determine how objects will be flattened and rasterized in an effort to preserve the appearance of transparency.

In the course of flattening, if Illustrator detects an object that contains transparency and overlaps an underlying object, it converts the overlapping area into a separate flat, opaque shape (and leaves the remaining, nonoverlapping parts of the original objects as is).

Illustrator tries to keep flattened shapes as vector objects. However, if the look of transparency settings can't be preserved in a flattened shape as a vector object, Illustrator will rasterize the shape instead. This will happen, for example, where two gradient objects with nondefault transparency settings overlap. The resulting flattened shape is rasterized in order to keep the complex appearance of transparency.

Default transparency flattener presets

[High Resolution] is suitable for high-quality color separations and film-based color proofs.

[Medium Resolution] is suitable for desktop PostScript color prints and proofs.

[Low Resolution] is suitable for black-and-white desktop printers.

Transparency to InDesign

When saving your artwork for **InDesign CS3,** use the native Illustrator CS3 (ai) format, which preserves the editability of transparency. Illustrator objects containing transparency will interact correctly with the content of, and any transparency in, the InDesign layout. InDesign will perform any needed transparency flattening at the time of printing.

To control how transparency is flattened for exported files:

1. Choose File > Document Setup.

2. Choose **Transparency** from the topmost menu **1**, then in the Export and Clipboard Transparency Flattener Settings area, choose a preset from the **Preset** menu (see the sidebar on this page), then click OK.
   or
   Click **Custom** to create a custom preset that saves with the file (see the following page).

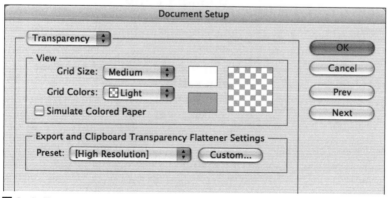

1 *In the* **Transparency** *option set of the* **Document Setup** *dialog box, you can choose an existing transparency flattener preset or create your own custom preset.*

To choose custom transparency flattener options:

1. When you click Custom in either the Document Setup dialog box (Transparency pane) or the Print dialog box (Advanced option set), the Custom Transparency Flattener Options dialog box opens **1**. Perform any of the following steps.

2. Move the **Raster/Vector Balance** slider to control the percentage of flattened shapes that will remain as vectors versus the percentage of shapes that will be rasterized. The Raster/Vector Balance settings apply only to flattened shapes that represent transparency. Vector shapes print with cleaner, higher-quality color and crisper edges as compared with rasterized shapes.

   Higher values (to the right) produce a higher percentage of flattened shapes as vectors, though complex flattened areas may still be rasterized. A higher percentage of vector shapes will result in higher-quality output, but at the expense of slower, more memory-demanding output processing.

   The lowest value (to the left) won't necessarily produce poor output quality. In fact, if a document is very complex and contains a lot of transparency effects, this may be the only setting that produces acceptable output. Low settings produce fast output at a low resolution.

3. In the rasterization process, the output quality is calculated based on two resolution settings. To specify the resolution for rasterized line art and text, enter a **Line Art and Text Resolution** value. For most purposes, the default resolution setting of 300 ppi is adequate, but for small text or thin lines, you should increase this value to 600 ppi. Transparent text is flattened and preserved as text objects; clipping and masking are used to preserve the look of transparency.

4. In the **Gradient and Mesh Resolution** field, specify the resolution for rasterized gradients and mesh objects. Gradients and meshes, like continuous-tone imagery, don't contain sharp details. The default value of 150 ppi is usually adequate; 300 ppi would be considered a high value.

   When the Raster/Vector Balance slider is below 100, due to transparency flattening, Illustrator may rasterize placed or embedded images at the resolution specified in the Gradient and Mesh Resolution field. This value will be used only for portions of an image that are overlapped by a transparent object; the remainder of the image will print at the original image resolution.

   When an EPS image is overlapped by an object that contains transparency, embed the image into the Illustrator document by clicking the Embed button on the Control panel. This will ensure an accurate printout of the image and the transparency effect.

   (Continued on the following page)

Custom Transparency Flattener Options

Raster/Vector Balance: ——————△———— Rasters ——— Vectors — [75] — (OK)

(Cancel)

Line Art and Text Resolution: [300 ▾] ppi

Gradient and Mesh Resolution: [150 ▾] ppi

☐ Convert All Text to Outlines
☑ Convert All Strokes to Outlines
☑ Clip Complex Regions

1 *Use the **Custom Transparency Flattener Options** dialog box to choose custom settings for the current file.*

Custom Transparency Flattener Options

5. With the Raster/Vector Balance slider between 10 and 90, portions of type that are overlapped by an object with transparency will be rasterized or converted to outlines, and may be thickened slightly. If those areas look noticeably different from type that isn't overlapped by transparency, try checking **Convert All Text to Outlines** to make all the type within a given font print in the same width, or move the type into its own layer above the transparent object.

6. With the Raster/Vector Balance slider between 10 and 90, any strokes that are overlapped by an object with transparency will be converted to outlines. Very thin strokes may be thickened slightly and may look noticeably different from parts of strokes that aren't overlapped by transparency.

Check **Convert All Strokes to Outlines** to convert all strokes in a document to outlines. This preserves the look of a stroke for its entire length but yields a larger number of paths in the file. An alternative to using this option is to apply Object > Path > Outline Stroke to selected strokes in your artwork.

7. When a file is sent to print, any areas of semitransparent objects that overlap other objects will be flattened and rasterized. The newly flattened areas, however, won't match the exact path shapes of the objects. Also, the resulting flattened object may contain a combination of pixel and vector areas, and color discrepancies ("stitching") between adjacent pixel and vector areas may result. If you check **Clip Complex Regions**, boundaries between raster and vector flattened shapes will fall exactly on object paths. This helps eliminate the signs of stitching but also slows down printing because of the complexity of the resulting paths. (*Note:* If the entire document is rasterized, no stitching occurs.)

8. Click OK.

Flatten an individual object

To control the flattening of a selected object, choose Object > **Flatten Transparency,** check Preview, then adjust the Raster/Vector Balance slider, the Line Art and Text Resolution value, and, if the object contains a gradient or mesh, the Gradient and Mesh Resolution value.

Preview the flattening

Via the **Flattener Preview** panel, you can see which transparent areas of a document will be flattened. Choose Window > Flattener Preview to open the panel. Click Refresh, and choose Show Options from the panel menu. Move the Raster/Vector Balance slider, if desired; check the appropriate options; then click Refresh again. From the Highlight menu, choose the type of object you want highlighted in the preview. You can save your settings as a preset by choosing Save Transparency Flattener Preset from the Flattener Preview panel menu.

➤ For more information about flattening and the Flattener Preview panel, see Illustrator Help. Or if you're using the Adobe CS3 Creative Suite, look for Documentation > Adobe Creative Suite 3 Design Premium/Standard > Designer's Guide to Transparency.pdf on the Content DVD.

Custom Transparency Flattener Options

Creating and editing presets

By creating a **preset** for your custom transparency flattener and Print dialog box settings, you'll be able to apply the same flattening or print settings to a series of documents quickly. For example, rather than choosing custom flattener settings via the Print dialog box (Advanced option set) or the Document Setup dialog box (Transparency pane) for individual files, you can create presets for different printing scenarios that you can choose for any file. Presets can also be exported as files for use by other users.

You can use the Edit > Print Presets command to create a new print preset, and any printing presets that you create via the Print dialog box can also be edited via this command.

To create or edit a transparency flattener, tracing, print, or PDF preset:

1. From the Edit menu, choose **Transparency Flattener Presets, Tracing Presets, Print Presets,** or **Adobe PDF Presets.** A preset dialog box opens.

2. *Optional:* Click New to create a new preset; or click an existing preset, then click New to create a variation (copy) of that preset.

3. Enter a **Name.**

4. Choose options. For the Transparency Flattener Preset Options dialog box **1**, choose settings as per the instructions on the previous two pages; for the Tracing Options

dialog box, see pages 155–157; for the Print Presets Options dialog box, see pages 378–389; or for the New PDF Presets dialog box, see pages 402–405. Click OK.

5. To edit an existing user-created preset (not in brackets), click the preset name, click **Edit,** change any of the settings, then click OK. *Note:* You can also edit the [Default] print preset, but not the default transparency flattener presets or the default PDF presets.

6. *Do any of the following optional steps:*

   To see a summary of settings for a preset, click the preset name, then look in the Preset Settings window.

   Click Delete to delete the currently selected user-created preset.

   Click Export to save the settings for the currently selected preset as a separate file.

   Click Import to locate and open an exported settings file.

7. Click OK.

➤ If your artwork contains transparency and you save it in the Adobe PDF format with compatibility set to Acrobat 4 (PDF 1.3), you must choose transparency flattener options (Advanced option set). With compatibility set to Acrobat 5 or higher, flattening won't be required.

1 *Choose options in the* **Transparency Flattener Preset Options** *dialog box.*

Create and Edit Presets

You can create a multipage PDF document by using the tiling option in the Print dialog box. Each PDF page will contain only the objects you place into the tile areas.

Creating a multipage PDF from page tiles:

1. With an Illustrator file open, choose File > **Document Setup** (Cmd-Option-P/Ctrl-Alt-P). In the Document Setup dialog box, choose Artboard from the top menu, create an artboard that will be large enough to contain all the art, then click OK.

2. Choose File > **Print** (Cmd-P/Ctrl-P). In the **General** option set, choose a **Media Size** for the PDF pages.

3. In the **Setup** option set, from the Tiling menu, choose either **Tile Full Pages** or **Tile Imageable Areas** 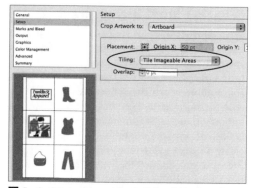, then click Done.

4. Choose View > **Show Page Tiling**. Drag your objects inside the page tile borders **2**, and delete any crop area by choosing Object > Crop Area > Release.

5. Choose File > Save As, choose Format: **Adobe PDF (pdf)**, then click Save.

6. The Save Adobe PDF dialog box opens. Leave the Adobe PDF Preset setting as [Illustrator Default], check **Create Multi-Page PDF from Page Tiles**, then click Save PDF.

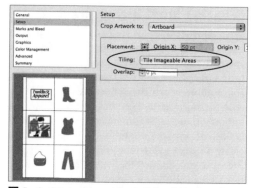

1 *In the Setup option set in the Print dialog box, choose Tiling: **Tile Imageable Areas.***

2 *With page tiling showing, each object was moved inside a page tile border.*

1 *Click an object with the **Crop Area** tool.*

2 *A marquee appears around the crop area.*

3 *The **crop area** displays in the document.*

Defining multiple crop areas NEW!

You can use the Crop Area tool to create multiple crop areas, but only one crop area can be active at a time. Create a crop area, then Option-drag/Alt-drag to define more areas. Option-click/Alt-click one of the crop areas to display its marquee and make it the active crop area; release Option/Alt to display only the active crop area marquee. To redisplay all the crop areas, hold down Option/Alt. When you click another tool, only the active crop area displays.

Creating custom crop marks

Commercial printers use crop marks (short perpendicular lines around the edge of a page) as guides when trimming the paper.

To control which section or object in your document prints, you can use the **Crop Area** tool to define a crop area, then choose Crop Area in the Print dialog box to print just the area you defined.

Note: Crop marks created by the Crop Area tool don't print. To create one or more sets of printable crop marks, use the Crop Marks filter (see the following page).

To use the Crop Area tool: NEW!

1. Choose the **Crop Area** tool (Shift-O).

2. Click a **layer** on the Layers panel, then click anywhere in the document to define a crop area for all objects on that layer, or click one **object** or **group** on that layer to define a crop area for just that object or group **1**.
   or
   Draw a **marquee** around the artwork that you want to create crop marks for.
   or
   Click on the artboard to set a crop area, then choose a size from the **Presets** menu on the Control panel. Fit Crop Area to Artboard defines a crop area that encompasses the whole artboard; Fit Crop Area to Artwork Bounds defines a crop area that encompasses all the objects on the artboard.

3. A crop area marquee will appear **2**. Areas outside the crop area will be covered in gray.

4. *Optional:* Drag a corner or side handle to adjust the size of the marquee, or drag it to a different location.

5. To display the crop marks, click another tool **3**.

6. To print the objects within the crop area you just defined, choose File > Print. In the Setup option set, from the Crop Artwork To menu, choose **Crop Area.** Only objects within the crop area will display in the preview area. Choose any other print settings, then click Print.

Crop Area Tool

To remove a crop area created with the Crop Area tool: NEW!

1. Choose the **Crop Area** tool (Shift-O).

2. Click **Delete** on the Control panel. Or to delete multiple crop areas, click **Delete All**.

➤ In Bridge, the file thumbnail and preview display only objects within the current crop area.

The **Crop Marks** filter places a set of 8 printable crop marks (4 pairs) around a selected object or objects. You can create more than one set of crop marks in a document using this filter.

To create crop marks for an object:

1. Select the object or objects that you want to create crop marks for.

2. Choose Filter > Create > **Crop Marks.** Crop marks will surround the smallest rectangle that could be drawn around the selection .

➤ Group the crop marks with the objects they surround so you can move them together. On the Layers panel, crop marks are listed as nested objects within a group on the uppermost layer in the document.

➤ To delete crop marks, drag the crop marks group to the trash.

➤ Unlike crop marks generated by the Crop Area tool, the Crop Artwork To menu in the Print dialog box (Setup option set) doesn't recognize crop marks that are generated via the Crop Marks filter; Illustrator treats such crop marks as artwork. Similarly, trim marks that are assigned via the Marks and Bleed option set are aligned with the edge of the printable area and are independent of any marks that you create via the Crop Marks filter.

1 *The Crop Marks filter was applied to two separate objects.*

Spot colors on raster effects

You can specify **spot colors** for the following Illustrator **effects**: Drop Shadow, Inner Glow, and Outer Glow. In the effect dialog box, click the color square. The Color Picker opens. Click the Color Swatches button to access the swatches that are currently on the Swatches panel, then click the desired spot color.

The Adobe Illustrator, Illustrator EPS, and Adobe PDF (1.4 or later) formats preserve spot colors and apply overprinting correctly. Spot colors applied to objects, raster effects, and grayscale images will appear on separate plates, whether you output the file from InDesign or directly from Illustrator.

(To colorize an embedded grayscale TIFF image with a spot color, see page 119.)

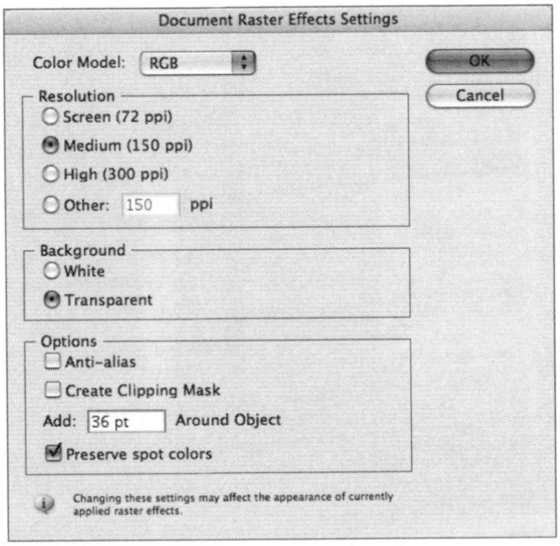

1 *Use the **Document Raster Effects Settings** dialog box to choose a **Resolution** setting for raster effects.*

Choosing a resolution for effects

All the Photoshop effects in the lower half of the Effect menu will rasterize upon export or output, as will the following effects on the Stylize submenu: Drop Shadow (if the Blur value is greater than 0), Inner Glow, Outer Glow, and Feather. The default **Resolution** setting for such effects is 72 ppi (a rather low setting that's suitable only for onscreen output), but you can choose a custom resolution value.

To choose a resolution for raster effects:

1. Choose Effect > **Document Raster Effects Settings 1**.

2. In the Document Raster Effects Settings dialog box, click another **Resolution** option, or click **Other** and enter a custom resolution value. The higher the resolution, the slower the output processing time. (This setting is also listed in the Graphics option set of the Print dialog box).

➤ To learn more about this dialog box, see page 290.

➤ Leave the resolution for effects at the default of 72 ppi while editing your document, then increase the resolution just before printing or exporting the file. A new resolution setting will affect all objects with applied effects that are rasterized, as well as resolution-dependent filters, such as Crystallize and Pointillize.

Raster Settings for Effects

Using the Document Info panel

On the **Document Info** panel, you can read information about the entire document or just about a selected object or objects.

To display information about an object or a whole document:

1. *Optional:* Select the object (or objects) that you want to read info about.

2. Display the **Document Info** panel 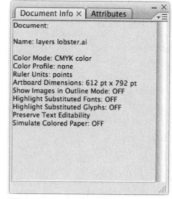 **1**.

3. To display information about a currently selected object, on the panel menu make sure **Selection Only** has a check mark **2**, or uncheck it to display information pertaining to all the objects in the document.

4. Choose **Objects** from the panel menu to list the number of paths, clipping masks, compounds, opacity masks, transparent groups, transparent objects, objects with graphic styles, meshes, and objects that contain brush strokes, as well as color, font, and linking info.
   or
   Choose another category from the panel menu to see a listing of graphic styles; brushes; objects containing spot colors, patterns, or gradients; fonts; linked or embedded images; or font details (PostScript name, font file name, language, etc.).

5. *Optional:* If the Selection Only option is checked on the panel menu, you can click any other object in the document to see info for that object in the currently chosen category.

6. *Optional:* Choose Save from the panel menu to save the currently displayed information as a text document. Choose a location in which to save the text file, rename the file, if desired, then click Save. Use the system's default text editor to open the text document. You can print this file and refer to it when preparing your document for high-resolution printing.

1 *Document information is always available on the* ***Document Info*** *panel, whether the Selection Only option is on or off.*

2 *The* ***Selection Only*** *and* ***Objects*** *options are checked on this* ***Document Info*** *panel menu.*

Document Info Panel

EXPORT 31

In this chapter, you'll learn how to save files in various formats for export to other applications: the EPS format for layout and drawing applications; the PDF format for a variety of output media; the Flash (swf), GIF, and JPEG formats for the Web; and the PSD format for Adobe Photoshop.

Saving to earlier EPS formats

If you need to save a copy of a file to an earlier Illustrator EPS format, for step 3 on the next page, choose **Illustrator CS2 EPS** or **Illustrator CS EPS,** and be sure to read the messages in the Warnings area at the bottom of the dialog box. The CS EPS and CS2 EPS formats preserve transparency, effects, and type features; the CS2 format also preserves live features, such as live blends and live paint; but saving a file in either of these earlier formats may cause changes to area type and a loss of editability.

Saving a file to one of the Legacy Formats (Illustrator version 10 or earlier), will result in a greater loss of editability; see Illustrator Help.

1 *This prompt will appear if there are objects containing spot colors stacked below objects containing transparency in your file, and you save it the Illustrator EPS format.*

To export artwork that contains transparency and any of the "live" features to InDesign CS2 or CS3, stick with the native Illustrator CS3 format (ai). This format includes both an Illustrator and a PDF version of the file and preserves transparency and "live" features. To prepare an Illustrator file for a drawing or page layout application that doesn't read AI files (such as QuarkXPress), save it in either the Illustrator EPS format or the PDF format.

Saving as EPS

The **EPS** (Encapsulated PostScript) format saves both vector and bitmap objects and is supported by most illustration and page layout programs. Furthermore, EPS files can be reopened and edited in Illustrator.

To save a file as EPS:

1. With the file open in Illustrator, choose File > **Save As** or **Save a Copy.**

2. From the **Format** menu, choose **Illustrator EPS (eps).** Choose a location for the file, then click Save.

   If your Illustrator file contains spot colors that interact with transparency, an alert dialog box will appear **1**. If you allow those spot colors to be converted to process colors in another application, the results may be unpredictable. Click Cancel and convert the spot colors in Illustrator (or click Continue if you know the spot color conversion won't be an issue).

(Continued on the following page)

EPS Format

399

The EPS Options dialog box opens **1**.

3. Keep the Version as **Illustrator CS3 EPS.** (Or to save to an earlier version, read the sidebar on the previous page.)

4. Choose a Preview **Format:**

   None for no preview. The image won't display onscreen in any other application, but it will print.

   TIFF (Black & White) for a black-and-white preview.

   TIFF (8-bit Color) for a color preview.

   In the Mac OS, you can also choose Macintosh (Black & White) for a black-and-white PICT preview, or Macintosh (8-bit Color) for a color preview in the PICT format, but these previews don't display transparent backgrounds.

Note: Regardless of which preview option you choose, color information will be saved with the file, and the file will print normally from Illustrator or any other application that you import it into.

If you chose the TIFF (8-bit Color) format, click **Transparent** to save the file with a transparent background, or **Opaque** to save it with a solid background.

5. If the artwork contains overprints (applied via the Attributes panel), from the Transparency: **Overprints** menu, choose **Preserve** to record overprint information in the EPS file, or **Discard** to save the EPS file without overprint information. See the sidebar on page 385.

1 *Choose Preview, Transparency, Font, and other options in the* **EPS Options** *dialog box.*

EPS Format

If the artwork uses blending modes or contains transparency, those areas will be flattened before the file is printed. From the **Preset** menu, choose **[High Resolution]**, **[Medium Resolution]**, or **[Low Resolution]** as the preset to be used for flattening transparency (see the sidebar on page 390). The High Resolution preset will produce the best quality printout.

Take a moment to read any messages 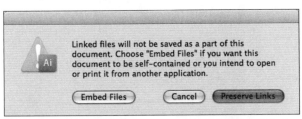 that you see in the Warnings area for the current settings. For example, you may learn that the document contains transparency that will require flattening, or how overprinting in transparent areas will be handled.

6. Under Fonts, check **Embed Fonts (For Other Applications)** to save any fonts being used as a part of the file so they'll display and print properly on any system, even where they aren't installed. Check this option if your Illustrator file contains type and you're going to import it into a layout application.

7. *Check any of these optional boxes, if available:*

Include Linked Files to embed a copy of any linked images used in the artwork into the Illustrator EPS file. With this option checked, you won't need the original (linked) image in order to print the EPS file from another program, but this does increase the file size.

(In any case, don't discard the original file that the image is linked to; you'll still need it to edit or print the file from Illustrator.)

Include Document Thumbnails to save a thumbnail of the file for previewing in the Open or Place dialog box in Illustrator.

Include CMYK PostScript in RGB Files to convert RGB objects in the EPS file to CMYK; this will make it possible to print the file from programs that output only CMYK color. *Note:* If you reopen the EPS file in Illustrator, RGB colors will be preserved as RGB.

Compatible Gradient and Gradient Mesh Printing to include instructions to help older PostScript printers print gradients and gradient meshes. Unless you're getting printing errors when printing gradients or meshes, leave this option unchecked!

8. Choose the **Adobe PostScript®** option that conforms to your printing device: **LanguageLevel 2** or **LanguageLevel 3**. (Choose LanguageLevel 3 if the file contains meshes and will be output to a Level 3 printer.)

9. Click OK. If you didn't check Include Linked Files and your file contains placed, linked images, an alert dialog box will appear **1**; click **Embed Files** or **Preserve Links**.

EPS Format

> ⚠ **Ai** Linked files will not be saved as a part of this document. Choose "Embed Files" if you want this document to be self-contained or you intend to open or print it from another application.
>
> (Embed Files)   (Cancel)   (Preserve Links)

1 *This alert dialog box will appear if you **didn't** check **Include Linked Files** in the EPS Format Options dialog box and your file contains placed, linked images. Here's a second chance to include those placed files.*

Saving as Adobe PDF

The versatile **Adobe PDF** (Portable Document Format) is a good choice for Web output and for other applications and platforms. This format is also useful for showing Illustrator artwork to clients, as the only software a user needs in order to view a PDF file is Acrobat Reader or Adobe Reader 6 or later (both of which are available as free downloads) or, in Mac OSX, the Preview application; they don't need Adobe Illustrator. Plus, your artwork will look as it was originally designed, as this format preserves all object attributes, groups, fonts, and type. PDF files can also be viewed in Adobe Acrobat, where edits and comments can be applied. Acrobat versions 6, 7, and 8 also preserve layers, and Acrobat 8 offers support for 3D features. The PDF format also supports document text search and navigation features.

Note: The instructions below are long-winded (yawn), but you can pick one of the default presets and be done with it by the end of step 3.

To save a file as Adobe PDF:

Saving as PDF using a preset

I. With your file open in Illustrator, choose File > **Save As** or **Save a Copy**.

2. From the **Format** menu, choose **Adobe PDF (pdf)**, choose a location for the file, then click Save. The Save Adobe PDF dialog box opens **1**.

3. From the **Adobe PDF Preset** menu, choose a preset that best suits the output medium (the Compatibility menu will display the default Acrobat version for the preset you choose):

Illustrator Default creates a PDF file that can be reedited in Illustrator or placed into InDesign or QuarkXPress. Fonts are embedded, and bitmap images aren't downsampled or compressed.

High Quality Print creates PDF files for desktop printers and proofing devices.

PDF/X-1a, PDF/X-3, and **PDF/X-4** create Acrobat-compatible PDF files that will be checked for compliance with specific printing standards to help prevent printing errors. PDF/X-1a and PDF/X-3 don't support transparency (files are flattened); PDF/X-3 and PDF/X-4 support embedded color profiles and color-managed workflows; PDF/X-4 adds support for transparency (files aren't flattened). If you need to keep your file fully editable in Illustrator, don't choose a PDF/X preset.

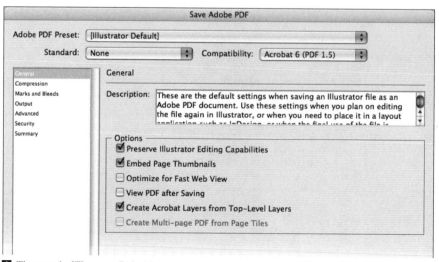

1 *These are the [**Illustrator Default**] settings in the **General** option set of the **Save Adobe PDF** dialog box.*

Press Quality is for high-quality prepress output. This preset embeds all fonts automatically, uses JPEG compression and Maximum quality, and preserves custom color and high-end image options. The resulting file size will be large, however, to accommodate all this data.

Smallest File Size creates compact PDF files for output to the Web, e-mail, or other onscreen uses; fonts aren't embedded.

➤ You can read about the currently chosen preset in the Description window.

If you're satisfied with the settings in the chosen preset, click Save PDF, or if you want to customize the preset, proceed with any or all of the remaining steps.

Saving as PDF using custom settings

4. Via the **Standard** menu, you can apply a PDF/X compliance standard to any non-PDF/X preset to ensure printing compliance. If you don't choose a PDF/X compliance standard, choose which version of Adobe Acrobat your file will be compatible with from the **Compatibility** menu. Note that not all applications can read Acrobat 7 or 8 files.

If you change any settings from the preset defaults, "[Preset Name] (Modified)" will appear on the Adobe PDF Preset menu.

5. Under **Options,** check any of the following:

Preserve Illustrator Editing Capabilities to enable the PDF file to be reopened and edited in Illustrator. This option limits how much the file can be compressed.

Embed Page Thumbnails to save a thumbnail of the file (or page) for display in the Open and Place dialog boxes.

Optimize for Fast Web View to enable the file to display quickly in a Web browser.

View PDF After Saving to have your system's default PDF viewer (usually Adobe Reader or Acrobat) launch automatically and display the file after you click Save PDF.

If the Compatibility option is Acrobat version 6, 7, or 8, check **Create Acrobat Layers from Top-Level Layers;** this will preserve the

ability to work with layers if the file is opened in one of those versions of Acrobat.

Create Multi-page PDF from Page Tiles to have each tiled area in your artwork become a separate page in the PDF file (see page 394).

To choose even more custom options, follow the remaining steps.

6. For online output (not print output), click **Compression** on the list of option sets on the left side of the dialog box, then choose options to control how your artwork will be compressed (downsampled) to reduce the file size (**1**, next page). From the menus under **Color Bitmap Images, Grayscale Bitmap Images,** and **Monochrome Bitmap Images,** choose an interpolation method for downsampling:

Do Not Downsample keeps the image at the size it was created.

Average Downsampling To divides the image into sample areas, averages the pixels in each area, and substitutes the average values for the original values.

Subsampling To replaces a sampled area with pixel data taken from the middle of that area, producing a smaller but not necessarily accurate file.

Bicubic Downsampling To replaces the sampled area with an average of the area's values, and often is more accurate than average downsampling.

For any of the interpolation methods, enter the desired **ppi** resolution, and the minimum resolution threshold an image must have in order to be downsampled.

Other settings in the Compression option set:

Choose a compression type from the **Compression** menus: None for no compression; a JPEG or ZIP option; or an Automatic option to let Illustrator choose the appropriate compression settings for the artwork—Automatic (JPEG) for the widest compatibility, or Automatic (JPEG2000) for the best compression. All the JPEG options are lossy (cause data loss). The ZIP option is

(Continued on the following page)

Adobe PDF Format

usually lossless (see Creating Adobe PDF Files > Adobe PDF Options in Illustrator Help).

7. For information about the **Marks and Bleeds** option set, see pages 382–383.

8. Click **Output** on the left side of the dialog box to control color conversion and profile inclusion in the PDF file:

In the **Color** area, choose color conversion settings. From the **Color Conversion** menu, choose **No Conversion** or a **Convert to Destination** option, depending on whether you want the output device or Illustrator, respectively, to convert colors to a destination profile. Choose **Convert to Destination (Preserve Numbers)** if the file has the same color space and embedded profile as the destination profile (e.g., when converting a CMYK file to a CMYK profile). If you opt for conversion, choose a destination profile from the **Destination** menu. *Note:* Unless you're accustomed to a color-managed workflow,

---

Save your preset!

Once you choose custom settings in the Save Adobe PDF dialog box, save them as a user-created preset by clicking **Save Preset** in the lower left corner. You can choose your custom preset from the Adobe PDF Preset menu for any file.

To edit a user-created preset, choose Edit > **Adobe PDF Presets,** click your user-created preset on the Presets scroll list, then click **Edit**.

---

it's best to leave these menus on the default settings.

The **PDF/X** options will be available if you chose a PDF/X preset standard. Unless your press shop instructs you otherwise, leave the **Output Intent Profile Name** menu set to the SWOP profile. The other fields are filled in automatically.

Note: For Web output, we suggest choosing Smallest File Size from the preset menu in

1 *Choose **Compression** options in the **Save Adobe PDF** dialog box.*

Adobe PDF Format

the General option set, in which case the Output options will be set correctly for you.

9. Click **Advanced** on the left side of the dialog box to access font, overprint, and flattening options.

The default PDF presets automatically embed all the characters in each font used in the file. If only a portion of the characters in those fonts is being used in your artwork, you can choose to embed just a subset of characters by entering a percentage in the **Subset Fonts When Percentage of Characters Used Is Less Than** field. This will reduce the file size. If you enter 50%, for example, the entire font will be embedded only if you use more than 50% of its characters in the file, and the Subset option will be used if you use fewer than 50% of its characters.

If Acrobat 4 is chosen as the Compatibility option and the document contains overprints, choose whether to Preserve or Discard **Overprints.** Similarly, if the artwork contains transparency, choose **Transparency Flattener** options (see pages 390–392). Acrobat versions 5 through 8 preserve overprinting and transparency automatically.

10. Click **Security** on the left side of the dialog box to restrict user access to the PDF. The following options are available only to non-PDF/X-compliant files:

Check **Require a Password to Open the Document** if you want the file to be password protected, and type a password in the Document Open Password field.

Note: Passwords can't be recovered from the document, so keep a copy of them in a separate location.

Check **Use a Password to Restrict Editing Security and Permissions Settings** if you want to maintain control over these options. Type a password in the Permissions Password field. The following Acrobe Permissions become available:

The **Printing Allowed** menu lets you control whether users can print the file. Options are None, Low Resolution (150 dpi), and High Resolution.

The **Changes Allowed** menu lets you specify precisely what users can and cannot alter.

Check **Enable Copying of Text, Images, and Other Content** to permit users to alter text or images.

Check **Enable Text Access of Screen Reader Devices for the Visually Impaired** to permit screen readers to view and read the file.

11. Check **Enable Plaintext Metadata** if you want the file metadata to be searchable by other applications (available only for Acrobat versions 6 through 8).

12. Click **Summary** on the left side of the dialog box to see a list of the settings you've chosen for each category. Expand any category to view those settings.

13. Click Save PDF, then give yourself a nice pat on the back.

Using the Export command

The **Export** dialog box gives you access to other file formats besides EPS and PDF. Some of them are discussed in brief on the following page.

To export a file:

1. With the file open, choose File > **Export.** The Export dialog box opens.
2. *Optional:* Change the file name in the **Save As/File Name** field. Illustrator will automatically append the proper file extension to the name for the chosen file format (e.g., .bmp, .psd, .tif).
3. Choose a file format **1**–**2** from the **Format/ Save as Type** menu, and a location for the new file.

   ➤ To create a new folder for the file in the Mac OS, click New Folder, enter a name, then click Create; in Windows, click Create New Folder, then enter a name.
4. Click **Export/Save.** Choose settings in any additional dialog box that opens, then click OK. A few file formats are discussed briefly on the facing page; following that, the Flash, GIF, JPEG, and PSD formats are discussed in depth.

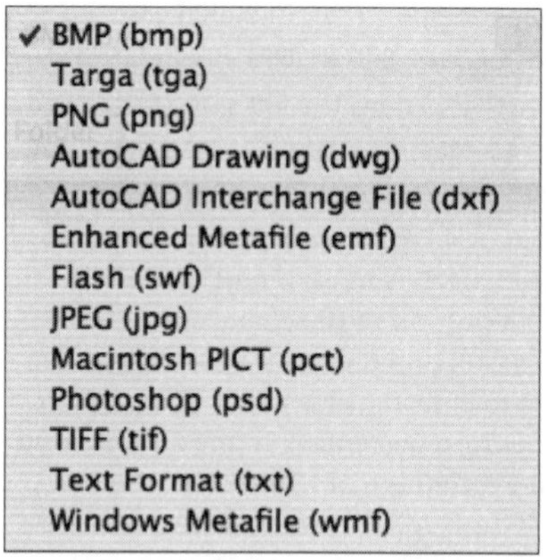
✓ BMP (bmp)
Targa (tga)
PNG (png)
AutoCAD Drawing (dwg)
AutoCAD Interchange File (dxf)
Enhanced Metafile (emf)
Flash (swf)
JPEG (jpg)
Macintosh PICT (pct)
Photoshop (psd)
TIFF (tif)
Text Format (txt)
Windows Metafile (wmf)

1 *Choices on the* ***Format*** *menu in the Mac OS*

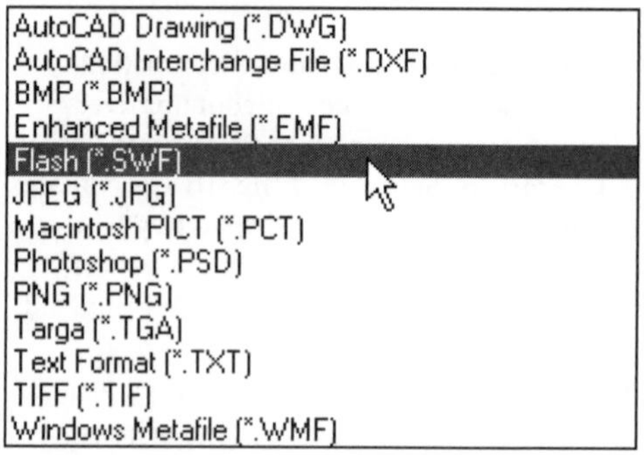
AutoCAD Drawing (*.DWG)
AutoCAD Interchange File (*.DXF)
BMP (*.BMP)
Enhanced Metafile (*.EMF)
Flash (*.SWF)
JPEG (*.JPG)
Macintosh PICT (*.PCT)
Photoshop (*.PSD)
PNG (*.PNG)
Targa (*.TGA)
Text Format (*.TXT)
TIFF (*.TIF)
Windows Metafile (*.WMF)

2 *Choices on the* ***Save as Type*** *menu in Windows*

A few file formats in brief

Rasterize

If you choose a raster (bitmap) file format in the Export dialog box, such as BMP, the **Rasterize Options** dialog box opens **1**. Choose a Color Model for the resulting file. For the file Resolution, choose Screen (72 dpi), Medium (150 dpi), or High (300 dpi), or enter a custom resolution (Other). Check Anti-Alias to smooth the edges of objects (pixels will be added along curved edges).

BMP (bmp)

BMP is the standard bitmap image format on Windows and DOS computers. When you choose rasterization settings and click OK, the **BMP Options** dialog box opens. Choose the Windows or OS/2 format for the desired operating system, specify a bit depth, and choose whether you want to enable RLE compression.

TIFF (tif)

TIFF, a bitmap image format, is supported by virtually all paint, image-editing, and page-layout applications. It supports RGB, CMYK, and grayscale color schemes, and offers LZW as a compression option.

If you choose the TIFF file format in the Export dialog box, the **TIFF Options** dialog box opens **2**. Choose a Color Model; choose a Resolution of Screen (72 dpi), Medium (150 dpi), or High (300 dpi) or enter a custom resolution;

and turn Anti-Alias on or off. Check LZW Compression if you need to compress the file; this lossless method doesn't discard or degrade image data. Choose your target platform in the Byte Order area, and check Embed ICC Profile if you've assigned such a profile to your file.

Enhanced metafile (emf) and Windows metafile (wmf)

A metafile describes a file, and functions as a list of commands for drawing a graphic. Typically, a metafile is made up of commands for drawing objects such as straight lines, polygons, and text, and commands to control the style of the objects. Use these formats to export simple artwork only. **WMF**, a 16-bit metafile format, is used on Windows platforms; **EMF**, a 32-bit metafile format which is also used on Windows platforms, can contain a wider variety of commands than WMF.

Microsoft Office

Choose File > **Save for Microsoft Office** to save your document in a PNG format that will be readable by Microsoft Word, PowerPoint, and Excel. The Save for Microsoft Office dialog box opens. Choose a location, enter a file name, then click Save. *Note:* This format makes transparent areas opaque.

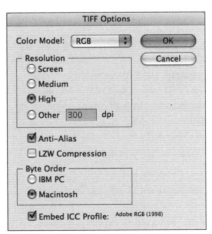

2 *The **TIFF Options** dialog box*

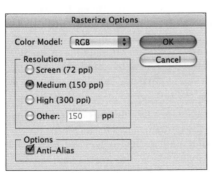

1 *The **Rasterize Options** dialog box opens if you choose a raster format in the Export dialog box.*

Exporting as Flash (swf)

The Adobe Flash application is used for Web animations and interactivity. The simplest way to get Illustrator objects into Flash is by using the Copy and Paste commands. All paths, strokes, gradients, type (designated as Flash Text), masks, effects, and symbols are preserved. And you can specify how layers are pasted.

Another option for exporting your Illustrator artwork to Flash is to save it in the **Flash (swf)** format. You can create objects for an animation on separate layers or via live blends, and then export the layers or blends as separate Flash frames or files. This vector graphics format produces compact and scalable files, and preserves Illustrator layers, text, and symbols.

To create a Flash (swf) file: NEW!

1. *Optional:* Place each object on its own top-level layer, and arrange the layers in the order you want them to appear in an animation.

2. Choose File > **Export.** The Export dialog box opens.

3. Type a name and choose a location for your file, choose **Format/Save As Type: Flash (swf),** then click Export/Save. The SWF Options dialog box opens (**1**, next page).

4. From the **Export As** menu, choose **AI File to SWF File** to export your entire Illustrator file as one Flash frame; or **AI Layers to SWF Frames** to export each layer in your Illustrator file as a separate Flash frame within a Flash document; or **AI Layers to SWF Files** to export each Illustrator layer as a separate Flash file consisting of one frame; or **AI Layers to SWF Symbols** to export each Illustrator layer as a symbol in a separate Flash file.

   Leave the default Flash Player 9 option as the choice on the **Version** menu.

5. Check any of the **Options,** such as:

   Clip to Artboard Size to export only the artwork that's within the artboard bounds.

   Clip to Crop Area to export only the artwork that's within a defined crop area.

Preserve Appearance to flatten objects and maintain the look of effects and transparency (this will limit editability).

Compress File to compress the SWF data to reduce the file size.

Export Symbols in the Panel to export the entire contents of the Symbols panel. Symbols without an instance in the exported frames will still be available in the Flash Symbol Library. **NEW!**

Export Text as Outlines to convert type to vector paths to preserve its appearance.

Protect from Import to prevent users from editing the exported SWF file. Enter a password in the Password field.

6. Choose a **Curve Quality** value (0–10) to control how accurate the vector curves will be in your Flash file. The higher the Curve Quality value, the more accurate the curves (and the larger the file size).

   To change the **Background Color** for the SWF file, click the color swatch, then choose a color from the Color Picker.

   Choose an option from the **Local Playback Security** menu to control whether the SWF file can access only local or only network files.

7. Click **Advanced** to display image and animation options (**2**, next page):

   If your file contains bitmap images or transparency that will become raster shapes when flattened, for the **Image Format,** click **Lossless** to preserve image quality, or click **Lossy (JPEG)** to compress the file and choose quality and other settings. Choose Lossless if you plan to edit the file in Flash, or if you're not going to edit the file, choose Lossy.

   Enter a screen **Resolution** value (72–600 ppi) for any bitmap images in the file. As the resolution increases, so does the quality and scalability, along with the file size.

8. If you chose AI Layers to SWF Frames in step 4, choose a **Frame Rate** (in frames per

second) for the rate of animation playback, then check or choose any of the following options:

Looping to have the animation loop continuously.

Animate Blends to have each step in a blend become an animation frame (you don't need to expand the blend in Illustrator). Click an export method: **In Sequence** to export each object in a blend to a separate animation frame, or **In Build** to have the first step become the first frame, the first and second steps become the second frame, and so on (the last frame will contain all the steps).

Layer Order: Bottom Up or **Top Down** to determine the order in which layers will be exported as animation frames.

Export Static Layers, then click a layer (or layers) to be used as a stationary background in all the SWF frames.

9. Click OK.

➤ Click Web Preview to preview the file and any animation in the default Web browser for your system.

➤ Some Illustrator effects, such as Drop Shadow, Feather, and Outer and Inner Glow, become rasterized on export. Evaluate your exported file in Flash to judge how the rasterization is affecting the image quality and file size.

1 *The Basic pane in the SWF Options dialog box*

2 *The Advanced pane in the SWF Options dialog box*

Optimizing files for the Web

If you're using Illustrator to create graphics for a Web page, that contribution will most likely be a logo or an illustration, or maybe buttons, graphics, or text to be used as navigation devices. Before placing elements like these into a Web page creation program, such as Adobe Dreamweaver or Adobe GoLive, you need to convert them from vector art into pixels. In this section, you'll learn how to optimize the conversion to pixels for efficient transmission and display online.

When preparing graphics for online viewing (as opposed to print), you need to choose an appropriate file size and format for optimal speed of transmission and image quality. Your goal will be to compress your images enough that they download quickly on the Web, while preserving their quality as much as possible. Note the change in image size as you choose options in the Save for Web dialog box.

Image size

The length of time it takes for an image to load into a Web page is related directly to its file size. The file size, in turn, is governed by the dimensions of the image in pixels and the amount and kind of compression you apply to the file. When choosing dimensions for your image, keep in mind that the Web page your graphics will be viewed on is even smaller than the 800 x 600-pixel area of the monitor.

➤ Web browsers always display images at 100% magnification and at a resolution of 72 ppi. Before optimizing your file, choose View > Pixel Preview to see how your vector artwork will look when rasterized for the Web.

Although the GIF and JPEG formats cause a small reduction in image quality as they compress files, the resulting smaller file sizes download more quickly on the Web. Vector graphics, in particular, tend to compress well because they're usually composed of solid-color shapes. For your Web design, resist the urge to add patterns or gradients, which can't be compressed as much. Your choice of file format also affects how much an image is compressed.

File format

GIF and JPEG, the two file formats most commonly used for optimizing Web graphics, are appropriate for different types of images:

➤ GIF is an 8-bit format, meaning it can save a maximum of 256 colors. It's a good choice when color fidelity is a priority (e.g., for type, and for vector shapes that contain solid colors). These kinds of graphics contain far fewer colors than continuous-tone (photographic) images, so the color restriction won't have a negative impact. And if your artwork contains transparency, you must choose GIF, as this format supports transparency whereas JPEG does not.

When you optimize an Illustrator file in the GIF format, the solid colors in your artwork translate into just a small portion of the maximum 256 possible colors (this set of colors is called the color table). Reducing the number of colors shrinks the file size, and the resulting file downloads more quickly.

➤ Because of its capacity to save at a 24-bit color depth, the JPEG format does a better job of preserving color fidelity in continuous-tone images (e.g., raster images that you've placed into your Illustrator file) than GIF. Another advantage of JPEG is that its compression model can shrink an image significantly without lowering its quality. When saving an image in this format, you can choose a quality setting; higher-quality settings produce larger files and lower-quality settings produce smaller files.

Unfortunately, the JPEG format, unlike GIF, doesn't preserve transparency or the sharp edges of vector objects. Furthermore, each time you optimize an image as JPEG, some image data is lost; the greater the compression, the greater the loss. (Always remember to optimize a copy of your file, not the original!)

You'll learn the actual optimization steps next.

In the **Save for Web & Devices** dialog box,
you'll find everything you need to optimize your
Illustrator graphics for the Web. Try using the
multiple previews in this dialog box first to test
the effects of different optimization settings.

To use the Save for Web & Devices previews:

1. Choose File > **Save for Web & Devices** (Cmd-Option-Shift-S/Ctrl-Alt-Shift-S). The dialog
box opens 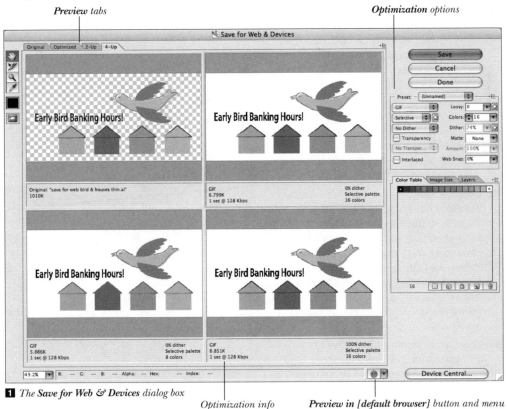.

2. Click the **4-Up** tab to display the original
image and three previews simultaneously.
Illustrator will use the current optimization
options to generate the first preview (to the
right of the original), then generate the two
other previews as variations on the current
optimization settings. You can click any preview and change the optimization settings
for just that preview (see the following page).
or

For a more definitive test preview, click the
Preview in [default browser] button at the
bottom of the dialog box. Your optimized
image will open in the default Web browser
application that's installed in your system.
Or to choose another browser that's installed
in your system, from the menu next to the
button, choose a browser name or choose
Other, then locate and open the browser.

Preview tabs

Optimization options

1 *The Save for Web & Devices dialog box*

Optimization info

Preview in [default browser] button and menu

We'll show you how to optimize files in the GIF format first, because it does a better job of optimizing vector objects and type than JPEG.

To optimize a file in the GIF format:

1. Save your file.

2. Choose File > **Save for Web & Devices** (Cmd-Opt-Shift-S/Ctrl-Alt-Shift-S).

3. Click the **2-Up** tab at the top of the dialog box to display the original and optimized previews of the image.

4. From the **Preset** menu, choose one of the GIF options. Leave the preset settings as is, then click Save. The Save Optimized As dialog box opens. Leave the name as is, choose a location, then click Save.
or
Follow the remaining steps to choose custom optimization settings.

5. From the **Optimized File Format** menu, choose **GIF** ■.

6. From the **Color Reduction Algorithm** menu, choose a method for reducing the number of colors in the image. We recommend the Selective option because it preserves solid colors and Web-safe colors.

7. Try lowering the number of colors to remove unnecessary colors from the color table. From the **Colors** menu, choose 16, or enter 16 in the field. If it looks as if some colors are substituted in the optimized preview, you can raise the Colors value to 32.

8. *Optional:* Dithering is a procsss by which Illustrator mixes dots of a few different colors to simulate a greater range of colors. For higher-quality gradients and soft-edged effects (but also a slightly larger file size), choose the **Diffusion** method from the **Dither Algorithm** menu, and choose a **Dither** value between 50% and 75%. (If you choose No Dither, gradients may exhibit banding.)

9. Check **Transparency** to preserve fully transparent pixels in the image. The Transparency option allows for the creation of nonrectangular image borders. With

Transparency unchecked, transparent pixels will be filled with the color currently chosen on the Matte menu. The GIF format doesn't preserve semitransparent pixels.

10. To control how the edges of the vector objects will blend with the background of a Web page, choose a **Matte** option. Set the Matte color to the color of the Web page background—if you happen to know what that color is. Any soft-edged effect (such as a Drop Shadow) on top of transparent areas will fill with this Matte color. If the

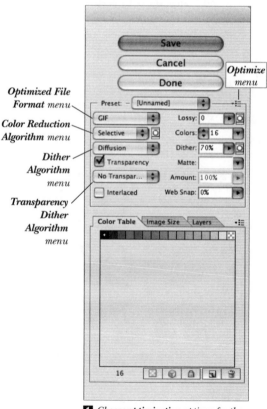

Optimized File Format menu

Color Reduction Algorithm menu

Dither Algorithm menu

Transparency Dither Algorithm menu

Optimize menu

■ *Choose **optimization** options for the GIF file format in the Save for Web & Devices dialog box.*

background color is unknown, set Matte to None; this will create a hard, jagged edge.

Another option is to choose Matte: None, then check Transparency and choose one of the three options on the Transparency Dither Algorithm menu. The result will look the same on any background.

11. Click Save. The Save Optimized As dialog box opens. Leave the name as is, choose a location, then click Save.

➤ To save the current (Unnamed) set of options, choose Save Settings from the Optimize menu, ⁑ enter a name, then click Save. Your saved set will now be available on the Preset menu in the Save for Web & Devices dialog box for any file.

JPEG is the format of choice for optimizing continuous-tone imagery (gradients, blends, and placed raster images). When optimized in this format, your file's 24-bit color will be preserved, and its colors will be seen and enjoyed by any viewer whose display is set to thousands or millions of colors. Two drawbacks to JPEG are that its compression method eliminates image data and that it doesn't preserve transparency.

To optimize a file in the JPEG format:

1. Save your file.

2. Choose File > **Save for Web & Devices** (Cmd-Opt-Shift-S/Ctrl-Alt-Shift-S). The Save for Web & Devices dialog box opens (**1**, next page).

3. Click the **2-Up** tab at the top of the dialog box to display the original and optimized previews of the image.

4. From the **Preset** menu, choose one of the JPEG options. Leave the preset settings as is, then click Save. The Save Optimized As dialog box opens. Leave the name as is, choose a location, then click Save.
or
Follow the remaining steps to choose custom optimization settings.

5. From the **Optimized File Format** menu, choose **JPEG.**

6. From the **Compression Quality** menu, choose a quality level for the optimized image.
or
Move the **Quality** slider to the desired compression level.

➤ The higher the compression quality, the higher the image quality (and the larger the file size).

7. Increase the **Blur** value to lessen the prominence of JPEG artifacts that may arise from the JPEG compression method, and to reduce the file size. Be careful not to over-blur the image, though, or your sharp vector shapes will become too soft.

(Continued on the following page)

Optimize as JPEG

8. Choose a **Matte** color to be substituted for areas of transparency in the artwork. If you choose None, transparent areas will appear as white.

Note: The JPEG format doesn't support transparency. To have the Matte color simulate transparency, make it the same solid color as the background of the Web page (if you know what that color is).

9. Leave the Progressive and ICC Profile options unchecked.

10. *Optional:* Check Optimized to produce the smallest possible file size.

11. Click Save. The Save Optimized As dialog box opens. Leave the name as is, choose a location, then click Save.

➤ To save the current (Unnamed) set of options, choose Save Settings from the Optimize menu, ⚏ enter a name, then click Save. Your saved set will now be available on the Preset menu in the Save for Web & Devices dialog box for any file.

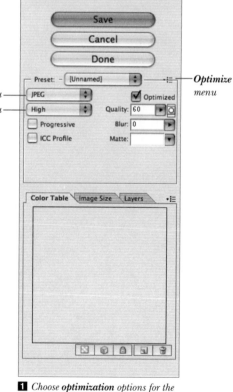

Optimized File Format menu

Compression Quality menu

Optimize menu

1 *Choose **optimization** options for the **JPEG** file format in the **Save for Web & Devices** dialog box.*

Optimize as JPEG

Creating smart type

If you create type in Adobe Illustrator CS3 and import it into Photoshop by using either of the two methods outlined below, it becomes a **Smart Object** layer in Photoshop. The contents of the Smart Object layer (which are embedded in the Photoshop file) can be edited easily at any time in the original application.

AI format

In Illustrator, make sure the type is on its own layer, then save the file in the **Illustrator Document (ai)** format. With a file open in Photoshop, use File > Place (in Photoshop or Bridge) to import the type file as a new Smart Object layer; it will appear on the Layers panel. Double-click the Smart Object layer and a temporary file will open in Illustrator. Edit, resave, then close the file, and the type will update in the Photoshop document.

PSD format

To create a Smart Object layer that can be edited as an independent Photoshop file, in Illustrator, choose File > Export, then choose Format: **Photoshop (psd)**. In the Photoshop Export Options dialog box, click Write Layers; check Preserve Text Editability, Maximum Editability, and Anti-alias; then click OK. Open a Photoshop file, then use File > Place in Photoshop or Bridge to place the .psd type file as a new Smart Object layer. If you double-click the Smart Object layer, the embedded file will open as a separate Photoshop file, with the editable type in a layer group. Edit, then resave and close the file, and the type will update in the original Photoshop document.

Exporting files to Photoshop

There are several ways to get an Illustrator file into Photoshop.

➤ For the greatest ease in future editing, make use of the **Smart Object layer** feature in Photoshop. A Smart Object layer is created automatically when you place an Illustrator AI file into Photoshop CS3 (via the Place command in Photoshop or Bridge); drag an object from Illustrator into Photoshop; or copy/paste an object into Photoshop and choose Smart Object in the Paste dialog box. When you double-click a Smart Object layer in Photoshop, the Illustrator artwork that you embedded in the Photoshop file opens in Illustrator for editing. Save the temporary file and the Smart Object layer updates in Photoshop—an effortless round trip!

➤ **Copy and paste** an object into Photoshop as pixels, as a path, or as a shape layer by choosing one of those options in the Paste dialog box. To ensure that the Paste dialog box will display in Photoshop, in Illustrator, go to Preferences > File Handling & Clipboard and check both the PDF and AICB options.

➤ **Drag and drop** an Illustrator object as a path outline into Photoshop by holding down Cmd/Ctrl as you drag.

➤ Export your Illustrator file in the **Photoshop (psd)** format (see the following page).

Last but not least, the **Photoshop (psd)** format, available as an option in the Export dialog box, converts Illustrator objects into pixels and preserves layers and transparency (well, pretty much; see the sidebar at right).

To create a Photoshop (psd) file:

1. Choose File > **Export**. The Export dialog box opens.

2. Type a name and choose a location for your file, choose **Format/Save as Type: Photoshop (psd)**, then click **Export/Save**. The **Photoshop Export Options** dialog box opens **1**.

3. Choose a **Color Model**.

4. Click a preset or custom **Resolution** option.

5. In the **Options** area, do any of the following:

Click **Flat Image** to flatten layers and have the artwork import as one layer in Photoshop. Or to export the Illustrator layers to Photoshop, click **Write Layers** and check **Maximum Editability**. If the Illustrator file contains type that doesn't have a stroke or effects applied to it, you can check **Preserve Text Editability** to keep the text editable in Photoshop.

Note: Although the Write Layers option preserves the stacking appearance of objects nested within a layer, only top-level layers will become layers in Photoshop. Hidden layers in the Illustrator file will become hidden layers in Photoshop.

Check **Anti-alias** to soften the edges of any curved shapes.

Check **Embed ICC Profile** to embed the current color profile in the file, if one was assigned.

6. Click OK.

Photoshop (psd) format

➤ The **Photoshop (psd)** export format preserves opacity masks and layers, and editable type that doesn't have a stroke or effects. Blending modes and transparency will look the same in Photoshop, although on the Layers panel in Photoshop, the imported layers will have a blending mode of Normal and an Opacity of 100%.

➤ If an Illustrator layer contains an object that Photoshop can't import as is (such as a stroke or an effect), that layer and any layers below it will be **merged** into one layer in Photoshop.

➤ **Opacity masks** from Illustrator are converted to layer masks in Photoshop (whereas a layer mask from a Photoshop file would be converted to an opacity mask if imported into Illustrator).

➤ **Compound shapes** translate easily between the two programs.

To learn more about importing Photoshop files into Illustrator, see pages 258–259.

1 *Choose options in the **Photoshop Export Options** dialog box.*

INDEX

A

acquiring images, 255–64
  with drag-and-drop, 264
  linked, 260–63
  methods, 255
  with Open command, 256
  from Photoshop, 258–59
  with Place command, 257
Add Anchor Point tool, 3, 137
Adobe PDF files. *See* PDF files
Adobe symbol libraries, 347, 349
Advanced Print dialog box, 389
AI (ai) format, 415
alert dialogs, 257, 308
aligning
  objects, 73, 95–96
  objects, by anchor points, 91
  objects, with smart guides, 90–91
  paragraphs, 240
  points, 144
  point type, 212
  strokes on path, 110
Align panel, 10, 95–96
anchor points
  adding, manually, 137
  adding, with commands, 138
  aligning, 144
  aligning objects by, 91
  converting, 135–36, 189–90
  converting on existing paths, 190
  corner, 22, 133, 135–36
  defined, 22
  direction handles, 135
  dragging, 134
  moving, 134
  preferences for display of, 367
  selected, 22
  selecting with Direct Selection tool, 82
  selecting with Lasso tool, 86
  smooth, 22, 133, 135–36
angle guides, 90
ANPA colors, 107
appearance attributes
  applying, 265–68
  blends and, 273
  choosing, 268
  copying, 273

  defined, 23
  editing, 269
  expanding, 278
  moving, 273
  multiple, applying, 268
  removing, 270
Appearance of Black preferences, 376
Appearance panel
  Add New Fill or New Stroke command, 253, 268
  attributes, 267
  Characters listing, 254
  Clear Appearance button, 270
  Contents options, 253
  deciphering, 267
  defined, 10, 265
  Delete Selected Item button, 270
  Duplicate Selected Item button, 268
  illustrated, 10, 265
  New Art Has Basic Appearance command, 268
  Redefine Graphic Style command, 275
  Reduce to Basic Appearance button, 270
  Stroke listing, 254
arcs, 76
Arc Segment Tool Options dialog box, 76
Arc tool, 3, 76
area type
  creating, 214
  illustrated, 214
  options, 247–48
  vertical, 214
Area Type Options dialog box, 247–48
Area Type tool, 3, 211, 214
artboard, 33
Art brushes, 304, 306
Art Brush Options dialog box, 304, 306
Art brush strokes, 297
Assign Profile dialog box, 57
Attributes panel, defined, 11, 91, 331

B

baseline shift, 24, 248
bevel join, 112
bitmap images
  acquiring, 255
  applying filters to, 281
  converting to Live Paint group, 164

Index

417

converting vector objects into, 290
black, appearance preferences, 376
bleeds, 382
blending modes
  changing, 339–41
  fill or stroke, 341
  illustrated, 339
  object, group, layer, 340
  restricting, 342
  symbol instance, 353
Blend Options dialog box, 311
blends, 309–16
  appearance attributes and, 273
  applying shading with, 316
  Control panel, 9
  creating via commands, 310
  creating with Blend tool, 314
  defined, 23, 317
  editing, 310, 312
  illustrated, 23
  Live Paint groups from, 164
  moving, 312
  object location, reversing, 313
  options, changing, 311
  orientation, 315
  outputting, 313
  path, reshaping, 312
  recoloring, 312
  releasing, 310, 315
  spine, replacing, 315
  stacking position, reversing, 313
  transforming, 312
Blend tool, 2, 311, 314
Bloat tool, 3
BMP (bmp) files, 407
bounding boxes
  hiding/showing, 93
  object transformation via, 123
  resetting, 132
Bridge, 37–50
  cache, 49, 56
  Content panel, 39, 40, 43, 44
  defined, 23, 38
  Favorites panel, 39
  file management, 47
  file search, 48
  Filter panel, 39
  Folders panel, 39, 40
  Keywords panel, 39, 50
  launching, 38
  Metadata panel, 39
  moving/copying files, 44
  opening files from, 40
  Preview panel, 39, 40
  stacks, 46–47

using, 38–39
window, 38, 42–44
workspaces, 41, 43–44
brushes, 295–308
  adding from libraries, 298
  applying, to paths, 297
  Art, 304
  Calligraphic, 302–3
  colorization, 305
  defined, 23
  deleting, 298, 308
  dragging, 297, 298
  duplicating, 305
  editing, 306
  libraries, creating, 308
  saving, 298
  Scatter, 300–301
  types, 295
  using, 295
Brushes panel
  Brush Libraries menu, 298, 308
  default, 295
  defined, 11
  Delete Brush button, 308
  display options, 299
  Duplicate Brush command, 305
  illustrated, 11, 295
  New Brush button, 300, 302, 304
  Options of Selected Object button, 307
  Remove Brush Stroke button, 270, 299
  Select All Unused command, 308
  thumbnails, 299
  using, 298–99
brush strokes
  applying, 295
  Art, 297
  Calligraphic, 302, 307
  editing, 307
  editing on objects, 307
  expanding, 299
  objects, scaling, 297
  Pattern, 297
  removing, 299
  Scatter, 297
butt cap (stroke), 112

C
cache (Bridge), 49
Calligraphic brushes, 302–303
Calligraphic Brush Options dialog box, 302–3
caps (stroke), 112
Character panel, 212
  Character Rotation value, 217
  defined, 18, 228
  Delete Selected Styles button, 246

Index

Font menu, 229
Font Size field, 230
Font Style menu, 229
Horizontal Scale field, 223
illustrated, 18, 228
Kerning option, 232, 233
Leading option, 231
Load Character Styles command, 246
No Break command, 239
Scale menus, 234
shortcuts, 228
strikethrough button, 229
Tracking option, 232
underlining button, 229
character styles
applying, 245
creating, 243
defined, 243
deleting, 246
editing, 243
illustrated, 243
loading, 246
overriding, 245
Character Styles panel, 19, 243, 245
Clipboard
export to Photoshop using, 415
moving/duplicating objects with, 93
on quit options, 375
clipping masks, 333–38
clipping paths
defined, 334
recoloring, 337
selecting, 335
clipping sets, 333–38
adding objects to, 335
Control panel, 8
copying objects in, 336
creating, 334
defined, 333, 334
releasing, 338
restacking masked objects in, 336
selecting, 335
taking objects out of, 337
closed paths, 22, 162
closing files, 36
CMYK color
color spaces, 53–54
management policies, 51
mixing numerically, 109
for print output, 102
proofing onscreen, 58
color groups
active, 176
colors, adding, 180
creating, 115

creating based on harmony rule, 177
creating via Live Color, 178–79
defined, 115
dragging, 116
naming, 115
restacking, 115
saving, 177
Color Guide panel
active color group, 176
Color Guide Options command, 175
colors, dragging from, 104
colors, limiting, 176
color variations, applying, 176
defined, 12
Edit Colors button, 178, 181, 183
Harmony Rules menu, 177
illustrated, 12
Save Color Group to Swatches Panel button, 177
using, 118, 175–77
variation options, 175
Color Management Print dialog box, 388
color management system, 51
color modes, 29, 103
Color panel
accessing, 101
color bar, 109
color models, 109
defined, 12
Fill box, 106, 118
illustrated, 12
Out of Gamut warning, 109
Stroke box, 106, 118
T (Tint) slider, 108
White/Black selectors, 104
Color Picker, 105
color profiles, 52, 57
color(s), 51–58
appending, 116
applying, shortcuts, 106
applying by dragging, 104
applying from a library, 107
applying via Color Guide panel, 176
applying via Color panel, 104, 105
applying via Live Paint Bucket tool, 166, 167
applying via Swatches panel, 104, 105
applying via Tools panel, 104, 105
applying with Eyedropper tool, 113
assigning via Live Color, 181–82
blending, 120
in blends, 312
for commercial printing, 102
editing via Live Color, 178–80
faces, in Live Paint group, 24, 161, 166, 170
global, 118
in gradients, 319–21

© DANIEL PELAVIN

Index

guide, 99
inverting, 119
layer selection border, 195
mixing numerically, 109
nonglobal, 118
for output medium, 102–3
print settings, 385
process, 102, 103, 107
reducing via Live Color, 183–84
Registration, 108
replacing, 118
sampling, 113
saving as swatches, 106
settings, choosing, 51–55
settings, saving, 54
settings, synchronizing, 56
smart guides, 91
spot, 102, 107
tint percentage, 108
for the Web, 102–3
Web-safe, 107
color-separating gradients, 320
color separations, printing, 384–85
Color Settings dialog box, 51, 53–55
color spaces
CMYK, 53–54
defined, 52
RGB, 53
combining objects, 147
compound paths, 254, 325–32
adding objects to, 331
compound shapes versus, 325, 330
Control panel, 8
creating, 329–30
defined, 23
illustrated, 23
released object appearances, 330
releasing, 332
reversing object fill in, 331
compound shapes
compound paths versus, 325, 330
copying, 326
creating, 192
defined, 23
expanding, 326
illustrated, 23
psd format and, 416
release, 327
Content panel (Bridge), 39, 40, 42
context menus, 26
Control panel, 8–9
defined, 8
illustrated, 8–9
moving, 8
moving objects via, 129

Convert Anchor Point tool, 3, 136, 151, 190
Convert to Shape effects, 285
copying
appearance attributes, 273
compound shapes, 326
files, 44
objects in clipping sets, 336
type, 221
corner anchor points, 22, 133
converting smooth point to, 136, 189
converting to smooth point, 135
direction handles, 185
joining, 145
crop areas
aligning objects to, 95–96
deleting, 396
illustrated, 395
multiple, defining, 395
printing objects within, 395
Crop Area tool, 2, 395
crop marks, 395–396
Crop Marks filter, 396
crosshair, 1
CRT display, 52
Crystallize tool, 3
curve segments, 22, 133
drawing with Pen tool, 187–88
point placement, 137
reshaping, 134–35
smooth and symmetrical, 187
custom characters, 222
Custom Transparency Flattener Options
dialog box, 391–92

D
dashed strokes, 111
Delete Anchor Point tool, 3, 137, 140
DIC Color Guide, 107
direction handles, 133, 136
anchor points, 135
corner points, 185
preferences for display of, 367
removing or creating, 136
rotating, 136
smooth points, 135, 185
direction points, 134, 135
Direct Selection tool, 69, 136, 169
defined, 2, 79
illustrated, 2
type object, select using, 225, 227
select points, segments using, 82
Divide Objects Below command, 149
docks, 6–7
Document Info panel, 12, 398

Index

Document Raster Effects Settings dialog box, 280, 397

documents
color mode, 29
color mode, changing, 103
creating, 29
information, displaying, 398
measurement units for, 25
naming, 29
orientation, 29, 32
profiles, changing, 57
proofing onscreen, 58
setup, 32–33
size, 29, 32
window, creating, 64

Document Setup dialog box, 32
Artboard options, 32
Orientation icons, 32
Size option, 32
Transparency options, 344, 390
Type options, 235
Units option, 25
Width/Height values, 32

drag-and-drop
objects between Illustrator files, 92–93
to Photoshop, 415
from Photoshop or Bridge to Illustrator, 264

Drop Shadow effect, 23, 152, 252, 288
Drop Shadow filter, 288
dual displays, 67
duplicating
brushes, 305
graphic styles, 274
layers, 204
objects, 92–94, 204
paragraph and character styles, 244
sublayers, 204
swatches, 117
symbol instances, 346
symbols, 354
type objects, 219
workspaces, 68

E

edges
clicking, 81
defined, 24, 161
dragging, 89
modifying with Live Paint Bucket tool, 167
path, 215

editing
appearance attributes, 269
Art brushes, 304, 306
blends, 310, 312
brush strokes, 307
Calligraphic brushes, 302–3
character styles, 243
colors, 178–80
effects, 282
gradients, 320–21
graphic styles, 275
in isolation mode, 84–85
linked images, 260
paragraph styles, 243–44
patterns, 122
presets, 393–94
Scatter brushes, 300–301, 306
symbols, 354–55
transformations, 131
workspaces, 68

Edit menu
Adobe PDF Presets command, 393
Assign Profile command, 35, 57
Color Settings command, 51, 53
Copy command, 93, 221
Cut command, 221
Define Pattern command, 121
Edit Colors submenu, 119, 120
illustrated, 4
Paste command, 93, 221
Paste in Back, Paste in Front commands, 93, 202
Print Presets command, 393
Redo command, 26
Tracing Presets command, 158
Transparency Flattener Presets command, 393
Undo command, 26

Edit Selection dialog box, 86
Edit Views dialog box, 63
Effect Gallery, 292–93
Effect menu
Distort & Transform submenu, 78, 131, 146, 152, 253, 289
Document Raster Effects Settings command, 280
Drop Shadow command, 252
Effect Gallery command, 281, 292
illustrated, 4, 279
Pathfinder submenu, 284
Stylize submenu, 72, 135, 252, 286, 287, 288

effects
adding, 283
as appearance attributes, 280
applying, 281
Convert to Shape, 285
defined, 23, 279
Drop Shadow, 23, 152, 252
editing, 282
Feather, 282
filters versus, 279–80
in graphic styles, 283
Illustrator, 280, 282

Inner Glow, 286
Outer Glow, 286
Pathfinder, 284
Photoshop, 280
reapplying, 281
Rectangle, 285
removing, 283
resolution, 397
Roughen, 152
scaling, 128
Scribble, 287
spot colors in, 397
in symbol instances, 353
Zig Zag, 146
Ellipse dialog box, 70
ellipses
creating by dimensions, 70
creating by dragging, 70
moving, 192
type on, 223–24
Ellipse tool
defined, 3
illustrated, 3
using, 70, 143, 192, 223
Width, Height fields, 223
embedded images, 261, 263
embossed letters, 254
endpoints, 145, 148
enhanced metafile (emf) files, 407
EPS files
opening, 256
Options area, 401
placing, 259
saving as, 399–401
EPS Options dialog box, 400–1
Eraser tool, 2, 150
Expand dialog box, 324, 364
Export dialog box, 406, 408, 416
exporting, 399–416
as Adobe PDF files, 402–5
Bridge cache, 49
as EPS files, 399-401
file formats, 407
as Flash (swf) files, 408–9
to Photoshop, 415–16
preset file settings, 158
printing and, 390–92
Eyedropper Options dialog box, 113
Eyedropper tool, 2, 113

F

faces, in Live Paint groups, 24, 161, 166, 170
Favorites panel (Bridge), 39
Feather effect, 282

File Handling and Clipboard preferences
Clipboard on Quit options, 375
illustrated, 375
Update Links menu, 260, 375
Use Adobe Dialog option, 35
Version Cue and Files options, 374–75
File menu
Document Color Mode submenu, 103
Document Setup command, 25, 32, 223, 235
Exit, Quit commands, 36
Export command, 334, 339, 406
illustrated, 4
New from Template command, 30
Open command, 37, 256
Place command, 154, 218, 257
Print command, 378, 380, 384, 386, 388, 394
Revert command, 36
Save a Copy command, 36, 399
Save As command, 34, 36, 399
Save as Template command, 31
Save command, 34, 36
Save for Web & Devices command, 411, 412, 413
files
Adobe PDF, 256, 393–94, 402–5
bmp, 407
cache, 49
closing, 36
copying, 44
copying swatches between, 116
deleting, 47
emf, 407
eps, 399–401
export formats, 407
exporting, 406
formats, 256
gif, 412-13
jpeg, 413–14
keywords, assigning, 50
linked, 35
moving, 44
opening, 37
opening, from Bridge, 40
optimizing for the Web, 410–14
psd, 415–16
renaming, 47
resaving, 36
saving as templates, 31
saving in Illustrator format, 34–35
searching for, 48
swf, 408–9
tif, 407
wmf, 407
fills
applying, 104–5
blending mode, 341

Index

color blending, 120
defined, 22
gradient, 319
illustrated, 22
multiple attributes, applying, 268
None, 104
opacity, 341
pattern, creating, 121–22
saving as swatches, 106
white/black, 104
Fill tool, 2
Filmstrip workspaces (Bridge), 41
Filter Gallery, 292–94
Filter menu
Create submenu, 291, 396
Distort submenu, 138, 289
Filter Gallery command, 281, 292
illustrated, 4, 281
Stylize submenu, 72, 288
Filter panel (Bridge), 39, 45
filters
applying, 281
Crop Marks, 396
defined, 280
Drop Shadow, 288
effects versus, 279–80
Object Mosaic, 291
Photoshop, 280
reapplying, 281
Roughen, 289
Twist, 289
Zig Zag, 146
Find dialog box (Bridge), 48
Flare tool, 3
Flash (swf) files, 346, 408–9
Flattener Preview panel, 13, 392
flattening
artwork, 210
individual objects, 392
previewing, 392
flipping objects, 126, 129
FOCOLTONE process colors, 107
folders, creating, 47
Folders panel (Bridge), 39, 40
Font Problems dialog box, 41
fonts
changing, 229
defined, 24
missing, 41
OpenType, 236
options, 34
point size, 230
printing, 386
styles, 24
fractions, 238

Free Transform tool, 2, 124
Full Screen Mode, 65
Full Screen Mode with Menu Bar, 65

G

Gap Options dialog box, 171
General preferences
Anti-aliased Artwork option, 366
Append Upon Opening Legacy Files option, 366
Constrain Angle option, 89, 125, 365, 366
Corner Radius option, 365
Disable Auto Add/Delete option, 137, 140, 365
Double Click to Isolate option, 84, 365
illustrated, 365
Keyboard Increment option, 92, 365
Reset All Warning Dialogs option, 366
Scale Strokes & Effects option, 125, 366
Select Same Tint option, 366
Show Tool Tips option, 366
Transform Pattern Tiles option, 125, 366
Use Japanese Crop Marks option, 366
Use Precise Cursors option, 80, 366
Use Preview Bounds option, 366
General Print dialog box, 378–79
GIF format, 410, 412–13
global colors, 118
glyphs, 24, 236–37
Glyphs panel, 19, 236–37
Gradient panel, 13, 319
gradients, 317–24
adding colors to, 321
applying, 317–18
color order, reversing, 322
color-separating, 320
color stops, 321
creating, 319–20
defined, 23, 317
deleting, 320
editing, 320–21
expanding into objects, 324
filling objects with, 318
libraries, accessing, 318
linear, 319
naming, 320
radial, 23
restoring, 322
saving, 321
spot colors, 320
spreading across multiple objects, 323
starting point, 320
swatches, 318
transitions, 322
Gradient tool, 2, 253, 317, 322, 323
Graph tools, 3
Graphics Print dialog box, 386–87

©DANIEL PELAVIN

graphics tablets, 303
Graphic Style Options dialog box, 274, 276
graphic styles
    accessing, 272
    applying, 271–72
    creating, 274
    defined, 24, 271
    deleting, 276
    Drop Shadow, 273
    duplicating, 274
    editing, 275
    effects in, 283
    libraries, 277
    links, breaking, 278
    merging, 276
    Pathfinder effects in, 284
    reasons for working with, 271
    symbol instances, 353
    updates, 275
Graphic Styles panel
    Break Link to Graphic Style button, 278
    defined, 13, 271
    Delete Graphic Style button, 276
    Graphic Styles Libraries menu, 277
    illustrated, 13, 271
    Merge Graphic Styles command, 276
    New Graphic Style button, 274, 283
    using, 272
    view, 272
grayscale images, colorizing, 119
grid
    defined, 100
    illustrated, 100
    preferences, 370
    showing/hiding, 100
    snapping objects to, 100
    transparency, 344
groups
    adding objects to, 85
    applying graphic styles to, 272
    blending mode, 340
    Control panel, 8
    creating, 84
    editing in isolation mode, 84
    isolating, 22, 80, 85
    in isolation mode, 202
    Live Paint, 161–74
    locking, 205
    merging, 209
    moving via control panel, 129
    opacity, 340
    restacking, 203
    selecting, via Layers panel, 202
    selecting multiple objects in, 202
    ungrouping, 85

    working with, 84–85
Group Selection tool, 3, 80
guides
    color, 99
    dragging onto one layer, 99
    hiding/showing, 99
    locking, 99
    objects, creating, 98
    preferences, 370
    releasing, 98
    removing, 99
    ruler, 97
    smart, 90–91, 371
    tips for working with, 99
    unlocking, 99
Guides & Grid preferences, 370

H

Hand tool, 2, 65, 223
hanging indents, 241
hanging punctuation, 249
Help menu, 5, 27, 28
HKS colors, 107
Horizontal Filmstrip workspace (Bridge), 41
horizontal scaling, 24
Hyphenation dialog box, 239
Hyphenation preferences, 372

I

Illustrator
    launching, in Macintosh, 27
    launching, in Windows, 28
    quitting/exiting, 36
    welcome screen, 27, 28
Illustrator menu, 4, 36
Illustrator Options dialog box, 34–35, 57
images
    acquiring, 255–64
    bitmap, 164, 255
    colorizing, 119
    drag-and-drop, 264
    embedded, 261
    linked, 260–63
    optimizing for the Web, 410–14
    Photoshop, importing, 258
    raster, 154
importing
    layer comps, 258
    Photoshop images, 258–59
    text, 218
    user-saved presets, 158
indentation, paragraph, 241
Info panel, 13, 102
Inner Glow effect, 286
inverting colors, 119

isolate, 22
isolation mode, 80
    editing in, 84–85
    exiting, 169
    groups, 202
    Live Paint group in, 170

J
Join dialog box, 145
joins, 112
JPEG format, 410, 413–14

K
kerning, 24, 232–33
keywords, assigning, 50
Keywords panel (Bridge), 39, 50
Knife tool, 3

L
Lasso tool, 2, 80, 86, 144
launching illustrator, 27
layer comps from Photoshop, 258
Layer Options dialog box, 205
layers, 193–210
    applying graphic styles to, 272
    blending mode, 340
    creating, 195
    defined, 22
    deleted, retrieving, 197
    deleting, 197
    duplicating, 204
    flattening, 210
    hiding/showing, 206
    locking, 205
    merging, 209
    moving, 207
    moving objects between, 204
    multiple, selecting, 199
    naming, 195
    numbering, 195
    objects, deselecting all, 88, 200
    objects, selecting all, 200
    opacity, 340
    Photoshop, 258–59
    printing, 378
    releasing objects to, 208–9
    remembering, 93
    restacking, 203
    selecting listings, 198–99
    selecting objects via, 200–2
    targeting, 266–67
    top-level, 195
    unlocking, 205
    unprintable, 205
    views, changing, 206

Layers panel, 193–210
    Compound Path listings, 330
    defined, 14
    Delete Selection button, 197
    functions, 193
    group selection via, 202
    illustrated, 14
    listings, locating, 201
    listings, selecting, 198–99
    Make/Release Clipping Mask button, 334, 338
    menu commands, 201, 207, 208, 209, 254
    New Layer button, 195
    New Sublayer button, 196
    object listings, 199
    object names, 194
    object selection via, 83, 200–2
    options, 194
    Paste Remember Layers option, 93
    selection area, 83, 84, 200–2
    selection square, 200, 204
    target circle, 200–2, 282
    thumbnails, 194
Layers Panel Options dialog box, 194
LCD display, 52
leading, 24, 231
libraries
    brushes, 298, 308
    gradients, 318
    graphic styles, 277
    swatches, 107, 117
    symbols, 347, 349
linear gradients, 319
lines, creating
    with Arc tool, 76
    with Line tool, 74
    for a Live Paint group, 164
    with Pencil tool, 162
    segments, creating, 75
Line Segment tool, 2, 75
linked images
    changing to embedded, 263
    Control panel, 9
    editing, 260
    in EPS files, 401
    going to, 261
    information, viewing, 262
    Links panel listing, 261
    locating, 261
    managing, 260–63
    missing, locating, 262
    placement options, 263
    replacing, 261
    scaling, 261
    updating, 262

©DANIEL PELAVIN

Index

Links panel, 15, 260–63
Live Color dialog box, 101
   accessing, 178
   assigning colors via, 181–82
   Assign tab, 181
   Color Mode menu, 178
   Color Reduction Options button, 184
   Colors menu, 183
   color wheel, 179–80
   Current Colors row, 182
   defined, 24
   editing colors via, 178–80
   Harmony Rules menu, 178, 181
   illustrated, 178
   New Color Group button, 178, 179, 182
   Preset menu, 183
   reducing colors via, 183–84
Live Paint Bucket Options dialog box, 165
Live Paint Bucket tool, 2, 166–67, 173
Live Paint groups, 161–74
   adding paths to, 170
   from blends, 164
   Control panel, 9
   converting bitmap images to, 164
   converting live trace objects to, 159
   creating, 164
   defined, 24, 161
   edges in, 161, 167
   exercise using, 173–74
   expanding, 172
   faces in, 161, 166, 170
   features, 161
   gap options, 171
   illustrated, 24
   isolating, 169, 170
   recolor, 167
   releasing, 172
   reshaping, 169
   from symbols, 164
Live Paint Selection tool, 2, 168
Live Trace, 153–60
   Control panel, 9
   defined, 24
   objects, converting to Live Paint group, 159
   objects, expanding, 159
   See also tracing
locking
   guides, 99
   layers, groups, objects, 205

M

Magic Wand panel, 15, 80, 87
Magic Wand tool, 2, 87–88
Manage Workspaces dialog box, 68

Marks and Bleeds Print dialog box, 382–83
marquees, dragging, 81
masked objects
   illustrated, 333
   restacking, 336
   selecting, 335
masking objects, 83, 333
Maximized Screen Mode, 65
measurement units, 25
Measure tool, 3
menus
   activation shortcuts, 5
   context, 26
   illustrated, 4–5
   See also specific menus
merging
   graphic styles, 276
   layers, groups, objects, 209
meshes, 317
Mesh tool, 2
Metadata panel (Bridge), 39
Microsoft Office file format, 407
miter join, 112
monitor displays, 52
moving
   anchor points, 134
   appearance attributes, 273
   blends, 312
   files, 44
   groups, 129
   layers, 207
   objects, 89, 128, 129
   objects between layers, 204
   panels, 7
   patterns, 122
   segments, 134
   sublayers, 207
   type, 221

N

Navigator panel
   Cmd-drag/Ctrl-drag in, 59
   defined, 15
   illustrated, 15, 59, 66
   moving illustrations via, 66
   View Artboard/Crop Area Only option, 66
   zoom settings, 59
New Brush dialog box, 300, 302
New Color Group dialog box, 115
New Document dialog box, 29
New Swatch dialog box, 121
New View dialog box, 63
nonglobal colors, 118

O

Object menu
    Arrange submenu, 204
    Blend submenu, 310, 311, 313, 315, 316
    Clipping Mask submenu, 334, 338
    Compound Path submenu, 329, 331, 332
    Expand Appearance command, 278, 299, 364
    Expand command, 164, 324, 364
    Flatten Transparency command, 344, 392
    Group submenu, 84, 224
    illustrated, 4
    Live Paint submenu, 164, 172, 173
    Path submenu, 94, 138, 144, 149, 162, 186, 329
    Rasterize command, 290
    Text Wrap submenu, 251
    Ungroup command, 85
Object Mosaic filter, 291
objects, 69–78
    adding, to clipping sets, 335
    adding, to compound paths, 331
    adding, to groups, 85
    adding/subtracting from selection, 81
    aligning, 73, 95–96
    aligning by anchor points, 91
    aligning with smart guides, 90–91
    blending fill colors between, 120
    blending mode, 340
    center point, hiding/showing, 91
    combining, 147
    copying, in clipping set, 336
    corners, rounding, 72
    creating, 70–78
    deleting, 69
    distorting, 124
    distributing, 95–96
    drag-dropping, 92–93
    drag-duplicating, 92
    duplicating, 92–94, 204
    erasing parts of, 150
    expanding gradients into, 324
    flipping, 126, 129
    grouped, editing in isolation mode, 84
    guide, 98
    hiding/showing, 206
    information, displaying, 398
    knocking out, 343
    line segments, 75
    masking, 83
    moving, 89
    moving, to new layers, 208–9
    moving between layers, 204
    moving horizontally, 128
    moving vertically, 128
    moving via Control panel, 129
    opacity, 340
    pasting, 202
    perspective, 124
    rasterizing, 290
    reflecting, 123, 124
    releasing from threads, 220
    releasing to layers, 208–9
    restacking, 203
    reusable, 24
    rotating, 123, 124, 129
    scaling, 123, 124, 126, 128
    scatter, 300–301
    selecting, 22, 201, 202
    shearing, 124, 129
    snapping to grid, 100
    spreading gradients across, 323
    tracing, 158, 160
    type, 83, 214
    unthreading, 220
    See also specific object types, paths
Offset Path dialog box, 94
opacity. *See* transparency
opacity masks, 416
Open dialog box, 37
open paths, 22, 329
Open PDF dialog box, 256
OpenType fonts, 236
OpenType panel, 20, 237–38
optimization, for the Web
    defined, 24
    files, 410–14
orientation
    blends, 315
    document, 29, 32
    print, 380
    type, 214, 216–17
Outer Glow effect, 286
Outline view
    defined, 62
    illustrated, 62
    layer display in, 206
Output Print dialog box, 384–85
overflow symbol, 213
overflow type, 219–20
overprinting, 385, 389
Overprint Preview view, 62

P

Page tool, 3, 33
Paintbrush tool, 2, 139, 141, 296
panels
    Align, 10, 95–96
    Appearance, 10, 253–54, 265–70
    Attributes, 11, 331
    Brushes, 11, 295–308

Character, 18, 212, 228, 229–34
Character Styles, 19, 243–46
closing, 6
Color, 12, 101
Color Guide, 12, 105, 175–77
Control, 8–9
Document Info, 12, 398
expanding/collapsing, 6
Flattener Preview, 13, 392
freestanding, 7
Glyphs, 19, 236–38
Gradient, 13, 317–24
Graphic Styles, 13, 271–72, 274
icons, dragging, 7
Info, 13
Layers, 14, 193–210
Links, 15, 260–63
Magic Wand, 15, 87
menus, using, 6
moving, 7
Navigator, 15, 59
OpenType, 20, 237
options, showing/hiding, 10
Paragraph, 20, 212, 228, 239–42
Paragraph Styles, 21, 212, 243–46
Pathfinder, 16, 147, 325–27
showing/hiding, 6
Stroke, 16, 101, 110–12
Swatches, 16, 101, 114–17
Symbols, 17, 345–64
Tabs, 21, 250
temporary, 8
Tools, 1–3
Transform, 17, 128–29
Transparency, 17, 152, 339–44
using, 6–7
widening/narrowing, 6
PANTONE colors, 107
Paragraph panel, 212
  alignment buttons, 240
  alignment shortcuts, 240
  defined, 20, 228
  Hyphenation command, 239
  illustrated, 20, 228
  Indent options, 241
  line-composer options, 239
  Roman Hanging Punctuation command, 249
  shortcuts, 228
  Space Before/Space After Paragraph fields, 242
paragraphs
  alignment, 240
  indentation, 241
  inter-paragraph spacing, 242
  line breaks, 240
Paragraph Style Options dialog box, 244

paragraph styles
  applying, 245
  creating, 243
  defined, 243
  deleting, 246
  editing, 243–44
  illustrated, 243
  loading, 246
  overrides, 245
  redefining, 245
Paragraph Styles panel, 21, 212, 243, 245–46
Path Eraser tool, 3, 141
Pathfinder commands, 327–29
Pathfinder effects, 284
Pathfinder Options dialog box, 327
Pathfinder panel
  Add to Shape Area button, 147, 152, 326
  Crop button, 328
  defined, 16
  Divide button, 327
  Exclude Overlapping Shape Areas button, 326
  Expand button, 326
  illustrated, 16
  Intersect Shape Areas button, 326
  Merge button, 328
  Minus Back button, 328
  Outline button, 328
  Pathfinder buttons, 327–28
  Release Compound Shape command, 327
  Subtract from Shape Area button, 326
  Trim button, 328
paths
  adding anchor points to, 137
  adding to Live Paint group, 170
  adding with Paintbrush tool, 139
  adding with Pencil tool, 139
  adding with Pen tool, 139
  applying brushes to, 297
  blend, 312
  building blocks, 133
  closed, 22
  combining, 325–32
  compound, 23, 325–32
  Control panel, 8
  converting points on, 190
  cutting, 149
  defined, 22
  deselecting, 81
  direction handles, 133
  duplicate, offset, 94
  edges, 215
  erasing, 141
  open, 22
  recoloring, 105
  reshaping, 141–43

Index

segments, 22, 133
selecting, 81
splitting, 148
stroke alignment on, 110
path type
creating, 215–17
effects, 216
options, 216–17
repositioning, 215
scaling, 230
Pattern brush stroke, 297
patterns
applying, 121
creating, 121
editing, 122
transforming, 125, 126, 128
PDF files
multi-page, creating, 394
opening, 256
preset, creating/editing, 393
saving as, 402–5
Pencil tool, 2, 139, 141, 162–163
Pencil Tool Preferences dialog box, 163
Pen tool, 185–92
adding paths with, 139
adjusting points while drawing with, 188
Cmd-click/Ctrl-click, 186, 188, 191
Cmd-drag/Ctrl-drag, 191
converting points with, 189
defined, 2, 185
deleting points with, 140
dragging, 187, 189
drawing curves with, 187–88
drawing polygons with, 186
illustrated, 2
Option-drag/Alt-drag, 189, 191
Shift-click, 186
tearoff toolbar, 135
Photoshop
copying/pasting objects into, 415
effects, 280
exporting files to, 415–16
filters, 280
issues, 259
layer comps, 258
multi-layer images, 258–59
placing files into Illustrator from, 258–59
psd format, 415
Smart Object layer feature, 415
Photoshop Export Options dialog box, 416
Photoshop Import Options dialog box, 258–59
Pixel Preview view, 62
placed images, 9, 258–59
placed text, 218
Placement Options dialog box, 263

Plug-ins & Scratch Disks preferences, 373
pointers, 1, 79
point size of type, 230
point type
creating, 212
defined, 212
scaling, 230
selecting, 226–27
shadow, 252
Polar Grid tool, 3
Polygon dialog box, 72
polygons, 72–73, 186
Polygon tool, 3, 73
preferences
Appearance of Black, 376
defined, 24
File Handling and Clipboard, 35, 260, 374–75
General, 80, 84, 92, 125, 365–66
Guides & Grid, 370
Hyphenation, 372
Plug-ins & Scratch Disks, 373
Selection & Anchor Display, 79, 367
Smart Guides & Slices, 90, 91, 125, 188, 371
Type, 231, 248, 368
Units & Display Performance, 25, 369
User Interface, 374
Preferences dialog box (Bridge), 42
presets
creating, 393–94
deleting, 393
editing, 393–94
print, 380
tracing, 158
transparency flattener, 390
workspace, 66
zoom level, 60
Preview panel (Bridge), 39, 40
Preview view, 62, 206
Print dialog box
Advanced options, 389
Color Management options, 388
General options, 378–79
Graphics options, 386–87
Marks and Bleed options, 382–83
Output options, 384–85
Setup options, 380–81, 394
Summary options, 389
printers, 378, 389
printer's marks, 382
printing, 377–98
artboard and, 33
to black-and-white printers, 378–79
with color management, 388
to color printers, 378–79
color separations, 384–85

color settings, 385
copies, 378
default setup, 33
define crop area for, 395
documents larger than paper, 380–81
exporting and, 390–92
flatness setting, 386
flattening options, 389
fonts and, 386
layers, 378
objects in crop area, 395
orientation, 380
overprinting, 385, 389
output size, 381
printer's marks, 382
scaling and, 378
settings, saving, 379
settings summary, 389
print presets, 379
process colors, 102, 103, 107
converting spot colors to, 108
editing, 118
libraries of, 107
mixing, numerically, 109
reducing artwork to one, 184
replacing, 118
tint percentage, 108
See also color(s)
projecting cap, 112
Proof Setup dialog box, 58
PSD (Photoshop) format, 415
compound shapes and, 416
creating files in, 416
defined, 416
opacity masks and, 416
smart type, 415
Pucker tool, 3
punctuation
hanging, 249
smart, 235

Q

quotation marks style, 235

R

raster effects, resolution, 397
raster images, tracing, 154
Rasterize dialog box, 103, 290
Rasterize Options dialog box, 407
recolor
blends, 312
clipping paths, 337
by dragging, 104
faces with Live Paint Bucket tool, 166
Live Paint group, 167

type, selecting to, 105, 227
Recolor Options dialog box, 184
Rectangle dialog box, 70
Rectangle effect, 285
rectangles
converting to costume mask (exercise), 191–92
creating by dimensions, 70
creating by dragging, 70
in pattern definition, 121–22
rounded, creating, 71
type in, 213
Rectangle tool, 2, 70, 121, 143
Rectangular Grid tool, 3
reference points, 126, 130
Reflect tool, 3, 125, 127, 192
rendering intents, 58
Reshape tool, 3, 142–43
reshaping, 133–52
blend path, 312
curves, 134–35
exercises involving, 143, 151, 152
Live Paint groups, 169
multiple paths, 142
objects, via commands, 146–47
with Paintbrush tool, 141
with Pencil tool, 141
quick, 141
with Reshape tool, 142
subpaths, 330
resolution, raster effects, 397
restacking, 203
RGB color
color spaces, 53
management policies, 51
mixing numerically, 109
proofing onscreen, 58
for Web output, 102
Web-safe, 107
Rotate tool, 2, 127
rotating
direction handles, 136
direction points, 135
objects, 123–24, 129
polygons, 73
scatter objects, 301
spirals, 78
stars, 73, 74
type, 217
Roughen effect, 152, 253, 289
Roughen filter, 289
round cap, 112
Rounded Rectangle tool, 3, 71, 153
round join, 112
ruler guides, 97

S

Save Adobe PDF dialog box, 394
  Adobe PDF Preset menu, 402
  Advanced options, 405
  Compression options, 403–4
  General options, 402–3
  Marks and Bleeds options, 404
  Options area, 403
  Output options, 404–5
  Security options, 405
  Standard menu, 403
  Summary options, 405
Save for Web & Devices dialog box, 411–14
Save Optimized As dialog box, 414–15
Save Selection dialog box, 86
Save Swatches as Library dialog box, 117
Save Workspace dialog box, 67, 68
saving
  as Adobe PDF, 402–5
  Bridge workspaces, 44
  color groups, 177
  colors as swatches, 106
  as EPS, 399–401
  files, as copy, 36
  files, as templates, 31
  files, for the Web, 408–414
  files, in Illustrator format, 34–35
  files, shortcuts, 35
  graphic style libraries, 277
  selections, 86
  swatch libraries, 117
  symbol libraries, 349
  workspaces, 67
Scale tool
  defined, 2
  illustrated, 2
  Option-Shift/Alt-Shift, 151
  smart guides with, 125
  Uniform: Scale field, 151, 223, 316
  using, 126–27
scaling
  brush stroke objects, 297
  effects, 128
  horizontal, 24
  linked images, 261
  objects, 123, 128
  path type, 230
  patterns, 126, 128
  point type, 230
  polygons, 73
  printing and, 378
  proportionally, 126
  spirals, 78
  stars, 74, 152

  type, defaults, 233
  type, scaling, 234
Scallop tool, 3
Scatter brushes, 300–1, 306
Scatter Brush Options dialog box, 300–1, 306
Scatter tool, 3
Scissors tool, 3, 148
Scratch Disks preferences, 373
screen display mode, 65
Scribble effect, 287
segments
  creating, 75
  curved, 22, 133
  moving, 134
  reshaping, 134, 136, 141–42
  selecting, 82
  selecting with Lasso tool, 86
  straight, 22, 133
selecting, 79–88
  anchor points, 82
  clipping paths, 335
  clipping sets, 335
  with commands, 82–83
  defined, 22
  with Direct Selection tool, 82
  layers, 198–99
  Layers panel listings, 198–99
  masked objects, 335
  masking objects, 83
  multiple layers, 199
  objects, 81
  objects, all, 88
  objects, all on a layer, 83
  objects, via Layers panel, 200–2
  pointer and, 79
  printers, 378
  segments, 82
  with Selection tool, 81
  stray points, 83
  strokes, 83
  sublayers, 198–99
  symbol instances, 364
  type and object, 226
  type but not object, 227
  type objects, 83, 227
Selection & Anchor Display preferences, 79, 81, 89, 367
selections
  deselecting, 88, 202
  inverting, 88
  saving, 86
Selection tool, 69, 169
  Control-click/right-click, 143
  defined, 2, 79
  illustrated, 3

© DANIEL PELAVIN

Index

Option-arrow/Alt-arrow, 92
Option-drag/Alt-drag, 92, 122, 172
Option-Shift/Alt-Shift, 92, 143
Option-Shift-arrow/Alt-Shift-arrow, 92
Shift-click, 81, 84
Shift-drag, 81, 89
type selection, 225
use illustration, 79
using, 81
Select menu
All command, 88, 221, 227
Deselect command, 88, 186, 188
Edit Selection command, 86
illustrated, 4
Inverse command, 88
Object submenu, 83, 297
Same submenu, 83
Save Selection command, 86
Setup Print dialog box, 380–81, 394
Shape Mode commands, 325–27
shearing, 124, 126, 129
Shear tool, 3, 125, 127
Slice Select tool, 3
Slice tool, 3
smart guides
aligning objects with, 90–91
defined, 90
display color, 91
in object transformation, 125
with Reflect tool, 125
with Scale tool, 125
with Shear tool, 125
when drawing with Pen tool, 188
using, 90–91
Smart Guides & Slices preferences, 90–91, 125, 188, 371
Smart Punctuation dialog box, 235
smart type, 415
smooth anchor points, 22, 133
converting corner points to, 135
converting to corner points, 136, 189
direction handles, 135, 185
joining, 145
Smooth tool, 3
soft proofs, 58
Spiral dialog box, 77
Spiral tool, 3, 77–78
splitting paths, 148
spot colors, 102, 107
accessing from libraries, 107
converting to process, 108
in gradients, 320
on raster effects, 397
reducing artwork to one, 184

replacing, 118
tint percentage, 108
tints, 309
Standard Screen Mode, 65
Star dialog box, 73
stars, 73–74, 151
Star tool, 3, 74
straight segments, 22
strikethrough type style, 229
Stroke panel
accessing, 101
alignment buttons, 110, 253
Cap buttons, 112
Dashed Line settings, 111
defined, 16
illustrated, 16
Join buttons, 112
Weight area, 110
strokes
alignment on path, 110
applying colors to, 104–5, 107, 109
attributes, changing, 110–12
blending mode, 340
caps, 112
converting to filled object, 329
dashed, 111
defined, 22
illustrated, 22
joins, 112
multiple, to characters, 253
multiple attributes, applying, 268
None, 104
opacity, 341
saving as swatches, 106
selecting, 83
white/black, 104
width, 105, 110
styles. *See* graphic styles
sublayers
creating, 196
defined, 193, 195
deleting, 197
duplicating, 204
merging, 209
moving, 207
multiple, selecting, 199
numbering, 195
selecting, 198–99
Suite Color Settings dialog box, 56
Summary Print dialog box, 389
Swatch Conflict dialog box, 116
swatches
copying between files, 116
deleting, 117

dragging, 114, 116
duplicating, 117
gradient, 318
locating, 114
naming, 106
saving a library of, 117
saving as a color group, 115
saving colors as, 106
Swatches panel
accessing, 101
defined, 16
Delete Swatch button, 117
display options, 114
dragging colors form, 104
illustrated, 16, 114
New Color Group button, 115
New Swatch button, 106, 117, 319
saving colors to, 106
Select Similar Options menu, 118
Show Find Field command, 114
Show Swatch Kinds menu, 114, 117
Swatch Libraries menu, 107, 117, 118
using, 114–17
View commands, 114
swatch libraries, 107, 117
Swatch Options dialog box, 118, 121
SWF Options dialog box, 408–9
Symbol Cruncher tool, 3
symbol instances
adding to symbol set, 350
applying graphic styles to, 353, 362–63
blending mode, 353
Control panel, 9
creating individual, 346
creating with Symbol Sprayer tool, 350
deleting from symbol set, 350
duplicating, 346
expanding, 349, 364
illustrated, 24
modifying, 353
moving, 353
multiple, creating, 346
opacity, 353
selecting, 364
temporary, 354
symbolism tools
Diameter and Intensity settings, 353
global properties, 351
in modifying instances, 353
types, 345
See also specific Symbol tools
Symbolism Tools Options dialog box, 351–52
symbol libraries, 347, 349
Symbol Options dialog box, 349

symbols, 345–64
advantages to using, 345–46
Control panel, 8
creating, 348
defined, 24
deleting, 349
double-clicking, 354
dragging, 346, 347
duplicating, 354
editing, 354–55
links, breaking, 355
Live Paint groups from, 164
measurement, 25
replacing, 348
Symbol Screener tool, 3, 345, 357, 361
symbol sets
adding instances to, 350
Control panel, 8
deleting instances from, 350
expanding, 364
modifying, 353
replacing symbols in, 348
Symbol Shifter tool, 3, 345, 356
Symbol Sizer tool, 3, 345, 358
Symbols panel
Break Link to Symbol button, 355
defined, 17
Delete Symbols button, 349
display, changing, 347
illustrated, 17, 345
New Symbol button, 354
Place Symbol Instance button, 346
Select All Instances command, 364
Symbol Libraries menu, 347, 349
Symbol Spinner tool, 3, 345, 359
Symbol Sprayer tool
defined, 2
dragging, 346
illustrated, 2, 345
options, 352
using, 350
Symbol Stainer tool, 3, 345, 360
Symbol Styler tool, 3, 345, 362–363

T

tabs, 249
Tabs panel, 21, 250
tab stops, 250
tearoff toolbars, 1, 3, 67
templates, 30–31
Templates folder, 30, 31
text
file formats, 218
importing, 218

placed, 218
tabs, 249
threads, displaying, 220
wrap, 251
Text Import Options dialog box, 218
Text Wrap Options dialog box, 251
threading type, 219–20
thumbnails (Bridge)
    adding to stacks, 47
    arranging, 46–47
    Bridge Content panel, 40
    Brushes panel, 299
    display, filtering, 45–46
    grouping into stack, 46
    labeling, 45
    Layers panel, 194
    rating, 45
    removing from stacks, 47
    resizing, 43
    sorting, 45
    stacks, expanding/collapsing, 47
    stacks, ungrouping, 47
TIFF Options dialog box, 407
TIFF (tif) files, 407
tiling, page, 381, 394
tint percentages, 108
tints, 309
tools
    Add Anchor Point, 3, 137
    Arc, 3, 76
    Area Graph, 3, 211
    Area Type, 3, 214
    Bar Graph, 3
    Blend, 2, 314
    Bloat, 3
    Column Graph, 2
    Convert Anchor Point, 3, 136, 151, 190
    Crop Area, 2, 395–96
    Crystallize, 3
    Delete Anchor Point, 3, 137, 140
    Direct Selection, 2, 69, 79
    Ellipse, 3, 70, 143, 192, 223
    Eraser, 2, 150
    Eyedropper, 2, 113
    Flare, 3
    Free Transform, 2, 124–25
    Gradient, 2, 253, 317, 322–23
    Group Selection, 3, 79
    Hand, 2
    Knife, 3
    Lasso, 2, 80, 86, 144
    Line, 3
    Line Segment, 2, 75
    Live Paint Bucket, 2, 164, 165–67, 173
    Live Paint Selection, 2, 168

Magic Wand, 2, 80, 87–88
Measure, 3
Mesh, 2
Page, 3
Paintbrush, 2, 139, 141, 296
Path Eraser, 3, 141
Pen, 2, 139, 185–92
Pencil, 2, 139, 141, 162–63
Pie Graph, 3
Polar Grid, 3
Polygon, 3, 72, 73
Pucker, 3
Radar Graph, 3
Rectangle, 2, 70, 121, 143, 191
Rectangular Grid, 3
Reflect, 3, 125, 126–27, 192
Reshape, 3, 142–43
Rotate, 2, 126–27
Rounded Rectangle, 3, 71, 152
Scale, 2, 125, 126–27, 223
Scallop, 3
Scatter Graph, 3
Scissors, 3, 148
Selection, 2, 69, 79
Shear, 3, 125, 126–27
shortcuts, 1
Slice, 3
Slice Select, 3
Smooth, 3
Spiral, 3, 77, 78
Stacked Bar Graph, 3
Stacked Column Graph, 3
Star, 3, 73, 74, 152
Symbol Cruncher, 3, 357
Symbol Screener, 3, 361
Symbol Shifter, 3, 356
Symbol Sizer, 3, 358
Symbol Spinner, 3, 358
Symbol Sprayer, 2, 350
Symbol Stainer, 3, 360
Symbol Styler, 3, 362–63
Twirl, 3
Type, 2, 211, 212–13
Type on a Path, 3, 211, 215
Vertical Area Type, 3, 211, 214
Vertical Path Type, 3, 211, 215
Vertical Type, 3, 211, 212–13
Warp, 2
Wrinkle, 3
Zoom, 2, 61
Tools panel
    defined, 1
    Fill box, 2, 105, 106, 118
    illustrated, 2
    Screen Mode menu, 2, 65

Index

showing/hiding, 1
Stroke box, 2, 105, 106, 118
tool tips, 26
TOYO Color Finder, 107
tracing, 153–60
Control panel options, 156, 159
converting to paths, 159
features, 153
objects, 160
options, applying, 155–57
presets, 158
previewing, 160
raster images, 154
releasing, 158
simple, 157
Tracing Options dialog box, 153, 155–58
Tracing Presets dialog box, 158
tracking, 24, 232–33
transformations, 123–32
blend, 312
via bounding boxes, 123
Control panel, 129
defined, 22
with dialog boxes, 126
editing, 131
Free Transform tool, 124
multiple, performing, 130
object copies, 126
preferences for, 125
random, 130
reference point, 126
repeating, 132
with smart guides, 125
Transform panel, 128–29
Transform Each dialog box, 130
Transform Effect dialog box, 131
Transform panel, 17, 128–29
transparency, 339–44
changing, 339–41
default flattener presets, 390
exporting and, 390–92
fill or stroke, 341
grid, 344
to InDesign, 390
object, group, layer, 340
objects affected by, 342–43
printing and, 390–92
symbol instance, 353
**Transparency Flattener Preset Options dialog
box,** 393
Transparency panel
accessing, 339
blending modes, 340–41
defined, 17
illustrated, 17

Isolate Blending option, 342
Knockout Group option, 343
Opacity slider, 152, 341, 342
TRUMATCH colors, 107
Twirl tool, 3
Twist filter/effect, 289
type, 211–24
adding, 227
appearances and, 226
area, 214, 247–48
attributes, 212
baseline shift, 24
baseline-shifting, 248
case, 238
Control panel, 8, 18
copying, 221
counters, 222
deleting, 227
double-clicking, 226
editable, Photoshop, 259
on ellipse, 223–24
embossed, 254
fill/stroke opacity on, 341
fitting to container, 233
horizontal, 213, 217
horizontal scaling, 24, 234
kerning, 24, 232–33
leading, 24, 231
moving, 221
in objects, 214
outlines, 222
overflow, threading, 219
paint attributes, 226
path, 215–17
point, 212
point size, 230
quotation marks style, 235
recoloring, 105, 227
in rectangles, 213
rotating, 217
with rough fill area, 253
scaling, 234
scaling defaults, 233
selecting, 225–27
smart, 415
smart punctuation, 235
spacing defaults, 233
special effects, 251–54
terminology, 24
threading, 219–20
tracking, 24, 232–33
vertical, 213, 217
vertical scaling, 234
wrapping, 251

Index

Type menu
Area Type Options command, 247
Change Case submenu, 238
Create Outlines command, 164, 222, 253, 332
Fit Headline command, 233
illustrated, 4
Show Hidden Characters command, 240
Smart Punctuation command, 235
Threaded Text submenu, 220
Type on a Path submenu, 216, 224
Type Orientation submenu, 217
type objects
Control panel, 8, 18
defined, 213
duplicating, 219
selecting, 83, 227
type on a path. *See* path type
Type on a Path Options dialog box, 216–17
Type on a Path tool, 3, 211, 215
Type preferences, 231, 248, 368
Type tool
create area type using, 214
create point type using, 212
create type in rectangle using, 213
create type on a path using, 215
defined, illustrated 2, 211
select type using, 225, 227

U

underline, 229
undos, multiple, 26
units, measurement, 25
Units & Display Performance preferences, 25, 369
User Interface preferences, 374

V

Variation Options dialog box, 175
vector objects, rasterizing, 290
Vertical Area Type tool, 3, 211, 214
Vertical Filmstrip workspace, 41
Vertical Path Type tool, 3, 211, 215
Vertical Type tool
defined, 3, 211
illustrated, 3, 211
point type, creating with, 212
type in rectangle, creating with, 213
View menu
Actual Size command, 61, 62
Edit Views command, 63
Fit in Window command, 33
Guides submenu, 97, 98, 151
Hide Bounding Box, 93
illustrated, 5
New View command, 63
Pixel Preview command, 62, 97

Proof Colors command, 58
Proof Setup submenu, 58
Show Bounding Box command, 123, 219
Show Grid command, 100
Show Page Tiling command, 33, 394
Show Rulers command, 25, 97
Show Text Threads command, 220
Smart Guides command, 125
Snap to Grid command, 97, 100
Snap to Pixel command, 62, 97
Snap to Point command, 97
Transparency Grid command, 344
Zoom In, Zoom Out commands, 60
views
changing, 62
creating, 63
deleting, 63
layer, 206
selecting for extra document window, 64
See also specific views

W

Warp tool, 2
Web
choosing colors for, 102, 107, 109
Flash (swf) format, 408–409
GIF format, 412–413
JPEG format, 413–414
optimization issues, 410
Save for Web & Devices previews, 411
saving files for, 408–414
Snap to Pixel command, 97
symbols, use for, 346
Window menu
Arrange Icons command, 64
Cascade command, 64
illustrated, 5
New Window command, 64
Tile command, 64
Type submenu, 18, 236, 243, 250
Workspace submenu, 41, 67
See also panels
Windows metafile (wmf) files, 407
working space color settings, 53–54
workspaces
in Bridge, 41–44
defined, 24
deleting, 68
duplicating, 68
editing, 68
preset, choosing, 66
saving, 67
settings, 59–68
using, 66–68
Wrinkle tool, 3

Index

z

Zig Zag effect, 146
zoom levels
    changing via Navigator panel, 59
    changing by clicking or dragging, 61
    preset, 60
Zoom tool, 2, 61

© CHRIS LYONS

GET UP AND RUNNING QUICKLY!

For more than 15 years, the practical approach to the best-selling *Visual QuickStart Guide* series from Peachpit Press has helped millions of readers—from developers to designers to systems administrators and more—get up to speed on all sorts of computer programs. Now with select titles in full color, *Visual QuickStart Guide* books provide an even easier and more enjoyable way for readers to learn about new technology through task-based instruction, friendly prose, and visual explanations.

Task-Based
Information is broken down into concise, one- and two-page tasks to help you get right to work.

Visual
Hundreds of screen shots illustrate the steps and show you the best way to do them.

Step by Step
Numbered, easy-to-follow instructions guide you through each task.

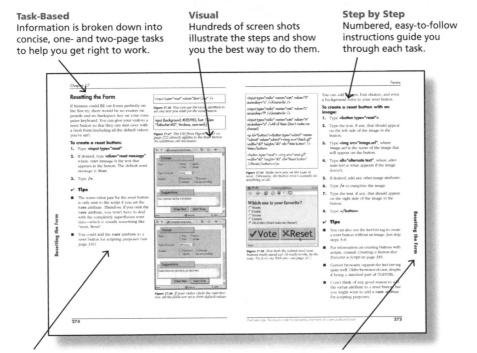

Tips
Lots of helpful tips are featured throughout the book.

Quick Reference
Tabs on each page identify the task, making it easy to find what you're looking for.

www.peachpit.com